BUDDHIST IDEAS AND RITUALS IN EARLY INDIA AND KOREA

Buddhist Ideas and Rituals in Early India and Korea

KWANGSU LEE

MANOHAR
1998

First published 1998

ISBN 81-7304-221-7

Published by
Ajay Kumar Jain for
Manohar Publishers & Distributors
2/6 Ansari Road, Daryaganj
New Delhi 110002

Lasertypeset by
A J Software Publishing Co. Pvt. Ltd.
305 Durga Chambers
1333 D.B. Gupta Road
Karol Bagh, New Delhi 110005

Printed at
Rajkamal Electric Press
B 35/9 G T Karnal Road Indl Area
Delhi 110033

To my father
Mr. Jong-suk Lee
and
my mother
Mrs. Myung-suk Kim

Contents

Preface

THE PRESENT WORK is based substantially on my Ph.D. work submitted to the University of Delhi in 1992. A number of studies have appeared on the history of Buddhism in early India and Korea. However, they have taken mainly normative ideology of Buddhism for manifestations of socio-economic entity. Our study therefore deals with the historical progress of Buddhism in socio-economic dimension which, we believe, is the most decisive factor forming religious tradition.

I would like to express my deepest gratitude to Professor K.M. Shrimali, my supervisor, who never tired of rendering sincere guidance at each step. Even hospitalization could not stop him reading through my numerous drafts and showing valuable new dimensions and directions. I was also introduced to some aspects of cultural contacts in the ancient world by the late Professor Devahuti. I would like to thank Professor J.P. Sharma at the University of Hawaii who has read the complete manuscript with care and made valuable suggestions. To Professors R.S. Sharma, D.N. Jha and P.S. Dwivedi, my teachers in University of Delhi, I express deep gratitude.

I am obliged to the Indian Council for Historical Research which granted me scholarship for several years. All the librarians and staff of libraries of University of Delhi, Archaeological Survey of India, Indian Council for Historical Research, National Museum and Jawaharlal Nehru University deserve my sincere thanks.

My greatest thanks should go to my parents, Mr. Jong-suk Lee and Mrs. Myung-suk Kim and all brothers and sisters who have supported in every endeavour of my long-time study outside home. Malay Neerab in St. Stephen's College, University of Delhi, who is in School of Oriental and African Studies, University of London, and all the classmates of M.A. in University of Delhi have helped and encouraged me. Most of all, my wife Jaehee, has stayed home alone letting me devote my full attention to this research. She deserves more thanks than words can express.

KWANGSU LEE

Abbreviations

ADM	*Aśoka and the Decline of the Mauryas*, by Romila Thapar.
AIAC	*Ancient India and Ancient China: Trade and Religious Exchange A.D. 1-600*, by Xinru Liu.
AIRTSC	*Ancient Indian Rituals and Their Social Contents*, by N.N. Bhattacharyya.
AISH	*Ancient Indian Social History: Some Interpretations*, by Romila Thapar.
AN	*Aṅguttara Nikāya*.
APIIAI	*Aspects of Political Ideas and Institutions in Ancient India*, by R.S. Sharma.
AS	*Arthaśāstra*.
BC	*Buddhacarita*.
'Buddhism'	'Buddhism in the Gupta Age', in *Essays on Gupta Culture*, ed. by Bardwell L. Smith.
BMMI	*Buddhist Monks and Monasteries of India*, by S. Dutt.
BS	*Buddhism and Society: A Great Tradition and Its Burmese Vicissitudes*, by Melford E. Spiro.
CIS	*Contribution to Indian Sociology*.
CTEI	*Cultural Transaction and Early India: Tradition and Patronage*, by Romila Thapar.
CTSA	*Culture, Thought, and Social Action*, by S. J. Tambiah.
Cvg.	*Cullavagga*.
Dāna	*Dāna: Gift System in Ancient India*, by Vijay Nath.
DEBS	*Democracy in Early Buddhist Samgha*, by Gokuldas De.
'Dhenukakata'	'Dhenukakata' in *D. D. Kosambi on History and Society: Problems of Interpretation*, ed. by S.J. Syed.
Divya.	*Divyāvadana*.
DN	*Dīgha Nikāya*.
DP	*Dhammapada*.
EBM	*Early Buddhist Monachism*, by S. Dutt.
EMB	*Early Monastic Buddhism*, by N. Dutt, 2 vols.

ER	*Encyclopedia of Religion,* ed. by Mircea Eliade.
Fa-hsien.	*The Travels of Fa-hsien or Record of the Buddhistic World,* tr. by H.A. Giles.
'Feudalism'	'Feudalism and Mahayana Buddhism' by A.K. Warder, in *ISHP.*
HIL	*A History of Indian Literature,* by M. Winternitz, 3 vols.
HIPI	*A History of Indian Political Ideas,* by U.N. Ghoshal
HTR	*History of Tantric Religion,* by N.N. Bhattacharyya.
IBE	*An Introduction to Buddhist Esoterism,* by Benoytosh Bhattacharyya.
IDETBJ	*India as Described in Early Texts of Buddhism and Jainism,* by B.C. Law.
IF	*Indian Feudalism,* by R.S. Sharma.
pro.IHC	*Proceedings of the Indian History Congress.*
IHR	*Indian Historical Review,* Delhi.
IHQ	*Indian Historical Quarterly,* Calcutta.
ISHP	*Indian Society Historical Probings,* ed. by R.S. Sharma.
I-tsing.	*A Record of the Buddhist Religion as Practised in India and the Malay Archipelago,* tr. by J. Takakus.
Jat.	*Jātakas.*
JAIH	*Journal of Ancient Indian History,* Calcutta.
JBORS	*Journal of the Bihar and Orissa Research Society,* Patna.
JBRS	*Journal of the Bihar Research Society,* Patna.
JIH	*Journal of Indian History,* Trivandrum.
Lal. Vis.	*Lalitavistara.*
KCEI	*Kingship and Community in Early India,* by C. Drekmeier.
Lg.SV	*Larger Sukhāvatīvyūha.*
LS	*Lankāvatāra Sūtra.*
LV	*Lalitavistara.*
Lud.	*A List of Brāhmi Inscriptions from the Earliest Times to about A.D. 400 with the Exception of Those of Aśoka,* by H. Luders.
'Mat.Back'	'Material Background of the Origin of Buddhism', by R.S. Sharma, in *Das Kapital Centenary Volume,* ed. by Mohit Sen and M.B. Rao.
'Mat.Mil'	'Material Milieu of Tantricism', by R.S. Sharma in *ISHP.*
MG	*Monastery and Guild: Commerce under the Sātavāhanas,* by Himanshu P. Ray.

MI	*Mauryan India,* by G.M. Bongard-Levin.
MN	*Majjhima Nikāya.*
MP	*Milindapañho.*
MS	*Manusmṛti.*
Mvg.	*Mahāvagga.*
Mvm.	*Mahāvaṃsa.*
Mvt.	*Mahāvastu.*
OYCTI	*On Yuan Chwng's Travels in India.*
P.E.	Pillar Edict of Aśoka.
PIIAI	*Political Ideas and Institutions in Ancient India,* by R.S. Sharma.
'Popular'	'Popular Buddhism', *IHQ,* vol. XXI, 1945.
Pre.Prac.	*Precept and Practice: Traditional Buddhism in the Rural Highlands of Ceylon,* by Richard F. Gombrich.
PSEHEI	*Perspectives in Social and Economic History of Early India,* by R.S. Sharma.
PTAI	*Political Theory of Ancient India,* by John. W. Spellman.
PTS	Pali Text Society.
R.E.	Rock Edict of Aśoka
'Religion'	'Religion, Ideology and Society' by K.M. Shrimali. *pro.IHC,* 1988.
RLPS	*Religion and Legitimation of Power in Sri Lanka,* ed. by Bardwell L. Smith.
Sagi.	*Samguksagi.*
Saun.	*Saundarānada.*
SAI	*Śūdras in Ancient India,* by R.S. Sharma.
SBCI	*Studies in the Buddhistic Culture of India,* by Lalmani Joshi.
SBB	*Sacred Books of the Buddhists.*
Sel.Ins.	*Select Inscriptions Bearing on Indian History and Civilization,* vol.I, by D.C. Sircar.
SHB	*Studies in History of Buddhism,* ed by A.K. Narain.
SN	*Saṃyutta Nikāya.*
SOB	*Studies in the Origin of Buddhism,* by G.C. Pande.
Soc.Org.	*Social Organisation in North East India in Buddha's Time,* by Richard Fick.
SP	*Saddharmapuṇḍarīka.*
SPS	*Suvarṇaprabhāsottama Sūtra.*
SSY	*Silla Sasangsa Yonku,* by Ki-baek Yi.
S.SV	*Smaller Sukhāvatīvyūha.*

Sut.Nip.	*Sutta Nipāta.*
Taisho.	*Taisho Shinshu Daizokyo.*
Thera.	*Theragāthā.*
Theri.	*Therigāthā.*
Vin.	*Vinaya Piṭaka.*
WCWR	*World Conqueror and World Renouncer*, by S.J. Tambiah.
Yusa.	*Samgukyusa.*

CHAPTER 1

Introduction

THE TRADITION of any religion makes its shape in accordance with history. Its form and social functions are not static but vagrant being inherently tied to space and time in each society. Therefore, in order to understand a religious tradition, we have to explore the relationship of exchange between religion and society in the form of cultural and social entities. The purpose of this work, thus, is two-fold. The first is a search for the tradition of Buddhism, 'tradition' being, according to Romila Thapar, 'the handing down of knowledge or the passing on of a doctrine or a technique. . . . The sheer act of handing on a tradition, is meticulously bounded by mnemonic or other devices to prevent interpolations or change. A tradition, therefore, has to be seen in its various phases.'[1] The second aim of this work is to explore the cultural contacts between India and Korea in early times, which may be taken to mean the 'behaviour patterns socially acquired and socially transmitted by means of symbols'.[2] In this work, it is aspects of the ideational and practical foundations of Buddhism and their roles in social formations in early India and Korea that we designate as behaviour patterns.

No proper study with a scientific and systematic approach has been taken up in this field till now. Many scholars of Buddhism have accepted the normative ideology of Buddhism as the manifestation of social reality. They are often unaware that the historical progress in social dimensions is decisive in forming religious tradition. Little attention has been paid so far to Buddhist studies in the context of the socio-historical milieu.

There are several ways in which we can approach the task of studying Buddhist tradition and its influnce outside India. In the first half of this century some eminent scholars noticed the connection between India's cultural contacts with the outside world and Buddhism. P.C. Bagchi, in 1944, gave an account of a thousand years of cultural relations between India and China tracing both land and sea routes to China and the first contacts between the two. He was the first Indian scholar who made available a complete picture of the cultural contacts between China and India through religion, both in religious and in secular matters such as astronomy, mathematics, medicine, etc. But he confined himself to largely discussing the elements of Indian influence on Chinese culture in the manner of comparative studies and his approach lacked scientific analysis. He ignored the socio-economic forces working behind the 'synthesis' of the two cultures. R.C. Majumdar, another votary of this approach, while stressing the infinite superiority of Indian culture in the spiritual field, attempted to establish a 'Greater India' in South-East Asia. His main interest did not lie in the study of the historical progress of Indian religion in society but in the manner and result of its spread. In his article 'Buddhism in South-East Asia',[3] he concentrated on discussing the manner in which South-East Asia became an Indian 'colony' through Buddhist influence. These two great scholars, influenced by the chauvinist nationalist resurgence of post-Independence India, attempted to show that the ancient Indian religion was a most superior and highly spiritual force. They ignored the fact that the study of civilization is not conceivable without a knowledge of the complicated role of religion in social history.

Kenneth K.S. Ch'en, in his work, *The Chinese Transformation of Buddhism* (1973), demonstrates 'how the Indian religion gradually became Sinicized'.[4] Though, on the one hand, Buddhism from India was a civilizing influence it was also, in its turn transformed or modified. In a similar but more systematic and intensified way, E. Zurcher in his book *The Buddhist Conquest of China* (1972) and article 'Buddhism in a pre-Modern Bureaucratic Empire: The Chinese Experience' (1980), emphasizes the way acculturation highlights various ways in which 'a huge and heterogeneous body of foreign beliefs and practices, itself subject to constant accretion, change and diversification came to be incorporated into'.[5] Concentrating on the cultural environment and the various types of interaction, he failed to realize that Buddhism, over many centuries and lands, had an unchangeable organic structure in which the transformation or modification or acculturation or whatever one might call it, continued to be made. We, thus, hesitate to adopt his approach in which the geographical factor rather than the socio-economic one becomes the criterion for characterizing Buddhism. His work, by emphasizing 'local genius or national character',[6] takes into account the output only, neglecting the organic structure of ideas and rituals. It is not a work 'of a substantial nature which did away with the territorial compartmentalization of Buddhism and which treated it more as a cultural system or as a civilizational factor of global dimension than mere religion and philosophy'.[7] Moreover, his book covers only the period from the first to the fifth century AD, not covering the entire time span of its own history, besides limiting itself to the main aspects of the particular type of Buddhism which developed in southern China.

The recent style of applying anthropological methods to Theravāda Buddhism makes rather modest progress in the study of Buddhism in society in South-East Asia. Anthropologists of religion usually study behavioural aspects and existing religious practices and institutions. Richard F. Gombrich in his *Precept and Practice* (1971), using classical texts as his primary sources has employed historical methods that supposedly identify the more authentic strata of the texts. He projects an image of Sri Lankan Theravāda Buddhism as an ethical system oriented toward an other-worldly *nibbāna* that is practised in its authentic form only by the monks. In the conclusion he clearly maintains that it is not the same as the distinction made between behavioural and textual Buddhism.[8] Melford E. Spiro belongs to that group of social psychologists who work on the religions of contemporary social groups with special stress on the ideas and practices of the people. In his *Buddhism and Society* (1971), he mainly follows the line of Weberian interpretation concerning what the authentic form of Theravāda Buddhism is. With this formation, he proceeds to provide an ethnographic description and analysis of Burmese Buddhism. He accepts nibbānic Buddhism only as the authentic religion and admits three other quite distinct religions, rather unauthentic in his view, as kammatic Buddhism, apotropaic Buddhism and esoteric Buddhism. Though in a remarkable effort he has reconstructed the tradition of Buddhism as a living religion by highlighting ethnographic description and interpretation, in characterizing the various aspects of the religion into separate independent systems he has faltered. Especially, we hesitate to accept the terms nibbānic Buddhism and kammatic Buddhism for they are not autonomous. Actually, the notions of nibbānic and kammatic are an invention of anthropologists which have no historical base. Religious tradition is not self-created. It grows out of the past and is composed of aspects chosen from the past. Religious forms, not to be separated from each other, are embedded in social realities throughout time and we should be aware of this reality in history. Here, we may refer to another notable scholar in this field, S. J. Tambiah. Taking ethnography as his primary focus, in the *World Conqueror and World Renouncer* (1976) and *The Buddhist Saints of the Forest and the Cult of Amulets* (1984), he has brought the tradition of Theravāda Buddhism to the fore through his research. In the first book he mainly discusses the dialectic relations between the Buddhist *saṃgha* and Thai kingship and polity. In the second he interprets the Buddhist tradition in a holistic manner with a more ethnographic focus. Though he approaches the task in too holistic a way, he has made an immense contribution to the study of Theravāda Buddhism and society, especially of its ritual systems. Adopting the attitude of Weberian anti-reductionism, he emphasizes the conjoining of the religious system with the economy, politics, social practices and cultural institutions of the times. He is a firm believer in Aśoka's 'benevolent' kingship inspired by Buddhist ideas and values.[9] Relating the rituals to kingship, he affirms that the study of ritual systems in relation to social structure and institutional environment is the anthropological task *par excellence.* His anthropological approach, both to texts and people in societies, can be used to study the present to illuminate the past, giving many valuable ideas to historians. Such an approach can furnishing valuable sources not available in ancient Indian history that historians of the religions of India may seek to reconstruct history by postulating a relationship between the past and the present. Yet, the essentials of the Buddhist tradition cannot be understood without juxtaposing it with its contemporary Brahmanical counterpart. Buddhism developed not in a virgin society but within the ideas and practices of the Brahmanical tradition, the study of which is essential in order to reconstruct the past in terms of the present. Such a combination is by no means absent in Tambiah's and other anthropologists' works on Buddhism.

Xinru Liu, examining a vast mass of material from original sources in the Sanskrit and Chinese languages, confirmed that 'the analysis of the structure of the trade reveals that Buddhist ideology and institutions played a considerable role in economic activities'.[10] In this respect, D.D. Kosambi[11] was the first scholar to study the involvement of Buddhist monks in economic activities with special reference to the trade routes in the western region of India. Examining both commercial and religious transactions, Liu offers new perspectives on the relationship between ancient urban society and religious ideas and rituals. Relating the Buddhist tradition to society in China, she showed that theological development and its concomittant practices influenced the various activities in the politico-socio-economic life in Chinese circumstances as well as in India. She firmly believes that Asian societies were never assemblages of self-sufficient villages and religion played a great role in the social progress of villages. In this respect, it would be noteworthy to add one more valuable work on religion in society, viz., Himanshu P. Ray's *Monastery and Guild: Commerce under the Sātavāhanas*. In this work, Ray emphasizes the role of monasteries which 'acted as pioneers and as centres providing information on cropping patterns, distant markets, organization of village settlements and trade'.[12]

The present work has been undertaken to highlight the relation between Buddhist ideology and institutions and socio-economic mechanisms in early India and Korea. An attempt is made to study not in a passionate but in an interconnected and systematic manner the transition of Buddhist ideas and the progress of its rituals in the context of its social basis. We believe that all religious ideas and institutions of a society are related to its secular activities. Thus, we contend the history of Buddhism cannot be an autonomous or self-sufficient discipline. There is no religious phenomenon which is irreducible in its own 'plane of reference'. For its adequate understanding, therefore, it is necessary to set up the ideational and practical foundations of the tradition in the socio-economic milieu. We try to see the essence of the Buddhist tradition through such a scientific approach.

Research on the history of Buddhism should, therefore, be focused on the socio-economic set-up of the period under review and ideas ought to be analyzed in terms of practical performing aspects in the particular period. The ideas and rituals of Buddhism were nothing but the living product of the material milieu of the society to which they belonged. Like amoeba, they incessantly metamorphosed. And the incessant change/metamorphosis of Buddhist ideas and rituals produced new significance at every time and in every place. However, the movement never broke free from the supporting structure. This is what has brought about the development of the various aspects of Buddhist culture in the Indian subcontinent and the places of Asia where Buddhism has held a predominant position in society for a long time. Also, the structure of Buddhism cannot be derived merely from the analysis of its manifestations, if any, at one particular time only. It has to be followed by research into other periods. Then we must try to interconnect them to find out the dynamics and vitality of the tradition which has lasted through the ages. People in religion have stuck to, or sometimes been urged to believe in, external shapes rather than the structure of the tradition. This is a myth which has to be exposed. In order to expose the myth, we have to seek simple facts from living society through time and place.

This work is based mainly on literary sources ranging from early Buddhist texts like *Nikayas* and *Dhammapada* to tantric texts, the precise dating of which is still problematic. Therefore, we have adopted the generally accepted chronology of the literary sources but in cases where there are differences of opinion we have indicated the reasons which have prompted us to adopt an unconventional dating.

Valuable information for this study, with regard to the manner of Indo-Korean contacts comes from the *Samgukyusa* (edited by Il-yon some time between 1281 and 1283) in which the narrative is more and more transformed into myth and legend. Yet, we have to be aware that the author, a national-priest, selected, distorted and imagined events in such a way as to improve the ethical picture of the events presented. Though history merges into myth and legend, the author, provides enough evidence to help establish certain historical truths. Comparison, investigation and renewal are the three main ways of examining this material, that is myths and legends. In addition to this, there are foot-notes and comments that criticize his own material as well as that of the others whom he quotes. In fact myth, in the sense of prototype history, preserves and gives significance to important aspects of the time of origin. Moreover, the interpretation of archetypes, themes and symbols can reveal the more emphatic assumptions of a society. Thus, the myths with which ancient texts are replete form an important source for the reconstruction of the history of religion in society.

In addition to the *Samgukyusa*, the *Samguksagi* compiled by Kim Pu-shik in 1145 is the other original source for our research. Unlike the *Samgukyusa*, the *Samguksagi* is based on the ideology of Confucianism, which ignores myths and legends and brands them as irrational. Though bearing some bias against Buddhist concerns, the *Samguksagi* supplies us with much valuable material for our research.

The time span of this research is from the sixth century BC to about fifth or sixth century AD in India which we call 'Early India' and from the first century to around ninth century AD in the Korean context, for which a detailed rationale has been provided in the second chapter.

NOTES

1. Romila Thapar, *AISH*, p. 8.
2. Ibid., p. 7.
3. *IHQ*, XXXII, 1956.
4. Kenneth K.S. Ch'en, *The Chinese Transformation of Buddhism* (Princeton, 1973), p. 12.
5. E. Zurcher, 'Buddhism in a pre-Modern Bureaucratic Empire: The Chinese Experience', in *SHB*, p. 401.
6. Ibid., pp. 5-6.
7. A.K. Narain, 'Introductory: Toward a New History of Buddhism', in ibid., p. xv.
8. Richard F. Gombrich, *Pre. Prac.*, p. 318.
9. S.J. Tambiah, *WCWR*, p. 60.
10. Xinru Liu, *AIAC*, p. 174.
11. 'Dhenukakata'.
12. Himanshu P. Ray, *MG*, p. 207.

CHAPTER 2

Indo-Korean Contacts in Early History

VARIOUS ACCOUNTS reveal that the ancient world was neither so large nor so separated as we are used to thinking. Long before the onset of the Christian era communication by sea and land had become brisk and regular. Military campaigns like those of Darius of Persia, Alexander and Emperor Wu of Han China opened up the routes thus erasing many demarcations between different cultures. Missionary activities contributed in broadening the way by increasing cultural communication. In this great activity, India played no mean role. The natural barriers of India were insurmountable only in theory. The mountain ranges in the north neither effectively checked any outside infiltration nor prevented the expansion of Indian civilization to the outside world. The Indian Ocean was navigated at an early date and hence it was easy for Indian traders and missionaries to proceed unhindered to East Asia across the seas.

In order to trace the origin of Sino-Indian contacts we have to go back to the time of Aśoka. Other than that we have only the Chinese legend from the Ch'in dynasty. However, our legends do not provide historical confirmation. Historically, the first contact between India and China was through the military march of the Chinese. It was cemented by commercial activities and broadened by Buddhist missionaries from India. Later on, India became a kind of dream land for many Chinese and Korean monks who continued to make the long journey to India despite hardships. There is hardly any evidence of violence between the two sides, only of trade and religious interchange.

The importance of this chapter on Sino-Indian contacts lies in the fact that Buddhism was introduced to Korea through China and thus became the main channel for the Koreans' relationship with India. Even if we do not want to get bogged down by the issue of Sino-Indian contacts, the beginning of their contacts must be established.

According to the Chinese tradition a band of eighteen Buddhist monks came to China during the latter half of the third century BC. This is not, however, generally regarded as a historical fact. Moreover, it is difficult to believe that the missionary route is prior to the existence of the trade route. The earliest Chinese historical record indicates that as early as the second century BC textile and bamboo products manufactured in China were being sold in the market of Bactria.[1] This was personally seen by Chang Ch'ien who was sent by emperor Wu of Han dynasty to form an alliance with the Yuechi, that is the Kuṣāṇas, against their common enemy Hsiung-nu. Further, he is reported to have said that these commodities were brought to Bactria via India. The objects might have come in ceremonial exchange for it was not an international trade route in the second century BC. Nevertheless, Chang Ch'ien's campaign marked the opening of concrete contacts between India and East Asia. A landmark in the history of this contact was achieved by the spread of Buddhism in East Asia in the succeeding periods.

Eurasian trade traffic along the famous Silk Road in the early Christian centuries inaugurated an era of frequent trade contacts between India and China. The demands from both sides stimulated the traffic through Central Asian routes. In this trade the Kuṣāṇas played the important role of intermediaries. Even though the volume of this exchange may not have been impressive its possible connection with another great change, the transmission of Buddhism from India via China, imparts it great significance.

The kinds of commodities transported along the trade routes between India and China shaped the nature of the trade. The commodities involved in the transaction were mainly luxury goods. While Chinese royal families and rich people, and after the popularization of Buddhism even ordinary men, demanded various precious stones, fragrances and incense, etc., Indian and Roman rulers and rich merchants demanded Chinese silk. The high profits from the transactions and the desire for rare commodities as symbols of prestige would have overcome the extreme physical hardships involved in traversing mountainous and desert routes and even encouraged people to invest in the risk-filled business of purchasing silk from China.

Coral, pearls and glass are among the Indian exports to China that are traceable in both literary and archaeological sources. In China coral had been an extremely valuable commodity since the beginning of the Christian era. It was considered to be the most precious and hence, the ideal item of tribute. Since India was the major market for Roman coral, it follows that the coral which arrived in China had come in mainly through India. Like coral, pearls were highly valued in ancient China. However, unlike coral, pearls originated in south India and Sri Lanka and it may have been more convenient to ship the pearl to south China via the Bay of Bengal and South-East Asia than overland to the north through Central Asia. Considering the heavy traffic along the west coast, south Indian pearls may have been exported to Barygaza also. Glass is another item which the rich Chinese yearned to possess. When the Indians exported crystal to the Romans some genuine crystal probably also reached China.[2] All these precious stones as Indian export items are traceable in both literary and archaeological sources. Pearls and conch-shells, products of the Indo-Sri Lankan straits are referred to in the *Arthaśāstra.*[3] The occurrence of cornelian in worked and unworked form in pre-third century BC levels at Anurādhapura in Sri Lanka points to its arrival from the Deccan as Sri Lanka does not possess any known sourçes of cornelian.[4] A large number of inscriptions dated to the second-first centuries BC found at Buddhist and Jain sites along the east coast refer to donations by lay devotees to religious establishments. The nature of the coastal trade is, however, evident from the find of gold leaves in a *stūpa* at Amaravati[5] and sixty-two pearls in a relic casket in a *stūpa* at Bhattiprolu.[6] Besides, incense appears in literary sources as a commodity from India but does not leave material traces. The so-called 'knobbed ware' and cornelian beads unearthed in burials in central Thailand are indicative of the vivid contact of South-East Asian people with the ports on the Bengal and Orissa coasts which were connected with the Deccan peninsula.[7] Perfume and incense traded in western Indian ports also appear in Chinese literature from the Later Han onwards. Bdellium, native to the dry region of western India, was imported into China under the name of *an-hsi-hsiang,* i.e. fragrance from Arsaces or Persia, and myrrh, another Indian product, was imported to china through Central Asian routes.[8] Similarly, it has been suggested that cinnamon and cassia were obtained from mainland South-East Asia or southern China.[9] It has been argued that sandalwood sent from Bharuch may have come from the dry regions of eastern Indonesia.[10] Cinnamon leaves, known to the Periplus as malabathrum, may also have been obtained from South-East Asia, as the plant is native to Malaya.[11] Silk, in large quantities, was the major product from China to India in the early Christian era. It is also estimated that much silk was transported to Roman markets through India in order to bypass the conflicts between the Roman empire and the Persians.

It is with the expansion of the Mauryan empire in the peninsula that coastal traffic becomes important. It is reflected in the Saṃgam literature dated between 100 BC and AD 250, where it is mentioned that the maritime trade was expanded very actively and wealth was accumulated by certain groups involved in it. These sources mention pockets of Paradvar settlements along the east coast of Tamilaham and associate the community with chank-pearl diving and fishing.[12] The Paradvar gradually diversified and increased their participation in coastal trade specializing in items like pearls, gems and horses and one section of this community figure as rich traders.[13] Twenty-two inscriptions, concentrated primarily in northern Sri Lanka and bearing the term *barata,* have been identified as belonging to the Paradvar of south India.[14] A study of historical developments along the east coast of the Indian subcontinent indicates shifts in power centres in the post-Mauryan period. Thus while the Orissa coast formed the major epicentre in the Mauryan and post-Mauryan period, the focus shifted to the lower Krishna and Godavari valleys under the later Sātavāhanas and to the Tamil coast with the rise of the Pallavas. The data certainly suggests that revenues from maritime trade across the Bay of Bengal contributed in no small measure to these shifts.[15]

The decline of the Roman empire and the rivalry between the Persians and the Romans made the volume of trade in the Gupta times less than it had been in the Kuṣāṇa-Sātavāhana times, when Pliny complains of the heavy drain of gold. Moreover, the introduction, into the Byzantine empire, of silk-worms brought secretly from China[16] played a decisive role in reducing Indian trade. The stoppage of the export of silk to the Byzantine empire drastically reduced whatever remained of the shrunken foreign commerce of north-western India in the Gupta times. So long as new articles did not take the place of silk there was no means of restoring the balance and retrogression in foreign trade was inevitable.[17] However, it is not likely that Indian trade collapsed entirely in this period. The Indian literature of the Gupta period testifies to the prosperity of the Ujjain region and its connection with trade. Based on the inscriptions of Samudra Gupta, Chandra Gupta II and Skanda Gupta it is maintained that the Saurashtra coastal region around Barygaza was still commercially active in Gupta times.[18] Fa-hsien formed a favourable impression of the west and middle Gangetic plains, while he could not help recording the depressing scenes witnessed in some of the cities on the middle Gangetic plain, which were all desolate. In summary, even when north India suffered a general urban decline in the Gupta period, certain cities along the trade route from Kashmir to the north Indian plain prospered. A major shift took place in the north-west, where the route through Kashmir connecting India to central Asia gained importance. As the seaports in western India continued to flourish the new Kashmir route brought both western India and the Gangetic plain closer to China.[19] The Sino-Indian trade not only survived warfare, shifts of trade routes, even regional de-urbanization of post-Kuṣāṇa and post-Han periods[20] but even flourished somewhat.

Although none of the items of Sino-Indian trade were necessary for human subsistence, the trade continued to flourish at least until the sixth century AD. Most of these items were required by privileged social groups, especially the urban elite for religious practices. Soon they became symbols of wealth and prestige in society. In the beginning, it was the royal family that craved and could afford these rare items from India but soon the taste spread from the court to the houses of aristocrats and rich merchants. Following the propagation of Buddhism, even people from the lower social strata wished to possess these items, especially fragrances and incense, for they were used widely in Buddhist rituals. Finally, the Buddhists became the major buyers of these foreign luxury goods.

It is generally believed that the Indians were afraid of undertaking sea-voyages and therefore remaind isolated. This belief originated in certain sects of the Brahmanical community and became rigid from the medieval period. But the Avadānas, the Nikāyas, the Jātakas, particularly *Janaka, Valāhassa, Samudda-Vanija* and *Saṅkha Jātakas,* bear witness to the sea-voyages undertaken in the post-Vedic period. They are often corroborated by Greek writings. Some of the Jātakas mention that the merchants from Varanasi and Rajagriha sailed down the Ganga and then went westward to reach the ports on the seaboard of Sobira in the gulf of Kutch while others travelled to Bharukaccha. From Sobira and Bharukaccha goods would be sent to Baveru, that is Babylon or Bahrain. As for the eastward sea-fairing activities, the route was open from Campa, Varanasi, and some other cities of the post-Vedic period to Suvarṇabhūmi, one of the states in South-East Asia, through the Ganga and the Bay of Bengal via Siṃhaladvīpa, that is, modern Sri Lanka. Manifestly, large ships carrying hundreds of men towards the east and west must have been in full activity as early as the sixth or fifth century BC.

Sea communication between the Indian Ocean and the China sea was established at the beginning of the first century AD if not earlier. In the first century AD the sea-route from India to the east ended at Tonkin, the most flourishing port of China. This route was not used by India alone but other countries like Rome and Parthia as well. Being the international route, the sea-route to China was utilized by Indians as frequently as that of Central Asia. And the men who utilized this route by this period were mostly merchants, the pioneers in the opening up of routes and carriers of nearly all aspects of culture. From the very commencement of the Christian era we have the unquestionable evidence of Pan-chao to show that the envoys of Wang-mang came to Kāñcī with costly presents to the king of the land and informed him that it was the desire of Wang-mang that he should send in return an embassy to China with a live rhinoceros as tribute. Clearly, there were political embassies from and to China from the initial years of the Christian era. There is reason to believe that the maritime contacts between China and south India reach as far back as the second century BC. A Chinese coin, most probably of the second century BC, has been found at Chandravalli in Mysore[21]. Chinese traders visited Kāñcī and bought pearls, glass, rare stones and other products not available in China and in exchange they mainly supplied gold and silk. Out of these, pearls were one of India's most important exports to China. In fact, Fa-hsien also has remarked on the advanced organization of the Ceylonese pearl fishery.[22]

The trade route by sea was quite well established and continued to flourish in the Gupta period. Fa-hsien mentions two port cities in the regions that he calls the 'Great State Campa' and the 'Tāmralipti State' whose commercial activities are indicative of the flourishing maritime trade. In fact, Fa-hsien went back to China on a merchant vessel. Besides, in P.C. Bagchi's list of more than a dozen Buddhist missionaries who went to China from India, half or so went there by sea-route.[23] Thus, it is quite natural to think that they, like Fa-hsien, made good use of trade vessels for their journey. Hsüan-tsang who visited Valabhipura, a renowned Buddhist centre in Saurashtra, observes that the people of the peninsula were a great commercial people and earned their livelihood by engaging themselves in sea-trade. When we consider that at this time they engaged in a large amount of trade we can be sure that a solid trade relationship existed between India and South-East Asia and China.

Sino-Indian contacts through land route commenced at almost the same time as sea-trade contacts. As a result of Chang Ch'ien's travels, the Han empire had pushed its diplomatic and military arms into Central Asia and in the succeeding years countries like Bactria, Ferghana, Parthia and Kuṣāṇa all sent envoys to the Chinese court. At this time the Kuṣāṇas were dominant in Central Asia and north India and had not only converted to Buddhism but had also become great patrons of the Buddhist Mission. In the wake of these diplomatic missions came merchants carrying various precious stones. It was at the court of the Kuṣāṇas that in 2 BC the Chinese met the Indian missionaries Kāśyapa Mātaṅga and Dharmaratna who made summaries of Buddhist doctrines for propagation in China. Later, these two Indian monks came to China during the reign of Ming-ti in AD 68 and composed four or five works in Chinese on Buddhist doctrines. The first Buddhist monastery in China was Po-ma-sse or White Horse Monastery.

For about seventy years after this first contact was made, we do not hear of any other missionary activities in China. The reason for this is not far to seek. Communications between the 'Western Countries' and China were still very uncertain on account of the political condition in Eastern Turkestan. In order to command the routes of Central Asia better, General Pan-chao carried out military operations for twenty years from AD 74 to 102 and Pan-yong, his son continued with them. The number of Buddhist missions to China increased considerably as soon as the routes in Central Asia were made secure by their military expeditions.

From the first century of the Christian era we hear of the regular arrival of Buddhist missionaries in the capital of China. The earliest missionary was Ngan She-kao, an Arsacid prince from Persia. Whether he carried on his study in India or somewhere else we do not know, but he translated quite a large number of Buddhist texts into Chinese. One hundred and seventy-nine translations of Buddhist texts are ascribed to Ngan She-kao. His translations were intended to meet the great need of the times. Buddhism was not yet well-known amongst the Chinese people. Thus he translated pious legends, discourses of the Buddha and small texts from the canon without bothering too much about the accuracy of his translations. His purpose was to give the Chinese people a general idea of the Buddhist religion in its various aspects. Towards the middle of the second century, for the first time, we find a Chinese Buddhist scholar named Yen Fo-t'iao amongst the translators in Po-ma-sse.

Under the Wei rulers, in the first half of the third century AD, the work of translation continued systematically and the Chinese people grew more interested in Buddhism. Indian scholars such as Dharmakāla, Saṅghavarman and Dharmasatya came to China at the request of Chinese monks. They translated a number of Vinaya works towards the middle of the third century AD. Their efforts are proof that the Chinese monks were eager to understand the Buddhist monastic discipline more precisely and thoroughly.

Dharmarakṣa, one of the most remarkable of monk-scholars, came to Ch'ang-ngan at the time of the unified Ch'in dynasty. He was born at Tun-huang which we know was the meeting place of the two worlds. He had assembled round him a number of Buddhist scholars from different parts of Asia such as Parthia, Khotan, Kucha, etc., not to speak of India. After the accession of Fu-kien of the Former Ch'in dynasty in AD 350, Buddhist activities received a new impetus. The famous Chinese monk Tao-ngan invited the Indian monks Gautama Saṅghadeva, Dharmanandi and Saṅghabhūti. What is more important is that Buddhism was officially introduced in this period to Koguryo, one of the three kingdoms in ancient Korea, by Chinese Buddhists. Wei Buddhism heavily influenced the formation of early Korean Buddhism.

Kumārajīva was the first to introduce, in a systematic manner, the Mahayana in China in the fifth century. In order to facilitate this, he translated some of the fundamental texts of Mahāyāna. Amongst the ninety-eight works which are attributed to him there is also a work of special importance, the *Brahmajāla Sūtra*, a Mahāyāna Vinaya code for the use of those who wanted to follow the path of the *bodhisattvas*. This text was one of the popular ones in China. He was the first to introduce in China the profounder aspects of Indian Buddhism. He realised that the texts translated earlier into Chinese were more or less diffuse and full of mistakes. It is an acknowledged fact that his translations were amongst the best.

The biography of Prince Ying of Ch'u contains a very significant piece of information conforming the existence of the Buddhist community in China before the arrival of Kāśyapa Mātaṅga and Dharmaraksa. What is more, this community consisted of monks and pious laymen in an outlying area of Kiangsu and Shantung. How did such an institution come about? The following hypothesis may be advanced. If the initial transmission between the Kuṣāṇas and the Chinese in 2 BC had been continued and extended, it would have provided over half a century for Buddhist missionaries to spread the law in China. However, another possibility is that Buddhism may have been introduced and developed in an independent manner through southern China. From the first century AD China had come into contact with India through Tonkin, the international port at that time. Unfortunately, Chinese historical records were compiled by orthodox Confucian scholars who disdained to notice the presence of a few insignificant foreign monks; hence their names and activities are not preserved in Chinese records and are lost forever.

In the second and third centuries AD, Buddhism spread rapidly in Tonkin. Records show that Mou-tseu, although a Taoist, migrated to Tonkin to avoid civil war and embraced Buddhism and his example was followed by others. About the middle of the third century, Saṃghabhadra became a Buddhist monk after the death of his father who had settled in Tonkin for purposes of trade. He is said to have converted Emperor Wu of Nanking and founded a Buddhist school there. Marajīvaka was another monk who came to Fu-nan in a merchant vessel and proceeded to Tonkin and Canton. He preached Buddhism wherever he went and contributed largely to its development all along the sea-route to China. Owing to the efforts of many other, lesser known missionaries about whom little information is available Buddhism had obtained a secure footing in Tonkin and south China by the end of third century AD. There were more than twenty *caityas* and five hundred monks in the district of Leileu. In the fourth century, the Eastern Ch'in dynasty flourished in south China which led to the further progress of Buddhism. This period witnessed frequent contacts between south China and South-East Asia. Eastern Ch'in is also known for spreading Buddhism to Paekche Korea.

Korea's contacts with India commenced latest by the fourth century. Relying on chronicles alone, we have the mention of three Indian monks who came to Korea in the ancient period. It has to be noticed that they were the first missionaries to each of the three kingdoms and these three names represent an exhaustive list of

Indian monks in ancient Korea. Though there is little to support it, there is a Japanese legend saying that an Indian monk named Ho-do, a translation of Sanskrit *Dharmapatha* or *Dharmamārga*, came to Japan through Paikje Korea. As in the case of Chinese Buddhism, ancient Confucian historians in Korea, too, did not record 'improper and outrageous happenings'.

The first Indian monk came to Korea from former Ch'in of China in 374. In spite of meticulous research, we have not been able to ascertain the Sanskrit name of the Indian monk. He is popularly known as Ado which does not seem to be a proper name but is perhaps a pseudonym denoting 'bald head'. One year after his arrival, two temples were erected in the capital of Koguryo. One is Songmun-sa and the other Ibulan-sa the latter being, in all probability, a transliteration of the Sanskrit name *Ipuṇya*. If we consider that after some time the name of this temple may have been changed into Hungbok-sa, with the meaning of 'Rise Blessing' temple, and that the term *bok* was a translation of the Sanskrit *puṇya*, with the 'i' denoting 'to be' or 'to arise from' in Sanskrit, we can assert that the name means *Ipuṇya*. It is maintained that Sun-do, the first monk who introduced Buddhism, the Buddha's images and Buddhist *sūtras* by order of king Fu-kien of former Ch'in in China, must have been an Indian or Central Asian.[24] Ten years after the advent of A-do, another Indian monk came to Korea in the first year of king Chimryu. His name is Maranant'a which must be a transliteration of the Sanskrit *Mālānanda*. He came to the other Korean kingdom of Paikje, whose king received him with full honour in his court. As for his origin, we have no source at all. And by what route he came from India to China is completely unknown. But since he was sent from the court of Eastern Ch'in in south China, which had frequent contacts with south India and Sri Lanka through the sea-route, there is a greater possibility of his hailing from south India. The third Indian monk visited Silla Korea via Koguryo in AD 417 during the reign of King Nulchi. He, too, was called A-do, together with another byname, Muk-ho-ja meaning 'dark complexed foreigner'. Further identification is not possible due to the paucity of source material. Besides these, there were other monks also from India. *Haedong-kosung-chon* or the Biography of Eminent Monks of Korea in Taisho[25] records the advent of three Indian monks during the reign of king Chik-pyong (579-631), viz., Bi-ma-ra-chik-che (which may be a variation of Vimalacitta) and Nong-gat'a, (which may be Lunghadha) from north India, and Bul-t'a-sunga, i.e. Buddhasaṇgha from Mathura.

In fact, India's original intercourse with East and South-East Asia had been inspired by trade and commerce as described above. The prospect of acquiring wealth first tempted Indian traders and merchants to explore the unknown territories beyond their own frontiers. Although it was soon overshadowed by missionary activities, merchants were the first conveyors of Buddhism and other aspects of Indian culture. Ancient Korea is no exception to this general norm. As for the possibilities of the spread of Buddhism in Korea, not by Chinese official envoys but by Indian merchants, a story from the *Samgukyusa* gives us a remarkable clue. The story goes as follows:

> During the reign of king Nulchi, the nineteenth Silla ruler, a *śramaṇa* named Muk-ho-ja came to Il-son county in Silla from Koguryo and hid himself from persecution in a villager's home. At this time, the emperor of Liang dynasty in south China sent an envoy, with robes and incense to the king of Silla. However, nobody in the court knew what the incense was for and how to use it. The king, therefore, asked a messenger to travel throughout the kingdom and find out if anyone had any information about the incense. Muk-ho-ja, hearing the news, came forward to say that the incense emitted a beautiful fragrance signifying that devotion had reached the plane of sacredness and nothing is better than *Triratna*. Therefore, if one prays with the incense burning one's wishes will be fulfilled.[26]

Regarding this story Shin Chong-won[27] argues that the reference to an envoy of Liang China is not correct, for the Liang dynasty had not been founded by this time. Also, if he was really a Chinese envoy, why didn't he know and inform the king of Silla about the usage of incense? Shin maintains that it must have been a merchant who had passed over the strange articles of Buddhism and due to its strangeness the incense must have reached the court. The merchant must have played a part in spreading Buddhism in Silla. Shin does not provide any details regarding the merchant, leaving room for him to be both Chinese and Indian. However, we think he must have been an Indian merchant. As we will show later, by this time commercial contacts between southern Korea and India were well established, either directly or via South-East Asia or south China. And if we take into consideration that the incense was one of the major items of Indian export, as stated earlier, the merchant should be an Indian. Therefore, before Chinese official envoys could transmit Buddhism, the Indian religion had, most probably, been introduced in southern Korea though it may not have been widely propagated. That is why, unlike the two other kingdoms of ancient Korea, Silla alone provides us stories conforming the existence of Buddhism prior to the official transmission from China.

The legend of princess Ho of Karak, an ancient Korean kingdom, in the *Samgukyusa*[28] is also relevant to our study of Indo-Korean contacts before the advent of Buddhism through China. The legend is part of the myth of king Suro, the founder of Karak or the Kaya kingdom. Il-yon, the compiler of the chronicle clearly indicates that it is a sketchy description taken from *Karakkukki*, a narrative by a magistrate of Kum-gwan county during the reign of Koryo king Mun-jong (1046-83). The important part of the myth goes as follows:

Since the creation of heaven and earth there had been no national name and no king of the people of Kimhae region. The nine kans or chiefs ruled over the 75,000 natives. In the eighteenth year of the Kien-wu era,[29] on the day of the bathing festival, the villagers heard a strange voice calling from Mt. Kuji. The voice declared that 'a heavenly god has commanded me to descend to earth, establish a kingdom, and become its king, and therefore I am here'. The nine chiefs and all the people danced with joy and looked up into the sky. The heaven opened and a purple thread descended to the earth, with a golden bowl wrapped in a red cloth tied to the end of it. When the cloth was removed the bowl was found to contain six golden eggs. The people worshipped the eggs and, having replaced the cloth, took the heavenly gifts to the house of Ado-kan, the head of nine kans. After some time they found that the eggs had hatched into six handsome boys. All the people bowed. The boys grew rapidly and after ten days the height of the boy who had hatched first had touched nine feet. He was crowned king with the title Suro. He named his kingdom Great Karak or Kaya kingdom, and the other five men became the rulers of the other five Kayas. After some time a queen of the Wanha kingdom laid an egg and it hatched a boy who was named T'alhae. T'alhae came over the sea to challenge Suro. They competed against each other in a magic contest which Suro won, after which he forgave the challenger.

In the twenty-fourth year of Kien-wu, on the twenty-seventh day of the seventh month, the nine chiefs requested the king to get married. The king replied, 'I was sent down from heaven to rule this land and so will get my spouse at divine command. Sail towards Mangsan-do or Mountain-viewed Island in the south and see what happens.' Reaching there, they found a ship with a red sail, flying a red flag. On the ship was a beautiful maiden with more than a score of attendants and servants. Getting down, she approached the temporary palace of king Suro. In the bed chamber she said, 'I am a Princess of Ayut'a. My family name is Ho and given name is Hwang-ok, and I am sixteen years old. In May this year my father and mother said to me, "In our last dream we saw a Heavenly-Emperor, and he commanded us to send you to Suro, the holy man." So, I started on my long voyage.' In that year the queen bore a son. The queen died at the age of one hundred and fifty-seven. Her two attendants from Ayut'a begat daughters and both died a few years later. All her servants died of homesickness and left no children. The king spent many lonely days in deep grief after her death and at last he also died at the age of one hundred and fifty eight.

Princess Ho, who came to be queen, had a very important role to play in the functions of fertility as well as divine kingship, both of which are not closely linked in early times. Suro, evolved from the heavenly egg, is the sky divinity which has been transmuted into the god of fecundity and sovereignty. Suro is also a mountain god while Ho is a sea goddess. Mountains share in the spatial symbolism of transcendence. They are 'high and supreme'. In this myth we find that Suro is bestowed divine kingship which it derived from the belief that the well-being of the social and natural order depends upon the vitality of the priest-king. The priest's or king's tenure of office was limited, in early times, to a prescribed period at the end of which he was put to death. In a series of ritual acts he had to have intercourse with the priestess or goddess-queen.[30]

Princess Ho, who came from the sea is nothing but the goddess of water, the one most essential to a fertility cult, while Suro is the god of the sky. They meet on the mountain, which is often looked on as the place where sky and earth meet and therefore, the point through which the *axis mundi* goes, a region impregnated by the sacred, a spot where one can pass from one cosmic zone to another. In this story, the structure of the fertility cult does not change but the goddess of the earth is replaced by that of the sea. In the Indian tradition the sea is the source not only of eternal life but sovereignty and sanctity. *Manusmṛti* states: 'In the beginning, only the water was created, and then, in the waters he laid his seed. And this became a golden egg. . . . In this egg Brahmā was born of himself, the ancestor of all living things.' Moreover, magico-religious power lies at the bottom of the sea and is given to heroes by female beings (*nagi*, 'princess smelling of fish').[31] Therefore, Princess Ho should be considered to be the mother goddess of the sea with fertility power as well as sacred powers for the throne.

Princess Ho is the one who came looking for a mate. In fact, the marriage is followed by sexual intercourse. It is noteworthy that in the *Samgukyusa*, quite a lengthy part of the story is circumstantial explanation of the marriage and the bridal night. We also find some passages related to the fertility cult. For example, the story states that on hearing the news of her arrival, King Suro ordered his officers to approach her in a boat pulled by oars made of the cassia tree which grows in the moon and with a helm made of magnolia. After receiving the king's request to come up to the temporary tent on the hill, Princess Ho leaves her ship and climbs a hill where she dedicates her pants to the Mountain Spirit.[32] Here, we notice that the oars made of the 'tree in the moon',[33] are another mark of the fertility cult, that is the lunar elements. The Indians believed that 'the moon is in the rivers' and 'rain comes from the moon'. That there was a connection between the moon, rain and plant life had been realized before the discovery of agriculture. The plant world comes from the same source of universal fertility and is subject to the same recurring cycles governed by the moon's movements. The fact that Ho dedicated her pants to the Mountain Spirit is also significant. The mountain is a symbol of the sky divinity, the counterpart of the mother goddess of the earth. Dedicating the pants is nothing but a metaphor for the rite or ceremony of sexual intercourse as a kind of fertility cult. In fact, sexual intercourse is regarded as a means, or rather a technique, of food-production. The magical or religious rites intended to secure the fertility of the fields were thought of as belonging to the special competence of women, the first cultivators of the soil, and whose power of child bearing was believed to have a sympathetic effect on the growth of the plant.

The ship of princess Ho bore a red-coloured flag and sail. The red colour is the symbol of blood and is treated everywhere in the world as having life-giving power. 'It is a worldwide custom for menstruating or pregnant women to daub their bodies with red ochre, which serves at once to warn the men away and to enhance their fertility. In many marriage ceremonies the bride's forehead is painted red . . . a sign that she is forbidden to all men save her husband and a guarantee that she will bear him children. . . . At initiation the girl is painted red from head to foot. So she is born again and will be fruitful. The symbolism becomes quite clear when we find, as we commonly do, that primitive skeletons were laid in the contracted or uterine posture. Smeared with the colour of life, curled up like a babe in the womb—what more could primitive man do to ensure that the soul of the departed would be born again ?'[34]

The motif of the cosmogonic egg is common to ancient India,

Indonesia, Iran, Greece, Phoenicia, Latvia, Estonia, Finland, Polynesia, West Africa, Central America, South America, Oceania and so on. The motif of the cosmogonic egg is widely available in Korean myths also though the idea of the birth of man replaces that of the creation of cosmos. We have five myths which contain the motif of birth from an egg out of which three can be grouped under one head and two under another.[35] The first group of the three has the common structure of the egg being produced by a woman regarded as profane, thrown away and preserved by some animals. This, we think, is the prototype of the idea of the egg-birth in ancient Korea.[36] The basic idea is not that of ordinary birth but rather a replication of the archetypal birth. Therefore, it is a model for the great king's birth. The egg of Hyokkose, the founder of Silla, and that of Suro are descended from heaven:

> King Suro was born from one of six eggs that came in a golden bowl wrapped in a red cloth which was threaded with a purple thread-band which descended from the heaven.[37]
>
> King Hyokkose was born from an egg of purple colour that a white horse left at the place where lightning-flash occurred. After leaving the egg, the white horse made a deep bow and went up to the sky.[38]

Here, we suggest that the motif of the sacredness (not simply uniqueness) of the egg-birth is the result of a mixture of Korean prototypes with Indian elements of the solar god and several other religious ideas.

Sūrya, the god of the sun, is man's true progenitor: 'When the [human] father thus emits him as seed into the womb, it is really the sun that emits him as seed into the womb.'[39] Thus, the epithet *viśvakarman* or 'all-creating' is applied to him. By his greatness he is the divine priest. The sun's chariot is driven by a divine horse, Etaśa, or by seven horses in the *Ṛg Veda.* Sūrya's horses radiate his rays. All the characteristics of the Surya myth are absorbed in the two Korean myths. Especially the horse and ray of the sun in Hyokkose's myth is good evidence of Indian influence. Hyokkose and Suro were maintained to be priest-kings who definitely needed the characteristic of divinity.

The name 'Suro' may be from the Sanskrit word *śūra* meaning 'to rule, possess supreme or superhuman power', or 'a god, divinity, deity', 'a sage, learned man'. It is also used as an ephithet of brave and divine kings or warriors like 'Śūravarman', 'Śūravīra', etc.

The golden egg indicates another element of Indian culture not found in any other myths. In India it was gold while in traditional China and Korea it was jade that the people regarded as the most precious thing. Gold has been highly valued in India from ancient times. In ancient China the symbol for the highest value was jade. In the social order it embodied sovereignty and power. In fact, there was no special term for gold, which was called *huangjin* or yellow metal. With the advent of Buddhist cultural influences, the Chinese began to associate gold with preciousness. Therefore, the golden egg is, in all probability, nothing but the incorporation of Indian ideas in the prototype to high value and sacredness.

Thread is another article much used by the Indians. Thread plays the role of a sacred article in Brahmanic tradition, such as the sacred thread in the *upanayana* ceremony when it is given to young boys before they start their course of Vedic studies. Those who accepted the thread were called *dvijas* or twice-born. Thus the thread is the symbol of one's being qualified for admission to the adult group which only can carry out all sacred functions. In the Suro myth, the thread plays the role of a chain connecting the sacred (eggs containing the king) with the secular (people of the world). In addition to this, the cloth in which the bowl is wrapped is red in colour which is the colour of blood in India as described above. It is a symbol of sacrifice and creation. Here, since the cloth contains the creation it bears the red colour. The use of the red colour in this manner is not found in any other myth of Korean prototype.

The event of the descending egg occurred on the day of the Bathing-festival in the case of Suro and in Hyokkose's case it was on this day that the egg was first bathed. It has been maintained that the idea of bathing came from China. If so, what makes the myths of Suro and Hyokkose contain the idea of bathing, although the northern part of Korea is far more easily influenced by Chinese culture? Since Harappan times,[40] Indians have believed that water has purificatory powers, not because of its intrinsic quality, but because it absorbs pollution and carries it away.[41] Thus, the flow of water determines its purificatory efficacy. Indians take a purificatory bath after they produce their children for they believe that the blood pollutes the mother. It is this idea which has been transferred to Korea at the time of king Suro.

King Suro was a bachelor when he ascended to the throne of the Kaya kingdom and was asked to marry the maidens recommended by the nine kans. He refused and instead selected a maiden from 'Ayut'a'. His doing so is indicative of the internal political situation which Suro faced. Since Suro was the man from the north, he had to control the native powers, i.e. the nine kans mentioned in the myth. To do so he must have tried some sort of marriage alliance and in order to keep some sort of check and balance among them chosen somebody not belonging to the strong families, i.e. the nine kans. Moreover, his power was challenged by somebody from outside his kingdom too. In the myth this situation is reflected in the story of the magic competition between Suro and Talhae who is considered to be the chief of the iron people from eastern Korea.[41] Overcoming all difficulties, Suro finally consolidated his political power. Since he changed the official names of the nine kans into Chinese, we know that he had succeeded in his task of consolidation. Finally, he became a king with tremendous power. Hence, myths naturally evolved around Suro and his exploits. He now becomes the king who is possessed of heavenly power and is master of the sacred Princess from India, the country with the more developed world-view.

After his coronation, according to the myth, Suro was advised in a dream, to meet a queen from the sea. And he met a Princess from Ayut'a and she became his queen. Here, the name 'Ayut'a' is clearly a reference to Ayodhya of India. It cannot be Ayuthaya of Thailand because the kingdom of Ayuthaya flourished at a period later than the year of the compilation of the *Samgukyusa.* Ayodhya is not the name of a kingdom or state but of a capital or major city of considerable antiquity. In fact the *Rāmāyaṇa,* in which Ayodhya figure prominently, provides the Asian people with the paradigm of a princess' abduction or her drifting in the sea. It can be suggested that Princess Ho in the legend is perhaps reminiscent of Sita[43] of the *Rāmāyaṇa.* The plot of the whole story is quite similar to the legend of prince Vijaya, the founder of Sri Lanka. According to *Mahavamsa* (Chs. VI and VII) and *Dipavamsa* (Ch. IX) the myth of King Vijaya goes as follows:

The Princess of Vaṅga, a kingdom in Bengal, was carried away by a lion of the Lāḷa kingdom in Gujarat, who begot on her two children, a son, Sīhabāhu and a daughter, Sīhasīvalī. The marriage between the brother and sister resulted in the birth of Vijaya. The prince Vijaya was so wild and lawless that he was banished from his native country, Sīhapura or 'lion's town'.[44] He set out southward with 700 companions and finally reached Sri Lanka. Prince Vijaya took for his wife a Princess of Pāṇḍya, a kingdom in south India, who, along with several officers of state and servants, set sail in a large ship which traversing the sea reached Sri Lanka.

The two chronicles justify the landing of Vijaya, which, as we have seen, make it coincide with the demise of Gautama Buddha in 483 BC. The validity of this synchronism may well be doubted but probably the records on this and other points, even if not absolutely reliable, are not very far from the truth. Whatever the exact year of the event might be, no one can deny the historical event. The chronicles are generally set in fourth and fifth centuries AD. Besides, Siṃhalāvadāna also relates the same event of the long sail from the mouth of the Gaṅgā to Sri Lanka. This great event was so popular that it became a fit theme for some of the paintings at Ajanta.

The idea of getting a bride, a Princess, from across the sea who reached the groom's country by ship, with a good number of companions, is strikingly similar to the story of the Suro-Ho marriage. Those arranging the marriage in the legend of Princess Ho, in the *Samgukyusa,* are her parents and the reason for selecting the groom are the groom's qualifications. These remind us of the requirements of a proper marriage in ancient India as approved by Manu. Out of eight forms of marriage, *brāhma, daiva, ārṣa, prājāpatya, āsura, gāndharva, rākṣasa,* and *piśāca,* the last four forms were condemned and the first four were approved. The father of the girl should freely select the bridegroom on account of his qualifications, and no party should be influenced by any consideration of wealth which the other might give. Here, we cite the words of Princess Ho in the *Samgukyusa* to show the correspondence of ideas, 'My parents told me . . . because Suro is a holy man . . . so go and marry him.' Though we find some later interpolations[45] suggesting that the marriage should take place because he is like a Heavenly Emperor, the main idea in the words of Ho is from the Indian marriage ideal.[46]

The red colour of the flag flown by Princess Ho is another proof of our contention. Red is the colour used in the marriage ritual. At the time of marriage, the husband places a red dot on his bride's forehead and fills the parting of her hair with the same colour. It is the symbol of the married woman in India, as the ring is symbolic of the wedded state in the West.

If we could demonstrate a similarity in the use of a symbolic or important number, we could be more certain of our thesis. The number of chiefs in the Kaya government is nine and the height of the first hatched boy, Suro, is also nine feet which cannot be the real size of the boy but is simply symbolic of his being extraordinary. In fact in India the number nine is very important. There are nine *licchavis*, nine *mallas*, and eighteen *gaṇarājas* of Kāśī and Kosala showing the significance of the number in terms of political organization. Nine is the expression of an ideal system. When Suro proclaimed the fitness of the land for rule, it was said 'to be the abode of the sixteen *arahants* and seven sages'. Sixteen might be equivalent to the *solasamahājanapadas* or sixteen great territorial states. In fact, in the Indian tradition, the number sixteen expresses completeness of features. In India, the number seven is regarded as sacred and used to express an indefinite plurality. Hence the number of *ṛṣis* or sages is seven, the *sapta-ṛṣis,* and that of sacred men is seven too, i.e. *sapta-vipra.* Thus in the *Ṛg Veda* and other Saṃhitas, the number of suns is seven, i.e. *sapta-sūryah,* the number of planets, of *mātris* or divine mothers, of streams, of oceans, of cities, of divisions of the world, of ranges of mountains, are all seven imbued with the significance of something sacred and brilliant. The Vedic tradition led to the Buddhist notion of *sapta-ratna* which is again related to brilliance. The number seven occurs at the birth of the Buddha. Mahāmāya, his mother, passed away after seven days of the child-birth. Therefore, it does not seem accidental that the body of king Hyokkose should become ashes and fall to the earth from heaven[47] seven days after ascending.

In Indian tradition the number three is divine as in the Brahmā-Viṣṇu-Śiva triad and the Buddha-Dhamma-Saṃgha triad. The *Ṛg Veda* mentions Viṣṇu's three strides and three is the number of the twice-born social classes in Vedic religious anthropology. Three-fold invocation of the deity is considered to be sacred in Brahmanical and Buddhist traditions. In Brahmanic prayers *śāntiḥ* is repeated three times at the end, and Buddhists perform their confession of faith three times. In addition to these, Buddhism conceives of *triloka* and of *trikāya.* Here, in our source too, the sacrificial offerings at King Suro's tomb continued for 330 years which is nothing but a complex of double three signifying divinity and zero signifying eternity. And the length of the silk on which King Suro is painted is three feet long. It was only after three days that tears of blood began to fall like rain from both eyes of that portrait as an expression of the discontent of the king's spirit with the sacrifices offered. And it was a thirty-foot long serpent that protected the king's tomb from a gang of thieves.

The idea of non-violence is introduced into the story when Suro fights against T'alhae. According to the Shamanic tradition the wicked should be destroyed fully. In the legend of sage Tamsi of Mt. Ch'il-chom, we are told that he declined beef supplied by King Kodung, son of Suro, but instead asked for some vegetables. Though this legend is tinged with the colour of Taoism, which is considered to be a later interpolation, it bears obvious affinity to the idea of non-violence or vegetarianism. Moreover, in this story, sage Tamsi is said to have uttered some sayings very similar to words in Sanskrit. All these factors establish without doubt some of the connections we have been suggesting. The similarities should not be considered to be accidental though this story was written down very late. Yi, Chong-gi maintains that a figure carved in Mt. Ch'il-chom must be the sage, and his features show Dravidian characteristics.[48]

Many elements in the story reveal the deep connection with India. Our story mentions a flag when the ship of Princess Ho appears. In fact, the flag is a common feature of Indian temples, be they Hindu, Buddhist or Jaina. Most of these flags are generally triangular in shape and usually of either ochre, red, white or yellow colour. The appearance of a flag in the story could indicate the existence of temples as well as a faithful and prosperous community carrying on its religious rituals and ceremonies without any obstruction.[49] In the Indian tradition a flag is a mark of a place which contains something sacred. It also denotes that a ceremony is to be performed. These connotations are absorbed in the flag of Princess Ho in the legend.

On her first night with Suro, Princess Ho brought out some mythical peaches and steamed dates after having searched for them for a long time. The date was a fruit which the Koreans had not even heard of at that time. The date is a fruit from a tree found in the Canary Islands and northern Africa and from the West Asia to South-East Asia and India.[50] It was not available in Korea in ancient times. Therefore, its mention as a gift prompts us to trace the origin of the ship.

In the third century BC there was a confederacy of tribes in the Kimhae area. This is generally accepted by scholars as it is supported by a good deal of archaeological remains like bronze implements and dolmens. The nine kans mentioned in the myth suggest that tribal-chiefs ruled and there was no absolute ruler among them. The setting-up of this tribal confederacy was due to the changing socio-political geography of the period. It was mainly due to the influx of people of the bronze culture from northern Korea who successively formed larger socio-political units outside Kimhae area. This situation naturally pressurized people of Kimhae and some others in the south to form a bigger political unit to suit the changing conditions. However, due to the lack of technology in the mode of production prevalent at the time, whether bronze or iron metallurgy, they could not form a more developed form of the state but only a kind of tribal confederacy.[51] This is the socio-political situation of Kimhae from the third century BC onwards uptil the rise of Suro.

However, in the first century BC or AD[52] people possessing advanced material culture or iron technology came down from the north. They succeeded in establishing several territorial chiefdoms. Suro was one of those who came from the north and finally founded Kaya. He collaborated with native tribes through marriage alliances and legitimized himself and his clan by insisting that he had descended from Heaven.[53] His clan must have been one of the conveyors of the prototype of the Korean myth whose main structure is the fertility cult and birth from egg. The myth of Suro is the product of the prevalent situation of the time.

King Suro had, as exemplified in the legend of T'alhae, difficulty in exercising political authority in his kingdom. Since he was the founder of the kingdom, he also needed political legitimacy to be able to consolidate his power. Mythological elements play an important part in the exertion of political control over others. For such purposes, the significance of cosmogonic myths is evident. Suro, too, utilized the prototype of myths in Korea which he must have been aware of, also adopting ideas from India or the so-called 'Indianized states of South-East Asia'. These ideas were obtained through the flourishing oversea trade of Kaya. Utilizing these prototype and alien ideas, he finally became the hero from heaven who got the heroine from the sea.

Suro's Kaya of Kimhae was situated on the bank of the Raktong river which regularly supplied a rich alluvial soil. It helped the Kaya attain great agricultural development. It also had the geographic advantage of being situated on the river where eventually developed into a good trading port. The port played an important role as a gateway to every important place from the upper Raktong region. At the same time, it was the key point in the Straits of Korea connecting southern Korea with the Japanese islands and China. Moreover, from the first century of the Christian era, the region was famous for the rich iron sand that enabled this area to develop the iron culture producing various iron weapons and iron-ore coins which were used as currency in the market.[54] Therefore, out of several Kayas, Suro's was most important power in the beginning, especially due to the sea-trade.

Kaya produced more refined wares which were the most advanced ones in southern Korea. The wares are decorated with various beautiful ornaments and bear witness to remarkable skills of manufacturing. Various kinds of crowns discovered from many tombs are enough to vindicate the claim of the advanced standard of the artisans and testify to the diversity of the crafts of Kayas. In particular, the existence of Kayagum or Kayaharp and the flourishing of music, arts and literature are good evidence of a sumptuous society and of the richness of the people. Such a society also tried to get articles from outside, which played an important role in the development of sea-trade.

From the beginning of the Christian era Kaya was the most active maritime state in Korea. The most popular trading articles were iron implements. *San-kuo-chi*, a Chinese chronicle informs us that trading ships sailed along the coast from Lolang of northern Korea to this area. In fact, Kaya exported large amounts of iron implements to various states of Korea, Japan and even China and imported other materials from these countries and supplied them to other tribal kingdoms of Korea. Various kinds of Chinese coins found in this region and some iron ore, used as currency, found in Japan are more than enough to support the claim of Kaya's flourishing sea-trade.[55] In fact it was an international trade at that time.

Meanwhile, in the early Christian era, there flourished some Indian or Indianized states in South-East Asia. Legend has it that the religious mission of the Buddhist monks Sona and Uttara was sent by emperor Aśoka in the third century BC to Suvarṇabhūmī, the 'Land of Gold'. However, it would be impossible to try to establish a precise date for the beginning of this process.

The Indians travelled to these regions both by land and sea. From very early times there was a regular trade-route by land between eastern India and China and also between Annam and India. The extensive trade along these routes led to the establishment of 'Indianized states' not only in upper Burma but also in the mountainous regions of the upper valleys of the Irawady, the Salwen, the Mekhong and the Red River as far as Yunnan. In South-East Asia,

Indian culture was not introduced for political reasons. None of the Indian type states in this area were ever dependencies of Indian powers. It was Indian merchants who opened the way for the expansion of Indian culture. In fact, they played a major role in the international trading network of Han China—Kuṣāṇa/Sātavāhana—Rome at that time. In our present state of knowledge, it is believed that extensive cultural contacts between the two civilizations had taken place some centuries before the Christian era.

We have seen that Korea came into contact with India through commercial activities as early as the first century AD but we do not hear of any Korean traders to India in the ancient period. Isolated attempts to visit India were made by some Buddhist enthusiasts from the sixth century AD, either with the purpose of learning Buddhism at first hand or to pay respect to the places hallowed by the memory of the Buddha. Moreover, Buddhist intellectuals faced serious problems in obtaining translations of Buddhist Sūtras and in formulating the proper disciplinary life in monasteries. Monk Kyom-ik was the first one to visit India with this purpose. In 526 he travelled to India to study the sacred texts further, especially the Vinaya texts. He visited a temple named Saṃghana in 'Central India' where he collected Sanskrit texts of Mahīśāsaka Vinaya. On his return journey an Indian monk, Devadatta, followed him to Paekche Korea where they translated seventy-two books of the Vinaya texts with the collaboration of eighteen eminent monks under the patronage of King Song of Paekche. Kyom-ik founded the Vinaya school in Korea.

From the eighth century onwards Korean Buddhists began to take a keener interest in India and Indian culture. In I-tsing's *Ta-T'ang Hsi-yu Ch'iu-fa Kao-seng-chuan* or *Biography of Eminent Monks Who Went to the Western Region in Search of the Law during the Great T'ang Dynasty* in the seventh century as many as eight monks out of fifty-five went up to India. This biography supplies us details of those Korean monks. A-nan-ya-bal-ma or Ānandavarman was the first one out of them who stayed at the Nālandā monastery studying the Vinayas and copying a large number of *sūtras*. He died thereafter having crossed the age of seventy. Hye-op or Jñanasaṃpada also spent some years in the Nālandā monastery where he studied Buddhism and devoted much time listening to religious discourses. Hyon-t'ae or Sarvajñadeva reached India through Tibet and Nepal. He made a pilgrimage to the Bodhi-Tree. Hyon-gak or Paramapūjya left for a pilgrimage along with Hyon-t'ae. Some days after reaching the monastery of the

Great Enlightenment he fell sick and died at the age of fifty. Hye-ryun or Prajñavarman left for India to pay homage to the sacred places of his religion. He lived in the Monastery of Faith in the city of An-mo-luo-pa or Amaravati for about ten years. Next, going east he visited the nearby Tukhara Saṃghārāma situated in north India. This Saṃghārāma had originally been built by the people of that country for the accommodation of Buddhist monks from Tukhara. The Saṃghārāma was very rich and had an abundant supply of all the necessities and comforts of life. No other monastery could surpass it in this respect. The pilgrim Hye-ryun remained there studying the Sanskrit language and became well versed in kosa. I-tsing's record says that two other Korean monks, whose names and origins are unknown, left Ch'ang-an, the Chinese capital, and reached the South Sea. They started their voyage to Śrīvijaya and P'o-lu-shih, the country on the west of Śrībhoga, fell ill and died there. Besides these, some more names are mentioned in the list of I-tsing's biography. Won-pyo, through land-route from China, Mu-ru via Eastern Turkestan, Pamir plateau and I-sin, returning with a large number of *sutras*, are some of the those names.

In ancient Korea, during the sixth and seventh centuries, Buddhism was so flourishing a paradise that the state supported it for the purpose of utilizing religion as state-ideology.[56] Monks devoted themselves mainly to studying the philosophy of Buddhism. The long distances separating Korea and India could not prevent them going into the Buddha's land in quick succession. The number of the lists which we have are not exhaustive of those who made a pilgrimage to India. A study of their numbers, ways, and their lives is still to be made. Due to scarcity of relevant sources in the two countries, not much work has been done on the subject. However, one could argue that the alien lifestyles of many Korean monks in India were impressive enough to leave a considerable influence on Indian culture, which also needs to be probed. Thus, we need not be surprised to find that Silla Korea was well-known to the Indians. I-tsing, in this respect, gives us valuable information: 'In Sanskrit the country Kye-kwi by-name of Silla is called Kukutaisola. Kukuta means chicken and Isola means honourable. Since chicken is worshipped in that country and people put its feathers on their hats for decoration, the name of country was given Kye-kwi.'[57] Here, we can refer the term *isola* to *īśvara* in Sanskrit without any difficulty.

The unification of the Three Kingdoms by Silla led to economic progress and social stability brought about by the sharp demarcation of the ruler and the ruled. The position of the peasants began to be undermined from this period. Among the ruling elite the Buddhists were the most prominent. The state patronized Buddhism, granting large amounts of land for Buddhist monasteries so that the Buddhists could develop the idealistic ethos of the religion. Thus, various schools of idealism prospered. This finally encouraged the monks to go to the advanced countries, viz., China and India to study their sectarian ideology. Among these, monk Won-ch'uk was the most prominent. He went to China for further study and with a thorough knowledge of Sanskrit he contributed a great deal to the development of the tenets of the *Vijñaptimātratā* school. His fame was so great that it spread as far as Tibet where his works are kept in the Tibetan Canon. Besides him, there were numerous other Korean monks in T'ang China. They even formed their own villages and monasteries in China.

Hye-ch'o was another prominent monk who went not only to China but as far as India and left a valuable record, *Wang-O-Chon-Ch'uk-Kuk-Chon* or *Memoir of a Pilgrimage to the Five Regions of India.* He left his motherland at an early age and reached China in AD 719 where he met and became a disciple of Vajrabodhi, a renowned master of Tantric Buddhism. He left for India some time shortly before 724. Hye-ch'o approached India via the sea-route across South China Sea. He started his travels in India via the eastern part of the country and made pilgrimages to holy places such as Sarnath, Kusinagara, Rajagriha and Bodh Gaya as well as important places such as Varanasi, Kannauj, etc. From here he went down south up to the capital of the 'south Indian kingdom' which has been identified as the kingdom of the Cāḷukyas.[58] Later he continued his travels and approached western India, which has been identified as the Valabhi[59] kingdom of the Kathiawar peninsular. Hye-ch'o headed for the northern part of India and visited Jalandhara, the Indus area, the Kashmir valley, Gandhāra, Kapiśā and several Central Asian states. Hye-ch'o arrived at An-hsi, the frontier city of the T'ang empire, which is identified by him as Kucha.

Such frequent pilgrimages by Korean monks to India were not the only a form of cultural contact between the two countries. The commercial activities of the early Christian era expanded after the fifth-sixth centuries which was the heyday of the three kingdoms in ancient Korea. In fact, in the fourth and fifth centuries the invasion by Hephathalites or White Huns damaged the urban centres in Bactria and along Amu Darya, bringing about its decline in the trade temporarily. However, communications between India and China continued and might even have improved. The waves of Hephathalites, Turkic tribes, Arabs and other pastoral people entering Central Asia from the fifth century onward did not block the prosperous trade of the Silk Road via Persia. Koguryo, extending its territory up to the far northern Manchu, met and struggled against the Turk empire of Central Asia which played a mediator's role in the Sino-Indian trade of luxurious items mentioned earlier. For this prupose, traders or official trade-missions of Koguryo must have made contacts with north-west India and Central Asia via the Silk Road. A mural painting in Samarquand in Central Asia clearly suggests the existence of Koguryo traders in this region.[60] In addition to this, a good deal of Indian luxury goods found their way in through Chinese trading missions. Archaeological remains reveal that the people of Koguryo imported various kinds of jewels, rare products of animal and plant origin such as lion-fur, peacock feathers, pomegranates, grapes, walnuts, etc.[61] Silla, which annexed Kayas in the sixth century, became a powerful kingdom with maritime activities. Due to lack of literary sources on the sea-trade we do not know much regarding the details of the trade such as its volume, items, etc. However, some archaeological remains suggest the contents of the trade. Roman glass, excavated in many tombs of Silla, might have been traded through Indian merchants. Flint glass was brought to Barygaza by Roman traders in the early Christian centuries, where Indian merchants handed it over to East Asian people. Though Indian workers must have been familiar with the technology of processing glass, most glass vessels found in Taxila were foreign imports. India was another major market for Roman coral. And the coral from Rome went to China and even further to Korea through north-western India. Yet, since Roman trade declined in Barygaza after the third century AD, Roman glass in Silla is unlikely to have come from here directly after that period.

From the eighth century, Korea witnessed rapid economic progress. The Koreans exported to T'ang China several items such as various kinds of luxurious silks, gold and silver artefacts, etc. They mostly imported luxury items such as emeralds, glass vessels, carpets, balm of Gilead, peacock feathers, etc. Some of the luxury items were handed over by Indian merchants but most arrived through Arabian traders who had the power of trade in the Indian Ocean and in West Asia in the pre-Turkish period. Indian traders are not mentioned anywhere in Persia and Central Asia, although we hear of Indian settlers in Alexandria at the beginning of the Christian era.

The history of Indo-Korean contacts starts at the beginning of the Christian era and reaches its climax during the seventh and eighth centuries. It commenced due to the influence of Indian culture in South-East Asia, and became well established through Buddhist activities. Lack of direct trade between the two was the main cause of the limited contact between them. In the early Christian era, Korean economy was not too vibrant but from the eighth century it picked up considerably. Without a prospering trade relationship, cultural contacts between the two countries could not assume significant proportions. Most of their contacts were indirect, with the Chinese playing the role of conveyors of Indian culture but paradoxically, sometimes China also became a barrier against direct Indo-Korean contacts. Even so, the cultural contact had such influence that Korean culture cannot be interpreted without understanding the Indian elements in it. Every aspect of Korean life bears traits of Indian culture.

NOTES

1. *Shih chi*, CXXIII, 3166.
2. Xinru Liu, *AIAC*, p. 61.
3. *AS*, VII. 12.
4. S. Seneviratne, 'Social Base of Early Buddhism in South-East India and Sri Lanka', unpub. Ph.D. thesis (Jawaharlal Nehru University, 1985), p. 522.
5. J. Burgges, *The Buddhist Stūpas of Amaravati and Jaggayyapeta* (rpt., Varanasi, 1970), p. 22.
6. A. Rea, *South Indian Buddist Antiquities* (Madras, 1984), pp. 7-11.
7. Himanshu P. Ray, 'Early Trade in the Bay of Bengal', *IHR*, vol. XIV, nos. 1-2 (July 1987 and January 1988), pp. 82-3.
8. J. Needham, *Science and Civilization in China* (Cambridge and New York, 1954), vol. V, pt. 2, p. 137.
9. L. Casson, 'Cinnamon and Cassia in the Ancient World', *Ancient Trade and Society* (Detroit, 1984), p. 237.
10. J.I. Miller, *The Spice Trade of the Roman Empire* (Oxford, 1969), pp. 86-7.
11. G. Lubrun, 'Betel Chewing', *Journal of Oriental Research*, vol. XVII (1947-8), pp. 160-7.
12. Seneviratne, op.cit., p. 486.
13. R. Champakalakshmi, 'Urbanisation in South India: the Role of Ideology and Polity', *pro-IHC*, 1986, p. 8.

14. C. Maloney, 'The Effect of Early Costal Sea Traffic on the Development of Civilization in South India', unpub. Ph.D. thesis (University of Pennsylvania, 1968), p. 112.
15. Himanshu P. Ray, op.cit., p. 89.
16. R. Pankhurst, *An Introduction to the Economic History of Ethiopia* (London, 1961), p. 47.
17. R.S. Sharma, *Indian Feudalism* (2nd edn., Delhi, 1980), p. 55.
18. H. Chakraborti, *India as Reflected in the Inscriptions of the Gupta Period* (New Delhi, 1978), pp. 101-3.
19. Xinru Liu, op.cit., p. 35.
20. For details on post-Han period, see Xinru Liu, op.cit., pp. 47-52.
21. Dipakranjan Das, *Economic History of Deccan* (Delhi, 1969), p. 264.
22. *Fa-hsien,* p. 66.
23. See P.C. Bagchi, *India and China* (2nd revd edn, Calcutta, 1981), pp. 255-77.
24. Byoung-Ik Ko, 'Han-kuk-kwa So-yok', *Che O Hoe Kukche Haksul Kangyonhoe Nonmunchip* (Seoul, 1977), p. 16.
25. *Taisho,* p. 1021 C.
26. *Yusa.*, III-iii, Adogira.
27. Chong-won Shin, 'Silla-ui Pulkyo Chonrae-wa Ku Suyong Kwajong-e Taihan Chaegomt'o', in *Paiksanhakpo,* vol. 22, (1977), pp. 143-4.
28. *Yusa.*, II-ii, Karakkukki.
29. AD 42.
30. See J.G. Frazer's *Dying God,* quoted in N.N. Bhattacharyya, *AIRTSC* (Delhi, 1975), p. 17.
31. M. Eliade, *Patterns in Comparative Religion* (London, 1958), p. 210.
32. *Yusa.*, II-ii, Karakkukki.
33. *Śāśin* in Sanskrit literally means 'containing hare'. This idea may have influenced Korean beliefs.
34. G. Thomson, *Studies in Ancient Greek Society* I (London, 1949), pp. 209-10.
35. See Yeol-Gyu Kim, 'Mindam-ei Chonki-chok Yu-hyong', in *Hankuk Minsok-kwa Munhak Yon-gu* (2nd edn., Seoul, 1972), pp. 71ff.
36. If we accept Eliade's opinion in his *Patterns in Comparative Religion* (op.cit.) in pp. 413-16 that of the myth of cosmogonic egg originated in India, and the Oceanian idea of man born of an egg only copys and repeats the motif of the creation of the Cosmos, the latter serving as a model for the former, the Korean prototype is nothing but a transformed prototype of India. The myth of the creation of the cosmos from an egg is given in the *Śatapatha Brāhmaṇa* and *Manusmṛti.*
37. *Yusa.*, II-ii, Karakkukki.
38. *Yusa.*, I-i, *Silla Sijo Hyokkose.*
39. *Jaimini Upanishad Brahmana,* iii, 10, 4.
40. However, the idea of the sacred bath is just an inference which is generally accepted.
41. Lawrence A. Babb, *The Divine Hierarchy: Popular Hinduism in Central India* (New York, 1975), passim.

42. Ki-dong Lee, *Hankuksa Kangjwa,* vol. I (Seoul, 1982), p. 103.
43. In the ancient hymns of the Vedas, sītā is simply the furrow which bears crops for men. In the *Arthaśāstra* of Kautilya (I.24) sītā is conceived as residing in seeds and plants. The superintendent of agriculture is mentioned as *sītadhyakṣa* (see N.N. Bhattacharyya, *AIRATSC*), p. 110. This is another kind of fertility cult. In the Korean myth, Princess Ho also plays the role of the Mother Goddess.
44. There is controversy regarding the location of this place; D.B.S.K. Aiyangar in *Age of Imperial Unity* (5th edn., Bombay, 1980) p. 235, located it in Magadha or Bengal following the tradition of *Mahāvaṃsa.* E.J. Rapson in *Cambridge History of India,* vol. I (Indian rpt., New Delhi), p. 549, locates in Gujarat.
45. In the later interpolation to the main story, some articles came to be connected with the legend of the advent of princess Ho. For example, a stone *stūpa,* named Basa or Pasa is attributed to princess Ho. The legend connected with the stone *stūpa* tells that it was brought to Kimhae by princess Ho in order to placate the anger of the Sea Goddess. This is definitely a later interpolation because at that time multi-storyed stone *stūpas* were not being constructed in India.
46. The similarity of the plot of the story is found in at least one other case. For example, the idea of 'to set a boat drift by a king with something left with boat praying whoever may take this and praying that someone would find the boat and perform a religious act using the materials do something' is common to the story of Hwang-nyong-sa-chang-yuk-sang (in *Yusa.*) and that of Bhaddakaccāna-Panduvāsudeva marriage (in *Mahāvaṃsa*). Comparative research on this topic in details seems to be done necessarily in near future under the other theme.
47. This must be rhetorical device of the act of cremation, that shows us the influence of Indian culture. Koreans did not cremate there dead especially great men like Hyokkose but buried their dead at that time. Here, the hidden expression for the custom of cremation is the striking influence of Indian culture. However, we are not sure whether this idea came into Korea during the initial contact with India, before the arrival of Buddhism through China or later, through Buddhism.
48. Chong-gi Yi, *Karak-kuk T'am-sa* (Seoul, 1972), p. 86.
49. Jagdish P. Sharma and Lee Siegel, *Dream Symbolism in the Sramanic Traditions* (Calcutta, 1980), p. 32.
50. *Encyclopedia Britannica,* vol. 3, p. 896.
51. Tae-sik Kim, 'Kaya-ui Sahoe Palchon Tankye', in *Hankuk Kodae Kukka-ui Hyongsong,* ed. by Hankuk Kodae Sahakhoe (Seoul, 1990), p. 89.
52. Ibid.
53. Ibid.
54. Ki-dong Yi, op.cit., p. 157.
55. Chong-hak Kim, *Hankuk Sang-go-sa Yon-gu* (Seoul, 1990), p. 237.
56. For details see Ch. 3.
57. *Taisho.,* no. 2066, p. 2b.

58. Yun-hwa Jan, 'South India in the VIII Century Hui-ch'ao's Description Re-examined', *Oriens Extremus*, vol. XII, no. 1 (1968), pp. 169-77.
59. Yun-hwa Jan, 'West India According to Hui-ch'ao's Record', *IHQ*, vol. 39, nos. 1 and 2 (1963), pp. 27-37.
60. Won-ryong Kim, 'Samarquand Afraciab Kungjon Pyokhwa-ui Sajoltan', *Kogo Misul*, nos. 129 and 130 (Seoul, 1976), pp. 162-7.
61. Ibid.

CHAPTER 3

The Political Idea of the Ideal King

BUDDHIST THOUGHT discounts secular values and stresses mental and spiritual discipline. Thus it does not offer much by way of a systematic contribution to political theory. Reform of earthly life is not a major concern of the sects, for peace and fulfilment are to be gained through detachment from the affairs of the world. Buddhist literature is basically moralistic. Early Buddhists, thus, called political science *khattavijjā*, 'the Kṣatriya science' assessing it to be *tiracchānavijjā*, 'low arts' and *micchājīva*, 'wrongful occupation'.[1] Buddhist canonists regarded politics as a systematized body of knowledge which can be identified, for all practical purposes with *arthaśāstra* (or more generally, 'the science of politics'), seeing it as a dismal science, based upon a creed of unbridled selfishness and ruthless cruelty for the sake of one's self-interest.[2] Following a stern and unbending code of ethics, they maintained the unqualified supremacy of moral law over governmental affairs. In other words, they saw politics as being antagonistic to ethics.

The origin of social and political institutions was accounted for in terms of periodic evolution, in the same way as in the Western theory of social contract. Challenging the Vedic dogma of the divine creation of social order, the *Aggañña Suttanta* propounds that in the original state of nature beings lived in a condition of god-like perfection. The institution of kingship, however, evolved when, as a result of the origin of property, the four evils of theft, censure, lying and violence appeared in society. It is explained that the people gathered together and elected the most handsome and capable individual as king who would be wrathful when indignation was right, would censure that which should rightly be censured and would banish him who deserved to be banished. In return the people agreed to give him a portion of their rice. He was called by titles such as Mahāsammata ('one chosen by the many'), Khattiya ('one who is lord of the field') and Rājā ('one who gratifies others in accordance with *dhamma*').[3] This view, which dominated early Buddhism, leads logically to the conception of a police-state in which the ruler's part is confined to the maintenance of public order, while that of the people is limited to contributing to his support.[4] On this point U.N. Ghoshal opines that it provides two important bilateral historical justifications for characteristic principles: the conception of the king's office as the grand safeguard of individual and collective security and that of the temporal ruler's quasi-contractual obligation of protecting his subjects.[5] The king's office is the foundation of the security of the people and his protecting the people is the natural and necessary obligation of the temporal ruler otherwise, the people would be free to kill the wicked king and place the wise youth on the throne.

A good number of passages in the Pali *Tipiṭaka* indicate, in impressive language, the immense significance of the king's attitude towards *dhamma* in relation to his whole environment. The stock description of an ideal king given in the *Nikāyas* is: *dhammiko dhammarājā çaturanto vijitāvī janapadadatthā variyapatto*: a righteous monarch who has conquered the whole world and under whom the country is stable and tranquil. The king must rely only on *dhamma*, honour *dhamma*, esteem *dhamma*, take *dhamma* as his standard and mandate and set the *dhamma* as watch and bar and ward for people living within his realm. This is significant in the sense that it defines precisely the relationship between *dhamma* and political power. *Dhamma*, in this context, implies a composite tradition of justice, impartiality, benevolence and non-violence.

In all their speculations on the nature and functions of the state, the early Buddhists perceive violence as the central, political problem. They acknowledge violence, force and arbitrariness as inherent in the exercise of power. Though *dhamma-vijaya* is favoured, the Buddha himself admits the difficulty of ruling without the use of force in any manner and under all circumstances. Nor is it known that the Buddha advised total disarmament of the state. However, the early Buddhists sought a solution to the problem of violence by making *dhamma* basis of the state in the hope that a constant awareness of *dhamma* would transform the very nature of the state. In this context *dhamma* comprises *dhamma* and *vidhāna*, a corpus of principles and a method of realizing them in practice. Since the reality of the power of the state was often likely to manifest itself in the violence of wars or expropriation and arbitrary conduct caused by the despotic ambitions of individual rulers, the early Buddhists sought to control, if not eliminate it, by advocating the virtue of *ahiṃsā* (non-injury), *pariccāga* (renunciation) and *sama* (equality). It is the combination of *dhamma* with *vidhāna* that makes a king a moral being which was the highest ideal projected by early Buddhist political theory. Thus, *dhamma*, in the political sense, requires ten ethical qualities in a king (*dāsarājadhamma*) comprising *sīla* (character/behaviour), *dāna* (charity), *pariccāga* (renunciation), *ajjava* (uprightness), *maddhava* (gentleness), *akkodha* (non-anger), *tapa* (austerity), *ahiṃsā* (non-injury), *khantī* (forbearance), and *avirodhanam* (non-opposition).

Besides, an ideal king is described as one who dispenses justice and carries out tours of inspection and provides proper treatment to the various classes of society as well as knows the proper time for the enjoyment of personal pleasures. The relationship between a king and his subjects is described to be similar to that between a father and his sons, an ideal echoed by Aśoka. The ideal king must observe *dhamma* towards mother and father, wife and son, relatives and ministers, draught animals, the realm, hermits and Brāhmaṇas, birds and beasts. He should apply himself to the promotion of the universal happiness of his subjects so as to extend its benefit down even to dumb creatures. Thus, the basis of the state being *dhamma* it became the duty of the state to eliminate poverty. The duties of the state are described as righteous protection and compassion, the former being its protective function while the latter is its ministrant aim. Thus, the early Buddhist concept of the state of *dhamma* has not the slightest of theocratic associations as is made clear in Ajātaśatru's assurance to Buddhist monks to go ahead with their plans for holding the First Council when he says: 'Mine is the authority of the state while yours is that of religion.' There is definitely no divinity associated with kingship.

The ideal king rules without *daṇḍa* for he resorts neither to mutilation nor punishes the errant with fines. Actually, in *rāja-dharma*, *daṇḍa* symbolizes the authority of the king and although often translated as force or physical coercion, it also carries the sense of authority and control over the enforcement of laws and punishment where these were not obeyed. Yet, in the Buddhist context *cakra*, as a symbol of the authority of law, is preferred to *daṇḍa*. This is well elaborated in the concept of the *cakravartin*. The origin of the concept of *cakravartin* is debatable. The *cakra* is known as a symbol of the sun which travels around the earth and rules over it, and thus, is the most important possession of Viṣṇu, the Brahmanical Lord, preserver of the world. The *cakra* was considered to be symbol of the legitimacy of power in ancient India and thus, the *cakravartin* held a similar position in the world of politics. Drekmeier, in this connection, points out that the *cakravartin*, as a product of the virile culture of the Vedic age, is the exceptional man who can remake the world—the 'the historical man' who emerges to save the dharmic order from whatever decay may be at work in the structure.[6]

The *cakravartin* is the *dhammiko dhammarājā par excellence*. He is the righteous conqueror because he has overcome his enemies as well as curbed his passion and anger. He is the *mahāpuruṣa* possessing all the signs of a super-normal stature. He is the proud possessor of the *saptaratna* or the seven mystic treasures. And he is handsome, long-lived, full of strength and beloved of his people. He is well-born and duly crowned and the country under his rule enjoys peace and plenty. His seven mystic treasures are the *cakra*, elephant, horse, jewel, woman, the householder and the leader or general. The horse and elephant are supernatural in their powers and can fly through the air. The woman is the most beautiful in the land and the jewel with its brilliance can turn darkness into light at any time and in any place. The householder is the richest man in the universe and the leader is invincible. The *cakra* is his chief emblem for it is the *cakra* that leads him to non-violent conquest in all directions. He acquires these treasures through mystic contemplation and communion and the source of all his charismatic power is *dhamma* itself. It is only when the king is righteous that the *cakra* appears before him. It cannot be passed on in hereditary succession and in the event of the abdication or death of the *cakravartin* it disappears. It leads the king in all the directions and wherever he goes the powers in the area acknowledge his paramountcy. As the mighty monarch appears in each quarter with his army, the rival kings therein offer their submission. And he does not exact tribute from them but simply advises them to observe the five precepts. The *cakravartin* allows them to retain their possessions on condition of their observance of the five moral precepts 'Ye shall' so goes his solemn admonition, 'slay no living thing, ye shall not take that which has not been given, ye shall not act wrongly in order to fulfill your material desires, ye shall not speak lie and ye shall drink no intoxicating drink'.[7] After his tour of conquest for *dhamma* when the *cakravartin* returns to the capital the *cakra* enters his palace and stands facing the seat of justice as the visible symbol of the rule of right and justice. Here, we see the association of the *cakra* with power and justice just as *daṇḍa* is associated with the king's power of punishment in Brahmanical thought. The symbol of the *cakravartin* is not the rod or punishment but the *cakra* or *dhamma*. With *dhamma*, the *cakravartin* is expected to eliminate the violence which is inherent in the power of the state and make of it an instrument of higher morality.

The best historical model of this concept is Aśoka, the third Mauryan emperor. It is debatable whether the Buddhist idea of the *cakravartin* in the *Cakkavattisīhanādasutta* is prior to Aśoka and an idea that inspired him to aspire to the model or conversely it was his political accumen that lay behind the idea of *cakravartin*. It seems, however, that Romila Thapar is right to hold that the idea of the *cakravartin* was not a fully developed political concept in the pre-Mauryan period and most of Aśoka's actions were not inspired by his ambition to be a *cakravartin*.[8] Several of Aśoka's political concepts such as on the *dhamma* tour of the king, *dhammavijaya, daṇḍasamatā, vyavahārasamatā,* paternalism and the welfare of the state, closely echo the ideas of the Buddhists on kingship and political authority. It is possible, therefore, that Aśoka's ambitious, all-embracing concept of benevolent kingship and the exercise of political authority is inspired primarily by Buddhist ideas and values, although it might not coincide perfectly with the Buddhist ideal of the king as *cakravartin*. Aśoka adapted a comparatively new religion in which he personally believed during a period of political and economic change.[9] Aśoka's *dhamma* played a positive role in defining kingship as the most productive and regulating force in the polity. In fact, precisely because Aśoka made a total claim for the role of the king, his policies simultaneously portrayed the other face of kingship, of wide-scale regulation and domestication and of political absolutism, which too have left their mark on the Buddhist polities of South-East Asia.[10]

The Buddhist idea of kingship prevented the emergence of dictatorship. Related to this, another concept to be taken into account is with regard to elective kingship. The words *yebhuyyasikā* in Pali and *yadbhūyaṣikā* in Sanskrit seem to mean putting to a vote and deciding by majority.[11] There is a clear reference in the *Uluka Jātaka* to a case where the birds were to vote on their choice of king.[12] On occasions, ministers might wield considerable power either as rulers or as selectors of the ruler. Succession by ministerial approval or restricted selection is mentioned quite frequently in Buddhist literature. The *Saṃvara Jātaka* has the courtiers saying to the dying king, 'When you are dead, my lord, to whom shall be given the White Umbrella?' He answers, 'All my sons have a right to the White Umbrella, but you may give it to him that pleases your mind.'[13] In another Jātaka we find the courtiers testing a seven-year-old prince to decide whether or not they can make him the king.[14] Ministerial influence on the king's rule and even on royal succession is also mentioned quite frequently in Buddhist literature. A legend in one of the Jātakas shows the king actually being deposed by one of his ministers because the king refused to give up his unrighteous conduct.[15] *Divyāvadāna* says that Aśoka wasted so much of his treasure on religious activities that finally the ministers deposed him and installed his grandson Samprati on the throne.[16] When a minor succeeded his father, the ministers held the real power of government until such time as the sovereign was capable of ruling.[17] Occasionally, ministers selected the future king from the royal family if the succession was disputed. There are stories in the Jātakas where the king hands over the kingdom and the duties of administration to the ministers and retires to the forest.[18]

The king's *dhamma* was believed to radiate into all spheres of activity. In ancient Indian tradition, not only the ends but also the means of the king's rule were within the range of political theory. The relationship between welfare, good rains, sickness, calamities, and death among the people, and the *dhamma* of the king is illustrated in a number of stories from both Brahmanical and Buddhist literature. The king was far more than merely the political head of the state. The king who followed *dhamma* presided over people of *dhamma* while a king who followed *adharma* presided over people who followed *adharma*. The Jātakas contain stories of kings banished by the people. The wicked king brought evil upon his kingdom and it may be that the subjects were morally justified in killing such a king in order that their own spiritual merit might not be diminished as a result of the king's folly. This idea is explicitly stated in a Jātaka which declares, in the words of Sakka, 'the unrighteous king is slain, now we have received from the hands of Sakka a king who is righteous. . . . This is your righteous king and from this time forth he shall rule in righteousness. If a king be unrighteous, God sends rain out of season, and in season he sends no rain; and fear of famine, fear of pestilence, fear of the sword—these three fears come upon men from him.'[19] The *Mahāvaṃsa* contains numerous illustrations to show that ministers and rebel princes had recourse to assassination as a method of gaining the throne.[20] *Milindapañho* lists a number of tortures and punishments which a person unfit to be king should undergo if he claimed the throne.[21]

Early Buddhist views on the ideal king as *dhammiko dhammarājā* are repeated in Māhāyana Buddhist works such as *Milindapañho.* Nāgasena, defining a king, says 'A king is one who in his turn proclaims laws and regulations according to the instructions laid down in succession by the righteous kings of ancient times, thus carrying on his rule in righteousness.'[22] And the view that politics is antagonistic with ethics is evident in *Buddhacarita* in which the author describes sensual indulgence as being in consonance with the principles of politics. In this work, the Buddha is made to remark that royal power is the abode of delusion and that it rests upon oppression. He adds that power intoxicates as well as obstructs *dhamma* by causing the oppression of others. He then points out that a gulf separates the *dhamma* of salvation with its emphasis upon quietude and the *dhamma* of kings with its emphasis upon *daṇḍa* or punishment, and he ends by indicating their essential incompatibility in the following emphatic words: 'If a king delights in quietude, his kingdom collapses; if his mind turns towards his kingdom, quietude is ruined; for quietude and security are incompatible like the union of water which is cold with fire which is hot.'[23]

The Mahayanists developed the principle of the ruler's obligation towards his subjects and the latter's willing submission to the former's political authority. Āryadeva, in his *Catuḥśataka*, puts to an imaginary king the bold and direct question: 'How can you be proud, you who are a mere slave of the multitude fed by the one-sixth share of the crops paid by the subjects?'[24] This clearly shows a remarkable development in the idea of sovereignty with the king functioning as the slave or servant of the people for wages. It embodies a moralist's stern repudiation of the ruler's claim to pre-eminence apparently based on the old *arthaśāstra* pattern, namely, that the king is the spring board of the whole administrative machinery.[25]

Following the tradition of early Buddhist ideas on the ideal king, Māhāyana Buddhists concentrated their emphasis on *dharma* as a king's foremost obligation. *Mahāvastu* emphasizes the basic idea that *dharma* is the best policy for the strength and prosperity of the kingdom.[26] The rule of righteousness imposes upon the king some characteristic principles and policies of government comprising protection of the good, impartial justice, friendliness towards neighbouring kings as well as temporal and spiritual benefit to all classes of his subjects. In *Milindapañho*, in the words of Nāgasena, the king is told to be one who rules and guides the world dominating over all other men, making his relatives rejoice and his enemies mourn.[27] When pleased with a hard-working servant, he gladdens his heart by bestowing gifts as well as censures and fines and executes the man who transgresses his commands. Proclaiming the right and the wrong principles according to instructions laid down in succession by righteous kings of old and ruling in *dharma*, he becomes dear to his people and by the force of his *dharma* establishes his dynasty long in the land. This makes clear that the king has not only the authority to reward and punish but to preserve all his belongings in the kingdom. His rule is justified only when his action is in the interest of his people and his kingdom's security and on the basis of *dharma*.

Following the tradition of *dharma* established by early Buddhism as the first policy of a king, the Mahāyāna Buddhists related the idea of kingship with the Brahmanical *arthaśāstra* tradition. The story of the three wise birds in *Mahāvastu* is a good instance of this.[28] The address of the first speaker is in the familiar *arthaśāstra-smṛti* tradition dealing with the moral qualifications of the temporal ruler (involving his freedom from passion) as well as the technique of his consultation with ministers. The second speaker refers similarly to the qualifications of the king's ministers (comprising wisdom and intelligence) as well as the principles underlying governance (including strictness in punishing criminals, firm supervision of officials and wide application of espionage). The address of the third speaker introduces the simple patriarchal-type government in contrast with that of organised bureaucracy put forward in the earlier Jātaka story no. 527. Here we have to observe that the author, agreeing with his predecessor, places the wisdom at the head of all the powers of a king. This statement, which means that the strongest state is the one ruled with the highest wisdom, brings the author's thought in line with the advanced ideas of Kautilya on the subject.[29]

Aśvaghoṣa, following tradition in his concept of kingship, considers a king to be an extraordinary being. The Buddha is made to say 'Be happy like Indra, shine even like the sun, flourish with your virtues, understand the highest good in the world, rule the earth; obtain long life, protect the sons of the good with Āryas and enter the glory of sovereignty.'[30] The author has assigned all divine and supernatural powers to the Buddha by glorifying his father, Śuddhodana, who is described as the counterpart of Indra.[31] He, with the beauty of the moon, attracted the gaze of his subjects.[32] He made his subjects happy by his conduct, like a cloud gladdening people with rain.[33] He illumined the earth with the blazing light of his fame.[34] He was endowed with rare qualities and virtues like those of Śakra.[35] He had extraordinary power and the glory of gods.[36] Not only is the king Śuddhodana but his queen Māyā and son Siddhārtha are also described by Aśvaghoṣa as endowed with divine powers. Queen Māyā was called Mahā Māyā, because of her resemblance to the incomparable Māyā.[37] To this divine couple was born Siddhārtha, who had a glorious form that surpassed all mankind and had the bull for his sign. In other words, he was a godlike son in human form. Such deification of the king corresponds with Manu's ideas who says that the king was created with the strength and qualities of Indra, Pavana, Yama, Sūrya, Agni, Varuṇa, Candra and Kubera.[38] In accordance with the *Manusmṛti*, a country without a king is described as being 'devoid of lustre, as the sky is without moon, though it may be full of thousands of stars.'[39] Agreeing with Kautilya, Manu and other *dharma sūtras*, Aśvaghoṣa elaborates in detail the mental and physical qualities of a king. The king is strong, resolute, learned in sacred lore, wise, brave, skilled in counsel, steadfast self-controlled and gracious.[40] He is noble, virtuous[41] and handsome yet not presumptuous; courteous yet straightforward, courageous yet forbearing, masterly yet without arrogance.[42] He considers *dharma* above self-reputation.[43] He is expected to follow *dharma, artha,* and *kāma* at the prescribed times.[44] He adheres to his promises with constancy.[45] He receives the unfortunate with kindness[46] and removes their misery.[47] He gives gifts regularly to the Brāhmaṇas[48] and takes a meal only after assigning the first portion to holy persons.[49] Describing the glories of Śuddhodana's reign after the birth of his son, Aśvaghoṣa says that since the event the king daily waxed mightier in riches, elephants, horses and allies, his enemies being turned neutral and those who had been neutral into allies, and his allies being firmly attached to him. During his reign the rain fell in the proper season and at the proper place and the crops grew without the labour of tilling. There was no begging and no turning away of those deserving alms. No one was disrespectful to his elders or lacking in generosity. Husband and wife did not transgress against each other and the people enjoyed the joy of deliverance from famine, fear and disease.[50]

Mahāyāna Buddhism developed the idea of the *bodhisattva* into a future Buddha. The *bodhisattva* is supposed to serve as an intercessor in the political realm while he awaits his incarnation and is related to the concept of the political messiah. Actually, the Buddha is *mahāpuruṣa par excellence* but his real role in the cosmological process is to reveal it. And the second *mahāpuruṣa* is the *cakravartin*, whose role is to roll the righteous wheel in the political process. The essential prerequisites for becoming either a Buddha or a *cakravartin* are identical. The Buddha in the sixth century BC is alleged to be the fourth of five Buddhas to appear in this world epoch and the fifth Buddha will appear five thousand years after the demise of this Buddha. Similarly, someday there will appear a *cakravartin* who will bring the universe under the rule of the law. Thus, any king can claim to be a Buddha or *cakravartin*. In almost every Buddhist country, many rebel kings from the peasantry legitimised their political authority by proclaiming themselves to be future Buddhas. Their charisma was based on the claim to being a *cakravartin* but some of the kings who are described as *bodhisattvas* were by no means saintly.

Mahāyāna Buddhism, under the influence of Brahmanism, raised the king's social status from that of high authority to that of divinity. In fact, Aśoka's title *devānaṃpiya*, 'beloved of the gods' may be the starting point of such a tradition. He repeatedly applies to himself the epithet *devānaṃpiya*, an action emulated by his grandson Daśaratha and by various kings in Ceylon after Tissa. Romila Thapar concludes that *devānaṃpiya* was a generally known royal title of the time.[51] The significance of this title lies in the fact that by claiming divine favour for the king it invokes a doctrine which was fully developed by Manu and Bhīṣma in the *Mahābhārata*. R.S. Sharma rightly points out that the title devaputra is assigned to the king to emphasize the divinity of the Kuṣāṇa rulers.[52] The king, in the *Suvarṇaprabhāsottama Sūtra*, is referred to as being born out of the thirty-three gods and therefore, he is called *deva* and styled *devaputra*.[53] In *Milindapañho*, the author describes a king as one held worthy of homage by the multitudes of beings, whether gods or men, who approach him and the king is exalted above all ordinary men.[54] Such is the adaptation of Manu's well-known doctrine of the divine creation of the temporal ruler out of the essence of the regent of the quarters, for the purpose of the thirty-three gods (a well-known Buddhist category of divinities), evidently is to acclimatize the Brahmanical theory to a new environment.[55]

The *Suvarṇaprabhāsottama Sūtra* provides us with the best example of the Mahāyāna ideas on kingship.[56] In this *sūtra* we are told that the king is installed by the gods so that the kingdom might not be destroyed by the practice of wickedness. The king should rule his kingdom in accordance with *dharma* and never practice *adharma*, and he should refrain from taking sides even at the cost of his life. In the event of the king's rule being unrighteous, unrighteousness increases greatly and the kingdom is afflicted with wickedness and strife, while the gods in heaven are wrathful and the kingdom falls a prey to the enemy's forces.

In the event of the king's neglect of that for which his kingship exists the winds do not blow regularly, the rains do not fall in season, the stars and the planets, the sun and the moon do not move regularly, the crops, flowers, fruits and seeds do not grow well, and famine visits the land. In such an event the gods in heaven predict swift destruction of the kingdom through divine wrath, while wickedness, strife and disease overtake the land. The king himself, in consequence, suffers bereavement in his family and his group of officials as well as in his elephants, horses and camels. In such an event meteors fall from the sky and a rival sun appears therein, while fear of the enemy's troops as well as famine increases greatly. When the king neglects to punish wrongdoing in his kingdom, he is found guilty at the bar of his heavenly parents, and he thereby ceases to be their son, while he fails to do his duty by his kingdom. There is no such terrible cause for the destruction of the kingdom as when the king fails to punish wrongdoers.[57]

Here we notice the neat dovetailing of the idea of *dhamma*, underlying the concept of ideal kingship of early Buddhism with the idea of the king being a divine creation found in Brahmanism, that leads to the peculiar ideas of Mahāyāna Buddhism on kingship. The king, thus, is a divine being for the fulfilment of righteousness. Moreover, he is the divine being who presides over the right cosmic order that is related to agricultural produce. In this respect, we know that the early Buddhist idea of king as protector of natural products enlarges in terms of divinity. Mahāyāna Buddhists, thus, expanded the range of the king's politico-social attributes to economic and even religious fields.

Since the time of the Guptas, Buddhist canonists have followed their predecessors' view on politics. Vasubandhu's *Abhidharmakośa* says that in the beginning the beings resembled the gods of *rūpa* and then gradually under the influence of greed and idleness they laid by provisions for themselves, and there arose among them the idea of property and finally dividing their fields they set up a protector of the same for a payment.[58] Following the canonist view Buddhaghosa also, in the fifth century, in his work *Visuddhimagga*, stands by the same logic on the relationship between the progressive fall of man and the rise of the institutions of property, ruler and the state. The authors in this period tell us how the fields were demarcated and alloted to individuals by mutual agreement. They truly follow the Pali canonists' theory of the creation of property rights by means of popular agreement and of the state by a governmental compact of a bilateral character. Āryaśūra too, in his *Jātakamālā*, repeats a principle which is as old as the Pali canonical text, that is the principle of antithesis and antagonism between politics and ethics on the ground that statecraft is dominated by the ends of wealth and pleasure instead of virtue and that it is based on a creed of merciless and shameless exploitation of the subjects by the ruler in his own interest.

By the middle of the sixth century AD the Korean people came into contact with a new kind of religious system which was highly developed and totally different from what they had known so far. As the three kingdoms competed with each other for paramountcy, they used all the available methods to maximize their political authority. In these circumstances, the rulers of the Korean kingdoms welcomed Buddhist ideas on kingship and political authority. Numerous attempts were made to follow the ideal of Buddhist kingship from the time that Buddhism was recognised as a state-religion though in actual life, like their predecessors in India, the kings presented a distinct contrast to the ideal. Many attempts were also made to choose from among the various ideas of kingship that Buddhism presented. Hence, many kings projected themselves as being associated closely with the Buddha and became his ardent patrons while at the same time, they pursued the single-minded quest for power unhampered by the concept of the ideal. In this context, early Korea is not an exception to all the other Buddhist countries.

In early Korea, only a few rulers projected the Buddhist ideal of the king or *cakravartin*. King Chin-hung (540-76), the hero of the unification of the three divided kingdoms could be taken as the best example of the historical reality of the ideal Buddhist king or *cakravartin*. We know that he was an ardent Buddhist from the following statement in the *Samguksagi* 'Since his coronation, he has devoted himself to the Buddha ardently and in his later days, became a monk.'[59] That King Chin-hung patronized Buddhism is evident from his having constructed monasteries, *stūpas*, etc. He also started the tradition of two Buddhist ceremonies, *Paekchwakanghoe* or the Ceremony of a Hundred Monks' Discoursing on Sūtras and *Palgwanhoe* or Uposatha or the Ceremony of Eight Precepts. These ceremonies turned out to be the most popular of Korean Buddhist ceremonies, leading ultimately to Buddhist ministers being instituted as national priests. Even though he was evidently a pious and ardent Buddhist king, we must not be hasty in concluding that he was also a *cakravartin* or ideal Buddhist king. Only after we have examined other aspects of his rule can the character of his kingship be properly understood.

King Chin-hung had two sons whose names were Tong-ryun meaning 'Copper *Cakra*' and Sa-ryun meaning 'Iron[60] *Cakra*'. Since it is the father who names his sons, the names Copper Cakra and Iron Cakra indicate that King Chin-hung must have been not only familiar with the concept of *cakravartin* but also anxious to fulfill the ideal. The inscriptions on his monuments, which were set up after his tour of border districts, are the main sources for determining the character of his kingship with relation to the idea of *cakravartin*. We have four extant inscriptions on stone monuments. Out of these the Hwangch'oryoung inscription shows us his political ideas best. The text of this inscription, according to the clearest letters decipharable is as follows:

Unless the breeze of purification blows, the righteousness of the world will be alienated from truth. Unless righteousness is studied thoroughly, evil will prevail in the world. Thus, the king, after the commencement of his reign, must exercise himself and render comfort to his people. Here, I have taken over the throne of honour and have been discreet in every respect lest I go against the Way of Heaven. I have expanded my territory into the four quarters and have protected the people and the land and led neighbours to swear to live together with trust and harmony by practising diplomatic friendship. On reflection, now, it seems righteousness did not reach all the people especially those who have newly became the citizens of the unified Empire. And it seems that those who enjoyed the benefits before the unification have suffered its absence. By the eighth month of this year I made a royal tour of the border areas in order to learn about the feelings of the people, to find out if they are loyal, trustworthy and diligent and to praise and reward patriotic people who have been brave in the battlefield and have devoted themselves to the kingdom.[61]

In this inscription of King Chin-hung it is practically impossible to miss the underlying ideal of the *cakravartin*. The ideas of righteous rule, royal tour, the emperor of the Four Quarters, protection of land and people, and diplomatic friendship with neighbours are clearly derived from Pali sources. Moreover, all of them are quite similar to the ideals advocated by King Aśoka, the most exemplary of the *cakravartin* in the Buddhist tradition. Especially notable is the fact that King Chin-hung visited the people, listened to their opinions and offered money or a prize which shows that he followed in the footsteps of Aśoka whom early Korean Buddhist kings admired as the ideal king. Chin-hung's inscriptions, also in the first person, remind us of Aśoka's inscriptions where the emperor speaks directly to his subjects. Besides, the erection of monuments and their utilization as a way of teaching and culturing shows us his strong will to attain *cakravartin*-hood or at least to follow the model of Aśoka. However, in this context, we should not miss the point that this attempt to follow either the *cakravartin* ideal or the historical Aśoka does not preclude the attempt to get legitimization and/or elevation of his power and authority in historical reality. Linking Aśoka's political ideas and policy to himself, King Chin-hung affirms the prestigious legitimization of his rule.

However, King Chin-hung, the greatest national hero of early Korean Buddhist kingdoms is also a most complex character whose actions, in fact, would seem an outright affront to the Buddhist sensibility. Warfare becomes King Chin-hung's mode of action as he ignites successive wars so as to bring the three kingdoms of early Korea under the parasol of one state. It is this waging of incessant wars that is the most evident affront to the Buddhist ideal of statecraft. The primary function of kingship in Buddhist thought is the maintenance of order. By living a life of contemplation and engaging in meritorious deeds and by setting an exemplary standard, the king serves to inspire the moral transformation of his subjects and thus ensures an orderly or peaceful realm. The ideal king was expected to cultivate the virtues of non-injury (*ahiṃsā*) and rule without the aid of force (*daṇḍa*) and weapons of destruction (*sattha*). Early Buddhist political thought insists on the principle of non-violence and non-injury as the ideal basis of statecraft and hopes to minimize the violence inherent in the exercise of power at all times, by restraining it with morality. King Chin-hung would be, by ideal standards, inviting disorder and in this manner, would ostensibly be antithetical to the portrait of that righteous and exemplary king, the *cakravartin* who lives in supremacy over this earth, to its ocean bounds, having conquered it not by the scourge, not by the sword but by *dharma*.

Between the year 551, in which he commenced his own rule following his mother's twelve years' regency, and 568 in which he completed his career of conquest, King Chin-hung wrested the Han valley, strategically the most important area; finally subjugated Great Kaya and brought all of the six Kayas completely under his suzerainty. For the first time he also brought the north-eastern part of the peninsula under his rule. Ironically enough, during this period he also devoted himself to many religious works such as constructing monasteries, performing the largest Buddhist ceremonies and so on. In 553 he laid the foundation-stone of the Hwangnyong monastery which was completed after fourteen years, in 566. In addition to this he constructed the four largest monasteries in early Korea. He also established, as has been mentioned before, two significant historic Buddhist ceremonies, the Paekchwakanghoe and Palkwanhoe. All of these activities were carried out simultaneously as he was waging wars.

The fact that he constructed the great Buddhist monasteries and performed some brilliant Buddhist meritorious acts at the same time as he was waging wars shows that King Chin-hung was different from both Aśoka and Duṭṭhagāmani, the Sri Lankan king who ruled between 161 and 137 BC and who performed meritorious works only after having renounced violent deeds. Whether their remorse was genuine or strategic is a matter of conjecture. Unlike the latter, however, Chin-hung's violence and meritorious deeds were concurrent. Then the question arises as to what made King Chin-hung perform meritorious works while committing violence? What kind of method did he adopt for justifying his continuing violence?

What is needed here is the study of the myth surrounding him for it could reveal valuable ideological assumptions. In the Sri Lankan myths regarding the three visits of the Buddha to the island, the Buddha is hardly a *mahākāruṇika*, the man of profound kindness but a persona endowed with violence who as a conqueror cleared up the island of Yakkhas. During his conquest the Buddha uses his supernatural powers to intimidate and harass the Yakkhas and shows his compassion only after the kingdom has been annexed. The Buddha's use of supernatural powers to harass the Yakkhas is comparable with the king's resorting to violence against foes. In explaining the need for the Buddha to take such extraordinary steps, it is stated that the Yakkhas were incapable of understanding the truth and were opposed to the *sāsana* and therefore had to be removed from the island. Thus the myth presents an ethical principle distinct from those found in the Pali canon, i.e. violence is permissible in the interest of the *sāsana*. According to the chronicle it was not for personal glory but for the establishment of the *sāsana*, to make 'the *sāsana* shine forth'[62] against those who do not understand the 'true doctrine' and are opposed to it, that violence is undertaken. This reinterpretation of the attitude towards violence facilitates the mediation of the practical behaviour of the king in Sri Lanka.[63] Needless to say the ideological background of Duṭṭhagāmaṇī's resorting to violence was this myth of the Buddha's presumed visits. And through Aśoka, who in the Sri Lankan chronicle[64] was depicted as a kinsman of the Buddha through Mahinda's entrance into the *saṃgha*, Sinhalese kingship is given political stature and deemed implicitly Buddhist.[65]

In Korea, the counterpart of the myth of the Buddha's visits to Sri Lanka is the myth of 'Buddha Land'. The myth which contains references to the Buddha, Buddhas, *bodhisattvas* and sometimes 'Aśoka' or 'India', supplied important ideological background to the political authority, sometimes even the king's violent actions. In the *Samgukyusa*, in one place, it is stated that:

> In the second month of the fourteenth year of King Chin-hung's reign . . . a large ship arrived all of a sudden at Sapo, Hagok-hyon. An official letter was found in it which read:
>
> Aśoka of Soch'uk[66] has set a boat adrift laden with 570 thousand kun[67] of iron and 30 thousand pun[68] of gold since he tried to cast three of Buddah's images but in vain, praying 'wheresoever may, let the country take these materials to cast images'.

With this came three models, one of Buddha's and two of *bodhisattva's* images. An official of Silla reported this, and the king sent an envoy to build a monastery named Tongch'uksa where the three images were kept. And the materials were sent to the capital city and the images were successfully cast. They were kept in the monastery Hwangnyongsa. . . . And the monastery Hwangnyongsa, in your country Silla, is a divine place where Śakyamuni Buddha and Kāśyapa Buddha had their abode and discoursed and lectured. Their stone pedestal still stands there.[69]

In this myth, we find a remarkable attempt at political legitimization through Buddhism. King Chin-hung is not simply depicted as an ideal Buddhist king but as one superior to King Aśoka who was admired as a paradigm of the ideal *cakravartin*, for the former accomplished what the latter failed to do.[70] Silla is designated as the land of Kāśyapa Buddha which implies that Silla existed as the land of the Buddha much earlier than India, the land of the present Buddha.[71] Therefore, the monastery built at the site where the ship of Aśoka arrived safely was named Tongch'uksa, literally meaning the monastery of east Chon-ch'uk.[72] Clearly, this is an attempt to upgrade the home country as superior or equal to India, which was degraded as So-ch'uk, west Chon-ch'uk. In this context, Silla is depicted as the land of *bodhisattvas* Mañjūśrī, Kṣitigarbha, Avalokiteśvara, Amitayus, and Vairocana. Raksan[73] and Mt. Odae are the places where Avalokiteśvara and fifty thousand Mañjūśris, etc., made their permanent abodes respectively.[74] The myth of the Buddha Land becomes the ideological background for the Buddhist king's legitimization of his kingship. It clearly embodies the message that the country belonged to the Buddha. Thus, it even rationalized anti-canonical actions, such as the resort to violence in the name of protecting *dhamma*. The myth of the Buddha Land performed the function of a political charter for the ambitious kings of ancient Korea.

Whatever the character of the myths may be, kings in early Korea were not divinized for purposes of political legitimization. This does not mean that the rulers were not aware of the notion of *devaputra*. The *Samgukyusa*, in this context, supplies us with a good illustration.[75] Here, in the words of King T'ai-tsung of T'ang China (626-49), General Kim Yu-shin is divinized as the son of Thirty-three Heavens. This clearly indicates that the significance of divination for the purpose of political legitimation was well-known. But simply because, 'Silla is a small country outside China',[76] their kings were not allowed to adopt the same title as was used by the Chinese kings. General Kim Yu-shin, one of the two greatest heroes of Korea, by virtue of unifying the three kingdoms as well as being the brother-in-law of King Mu-yol, another hero of the Koreans, therefore acquired legitimacy by being called *devaputra*, that is, the son of Thirty-three Heavens. Though the early Korean kings knew of the Buddhist method of divination for political purposes, they could not make full use of it in their contemporary geo-political circumstances.

King Pop-hung, literally meaning '*dharma* arising' who ruled between 514 and 540 is credited with the official recognition of Buddhism as a state-religion even though to do so he had to execute one of his court officials. Together with the recognition of Buddism, he started his military campaigns and subjugated some small chiefdoms in which the main state of six Kayas was included. His military campaigns were not claimed to be for personal glory but for the 'creation of an earthly paradise which would provide comfort and long life to citizens by the establishment of state-religion'. This strategy developed into the idea of Buddhism as '*rāṣṭrapāla dhamma*'[77] which has become the most characteristic feature of Korean Buddhism down the ages. This notion of '*rastrapala* Buddhism' has been deeply enmeshed with the idea of 'Buddha Land', supplying the ideology of justification for a Buddhist king's non-Buddhistic policy, such as resort to violence. Of the five secular precepts of monk Won-kwang; viz., (i) to serve the king loyally; (ii) to honour ones parents with filial piety; (iii) to make a friend with sincerity; (iv) to fight at the battle-field without retreat; and (v) to kill living things with discrimination, we see that a new principle the fifth has been presented which enables a distinction to be drawn between permissible and non-permissible types of violence. If we take note that monk Won-kwang was the political counsellor of King Chin-p'young, another famous Buddhist king in early Korea reigning between 579 and 632, we will see that this principle, which is not found in the Pali canon, is manifested as basic and vital for the justification of violence by early Korean Buddhist kings.

At one place in the *Samgukyusa*, the royal family of Silla is proclaimed as being descendend from a Kṣatriya,[78] a clan to which the Buddha also belonged and whose duty was to protect the people and the land with violence if necessary. This tradition clearly shows that by establishing this connection with the Kṣatriyas, Korean Buddhist kings attempted to protect themselves as warriors who could resort to violence when necessary while at the same time projecting themselves as Buddhist kings. Needless to say, this kind of connection is established not only for the purpose of elevating the genealogical status of the royal family but also to facilitate the mediation of the contradiction between the ethical ideal and the practical behaviour of the king. These myths were resorted to when the kings were threatened by enemies and invasions. In this respect, it is noticeable that this attempt to identify the Silla king with the Kṣatriyas continues, in the *Samgukyusa*, with: 'Go back and erect the nine storyed *stupas*; then the neighbours will surrender and the nine countries will pay tribute.'[79]

The association of the king with the *bodhisattva* provides another ground for the justification of the king's resort to violence. Kung-ye, a rebel king, in the post-Three Kingdoms period, in the ninth century, provides us the best example in this context. Before his accession to the throne, Kung-ye was a monk. He founded the Later Koguryo dynasty proclaiming its name as Ma-Chin (derived from the Sanskrit Maha-Cina or Great China), i.e. the Great East as South-East Asia was called 'Greater India'. And Kung-ye declared himself to be *bodhisattva* Maitreya and his two sons as two other *bodhisattvas*. According to the chronicle, he rode only on a white horse with ornaments of silk on its head and tail. He ordered two hundred *bhikkhus* to follow him, chanting Buddhist invocations whenever he went out. And he is credited with the authorship of twenty Buddhist works which unfortunately are not available now. He is also supposed to have given discourses on these works to the people. Moreover, he has been described as a merciful general-king, sharing every happiness and sorrow with his soldiers at the time of both labour and rest. From this source, we also come to know that he tried to realize the Buddhist paradise in which *bodhisattva* Maitreya descends upon the earth and *cakravartin Saṃkhya* rules. Through this method, he came to attain the status of the leader of the laity in a political as well as religions sense which the *saṃgha* recognized. However, it is a paradox of history that after the attainment of such religious merit, he proved to be a most non-religious king. In his later years Kung-ye, king of *bodhisattva* Maitreya, was by no means saintly. His aspiration to *bodhisattva*-hood did not prevent him from executing one of his monks who ridiculed his Buddhist works and lectures, and from killing his wife and two sons. We know that even the king who wielded the sword with vigour and executed his people cruelly was recognized as a future Buddha, Maitreya, which is one of the most characteristic components of the ideal world ruled by a *cakravartin* described in Buddhist literature. It is quite clear that by this time (around the ninth century) the contradictions between the warrior king and the Buddhist ideal king had already been mediated.

It is in this context that we should examine the essence of the relationship of the *saṃgha* with secular society. The picture of the *saṃgha*-laity relationship as revealed in the Vinaya texts reflects a stage of development where the two had evolved ongoing and mutually beneficial contacts in day-to-day life. The *saṃgha* was no longer a group of people who had renounced household life and lived outside the bounds of organized society. The life of the *saṃgha* involved a dependence on householders who alone could supply the *saṃgha's* everyday needs. Furthermore, the institutions of renunciation and ordination inevitably brought the *saṃgha* into contact with the state and its bureaucracy, which led to the formulation of rules prohibiting the entry of persons who had opposed the ruler. In order to secure sustained assistance from the householder, early Buddhists had to offer their patrons a distinct spiritual ideal, such as that of merit-making which the *saṃgha* alone could confer. These circumstances created a mutualistic symbiosis eventually resulting in the socialization of an organization that had begun its career on an a-social basis. We will now examine this symbiotic relationship between monarchy and *saṃgha* with special reference to the *saṃgha's* participation in politics, leading to *adharma*, that is, violence.

The tradition of Buddhist political thought in Korea in the early centuries did not prohibit involvement in the political life of the country. The establishment of Buddhism in Korea depended heavily on royal patronage, sanction and support, which meant that Buddhism had to make peace with the temporal power. Even when a certain monarch had serious moral shortcomings, as in the case of the rebel King Kung-ye, in the post-Three Kingdoms period, the Buddhist *saṃgha* did not oppose his authority and sometimes even tended to consider him virtuous and pious so long as he supported the *saṃgha* and *dhamma*. Buddhism as such could not be a threat to royal authority. In other words, the *saṃgha* never embarrassed the monarch by passing ethical judgements on political issues. The king, as the patron, saw to it that Buddhism did not step outside its boundaries. Therefore, though there were devout kings and ministers and even monk-ministers, they conducted political affairs with little reference to Buddhist principles.

In early Korea, cases of eminent monks' participation in politics, the world of *adharma*, are not rare. The best example of this is monk Won-kwang. Although a monk, at the command of King Chin-p'young, he wrote an official letter to request Sui China to dispatch troops, justifying his actions by saying 'It is not the way of monks to destroy others in order to save themselves. But how can I disobey you as long as I am your subject in your land!'[80] He did not try to excuse himself through any pedantic interpretation of the precepts of Buddhism. Instead he willingly compromised himself as he was faced with a historical reality he could not wish away. It will be remembered that it was monk Won-kwang who formulated the 'Five Secular Commandments' out of which the fifth one, 'to kill living things with discrimination' and the fourth one 'to fight at the battlefield without retreat' were already indicative of his attitude. Thus, under the guise of *rāṣṭrapāla* or protecting the country, adharmic practices were fully justified in the Buddhist system as it developed in Korea.

It is well-known that not merely did monks support warfare in spirit but they actually participated in the very activity. In this context, the fifth precept of the 'Five Secular Commandments' of Won-kwang supplies sufficient ideological backing for the idea. Won-kwang was, in his time the leading monk, revered not only by monks but by the laity and society in general. The monk-minister, like the national-priest, was a military officer rather than a civil servant whom the government expected to act as a military strategist or sorcerer.[81] Monk To-ch'im was dispatched to the court of the neighbouring kingdom as a spy, to help his king to plan his assault on the enemy with ease. Such activities are definitely opposed to the Buddha's teaching. That monks should indulge in them is even more deplorable. Though the Buddha admits the difficulty of ruling without the use of force and never advised the total disarmament of the state, he did expresses his disapproval of the institution of war by forbidding monks from witnessing any parades and reviews. Therefore, the participation of monks in a battle is far more reprehensible, being rather an extreme kind of adharmic action.

Sovereignty was, thus, the source of manifold works of merit at the same time as it was the source of many injustices as if it were sweet food mixed with poison. The *saṃgha's* historic dependence upon the monarchy for support, protection and confirmation of the faith was not an unmixed blessing. The solemn charge given to the king was that of helping to maintain a strong and united order. That is the reason why kings in every Buddhist country made use of officials to force the unity of the *saṃgha*. Sectarian conflicts appear to have become entwined in political faction fights given the inevitable competition for patronage.[82] The king was head of the state with power to purify the *sāsana*, which he often did. The monarch, in turn, was kept responsible by the *saṃgha*. However, the ideal of reciprocity that endured cannot be questioned. No one can deny that there was little friction between the *saṃgha* and the monarchy as long as the monarchy was favourable to Buddhism. In essence, it was a symbiosis rooted in tradition and having far reaching consequences. It also demonstrated what it meant to be a Buddhist community in the best sense of the word, a *sāvaka-saṃgha* or ideal social order.[83]

A great deal more could be said about the king's protection and support of the *saṃgha*. Early Korean history witnessed full-fledged royal patronage to the *saṃgha*. Ideally, too, the ruler was expected to be the *fidei defensor*, protecting *dhamma* from heretical incursions, settling disputes among the *bhikkhus*, encouraging the teaching and spread of the doctrine. There were roughly two kinds of royal patronage in early Korea. At first kings supported the *saṃgha* in material terms, such as by constructing monasteries and granting lands and/or finances. The land grant and/or finance grant was the earlier form of the king's material support to the *saṃgha* that gradually lost its use once the *saṃgha* itself came to be a flourishing institution with its own economy. Gradually, the size of the farms that belonged to the Buddhist *saṃgha* increased as donations by the rich poured in so that finally it became possible for the *saṃgha* to run its own economy. Finally, the *saṃghas* took over the business of money-lending and rice-lending, which was, paradoxically enough, prohibited severely by *their* lord, the Buddha in his days in the sixth century BC in India. Such business activities made the *saṃghas* very affluent and finally left them corrupt. These became the most critical points which caused severe affront to the Buddha's teaching. The involvement of the *saṃgha* in economic activities on a large scale and corruption in the *saṃgha* itself were some of the major factors which caused the decline of Buddhism in medieval Korea.

In spite of this, however, Buddhist patrons accumulated their merit by encouraging Buddhism in spirit too. It was the king's initiative which led to the introduction of the Buddha's *śarīras* from China. Kings prompted monks to go to China and India to study Buddhism further and bring the *Tripiṭaka* from those countries. They also sent monks to Japan to introduce Buddhism there and teach its philosophy to the members of the royal family. Kyom-ik from Paekche was the earliest monk who visited India and brought Vinaya texts in 524. Hye-ch'o was another monk who visited India to study Buddhism. The records he has left now form an invaluable source for the reconstruction of Indian history in the eighth century. In addition to these there are also, as mentioned in I-tsing's *Biography of Eminent Monks Who Went to the Western Region in Search of the Law during the Great T'ang Dynasty*, eight Korean monks (out of a total of fifty-five, the rest being all Chinese except one from Sogdiana, Central Asia) who visited India. If we take into account the fact that Korea is much further away from India than China and that the record of I-ts'ing concerns mainly his own people, that is Chinese monks, it will become easier to estimate the enthusiasm of Korean monks at that time. Eminent monks to the Japanese court and the royal family included Monk Hye-gwan, who became the teacher of the crown prince-regent Shotoku (593-622) and who opened the Mādhyamika school in Japan. Kwan-ruk, another monk from Paekche became the first head-priest in Japan. These instances provide enough proof of the kings' full-fledged support to the *saṃgha* as patrons supplying a valuable ground of symbiosis between them and the *saṃgha*. Finally it must be mentioned that the Vinaya school flourished most in early Korea and was of great importance. The stress on the observance of Vinaya rules was so attractive to the kings that they utilized it to control not only monks but lay people as a whole.

NOTES

1. *DN*, I.1.27.
2. U.N. Ghoshal, *HIPI*, p. 66.
3. *DN*, III, p. 93.
4. U.N. Ghoshal, *HIPI*, p. 64.
5. Ibid., pp. 64-5.
6. C. Drekmeier, *KCEI*, pp. 162-3.
7. *DN*, II. pp. 169f.; *DN*, III.62f.
8. Romila Thapar, *ADM*, p. 146.
9. Ibid., p. 215.
10. S.J. Tambiah, *WCWR*, p. 62.
11. John W. Spellman, *PTAI*, p. 52.
12. *Ulūka Jāt.*, no. 270.
13. *Saṃvara Jāt.*, no. 462.
14. *Gamaṇi Caṇḍa Jāt.*, no. 257; *Padañjali Jāt.*, no. 247.
15. *Maha Sutasoma Jāt.*, no. 537.
16. *Divya.*, p. 384.
17. *Udaya Jāt.*, no. 458; *Mvm.* VIII, 4.

18. *Gaṇḍatindu Jāt.*, no. 520; *Ekarāja Jāt.*, no. 303.
19. *Maṇicora Jāt.*, no. 194.
20. *Mvm.*, XXXIV, XXXV, XXXVI.
21. *MP*, VI, 17.
22. Ibid., IV, 5.27.
23. *BC*, IX, 12-49.
24. *Catuḥśataka.*, IV, 77.
25. U.N. Ghoshal, *HIPI*, p. 342.
26. *Mvt.*, I, 274-82.
27. Ibid., IV, 5. 27.
28. Ibid., I, 274-82.
29. U.N. Ghoshal, *HIPI*, p. 266.
30. *BC*, XI, 70.
31. Ibid., I, 2.
32. *Saun.*, II, 22.
33. Ibid., II, 30.
34. Ibid., II, 39.
35. Ibid., II, 45.
36. Ibid., II, 49.
37. *BC*, I, 2.
38. *MS*, VII, 4.
39. *Saun.*, I, 60.
40. *BC*, II, 33, 34.
41. Ibid., II, 21.
42. Ibid., II, 4.
43. Ibid., II, 20.
44. *BC*, X, 28.
45. *Saun.*, II, 13.
46. Ibid., II,10.
47. Ibid., II, 16.
48. Ibid., II, 31.
49. Ibid., II, 19.
50. *BC*, II, 1-16.
51. Romila Thapar, *ADM*, pp. 226-7.
52. R.S. Sharma, *APIIAI*, p. 227.
53. *SPS*, XII, 5-12.
54. *MP*, IV, 5-27.
55. U.N. Ghoshal, *HIPI*, p. 262.
56. *SPS*, XII, 13-73.
57. Ibid.
58. *Abhidharmakoṣa*, III, 98.
59. *Sagi.*, IV-iv, Chin-hung-wang.
60. Cheol-chun Kim, 'Silla Sangdae Sahoe-ui Dual Organization', *Yoksahakpo*, no. 2, 1952, p. 91.
61. Nam-son Choe, ed., *Shinjong Samgukyusa*, Purok (Seoul, 1933), pp. 13-15.
62. *Mvm.*, 25, 2-3, 17.

63. R.A.L.H. Gunawardana, 'The Kinsmen of the Buddha: Myth as Political Character in the Ancient and Early Medieval Kingdoms of Sri Lanka', in Bardwell L. Smith, (ed.), *RLPS*, (Chambersbourg, 1978), p. 99.
64. *Mvm.*, 5, 196.
65. Alice Greenwald, 'The Relic on the Spear: Historiography and the Saga of Duṭṭhagāmanī' in Bardwell L. Smith (ed.), *RLPS*, p. 15.
66. Italics mine, for emphasis.
67. 601.04 gm.
68. 0.375 gm.
69. *Yusa.*, III-iv, Hwangnyongsa Changyuk.
70. Yong-tae Kim, 'Silla Pulgukt'o Sasang', in *Hankuk Pulgyo Sasangsa* (Seoul, 1975), pp. 155-6.
71. Ibid., p. 151.
72. Chon-ch'uk, a transformed name of Sindhu was the name of India in traditional East Asia. It abridges as ch'uk when it adds a prefix and/or suffix.
73. Transliteration of Potalaka.
74. *Yusa.*, III-iv, Raksan Idaesong Kwanum Chongch'ui, Choshin; *Samgukyusa*, III-iv, Taesan Oman Chinshin.
75. *Yusa.*, I-i, T'ai-jong Ch'un-ch'u-gong.
76. Ibid.
77. Sanskrit equivalent for *hokuk*, meaning 'protecting country'.
78. *Yusa.*, III-iv, Hwangnyongsa Guch'ungt'ap.
79. Ibid.
80. *Sagi.*, IV, Chin-p'yong-wang.
81. Ki-baek Yi, *SSY*, p. 37.
82. Romila Thapar, 'Religion and the Social Order', *CIS* (n.s.) 21, 1 (1987), p. 162.
83. Bardwell L. Smith, *RLPS*, p. 57.

CHAPTER 4

The Idea of Merit-Making and Donation

THE INSTITUTION of gift-making, holds a remarkable place in ancient societies. Though the nature of gift-exchanges in societies has changed as societies change, it has never lost its main characteristic of reciprocity from the beginning of time till now. The attitude towards exchanges in primitive agricultural society changed with the advent of advanced agricultural societies. In a similar manner, the nature of exchanges in a society dominated by the commercial ethos differs from that of an agriculture-based society. According to Marcel Mauss gift-exchanges in which certain categories of people are involved in almost ritualized social and economic relations are embedded in the larger continuum of social and economic relations.[1] Gift-exchange would, therefore, tend to become less embedded in those primarily agricultural societies which experienced the gradual impinging of changing attitudes to land and the ownership of land and where land slowly emerges as the major economic unit.[2] The exchange is not impersonal as it is linked to an individual or a particular group. And the accepted token of wealth is significant since wealth is a demonstration of status; it is a means of controlling others by winning followers and by placing those who accept the gift under obligation.[3] The exchanges precluded accurate calculations of direct returns but never obliterated the concept of a more general return. The symbolic motivation in making a gift was the belief that it is reproductive and the donor would receive the same in larger quantity. Though in theory all gifts are voluntary, disinterested and spontaneous yet in practice they are obligatory and interested.[4]

In early societies influenced by Buddhism, the transactions between the mundane and sacred worlds were realized between the *saṃgha* and the laity. It was on alms exclusively from lay society that the large number of renouncers led their lives in the beginning. And the lay people in society who gave up the ultimate goal came to insist on their own share in soteriological terms owing to their gift-making. This took the form of reciprocity under the parasol of the idea of merit and its practice that is *dāna*.

The idea of exchange of donation for merit may have come from the Buddhist tradition or may have grown independently as a result of changing social forms. Whatever the cause of evolution may be, the basic understanding of the workings of donation-merit can be traced back at least to the time of the Buddha. By *c.* 600 BC donations appear to have increasingly formed an important part of the new emergent economic order which was marked by remarkable technological growth, surplus production and a widening gap between the producers and the consumers. In the beginning Buddhist ascetics, following the *Śramaṇa* tradition, took no part in production and were forbidden ownership of houses, fields, cattle, and any contact with gold, silver and trade. They had to live on alms alone. The ascetics, however, had to reckon with the monsoons when climatic conditions which made an annual break in their wanderings inevitable. During the rainy season they had to suspend wandering and remain in retreat which the Buddhist called *vassāvāsa*. Being professed almsmen, the *bhikkhus* would naturally make their *vassā* settlements in localities where alms were available. Normally these settlements were located in both towns and villages where the *bhikkhus* could live in congregations of their own and subsist on alms. The problem of accommodation for the rain-retreat, however, was not the same in the town as in the countryside. In the country, the erection of a boundary would be the first task of the monks and they themselves would have to build shelters. In the town or city, on the other hand, could be found wealthy lay devotees inclined to donate to the monks as an act of piety, permanently or for use during the *vassā* period, their own private parks or pleasure gardens.[5] Thus, at the time of the Buddha, the demarcation between the two modes of living, though not markedly different, was largely the result of merit and its working mechanism.

The widespread notion of earning merit through donations was due mainly to the adoption of the Buddhist faith by Aśoka. The idea received its fullest elaboration in the vast collections as the Jātakas, Avadānas, etc. The Jātaka stories, full of the spirit of earning merit through donation, were popular at the time of Aśoka. The theme is also represented on the ancient reliefs of the stone railings of the Bharhut *stūpa*, Bodh Gaya and the stone gateways at Sanchi.

Rites of piety and devotion, quite apart from monastic practice, are shown in those sculptures. The motifs of the Bharhut and Sanchi railings were furnished by the stories of the Jātakas and Avadānas that clearly show the elements of *bhakti* and worship. It shows a faith visibly merging into worship in the symbolic form such as the *stūpa*. With the spread of the Buddhist faith, people came to erect huge *stūpas* (none of which were built at the outset of the religion) complying with the spiritual demand of common believers. Around the *stūpas* were built shrines which were called *caitya,* whose meaning seems to have been a building to pile up merit—the root comes from the Sanskrit root, *ci,* 'to heap up'. The growing Buddhist movement took root among the common people after the reign of Aśoka, owing to the close relationship between the *saṃgha* and the laity supported by the idea of merit which has long been one of the prominent features of Buddhism. The worship of relics enlarged the scope of the potential power of merit-making. Out of the numerable meritorious activities that men can perform, *dāna* has long been considered as the most meritorious one. In many ways, this is the Buddhist act of merit *par excellence.* Lay persons practice it by giving to the monks support of a more material kind while monks engage in it by giving *dharma* to lay persons in the form of sermons or preaching or advice or by the example of their own lives. From the time of Aśoka, *stūpa* worship also became a popular method of merit-making. The laity, in addition to providing food and abodes for the *saṃgha,* had to pay for the construction and decoration of *stūpas* as well as the jewels to be buried along with the relics.

As lay devotees began to expect more in return for their donations under the transformed doctrines of spiritual goal in Kuṣāṇa times, there appeared the phenomenon of collective donations by lay organizations. Under the commercial ethos of the times and related to the brisk development of guild organizations, lay associations sprang up in urban centers. It is likely that the substantial donations motivated lay devotees to organize themselves according to the model of their own guild. As for collective donations, more evidence of merchants' donations survives in the western Indian caves than it does in the north, denoting a deep relationship between commerce and religious activity.

By the early Christian centuries, monasteries had also become refuges for those wishing to escape economic problems. Nagasena clearly states that there were some who had joined the *saṃgha* to avoid being robbed.[6] The Buddha's word, in the form of a prediction in the *Theragāthā*[7] that some day monks would receive gold, silver, fields, slaves and servants, etc., is nothing but the depiction of the monks' life at the time when the work was composed, between the third century BC and first century AD. Thus, there were some monks who possessed their own private property in the monasteries. Naturally, the monks also held the position of donors. *Majjhima Nikāya* gives us a good instance of the monk as a donor, when a monk says 'Moreover Udena, the king of the Aṅga country, gives me a regular daily allowance out of which I will give you a regular allowance.'[8] What is even more interesting is that joint donations of monks and nuns also took place, meaning that they continued to make contributions through their own private property. However, the accumulation of the private property of monks in the *saṃgha* became a serious problem. The monks were so rich that they were criticized in the *Mahāvagga*: 'These *Sākyaputtiya samaṇas* are becoming storers up of goods like the Magadha king Seṇiya Bimbisāra.'[9] The *Vinaya Piṭaka*[10] states that the use of gold and silver was not allowed to the monks. They were neither allowed to accept it nor to take charge of it. The *saṃgha* authority, therefore, regulated that monks should not take any goods donated to the *saṃgha* in order to prohibit individual monks from possessing private property. The *Pātimokkha* reads: 'In case a robe should fall to the lot of a *bhikkhu*, as a special gift; ten days before the Kattika-temāsa full moon, that *bhikkhu* may take it, considering it as a special gift; and when he has it, he may keep it till the ritual of the robe time. Should he keep it beyond that, it is a *pācittiya* offence, involving forfeiture.'[11]

The intensified dependence of the *saṃgha* on lay society due to their materialized structure led the monk-community to keep up not a casual but a regular intercourse with lay society. At the time of rites and ceremonies, for instance on Uposatha day, two features came into relief: the laity's support to the Buddhist *saṃgha* and the *saṃgha's* ministration to lay society. The main ideology behind the brisk contact between the two on Uposatha day was the merit mechanism. In order to secure sustained material assistance from the laity the *saṃgha* had to emphasize the distinct spiritual mechanism of donation-merit. It was this mechanism, with its great momentum, that brought about the popularization of the non-theistic religion and helped in its propagation in all the places in the initial stages.

Moreover, constituting a circular process, the institution of gift-making formed an important link in the distribution of wealth. We learn from contemporary sources how wealthy *setthis* and merchants, out of their religious zeal as well as their wish to earn merit and fame, vied with one another in lavishing wealth on religious orders as well as on the infirm and destitute, which otherwise might have remained locked in their coffers.

The institution of *dāna* created another form of subsistence for the monks who renounced the task of production. Instead, taking to alms-seeking they lived on goods produced by others. Thus, it led *Therīgāthā* to reprove the recluse's life: 'Fain to work are they, the lazy crew. They make their living off what others give.'[12] The Vinaya records how a potter making many bowls for the monks, could not make other goods for sale, and was unable to earn his living and his wife and children suffered.[13] As a result of increasing mendicancy there may have been a considerable decline in the number of people engaged in active production and also a corresponding increase in the economic burden which the rest of the producers had to bear. The widespread alienation of able citizens from the production structure of society led Kautilya to prescribe a fine on all those who either renounced home to become ascetics without providing for their sons and wives or induced a woman to renounce home.[14]

The increasing material reliance of the *saṃgha* on lay society created changes in Buddhist ideology which had to offer its patrons a distinct ideal of soteriology with special reference to merit-making. In early Pali texts, Buddhist patrons, mostly merchants, do not expect any direct rewards from the Buddha. Nāgasena explicitly states in the *Milindapañho* that the Blessed One is set entirely free and therefore accepts no gift; nevertheless, acts done to him, notwithstanding his having passed away and not accepting them, are of value and bear fruit. The orthodox position then was that the Buddha's attainment is symbolized in his images and by his relics and when men pay homage to them goodness arises within them because the relics and images act as a field of merit in which men can plough, plant and produce fruits.[15] He debates whether there are rewards for a lay devotee and more specifically whether a Buddhist lay adherent can achieve *arhatship* owing to merit. At one point Nāgasena claims that a layman can achieve *arhatship* only on the same day, i.e. he cannot enjoy *arhatship* in this life. His being a layman makes it impossible for him to be an *arhat.*[16] On another occasion Nāgasena admits that a layman can gain *nirvāṇa* in his next incarnation because of the merit he has achieved in his former lives. Since no one can achieve *nirvāṇa* in one life, and if one has already accumulated sufficient merit in former lives to reach *nirvāṇa*, it is justifiable to remain a lay person and enjoy sensual pleasure in one's last life before *nirvāṇa*. The main advantage of joining the *saṃgha* is to hasten the accumulation of merit.[17] Nāgasena's conflicting opinions about the religious status of lay adherents suggest a possible trend in which Buddhist believers hoped for increased recognition of their patronage in the form of earning merit. Yet, at this early stage, nothing suggests that by virtue of their donations laymen could share the greater merit gained by monks. According to the *Mahāvastu*, which introduced the concept of the eternal Buddha making the historical Gautama Buddha only one manifestation of the eternal Buddha, the worship and patronage of a Buddha appearing in this world offers tangible benefits. A king who builds a palace of precious materials for a Buddha has the full right to claim Buddhahood by virtue of this act of merit.[18] In the *Mahāvastu* the purpose of worship and making donations is no longer limited to the attainment of *nirvāṇa*. The text promises that worshippers and donors will attain kingdoms, wealth, the status of gods, and many other desires.[19] There are also many lands of the Buddha where life is more pleasant and interesting than in the pure state of *nirvāṇa* and since *nirvāṇa* could only be achieved after the effort of many life-cycles, these rewards were more appealing to common lay devotees. The early part of *Saddharmapuṇḍarīka* develops the idea that the wisdom of the Buddha is very hard to obtain and that only the Buddha knows all. Hence memorizing Buddhist teachings and principles is not essential for preaching and converting. Once the way of approaching the Buddha through wisdom was ruled out, both the monks in the Order and laymen in society were able to communicate with the Buddha only by worship of which the main part is the act of donation. Thus, the emphasis on worship came to obtain considerable weight as shortening and simplifying the process of accumulating merit.

From the beginning of the Christian era, under the commercial ethos of the Kuṣāṇas, the idea of merit was no longer restricted to what an individual could achieve through his own efforts. The appearance of the *bodhisattvas* as future Buddhas, especially of Avalokiteśvara, was a crucial point. That the *bodhisattva* could save other people through accumulated merit implied that merit, like goods, could be transferred and exchanged.[20] Cleatly, contemporary commercial features developed in conjunction with the highly flourishing urban culture and mercantile economy of the Kuṣāṇa period had penetrated Buddhist ideology by this time. At the same time, dedication of merit appeared as one of the pivotal doctrines of the new Buddhism of this period. Evidently it served a social function: it made participation in Buddhist ritual a social encounter rather than a private experience. Such radical changes show that Buddhism had become aware of the potential for conflict between the *saṃgha* and lay society. Therefore, the overwhelming acceptance of merit transfer, despite its doctrinal inappropriateness to Buddhism, may be seen as a solution to this conflict.

The new mode of subsistence of the renouncers, totally dependent on alms, could not have been totally inbred and exclusive. In fact, every donation was a form of economic activity, whether it was of wealth or labour but most donations were made for non-functional, unproductive purposes and did not promote the cause of production. All things essential and luxurious, movable and immovable, finished and unfinished constituted items of gift. Variations and increase/ decrease in gift-items may be seen as indicative of particular periods. Gift articles in an agricultural economy of the sixth century BC, were usually foodgrains, dairy-products, precious metals, means of irrigations, etc. In urban economy of the post-Mauryan period[21] it would be land, stone artifacts, monetary endowments, etc., and agricultural and landed properties in Gupta and post-Gupta period. Though it provided a good deal of employment to masons and sculptors, it did not promote the cause of production and adds to the wealth of the state. From the sheer economic point of view, the giving of gifts was unproductive. The religious beneficiaries, the Buddhist monks, could not be expected to reciprocate in equal measure. What the *bhikkhu* or the *saṃgha* could provide to the donor in exchange could not be compared in economic terms.

Yet, other kinds of gift were not unknown. Members of the royal family often invested money in a guild, the interest on which went towards financing some aspect of the Buddhist *saṃgha.* Here a different kind of nexus is established which still draws on patronage, but of a less obvious kind, and brings together royalty, commercial interests and the *saṃgha.* In this case the gift plays a dual role—as donation as well as investment.[22] In any case, it may have strengthened the donors ideologically and psychologically in pursuing their normal avocations. The practice of donation, thus, facilitated commerce by making capital available for commercial enterprise. Gift-making led to the utilization of much hoarded wealth for more useful purposes, or at least partly prevented some of the wealth from being buried underground. As Vijay Nath points out, 'it was the post-Mauryan practice of investing money with trade and craft-guilds and allotting only the regular interest that was drawn from it for the maintenance of charitable and religious institutions, which not only kept liquid capital from going out of circulation but also furnished ready capital to the guild with which that sum was deposited'.[23]

Here we need to mention the peculiar role of the gift which resulted in a very substantial increase in social relations. *Gahapatis, seṭṭhis,* individuals and communities of traders, artisans, guilds of craftsmen and so on, the main patrons of the *saṃgha* were status seekers. They sought upward social mobilization in a period of social change through gift-making in the form of wealth or labour. Some of these artisans and guilds were, doubtless, also seeking both status and publicity by recording their donations. In this structure, we note that the *saṃgha,* paradoxically enough, played the role of a source of authority on social life.

In this environment, to achieve the Mahāyāna goal of better rebirth which depends on merit accumulation through worship, the type of articles which can be donated is changed. In the beginning, it was only the bare necessities such as alms bowls, cooked-food and drink, clothing, fuel-wood, medicine and shelter, etc., that were allowed to be gifted to the *saṃgha* and that too in limited numbers. Some seemingly luxury articles but in fact necessities for the *bhikkhus,* like sandalwood for medicinal purposes,[24] sheep/goat/deer skin for coverlets in Avanti and southern regions[25] could be donated. Gradually, the disappearance of the ascetic spirit which characterised the incipient stage brought about an increase in the number of non-essential items which were acceptable such as vessels made of various materials,[26] fans,[27] umbrellas,[28] oil for the head,[29] sunshades,[30] looms,[31] spitoons,[32] and various kind of unfinished goods. Various Buddhist texts in Sanskrit show that the major luxury items of donation were derived from the material development in the urban culture of the Kuṣāṇas. The increase in the donation of such luxury goods suggests the advance of technical skills required for those items. Our sources bear witness to a gift of heavenly silk[33] and shoes of various hues like the wings of a partridge.[34] Needless to say, the donation of images, pillars, gateways and railings in good numbers during this period attests to the development of various technologies and crafts such as masonry, carpentry, metalsmithy and sculpture.

During post-Mauryan times, there was an increase in the popularity of precious metals such as gold and silver and various precious stones as gift items. In this context, Vijay Nath assumes that strong social or ritual compulsions must have worked behind the popularization of gold as a gift-item.[35] She maintains that the use of precious stones as gift-items, in spite of their scarcity, suggests the existence of some rigid social mores or ritual based religious dictates which would have acted as strong moral inducement to make a person part with the precious commodity.[36] In this regard, we may invoke the development of the concept of *sapta-ratna*. Originally the *sapta-ratna* was the traditional Buddhist concept of state machinery whose constituents were the *cakra* (wheel), *hastin* (elephant), *aśva* (horse), *mani* (jewel), *strī* (lady), *gahapati* (householder) and *parinayaka* (leader). It is not clear when and how it began to designate seven kinds of precious items, i.e. *suvarṇa, rūpya, vaiḍurya, sphaṭika, mukta, lohitika, musargalva*. The concept of *sapta-ratna* as precious stones or jewels seems to have attained maturity since the early Christian era when the precious stones became important items in the commercial environment. Thus, the standardization of the *sapta-ratna* paralleled the development of Eurasian trade from the Mediterranean to East Asia. Most of the components of the seven treasures were items either brought to north and north-west India by trade, or highly popular in markets of other countries. The trade of luxury goods, including the seven treasures, stimulated the standardization of the *sapta-ratna* concept and of other necessities for Buddhist rituals and ceremonies.[37]

The link between Buddhist ritual practices and trade in luxury goods shaped the close relationship between Buddhist monasteries and the laity. Monasteries were important purchasers of clothes and other commodities for the monks and retainers, and of costly material for rites and ceremonies. *Stūpas* in ancient India were not merely bare stone structures. The descriptions of pilgrims and the precious items found scattered around *stūpas* suggests that they were decorated with gold, silver, glass and other ornaments made of a variety of precious stones. In addition to luxury goods, monasteries favoured various kinds of fabrics, including imported ones, for elaborate monastic rituals and the complex life led in them. The fabric used in the making of the *cīvaras* could be linen, cotton, silk, woollen cloth or hemp. A piece of silk found in a Buddhist relic casket dated to the early centuries AD in Nagara is evidence of the role of silk in Buddhist rituals.[38] Moreover, silk banners were indispensable for Buddhist ceremonies.

From post-Mauryan times onwards we notice a conspicuous change in the nature of gifts, suggesting the considerable decline of foreign trade in luxury goods. We notice that movable items particularly luxury goods, were gradually replaced by immovable, landed properties. The thick forests of the earlier period were being fast replaced by agricultural fields, artificially developed parks, gardens, fruit-groves, etc.[39] In fact, the idea of land as gift to religious figures has a comparatively long history. There are instances of land gifting before the land grant of Gautamīputra Sātakarṇī in second century AD. In fact, it was from the post-Vedic period that the practice of granting tax-free land and village revenue to religious beneficiaries began. Early Pali texts of pre-Mauryan period attest to the number of villages granted to Brāhmaṇas by some rulers in north-east India. A Sātavāhana inscription of the first century BC refers to the grant of a village as a gift during the *aśvamedha* sacrifice.[40] Such donations, however, merely meant the transference of the right to collect the tax from the village and not the right to the land as such.[41] The idea and practice of land as gift with the actual relinquishment of the king's right over it started taking shape in the early centuries of the Christian era with the tendency towards feudalization. The gifting of land to religious institutions and individuals as a substitute for luxury goods and as the most valuable property in society dates, thus, from the beginning of the early Christian centuries.

The majority of the land-grants from the post-Mauryan period onward were made by kings due to the growing size of the royal lands as well as augmentation of estate authority over private land-holdings. Sātavāhana ruler Gautamīputra Sātakarṇī was the first historical figure who granted whole villages, which were exempted from many kinds of taxes, to Buddhist monks. The land was protected from unofficial intruders and could not be disturbed by royal troops and district police. The grant of villages to the monasteries should be seen against the backdrop of the expanding rural economy and the need of the state to moniter new settlements. It might also have promoted state interests instead of entailing any loss of revenue, for the lands were mainly waste ones. Besides, from first century AD onwards, there were increasing donations of land to religious establishments by lay devotees, i.e. rich *negamas* and *seṭṭhis* though the number of land-grants made by them were smaller than those by princely donors.

Land-grants supplied Buddhist monasteries with a regular income. This independence from constant alms-seeking further facilitated the expansion of the monasteries and their preaching activities. D.D. Kosambi notices that the influence of monasteries extended beyond religious matters. They possibly also supplied (on profit) essential provisions and loans (at interest) of indispensable capital to trade-caravans. The monasteries themselves were untaxed and their possessions not in danger of arbitrary confiscation by kings or officials as might be the lay merchant's hoard.[42] Examples from ancient societies show that there is a close connection between landed wealth and commercial capital and it was the possession of the former that made large-scale investment in trade and money-lending possible.[43]

Monasteries continued to be important institutions. Although most grants, in this period, were executed in favour of the Brāhmaṇas, some were executed in favour of Buddhist monks as well. The land-grants also facilitated agricultural expansion and the process of cultural expansion. Actually, religious institutions—of which monasteries were the most developed—were amply suited to the consolidation and integration of agricultural settlements on account of their ability to forge channels of communication. These channels could not only be used to popularize improved methods of agriculture and cropping patterns but also to reinforce the authority of the state. It was perhaps for this purpose of supervising and maintaining control that the Sātavāhanas gifted villages to the *saṃgha*.[44] One of the most important factors that contributed to the rise and growth of landowning monastic institutions was the grant of *agrahāras* by the king for religious and educational purposes. Thus, royal patronage gradually came to predominate in Gupta times and it superseded community patronage in post-Mauryan times. The period between the fifth and seventh centuries witnessed the rise of landowning monasteries in large numbers. Hsüan-tsang informs us that the Nālandā *vihāra* was maintained out of the revenues of about a hundred villages granted to this institution. By the time of I-tsing this number seems to have risen to two hundred.

The *saṃghas* established close economic relations with lay society for the purpose of administering the monastery's enormous accumulated wealth, ranging from villages to cattle. Owning permanent property relieved Buddhist monasteries of their dependence on steady donations, both to maintain buildings and to supply provisions for the *saṃgha*. Moreover, the practice of perpetual endowments from the laity, which invested with trade and deposited with different craft-guilds, would have not only ensured a permanent income for the *saṃgha* but would also appear to have placed that much capital for the immediate use of that guild. Playing a crucial role in the contemporary economic system, when there were no banks and when the safest mode of saving money was to bury it underground, monasteries had either to lend money out or invest it for the purpose of earning interest on the donations. The practice of making permanent endowments in favour of religious beneficiaries and the investment of the donated amount with some guild which stood in need of the capital made *saṃghas* take on the major task of financing. A monetized economy including cash transactions must have existed. The cash income that the monastery needed for its expenses was derived from the sale of produce from monastic estates and from investments like money deposited in guilds which brought in a regular income as interest.[45] Some Buddhist monasteries, for a long time, were even associated with the consumption of liquor[46] some of which was even expensive, imported liquor.[47] If monasteries could purchase and sell this commodity, which was banned for the monks, they probably also traded in other items. Trading in incense and precious stones for use in Buddhist rituals would be a much less serious violation of Buddhist rules than trafficking in wine. Buddhist monasteries, particularly those situated along the route of trade, functioned as financial institutions, using its treasury to generate profits. Himanshu P. Ray makes a convincing case to show that Buddhist monasteries in western Deccan were closely dependent on the trade routes.[48]

The Buddhist *saṃgha,* after finally having settled down as a financial institution playing the role of a bank in modern terms, came under increasing pressure to put its property at the disposal of society or to participate in economic activities for the benefit of society. The *saṃgha* naturally expanded its role as a donee, making charitable use of monastic grain for the relief of famine, scarcity or individual distress among laymen. The accounts of Fa-hsien record that in the city of Pataliputra, elders and householders opened charitable houses attached to Buddhist institutions, providing medical care to poor people for the purpose of merit-earning.[49] In cases when the *saṃgha* refused to do so, rulers often issued edicts to regulate or prohibit gifts to the *saṃgha* or confiscated the property in the name of purification. It is after village settlements using the heavy plough had become much denser that the same monasteries became a drain upon the revenues and resources of the country, without mitigating features.[50] By that time, however, it was much too late to reverse the trend towards degeneration that had set in (under the guise of theological differences) with the gain of wealth and the taste for luxury.[51]

I-tsing leaves us in no doubt that the monasteries got their lands cultivated by temporary tenants. He also gives some idea of the nature of the tenure on which the cultivators were assigned land. He states that the *saṃgha* provided bulls and fields, and generally received one-sixth of the produce. He does not indicate whether the cultivators were also provided with ploughs, seeds, manure and other equipment for agriculture. All this required a large number of functionaries. The head of the monastery was given the appropriate title of *bhoga parikṣa* and he was both the religious head as well as the superintendent of the administration of the monastery. The administration had a separate hierarchy of Brāhmaṇa priests, office-bearers such as accountants and treasurer, artisans such as goldsmiths, stonemasons, carpenters and various menial workers from the Śūdras. The religious and administrative officers were hereditary and were paid with endowments of land or a share of the offerings.[52] Monasteries, thus, developed into semi-independent areas enjoying immunity on religions grounds. They were gradually converted into medieval *mathas,* rich enough to tempt the Turkish invaders.

There is no doubt that the early Koreans, after the advent of Buddhism in AD 372, have possessed texts such as *Sukhāvatīvyūha, Saddharmapundarīka, Mahāvastu,* etc., which, as we have examined earlier, promoted the idea of merit-making and the practice of donation. However, it was only by the time of Unified Silla, between the mid-seventh and mid-tenth century that the idea and practice became widely prevalent. Silla witnessed the popularity of Amitābha Buddha, of the cult of Land Bliss or Western Paradise. The enthusiasm for the cult, amongst both the elite and the common people, was not different although the style of their approaches to the cult varied. The happiness promised and the easy approach are so alluring in comparison to earlier thought that the more conservative theorists feared that Buddhists would lose sight of the final goal of *nirvāṇa* and opt to stay in the land of bliss in the west. The elite, who stored up wealth, wished to accumulate merit to be able to enter the Western Paradise for this method was in consonance with the sacred texts and models, both in India and Korea. To the common people, it was an attractive faith largely because they could not comprehend the difficult and complex doctrines of Buddhism. Moreover, all the people from the top to the bottom, who realized the vanity of life after the incessant wars, sought some sort of compensation for their troubled lives through the cult. The popularity of the cult gave birth to stories of people reaching the Western Paradise and even attaining Buddhahood owing to their repeating the name of Amitābha Buddha with sincere faith. Repeating the name of Amitābha Buddha was heavily bound up with the practice of donation. Like their predecessors, the Kuṣāṇas in India, the donors of Silla also expected their donations to bring benefits in their future lives and to their deceased relatives. Some of the aspirations of the donors included the prosperity of the state and their religion, health and longevity, both for themselves and their king, good harvests, gain of office and purification from sins.

Thus, at the time when the cult of Western Paradise of Amitābha Buddha enjoyed great popularity, from the eighth century onwards, we have examples of the practice of donation to monasteries in large numbers. When Kim In-moon, the brother of King Mun-mu who achieved the perfect unification of Korea after the war against T'ang China, was put in a jail in T'ang China, his family and relatives[53] built a temple for him. Temple Minjang was built by Prime Minister Minjang out of his own house. Temple Yudok was also donated by Choe Yu-dok. Kwi-chin made his house a temple by donating land and labour to the temple. *Śramana* Shin-hyo made the temple Hyogawon out of his own house. Monk Cho-shin built Chongt'osa from his private funds. Kim Chijon built the temple Kamsan out of his lands in Kamsan. The Changsusa temple was built by Kim Tae-song and the temple Howon by Kim Hyon out of their own properties. Temples Honghyo and Yangch'an are similar examples of temples of dedication. The instances cited here are only from the extant sources and such donations to Buddhist *saṃghas*, and of dedicating temples, must have been far larger in actul numbers at the time of Silla, especially during the eighth century, the period when the economy flourished most.

Donors donated several other kinds of objects too, sometimes individually, sometimes in groups, that is, through lay associations. Monk Myong-rang decorated *stūpas* and statues with one thousand tael of gold donated by a dragon-king.[54] Though we cannot designate the exact character of the dragon-king, it is assumed that he must have been a local petit-power as Woo-sung Yi's analysis[55] shows. Decorating Buddhist monument was one of the many forms of worshipping Buddha encouraged by the *Mahāvastu* and *Saddharmapuṇḍarīka*, the most popular texts in early Korea. These texts, the result of a few centuries' votary movement in north India, also inspired early Korean donors several centuries later. After the death of her husband in 799, the queen of King So-song donated six of her luxurious royal gowns as well as treasures from the privy purse for the carving of an image of Amitābha Buddha and several statues of lesser divinities associated with him, to be enshrined in a hall of the Mujang temple. In this case, the royal privy purse is identified with the state exchequer for the concept of the state was never fully developed in ancient Korea. The *Samgukyusa* says 'monk Won-kwang received personal gifts from people and he always gave them away to be used for the maintenance of temples.'[56] Monk Son-yul 'used the donation received from local people to pay for the copying of six hundred volumes of *Mahāprajñāpāramitā Sūtra*'[57] and also 'was offered a bottle of sesame oil and a roll of hand spun silk to light a lamp and to pay for the copying expenses'.[58] Kim Taesong donated his small paddy field, which he had acquired from his servant-salary, to the temple with the hope of having better living conditions in the next life. These examples show us that donations from common people's too were popular in this period when Buddhist culture reached great heights in various spheres. A fairly popular movement of the common people donation seemed to be in vogue, notwithstanding the comparative paucity of available sources. The following are good examples: A rich person, Pok-an donated fifty pils[59] of cloth in the reign of King Shim-mun (681-91). Kim, a high officer of the court, donated 15,595 soks[60]of grains to temples of Pong-unsa, Pojangsa, etc., during the eighth and ninth centuries. At this time there must have also existed the practice of the rich donating property with the aim of being exempted from various taxes.[61] The king was the most prominent figure among various kinds of individual donors. King Hyo-so (692-701) donated to Paegyul temple two sets of gold dishes each weighing fifty nyangs,[62] five fine robes, three thousand rolls of gray hamper cloth and one thousand kyongs[63] of farm land.[64] King Kyong-dok (742-64) donated 120,000 pounds of copper for the casting of a bell dedicated to his deceased father, King Song-dok. He granted rice fields and many other gifts to Minjang temple in AD 745. He also bestowed on monk Chin-p'yo 77,000 large bags of rice and his queen and her family also presented the monk with five hundred rolls of silk and fifty tael of gold. Wang-kon, a King of Later Koguryo, who became the founder of the Koryo dynasty after Silla, granted five hundred kyol[65] of lands each to Chakkot and Hyein temples.

More characteristic than donations made by individuals were those made by lay associations. In India, lay associations sprang from the formation of guild/caste organizations in the urban centres of the Kuṣāṇas. The increasing responsiveness of the Buddhist *saṃgha* towards the laity facilitated their birth. The lay associations also intensified contact between Buddhist monasteries and lay devotees. As Buddhist doctrine promised more rewards to donors, so too, monks became more active in attracting converts and soliciting donations. It is likely that it was the monks who initiated the system of collective donations. The attraction of making substantial donations motivated lay devotees to organize themselves according to the model of their own guilds and that of the *saṃgha* administration. Although there is no direct evidence that monks encouraged lay associations to make donations, some inscriptions show that monks were active in encouraging donations by the 'masters of a *vihāra*'. Because Buddhist monasteries in the Kuṣāṇa period did not own sizeable amounts of landed property or other permanent property which could provide a regular income and because they conducted many expensive religious activities, they may well have relied on regular donations from the urban laity. The significance of the lay associations is that by organizing many moderate income donors into groups and by enlarging the contact of Buddhist monasteries with minor traders, they enabled monasteries to receive many donations which facilitated large scale constructions.

A few extant inscriptions giving information on lay associations at the time of the Three Kingdoms allow us to speculate about the character of the contemporary lay associations in Korea. An inscription on a Tathāgata statue made in 539[66] or 599[67] in Koguryo informs us that it was dedicated to the temple by a 40-member lay association led by two masters of a *vihāra* and one alms-monk.[68] Another inscription on a statue, inferred to be made in the year 673 in Paekche, tells us that the lay association was formed by the Chon family as a central power at Yon-gi district and it had at least 50 members led by three masters of a *vihāra*.[69] After the unification of the Three Kingdoms there appeared a good number of lay associations. In the beginning they were affiliated to government authorities. In 705, King Song-dok ordered five learned monks to transcribe the *Hwaom-kyong* or *Avatamsaka Sūtra* and to organize a lay association with the name of Hwaom-sa or Hwaom society. To pay the recurring expenses of the society, he made it a rule to contribute one hundred som[70] of rice and one som of purified oil from the neighbouring hyons or prefectures regularly each spring and autumn. The king also established a large *jangwon* or manor of fifteen kyol of land plus six kyol of forest-land and two kyol of farm land, yielding firewood, chestnuts and grain.[71] There were also such government-backed lay associations as Wont'ong-sa, Kumkang-sa, Sujong-sa, Paengnyon-sa all of which were organized around Mt. Odae. Unlike the earlier ones, these lay associations had their own names and had a specific relationship with each monastery. Though these societies were not organized at the laity's own initiative, they were like the fully developed lay associations of later times, material supporters of the various activities of a monastery. These included the erection of *stūpas*, the establishing and repairing of monasteries, reading, reciting, copying of texts and lecturing, ceremonies, festivals and so on. It was believed that these acts helped to accumulate merit.

After the eighth century, non-governmental lay associations began to appear. They organized material support to a specific monastery on a large scale. The prototype of such non-governmental lay-associations is given in the following story of the *Samgukyusa*: 'Monk Chin-p'yo decided to found temple Kumsansa and had descended the mountain from his hermitage as far as Taeyonjin, when a dragon-king emerged and presented him with a robe of jade and guided him to Kumsan forest with an escort of 80,000 people. Soon men and women gathered from all directions and within a few days the temple was completed.'[72] One can assume that the dragon-king was a rich petit-power of the district who must have donated the land in Kumsan forest in addition to a jade-robe, and people thronged to organize a lay association to raise material for the construction of the temple. The figure of 80,000 may only be figurative, to indicate a great multitude of people.

At another place the *Samgukyusa* says 'during the reign of King

Kyong-dok, tens of men-devoted laitys grouped themselves and organized an association in Kang-ju and established a monastery called temple Mit'a or Amitābha, in a grove of trees and began to worship Buddha even in order to enter the Western Paradise'.[73] Affiliated to the cult of Pure Land, the lay associations extended their scope by enlarging their membership. The aforesaid story from the *Samgukyusa* also tells us, 'Tongnyang P'alchin, an incarnation of Avalokiteśvara, organized one thousand men and divided them into two, one for "noryok" or "effort" and one for "chongsu" or "mental cultivation".'[74] Here it is difficult to define 'effort' precisely. Most probably it means 'material support', for its companion word in the sentence is 'mental cultivation'.[75] The first part of 500 lay persons must have supplied material to the other part's work, i.e. 'mental cultivation' such as lecturing on texts, reading, reciting and transcribing texts or extensive praying, meditation, etc. The first may have devoted themselves to repairing monasteries, statues, *stūpas*, building new halls for the latter's work, supplying food, robes, etc., when necessary. An inscription on a Buddha statue in Ch'olwon, installed in 865, informs us that the lay association had as many as 1,500 members to get this statue of Birojana or Vairocana Buddha installed[76] who must have offered money, grain, clothes, etc., for the purpose.

Lay associations were important means for common people to accumulate merit in order to attain a better life in the next birth as well as functioned as a decisive means for the *saṃgha* to keep in touch with the laity or mundane world or earthly-economic affairs. The donations made by lay associations with strong family and territorial ties centered on specific sects. Monks represented both, the rural-based Buddhist laity as well as urban-based groups. Whatever their composition, the purpose of lay associations was to organize donations and they played a great role in popularizing Buddhism in society.

During the period under survey, there developed another kind of institution for the purpose of merit-accumulation by means of donation. Called po, it was a kind of foundation. Donors, including kings and monks deposited money, grain, land, etc., to a *saṃgha* which was used as the principal capital, which is called po. Po and its increased and accumulated wealth were supposed to be utilized to support specific works performed in a monastery.[77] Monk Won-kwang installed Chomch'al-Po or Po of Divination Ceremony between 600 and 637. He made it a perpetual institute or foundation to which a pious nun donated one hundred kyol of land. King Hyegong (765-79) donated land of thirty kyol to Chui-son temple as Kong-dok-Po or Po of Honouring Merit in order to pray for the peace of a deceased general. In the year 931 Wang-kon praised the loyalty of two monk-brothers and donated some kyol of land as Kiil-Po or Po of Parents' Sacrifice to T'albaek temple.

Though the available sources on Po in this period are not enough to allow us to draw any definitive inferences, the majority of the form of property of po should have been land. It became a regular channel through which donors donated land and the *saṃgha* received and accumulated landed property. Moreover, under the contemporary conditions of the main mechanism of state-ownership of land, it was also possible to keep and accumulate a monastery's landed properties, delimiting state landed properties.[78] In due course its scale grew rapidly, its forms of properties diversified and included money, grains, etc., in addition to landed property. Its functions, too, became more complex, performing the role of capital under a pre-capitalist economic system.[79] In other words, the *saṃgha* let po function as the capital of the monastery by loaning and transferring capital on interest.

Our examination so far allows us to maintain that various types of donations flourished from mid-seventh century onwards, especially under the reign of King Kyong-dok. From this time onwards also, the Buddhist religion changed its main character from a rather political ideology of the ruler, used to legitimize royal authority and state-protection to a practical religion of the people through which they sought to better their lives in the next birth or in the next world. The change spread and made widely prevalent the idea of merit-making and the practice of donations through which people believed they could attain their goal. Simultaneously, the economic conditions of society too improved. The unification of the three kingdoms brought about an increase in productive labour and arable land. At the same time, the end of successive wars of attrition led to the utilization of abundant iron in Kyongju, Yongdok, Ulsan districts[80] to make iron tools for agriculture rather than weapons. And after having attained victory in war, the government began to grant land to the nobility in which the rights of taxation and labour-mobilizing were included. The nobles, having obtained a number of war captives, could use them as their private, domestic slaves.[81] Moreover, large numbers of poor people, who became even poorer due to the excessive exploitation by the ruling class because of successive wars, came to be enslaved under the mechanism of usury. They brought about a rapid increase in agricultural production, which enabled the ruling class to accumulate wealth rather quickly.

'The more extensive growth of cultivation and cattle rearing in the countryside'[82] led to the growth of towns and trade ports. Villages produced larger amounts of grain and supplied the surplus to large numbers of artisans, leading to the diversification of crafts and to merchants conducting brisk inland and foreign trade. The remarkable flourishing foreign trade with T'ang China resulted in the appearance of big merchants. The most characteristic aspect of foreign trade at the time was the import of luxury goods such as fine cotton cloth, silk, items of gold and silver, Chinese tea, etc., from China and emerald, woollen carpets, peacock tails, kingfisher feathers, turtle backs, rosewood, frankincense, etc., from Arabia, Persia, Tashkent, India, Sri Lanka, Philippines, Java, Borneo, Sumatra and so on, through the mediation of Arab merchants in some ports of China[83] and even in Silla Korea.[84] The import of such luxury goods from almost all over the Old World are enough to convince us of the rich people's abundant accumulation of wealth.

Donations leading to the establishment or repairing of monasteries or pavillions, grant or contribution of land, manufacture of statues, *stūpas*, bells, relic caskets, etc., the offering of money, cloth, clothes, grains, etc., to temples necessitates the first inevitable condition, that is, a sufficient propertied class. Then it needs the promotion of the idea of attaining salvation through the donation. Since the mid-seventh century, especially during the time of King Kyong-dok, Korean society fulfilled both these conditions. There were enough rich people devoted to the cult of Amitābha 'with the wish for their lasting happiness in this world and for their attaining Pure land after the end of this world'.[85]

Once such ideas and practices became prevalent amongst the rich, it was inevitable that they would spread quickly to other sections of society. The following story in the *Samgukyusa* confirms our contention:

Kim, Tae-song's mother was too poor to feed him, so she gave him to a rich neighbour named Pok-an as a daily labourer. Tae-song worked so hard that his master liked him very much and gave him a small plot of rice field to feed his mother and himself. About that time, Chomkae, a virtuous monk from Hungnyun temple, visited the house of Pok-an and asked for a donation for a great ceremony at the temple. Pok-an gave him fifty rolls of cotton cloth. The monk bowed in thanks and said, 'You like to donate. The Buddha is so pleased with your donation that he will reward you ten thousand times what you have donated, and bless you with longevity and happiness.[86]

The idea that one receives in reward 10,000 times what one donates, suggested in this story, is not to be found in any of the Buddhist texts, yet it played a most decisive role in promoting the culture of donation in early medieval Korea. It goes without saying that donations were not the only merit-making activities practised in early Korea. In addition to *dāna*, people practised *dasakusala-kamma* or the ten meritorious deeds.[87] However, in early medieval Korea, as in other Buddhist countries, it is mainly the ideology of donation that indicates the symbiotic relationship between the *saṃgha* and laity.

NOTES

1. Marcel Mauss, *The Gift* (New York, 1967), pp. 45ff, 53ff, 71ff.
2. Romila Thapar, *AISH,* p. 107.
3. Ibid.
4. Cf. Marcel Mauss, op.cit., p. 1.
5. S. Dutt, *BMMI,* p. 54.
6. *MP,* II. 1, 6.
7. *Thera.*, CCLVIII, p. 337.
8. *MN,* XCIV, 163.
9. *Vin., Mvg.*, VI, 15, 9.
10. *Vin., Cvg.*, XII, 1,1.
11. *Vin.*, Pātimokkha, Nissagiya Pācittya Dhamma, 28-30.
12. *Theri.*, LXVII, Rohini.
13. *Vin.*, Nissaggiya Pācittiya Dhamma, 22.
14. *AS,* II, 1. 29.
15. *MP,* IV-1.
16. Ibid., VI-1.
17. Ibid., IV-54.
18. *Mvt.*, I, 49-50
19. Ibid., II, 363-97.
20. Xinru Liu, *AIAC,* p. 101.
21. Vijay Nath, *Dana,* pp. 120-54.
22. Romila Thapar, *CTEI,* p. 30.
23. *Dāna,* p. 187.
24. *Vin., Mvg.*, VI, 11. 2.
25. Ibid., V, 13. 6
26. *Vin., Cvg.*, V, 16. 2.
27. Ibid., V, 23. 2.

28. Ibid.
29. *Vin., Mvg.*, VI, 13. 1
30. *Vin., Cvg.*, V, 13. 3.
31. Ibid., V, 21.
32. Ibid., VI, 20. 2.
33. *Vidhurapandita Jāt.*, no. 545.
34. *Vin., Mvg.*, V, 2. 3.
35. Vijay Nath, *Dāna*, p. 142.
36. Ibid., pp. 141-2.
37. Xinru Liu, *AIAC*, pp. 92ff.
38. R.N. Mehta, *Excavations at Devnimori* (Baroda, 1966), p. 186.
39. Vijay Nath, *Dāna*, pp. 144-5.
40. *Sel.Ins.*, p. 188, 1, 11.
41. G.M. Bongard-Levin, *A Complex Study of Ancient India* (Delhi, 1986), p. 129.
42. 'Dhenukakata', pp. 208-9.
43. M.G. Raschke, 'New Studies in Roman Commerce with the East', *Aufsteig und Niedergang der Romischer Welt*, (Berlin, 1978), p. 645, cited in *MG*, p. 102.
44. *MG*, p. 101.
45. R.A.L.H. Gunawardana, *Robe and Plough, Monasticism and Economic Interest in Early Medieval Sri Lanka* (Arizona, 1978), p. 321.
46. F.R. Allchin, 'Evidence of Early Distillation at Shaikhan Dheri', *South Asian Archaeology*, 1979, pp. 776-9.
47. Xinru Liu, *AIAC*, p. 122.
48. *MG*, passim.
49. Fa-hsien, pp. 47-8.
50. 'Dhenukakata', p. 61.
51. Ibid.
52. Romila Thapar, *CTEI*, p. 35.
53. Literally it is 'kuk-in' or 'people of a country', but Ki-baek Yi interprets it as relatives. See *SSY*, pp. 151-3.
54. *Yusa.*, V-ii, Myong-rang Shinin.
55. Woo-sung Yi 'Samkukyusa Sojae Choyong Solhwa-ui Il Punsok', *Kim Jae-won Paksa Hoegab Kinyom Nonch'ong* (Seoul, 1969), pp. 89-127.
56. *Yusa.*, IV-v, Won-gwang Sohak.
57. *Yusa.*, V-vii, Son-yul Hwansaeng.
58. Ibid.
59. One p'il = 40 yards.
60. One sok = 47.6 US gallons.
61. Tae-don Noh, 'Tong-ilgi Kwijokui Kyongche Kiban', Hankuksa, III, p. 165.
62. One nyang = one tael.
63. One kyong = 100 plot.
64. *Yusa.*, III-iv, Paegyulsa.
65. One kyol = one kyong.
66. Won-ryong Kim, *Hankuk Misulsa* (Seoul, 1968), p. 71.

67. Su-yong Hwang, 'Koguryo Kumdong Pulsang-ui Shinnye Ijwa', *Hankuk Pulsang-ui Yon-gu* (Seoul, 1968), p. 71.
68. Mun-kyong Kim 'Samguk-kwa Silla Sidae-ui Sinang Kyolsa', *Sahakchi*, vol. 10, 1976, p. 56.
69. Ibid., p. 63.
70. One som = one sok.
71. *Yusa.*, III-iv, Taesan Oman Chinsin.
72. *Yusa.*, IV-v, Kwandong P'ung-ak Palyonsu Sokki.
73. *Yusa.*, V-vii, Uk-myon-pi Yombul Sosung.
74. Ibid.
75. Mun-kyong Kim, op.cit., p. 70.
76. Ibid., p. 71
77. Sam-su Kim, 'Po-ui Chon-gi-chok Chabon Kinung-e Kwanhan Chonggyo Sahoehak-chok Yon-gu', *Munhak Chongkyowa Kyongje* (Seoul, 1979), p. 156.
78. Nam-woon Paek, *Choson Sahoe Kyongchesa* (Tokyo, 1933), p. 813.
79. Sam-su Kim, op.cit., p. 155.
80. Yong-bom Yi, 'Ch'oyong Solhwa-ui Il Koch'al', *Chendanhakpo*, vol. 32, 1969, p. 23.
81. We would not call this a slave society.
82. Yong-bom Yi, 'Samkuksagi-e Poinun Islam Sangindul-ui Muyokp'um', *Yi Hongjik Paksa Hwagap Kinyom Nonmunjip* (Seoul, 1969), pp. 96-102.
83. Ibid.
84. Yong-bom Yi, 'Ch'oyong Solhwa-ui Il Koch'al', op.cit., pp. 25-31.
85. Ki-baek Yi, *SSY*, p. 180.
86. *Yusa.*, V-ix, Taesong Hyo Isepumo.
87. Pre. Prac. gives us 'dasakusalakamma' as following: giving (*dāna*), observing the moral precepts (*sīla*), meditation (*bhavana*), showing respect to one's superiors (*apacayana*), attending to their needs (*veyyavacca*), transferring merit (*pattidana*), rejoicing at the merit of others (*pattānumodāna*), listening to *dhamma* (*dhammmasavana*), preaching *dhamma* (*dhammadesana*) and having right beliefs (*diṭṭhijjukamma*).

CHAPTER 5

Ideas of Social Differentiation

THOUGH BUDDHISM supposedly has a streak of Śramanism,[1] and is somewhat a-social, it has never totally neglected the major social concerns. The Buddha and his disciples renounced worldly society in favour of a spiritual society which is represented by the Buddhist *saṃgha*. But this did not make them apathetic or indifferent towards society. Therefore, it would be futile to try to understand the essence of Buddhism without its social dimension.

India has witnessed the peculiar development of a sharply stratified society. The theory of social classes manifest in the concept of *varṇa* derives its ethical foundation from the doctrine of *karma* which becomes a great sociological force moulding the social and economic reality. We will, therefore, undertake an analysis of the concept of *karma* in its historical context and unravel its sociological implications. The Buddha's views on social classes was expressed frequently in early Buddhist texts. He has dealt with the origin and organization of society in varying degrees of detail in several important dialogues and passages in the canon. First, the Buddha recognised the contemporary social stratification. However, he explained the rise of class-divisions, not as in the Brahmanical canon through the dogma of Divine will but rather through rational principle, namely the voluntary selection of occupations by the classes concerned under the influence of their respective norms or standards.[2] But, the sharp and ironical tone that he has used in the Pali *Tipiṭaka* gives us a clear idea of the importance he attached to the social questions.

In the *Āmagandha Sutta* of the *Sutta Nipāta,* the Buddha argued that defilement does not come from eating this or that, prepared and given by this or that person, but from evil deeds and words and thoughts.[3] Here we find that the Buddha clearly denied the spirit of 'repulsion' which is, according to Celestine Bougle, one of the three prime constituents of caste; the other two being hierarchy and hereditary specialization.[4] The Buddha also refuted the hereditary character of the system which is based on a theory of creation first referred to in the *Puruṣa Sūkta* of the *Ṛg Veda*. He maintained that human beings are born from parents and not from imaginary beings. As regards Brāhmaṇas, he pointed out that they were born of mothers who had to undergo the same natural process as others in the matter of conception, delivery and so on. He said, 'the wives of Brāhmaṇas are known to have their periods, conceive, lie in and give suck. So how do they maintain all this when they are themselves born of woman like everybody else?'[5] Again, he maintained that 'Yet, it is these very woman-born Brāhmaṇas who say that . . . Brāhmaṇas are the genuine children of Brahmā, born from his mouth, his offspring, his creation and his heirs. This is false through and through.'[6] In another place, the *Vāseṭṭha Sutta* of the *Sutta Nipāta*, the Buddha has explained the hereditary occupational character of the caste system in detail. Here, the Buddha has shown that caste distinctions are without any basis and the distinctions sought to be maintained by caste institutions are arbitrary in character. The Buddha argued so with reference to the Brāhmaṇa community itself. Besides being priests and teachers, the Brāhmaṇas of the day would follow various professions such as farming, trading and so on. In this respect, the Buddha asserted that men who work as cow-keepers, mechanical artists, traders, or are husbandmen, artisans, traders, servants, and so on respectively—none of them is truly a Brāhmaṇa.[7]

Buddhist texts maintain that for a Brāhmaṇa the ideal is to be an ascetic who owns no property. The *Sutta Nipāta* tells us that most Brāhmaṇas had ceased to observe their ancient *dhamma*.[8] In the *Brāhmaṇavagga* of *Dhammapada* and the *Vasalasutta* of the *Sutta Nipāta*, there are full descriptions of the Buddha's conception of a Brāhmaṇa. He defines a Brāhmaṇa as a man who is free from fear, shackles, taints, passion, anger, etc., and who is meditative, settled, pure, controlled in body, speech and mind, and who knows the end of his sufferings and so on.[9] Brāhmaṇas are denounced for their greed for wealth in various stories of the Jātakas. In many of these stories, Brāhmaṇas are usually described as men of mean character and being corrupt, they are often led to lose their honour in society. They not only eat beef but indulge in the most despicable deeds—even Brāhmaṇa housewives are shown as being grossly corrupt, even behaving like prostitutes. In the various writings of the Buddhists of the time we find repeated assertions that the Brāhmaṇas were corrupt, greedy, vulgar and im-moral and often lost their privileges. In contrast, the Kṣatriyas are depicted as virtuous, honest and noble.

This shows us that the Buddhists beleived that the Kṣatriyas were still as honourable and worthy of their status as they had been in the earlier ages. It is, therefore, the claims of the Brāhmaṇa's superiority in the hereditary hierarchy that the Buddha wished to explode. The Buddha pointed out that like others the Brāhmaṇas too had to suffer the consequences of their misdeeds. He said that if there was any inherent superiority in the Brāhmaṇas, they would neither commit such deeds nor would they suffer for them, but since they do commit such deeds they must indeed suffer the consequences thereof. In the *Majjhima Nikāya,* the Buddha cleary maintains that for the same offence the members of different castes had to undergo the same punishments.[10] The Buddha pointed out that the real worth of a man was to be judged not according to his birth in this or that family nor according to the so-called caste distinctions, but according to his conduct. The Buddha set conduct as the criterion determining superiority or inferiority.

It has been suggested by Rhys Davids that the caste system was not yet fully established by the time of the Buddha. 'The key-stone of the arch of the peculiarly Indian caste organization—the absolute supremacy of the Brāhmaṇas—had not yet been put in position, had not, in fact, been yet made ready. The caste system, in any proper or exact use of the term, did not exist.'[11] This conclusion, however, does not seem to be sufficiently warranted. The fact seems to be that the Buddhists represent the caste hierarchy in a manner different from the Brahamanical texts and evaluate the idea and the hierarchy itself differently.[12] In fact, the Buddha firmly believed that the idea of intermarriage and commensality were the touch-stones of the caste system. Thus, according to him the Brāhmaṇas were inferior to the Kṣatriyas not only because a woman of impure ancestry would be accepted by the former though not by the latter, but also because the latter would not eat with her or her progeny while the former would. And moreover, according to the Buddha, it is because the Brāhmaṇas accepted the offspring of an intermarriage between a Brāhmaṇa and a Kṣatriya while the Kṣatriyas did not, and that the status of the Kṣatriyas was higher than that of the Brāhmaṇas. Refuting Brahmanical claims to superiority over the other three *varṇas,* the Buddha argues that as regards descent the Kṣatriyas are higher and Brāhmaṇas lower. In various Suttas his rather chauvinistic pro-Kṣatriya attitude or hostility to the Brāhmaṇas is amply demonstrated. In many cases the Brāhmanas are pictured as greedy, shameless and immoral and serve as a foil to the Kṣatriyas who play the part of virtuous and noble humanity.[13] In the *Ambaṭṭha Sutta* of the *Dīgha Nikāya* we are told that the Brāhmaṇa Ambaṭṭha went to the Buddha and accused the Śākyas of being rude to the Brāhmaṇas. In answer, the Buddha praised the Śākyas and tried to humble the pride of Ambaṭṭha by describing the Kanhayana *gotra* to which he belonged, as having been founded by the slave of King Ikṣvāku. The reason why the first *khattiya* was elected to the position of king or *mahāsammata* was that he was 'the most handsome, the most favoured, the most attractive, and the most capable'. Despite the fact that the Buddha was critical of Brāhmaṇas, the Brāhmaṇas were held in high esteem, and the word itself came to mean not only a man of a certain descent, but exclusively a man of a certain character and insight. The Buddha himself used the word in this sense and the very choice of this word as a title of honour must have actually afforded fresh strength to the veneration which the word inspired, because Buddhism did exercise wide influence for many centuries through and beyond the Gaṅgā valley. Rhys Davids rightly points out that the very means the Buddhists adopted to lend weight to their doctrine of emancipation became a weapon to be used against them.[14]

However, the Buddha never questioned the superiority of either the Brāhmaṇas or the Kṣatriyas over the Vaiśyas and the Śūdras. Buddhist writings project the Kṣatriyas and the Brāhmaṇas as high born, i.e. twice-born with the other two *varṇas* as the low-born, i.e. once born. The Buddha declares that the Kṣatriyas and Brāhmaṇas take precedence over the Vaiśyas and the Śūdras.[15] In a Buddhist text *gotras* are associated only with the Kṣatriyas and the Brāhmaṇas.[16] In a Jātaka story, the Buddha is quoted as saying that Buddhas have never been born in the *varṇa* of Vaiśyas or Śūdras, but always in the *varṇa* of Kṣatriyas or Brāhmaṇas. 'Since the Kṣatriya *varṇa* is now the highest one, I shall be born again as a member of that *varṇa*.'[17]

It should now be our task to find out how the Buddha implemented his ideas in practical life. First, on the question of recruitment into the *saṃgha* the Buddha ignored all advantages or disadvantages of birth, occupation, and social status. His *saṃgha* was a spiritual society wherein men came together after renouncing the desires of the material world, to attain the highest spiritual goal. Monks and nuns could come from any caste. This was apparently not a Buddhist innovation, for it was common practice among those who led a wandering life and became hermits. The organization of the *saṃgha* was far from being autocratic. Based on the doctrine of complete individual responsibility for one's actions, the Buddha denied to himself any prerogative of guardianship in relation to the community and refused to appoint a successor to assume such responsibility.[18]

The *saṃgha* was in effect a community within which ancient freedoms could be preserved at the price of yielding up the worldly life in society at large. It was, thus, an ideal society, a model to be emulated by worldly people. As such, there were no conflicts, clashes or distinctions as are common in ordinary society. A good number of people from the lowest caste were welcomed therein. And that members of the lower caste actually got into the Buddhist order is attested to by a number of instances.[19] Upāli was a barber, Sunīta a flower-sweeper, Sati the son of a fisherman, Nanda a cowherd, Capa the daughter of a deer-stalker, Puṇṇā and Puṇṇikā were slave girls, Sumaṅgalamata was the daughter of a worker in rushes and Subha the daughter of a smith. One monk is described as a former vulture-trainer.[20] Mātaṅga, the son of a Caṇḍāla, is said to have reached the highest level, which many Kṣatriyas and Brāhmaṇas could not attain and acquired infinite bliss.[21] In the list of the authors of *Therāgāthās* and *Therīgāthās*, at least 10 out of 259 *theras*[22] and 8 out of about 59 *theris*[23] belonged to sections of society which may be regarded as Śūdras. They included an actor, a Caṇḍāla, a basketmaker, a trapper, a prostitute and a woman slave. In the beginning there was no room for caste distinction in the *saṃgha*. In this connection, it is well to bear in mind the famous saying of the Buddha:

> Just, O *bhikkhus*, as the great rivers—that is to say, the Gaṅgā, the Yamunā, the Aciravatī, the Sarabhū and the Mahī—when they have fallen into the great ocean, renounce their names and lineages and are thenceforth reckoned as the great ocean—Just so, O *bhikkhus*, do these four castes—Kṣatriyas, Brāhmaṇas, Vaiśyas and Śūdras—when they have gone forth from the world under the doctrine and discipline proclaimed by the Tathāgata, renounce their names and lineage and enter into the number of the Śākyaputtiya Samaṇas.[24]

The Buddha's opening of the door of his *saṃgha* to every caste and to men at any time of their life was so revoltuionary that the existing social order was threatened. The Brahmanical system, afraid that renunciation at an early age would upset the requirements of society, maintained that the true value of renunciation was available only afer a socially fulfilled life.[25] Thus, the Buddha's doctrine of renunciation irrespective of caste, instead of creating a favourable atmosphere, evinced much hostile criticism, if not direct opposition, from the people of Rajagriha who regarded him not as a saviour but as one who came to depopulate society by depriving wives of their husbands and noble families of their sons.[26] According to a Jain canon some of the main causes for the renunciation of the world were poverty, sickness, sudden anger and insult.[27] There might have been some truth in the following abuse hurled by householders at monks: 'those who become *śramaṇas* are the meanest workmen, unable to support their families, low-caste men, wretches, idlers'.[28] In order to discourage the influx of such people into the *saṃgha*, it was said that a miserable man who became a monk in order to get food from others would be reborn as a boar greedy for wild rice.[29] A Buddhist text informs us that in the realm of Bimbisāra the *saṃgha* enjoyed special protection from the king on account of which at times prisoners, thieves, persons condemned to the punishment of whipping, debtors and runaway slaves took refuge in the Buddhist order and got themselves ordained.[30] A passage in the *Dīgha Nikāya* makes it clear that members of the lower orders sought an end to their misery by becoming Buddhist monks.[31] In one text the Buddha poses the question to a king as to what treatment he would meet out to a man who had joined the order, whom he would have treated as a slave-servant under ordinary circumstances. The king confesses that he would treat him as a person worthy of honour and respect and would offer him a seat, robes, a bowl, a lodging place and medicine.[32] The above discourse of the Buddha leaves us in no doubt that the life of a renouncer offered to the members of the lower orders not only prospects of immediate relief from poverty, but was also supposed to earn them enough merit to enable them to lead a happier life in the next birth. It is significant that there is no mention of Brāhmaṇas and Kṣatriyas in this connection, which may suggest that in joining the *saṃgha* the poorer sections of the Vaiśyas and the Śūdras were generally moved by materialistic interests.[33] However, when these cases were brought to the notice of the Buddha, he laid down that such people should not be admitted into the order. The rules of the *saṃgha* did not favour the admission of considerable sections of the labouring masses who, in joining the *saṃgha*, were running away from their worldly obligations. There was no permission either for a slave or a debtor to join the *saṃgha*, unless the former had been manumitted by his master and the latter had cleared his debts. But, the discourse of the Buddha to Ajātaśatru in the *Dīgha Nikāya* points up the ambiguities on the question of the admission of slaves to the *saṃgha.*[34] The negative answer of King Ajātaśatru to the question of the Buddha whether the former could claim an ex-slave, who had become a member of the *saṃgha* and compel him to work again as a slave may suggest the possibility of a *dāsakammakāra* joining the Buddhist church without the permission of his master. However, such cases were probably rare.[35]

Besides stabilizing the existing social and economic relations, Buddhism tried to improve the position of slaves in other ways too. Whereas the *Dharmasūtra* forbids trade in human beings only to the Brāhmaṇa, who can, however, exchange slave for slave,[36] it is clearly stated in the *Aṅguttara Nikāya* that trade in human beings is prohibited even for their lay devotees.[37] Buddhism tried to inculcate among its followers a spirit of generosity and kindness towards its employees. Thus a passage in the *Dīgha Nikāya* enjoins that employers should treat their slaves and workers decently. They should not be given tasks beyond their strength. They should receive food and wages, be cared for in times of sickness and be given occasional holidays and a share in the unusual delicacies enjoyed by the master.[38] A Jain text states that wealth should be accumulated not only for the sake of kinsmen and kings but also for the use of *dāsas, dāsīs, kammakaras* and *kammakarīs,* suggesting thereby that the latter deserve to be well looked after by the employer.[39] Such an instruction was required for the consolidation of the new social formation marked by the appearance of the state and of clear-cut social classes, for in a tribal society wealth is meant primarily for distribution among kinsmen.[40]

Nevertheless, Buddhism could not bring about any fundamental change in contemporary society. The Buddha's impact on the prevailing social structure and apparent social evils and injustices was minimal. In the final analysis the Buddhists could not effect any significant change in the position of the lower orders and those who were oppressed in the newly risen unequal society based on the power of wealth. The proportion as well as the importance of such people in the Buddhist church was negligible. The Buddha did not reject the notion of the caste system but gave it his own interpretation. In *Aggañña Sūtta* of the *Dīgha Nikāya* he rejects the theory of the divine origin of the caste system and instead ties it up with the evolutionary process. In this Sutta, he opines that all castes arose because of the laziness and greed of men. The first to emerge were the *khattiyas*, so-called because their job was to look after the fields. And the first *khattiya* was elected to the position of king or *mahāsammata*. Next arose the Brāhmaṇas who became abstainers from worldly pursuits. Then came the *vessas* who engaged in various trades and the *suddas* who subsisted on hunting. Here it is clear that the Buddha did not question the wisdom of organizing society into four *varṇas*. In this respect we find Romila Thapar right in pointing out that the Buddha made a distinction between caste as the frame of the socio-economic structure, which he accepted and the notion of the relative purity inherent in the upper castes, which he rejected.[41] The Buddha theoretically rejected the principle of determining one's social status on the basis of birth in a caste but this was not an unqualified rejection and was applied in the case of Brāhmaṇas only. He accepted the concept of social superiority or inferiority on the basis of *kula* or family, which in his thinking was determined by one's birth. In the *Ambaṭṭha Sutta*, he tries to convince the Brāhmaṇa Ambaṭṭha that he was inferior to the Śākyas because he had been born in an inferior *kula*.[42] The Buddhist point of view expressed in this text clearly places the Kṣatriyas above the Brāhmaṇas in social hierarchy and at the same time decries the caste hierarchy in favour of spiritual learning and achievement.

Buddhism merely tries to show that caste is of no value in the search for emancipation. It did not attack the basis of slavery and did not try to abolish the social, economic, political and religious limitations of the Śūdras. The Śūdras, from the post-Vedic period, had been deprived of the remnants of their tribal rights and saddled with disabilities in every aspect of society. Buddhist texts repeatedly describe the members of the first three *varṇas* as opulent but leave out the Śūdras, the *dāsas* and the *kammakaras*. The Buddha is described as having visited the assemblies of the Brāhmaṇas, the Kṣatriyas and *gahapati* devotees, but the assembly of the Śūdras is not mentioned. In spite of these limitations, however, it is perhaps right to say, as D.P. Chattopadhyaya does, that Buddhism was destined to become the biggest socio-religious movement in Indian history. He believes that the Buddha's attitude to the injustices of the caste system and his attack upon Brahmanical ritual was significant for its appeal to the people.[43] However, Chattopadhyaya also argues that the Buddha only created an illusion of liberty, equality and fraternity because he modelled his *saṃgha* on tribal values, whereas in reality these values were being trampled upon in the world outside the *saṃgha.*[44] Therefore, even in a *saṃgha*, the spirit of equality was true only theoretically. Thus, the distinctions of caste and the value of high birth were in no way extinguished, though it may be going too far to assert that social organization in India was not in the least altered by the Buddha's appearance.[45]

In the Mauryan period, owing to the country's economic development and the growth of towns, the position of wealthy Vaiśyas, who had waxed rich, began to approach that of the Kṣatriyas and Brāhmaṇas. On the other hand impoverished Vaiśyas began sinking to the level of the Śūdras who, even if they could succeed in raising their material level, still remained at the bottom of the social ladder. Therefore, it is natural that the Brāhmaṇas retained their influence mostly in villages and avoided city life. Nevertheless, a decline in the role of the Brāhmaṇas, particularly in the Mauryan period does not mean that they lost their influence or their privileges completely. True, in the political and ideological spheres they were compelled to lower their claims under the influence of the Kṣatriyas and the consolidation of Buddhism. However, in the economic and social areas they still retained much of their position. Naturally, as *Majjhima Nikāya* mentions quoting the Buddha, two of the *varṇas*—Kṣatriyas and Brāhmaṇas—held a special position[46] and they rooted this position firmly in society as the ruling classes. It is interesting that disputes between Buddhists and Brāhmaṇas did not lead to any acute social conflicts.[47] It is no wonder that the Brāhmaṇas and Kṣatriyas favoured a union to consolidate their positions. The *Manusmṛti* reads, 'the Brāhmaṇa and Kṣatriya, having united, flourish in this and in the other world'.[48] Kautilya also recognized that 'Kṣatriya power, made to prosper by the Brāhmaṇa (chaplain), sanctified by spells in the four councils of ministers (and) possessed of arms in the form of compliance with the science (of politics), triumphs, remaining ever unconquered'.[49]

In the subsequent period, the Buddhists, with the skill of the ambidextrous, maintained the idea of the equality of the people as well as Kṣatriya chauvinism, and gave a new shape to Buddhism. They assigned countless superhuman qualities to their Lord and made him excel the heroes of popular epics, such as the *Rāmāyaṇa* and *Mahābhārata*. One of the most notable works of the period is *Mahavastu* in which the Buddha is endowed with superhuman qualities. Another important work exhibiting a similar trend, the *Lalitavistara* in which 'the life and work of the Buddha on earth is termed as *lalita* or the sport of a supernatural being', traces the development of the Buddha-legend.[50] In these works we notice the Buddhist attitude of the time and the partiality for the Kṣatriyas, which was a product of the preceding phase. What is emphasized and eulogized is the Buddha's Kṣatriya heritage rather than any ideology of social equality. In one of the Jātaka tales, it is said that the Buddhas have never been born in the Vaiśya or the Śūdra castes, only in one or other of the two highest castes, the Kṣatriyas or Brāhmaṇas and because just now the Kṣatriya is the highest[51] he has been born in a Kṣatriya family. The same view is found in the *Lalitavistara*.[52]

In this period, the attempt at founding a casteless society in the Buddhist *saṃgha* suffered a set back. Actually, the Buddha wanted a healthy and harmonious relation between society and his order.[53] He, therefore, banned these who wanted to join the *saṃgha* for materialistic interests or who went against the social order. Following the stand of their Lord, the rules of the *saṃgha* could not favour the abolition of the existing social order. The *saṃgha*, trying to stay in close relation with lay society, could not maintain its incipient pristine and ideal character. Caste-based divisions in the *saṃgha* were not unheard of.[54] The *saṃgha* was an association of renouncers, but these renouncers were no longer ascetics. They created a parallel social stratification of society. With the passage of time, the Brāhmaṇa members of the *saṃgha*, by virtue of their literacy got hold of the leadership. It appears that during the early medieval period, the feudal character of society infiltrated into the *saṃgha*. The hierarchical organization of the Buddhist monasteries followed, more or less, the model of the prevalent, social structure. They were not exactly on the lines of churches in medieval Europe, but all the same, with grants of land free from royal interference in the maintenance of law and order, temples and monasteries grew into later *maṭhas*, which assumed a feudal character.[55]

The best instance of the assimilation of Buddhism into the feudal culture is witnessed in the rise of the *boddhisattva* as a saviour.[56] From about the first century AD. Mahāyāna Buddhism offered an ideal of benevolent lords in the form of buddhas and especially *bodhisattvas* (in whose names the word *īśvara*, 'lord', often appears). It was desired that the lords of this world, the kings and landowners, should provide a corresponding ideal of submissive trust for those who hoped to be protected and made happy by them.[57] The cult of Amitābha or the doctrine of *Sukhāvatīvyūha* is related to this trend.

Sukhāvatīvyūha is splendour, gay, bright and enjoyable enough to attract ordinary people who can hardly comprehend the absolute, dry soteriology of *nirvāṇa*. The simple contents of *Sukhāvatīvyūha*, thus, made this cosmology accessible to many uneducated people and the texts promise full success to the people through simple worship and donation. The flourishing cult of *bhakti* in the early medieval period was deeply related to such trends in religious development. In this cult, an important change is seen in the Śūdra's right to make gifts. A Śūdra who practices truth and sincerity, honours *mantras* and Brāhmaṇas and makes gifts, attains heaven and even Brāhmaṇahood in the next birth.[58] A Śaiva prostitute and a Śūdra goldsmith made gifts, as a result of which the former attained the reign of Śiva after death and the latter became a paramount sovereign named Dharmamūrti.[59] A Buddhist commentary of the fifth century AD provides instances of at least a dozen persons of the lower orders who enjoyed the pleasures of heaven and the joys and comforts of the Buddhist *vimānas* as a result of their gifts to the Buddha, the *bhikṣus* or the *saṃgha*.[60] The most advantageous character of this system is the easily attainable other world which is the only hope and protection of humble people from this world's hard oppression. There is no need to make persevering efforts for anyone, regardless of his socio-economic status, who sets his mind on Amitābha or some other Buddha or *bodhisattva* can be reborn in the Buddhist heaven.

With this trend of the feudalization in Buddhism, the strong impact of the wide ranging *varṇa* restrictions became noticeable in monasteries. They lost the reformative spirit, particularly with regard to dining. Though they could approach families of all the four *varṇas* for a meal, hard restrictions were put on the rules for begging food. It shows us that the spirit of repulsion with regard to dining, the basic pole of the caste system in early India, had seeped into Buddhism. The injunctions contained in the Buddhist text *Vimuttimagga*, of first-second centuries AD that the covering of his bowl by a monk on seeing a Caṇḍāla did not amount to a transgression of the alms-seeking rules[61] clearly suggests that the donor's qualifications had come to be governed by *varṇa* prejudices. Thus, even the Buddhists, who in theory sought to attack the caste system, could not remain totally indifferent to it. In Buddhist canonical texts we do not come across any specific instance of a Caṇḍāla being offered gifts, even though notices of alms being given to destitute and inferior beggars are plentiful.[62] The omission seems all the more significant when even in the *Mahābhārata* it is conceded that offerings to dogs and Caṇḍālas are never totally devoid of merit.[63] Aśvaghoṣa, who severely attacked caste distinctions, acknowledges a Śūdra's right to receive gifts only if the latter has crossed the dreadful ocean of the five senses.[64]

The descriptions of the Kali age in several early Purāṇas in the period under discussion, show that the society practising *varṇa* was marked by strong social conflicts. Manu tried his best to preserve Brahmanical society. In this Kali age, the clear distinctions between the functions of the Vaiśyas and the Śūdras were being gradually obliterated. Manu lays down that if, in times of distress, a Vaiśya finds it difficult to support himself by his lawful occupations he should take to the occupations of the Śūdras, i.e. live by serving the members of the twice-born caste. This Brahmanical view on social distinctions was shared by contemporary Buddhists. The existing inequality is accepted as something usual in Buddhist writings. The spread of Buddhism, thus, did not attack the caste basis of social organization. In the *Milindapañho* cultivation, trade and tending of cattle are described as the functions of the ordinary folk such as the Vaiśyas and Śūdras, there being no separate mention of the functions of the two classes.[65] It also states that a person who is low born is not fit to become king.[66] This is in consonance with Manu who prescribes that Brāhmaṇas should not accept presents from a king who is not descended from the Kṣatriya race.[67]

In the early Christian centuries Buddhists held a different view. They rather faithfully followed the ambidextrous attitude of the Buddha and his early followers. The *Śārdūlakarṇāvadāna* of *Divyāvadāna*, translated into Chinese in AD 265, is a good example of refuting the caste system in the works of the transitional period. The author denies caste distinctions in relating the love story between Ānanda and a Caṇḍāla girl. He severely criticizes, in the form of the Buddha's speech, the caste system, pointing out that between members of the various castes there exists no such natural difference as between diverse species of animals and plants. *Kalpanāmaṇḍitikā*, the work of Kumāralāta, translated into Chinese by Kumārajīva in about AD 405 refutes the caste system with quotations from the *Manusmṛti*. In this work the Buddha is shown as filled with mercy towards everybody. He mercifully initiates the man whom Śāriputra denies due to the lack of good deeds in his previous lives.

Vajrasūci also gives us some information on the attitude to caste distinctions, especially with regard to Śūdras.[68] It refutes the caste system sharply. Criticising the Vedas, the *Mahābhārata,* and the *Manusmṛti* it contends that if a Brāhmaṇa does not cultivate truth, asceticism, sublimation of passions and compensation for all beings, he is like a Caṇḍāla[69] and that good conduct can help a man attain Brāhmaṇahood in the next birth.[70] The text avers that Brāhmaṇas are to be found even in the families of the Kaivarttas, Rajakas and Caṇḍālas, among whom the rites of *cūḍakarṇa, muñja, daṇḍa, kāṣṭha,* etc., are performed.[71] It further states that Kṣatriyas, Vaiśyas and Śūdras are seen sacrificing and officiating at sacrifices, studying and teaching, and accepting gifts.[72]

We do not think that such radical, anti-caste views reflect faithfully the true Buddhist position on social stratification. Such revolutionary views, that went against contemporary thought and practices, owed a great deal to the Vaiṣṇava sect. Unlike the old orthodox form of Brahmanism, Viṣṇuism and Śivaism, in post-Gupta times, did not push the Śūdras and untouchables out of sight, but extended to them the privilege of knowing God and attaining liberation.[73] The Vaisnava texts never fail to emphasize that women and Śūdras can attain emancipation through their devotion to Kṛṣṇa, Nārāyaṇa or Vāsudeva. If a person of low birth utters the name of God even once, he is liberated from bondage.[74] Bhagavan is represented as claiming that the whole world, from the Brāhmaṇa to the śvapaka is purified if devoted to Him.[75] Śivaism also maintained a similar position. The same assertion is made with regard to all the four *varṇas* if they recite the hymns dedicated to Mahādeva.[76] If Vaiśyas, women and Śūdras listen to the story of the Dakṣa-Śiva conflict from the Brāhmaṇas, they find a place in the Rudra-loka.[77] Like the members of the three higher *varṇas,* a Śūdra devotee of Śiva is also promised the status of Gaṇapati.[78] It is Tantricism that infiltrated into Viṣṇuism, Śivaism and Buddhism and did not recognize *varṇa* distinctions in the matter of religion. The post-Gupta Tantric texts shifted their emphasis from ritual observance to good conduct, which it claimed determind social status. Protesting against social norms and a way of life dominated by the caste system imposed by the Brahmanical law-givers, they maintained that there was no need to search for God outside human existence, that external rites and ceremonies were false and that the caste system was meaningless. Within the fold of Buddhism there developed a special Tantric way the aim of which was to attain *siddhi* and allow men to become *siddhas*. According to the tradition there were eighty-four *siddhas* who were endowed with supernatural powers which they had achieved through meditation and physical exercises. The *siddhācāryas* did not care for social distinctions and the caste system. The followers of *Hevajra yoga* regarded everyone as a Buddha and did not differentiate between high and low. But the influence of the reforming sects of Tantricism should not be exaggerated. They did not question the fundamental theory of *karma*, which provided the doctrinal basis of the Brahmanical social order. In the course of time Tantric reformism on social evils began to wither away. Tantric Buddhists could not substantially alter the servile position of the lowest members in the caste structure. They tried to contain social discontent rather than channelize it into revolutionary directions. By promising religious equality in place of other forms of equality, they helped to reconcile the lower orders to the existing social system.

The record of I-tsing, however, provides us with another invaluable point for study in the practice of caste distinctions in early-medieval Buddhist *saṃghas*. He gives an account of the monks' ideas on purity and pollution. According to him, after having attended a funeral, the monks went from the cremation ground to the pond outside the monastery for bathing. If there was no pond then they went to a well to wash themselves. Then they returned to their apartments where they cleansed the floor with powdered cow dung.[79] This example clearly brings out the monks' attitude towards caste. In fact, in Brahmanical beliefs, water is the great purificatory agent. The laws of Manu say 'when he has touched a caṇḍāla, a menstruating woman, an outcaste, a woman who has just given birth, a corpse . . . he purifies himself by bathing'.[80] And, here, in I-tsing's record, the fact that the monks washed themselves after cremating the dead body indicates their recognition of the notions of purity-pollution. In another example, describing the Uposatha day, I-tsing says that only copper utensils are used as a rule. Earthenware which has been used already should be thrown away into a ditch, for used vessels should not be possessed at all. Left over food was not kept for later use and was never offered to another person. Priests and laymen alike washed their hands and feet before meals. They sat on small chairs, which were ranged at such a distance from each other that one person would not touch another. And blocks of wood would be used for minor members and novices of the *saṃgha*. After finishing, the meal they generally washed their hands and rinsed their mouths properly. Pea-flour or mud would be rinsed for washing lips and the mouth would be rinsed two or three times with water from a jar. No contact would be made with each other until they had been purified. If anybody touched another person before rinsing his mouth, the person touched would be defiled and had to rinse his mouth.[81] Three kinds of cleansing material, i.e. pea-flour, dry-earth and cow dung were used for scrubbing jars used for keeping water. I-tsing states that India had abundant pools. In one *yojana* he saw twenty or thirty bathing places of various sizes. The Chinese traveller saw ten great pools near the Nalanda monastery.[82] To remind Buddhist monks of the bathing hour a bell was sounded every morning and sometimes several hundred and sometimes several thousand Buddhist monks would go together with bathing-sheets to the pools to take a bath.[83] The various rules and regulations and the bathing practices of this time were rooted in the practice of the Buddha. The Buddha continued with the custom of bathing which is necessary in Indian climatic conditions. However, it was also seen as being medicinal, taken in order to cure a disease, as I-tsing states.[84] Bathing with the idea of purification was the result of the incessant contact with lay society which was entrenched in the Brahmanical milieu.

Among the dominant ideas that greatly contributed to social stratification in Korea, one may distinctly point out the doctrine of *karma*, especially in relation to the concept of rebirth in the Buddhist time frame. Since *karma* is intimately related to merit, it is very important to understand the relation between the concept of *karma* and that of merit. However, the doctrine of *karma* has also played another role in society. It promises a better/worse status in a future life according to meritorious/demeritorious actions performed in this life. Even the wicked could possess great fortune because of their merit acquired in previous births and *vice-versa*. *Karma,* thus, played its own role as a theory of value in the ethical and spiritual areas of life, whose implications were worked out in some detail by the Buddha and his followers in their attack on the caste system. This is clearly reflected in the Buddha's observation that 'not by birth does a man become an outcaste; nor by birth alone does he become a Brāhmaṇa; it is by deeds that a man becomes an outcaste and also by deeds alone can a man be called a Brāhmaṇa'.[85] *Karma* tended to cut across the bonds of various social units as it postulated a creed that held valid for all men irrespective of their other connections. It attempted to posit a system of ethics of universal application. It was a message of hope for man, who by the sheer dint of his own personal exertion could make his own destiny.

The basic issue in the acceptance of Buddhism in early Korea was the seeking of material blessings and consolidation of privileges in this world. Some clues can be obtained from a royal edict of King Ashin of Paikche, 'Seek blessings in the worship of the Buddha.'[86] The message of Paikche King Song is another good source: 'This (Law of the Buddha) is the utmost and best one among all the doctrines . . . if you wish, everything is achievable . . . if you pray with determination, nothing would be insufficient.'[87] Through this, one can easily identify the nature and character of Buddhism which flourished in the royal courts, which was to rationalize its physical and material demands. The royal court happened to be the most active force behind the introduction of Buddhism because the Buddhist view of *karma* lent powerful support to status-quoist forces. It legitimized political regimes based on social differentiation. The difference in social ranks was given moral justification by interpreting one's position in terms of 'just retribution for the merits and demerits of the past life'. It was even regarded impious to blame the inherent poverty, inequality and injustice in society. Thus, while it helped in the consolidation of existing privileges, it opposed any attempt to change the existing social order in spite of many rampant evils and oppression.

Such a highly rationalized world-view was totally different from that of Shamanism which had been the main mechanism for the justification of authority by the old aristocracy. Since the aristocracy, comprising heads of clans, was struggling for the paramountcy of power, the royal family—a newly risen group, was searching for a new ideology for its own legitimization. This reminds us of very similar conditions in India in the sixth century BC when the struggle between the Brāhmaṇas and Kṣatriyas came to the fore. In India, too, Buddhism came into being as an ideology for the latter, the newly risen class, against the old power. Therefore, the fact that the Buddha disapproved of the 'pure blood' of the Brāhmaṇas was especially appealing to the royal families in early Korea who tried to enforce their ideological stand by denying the authority of the 'pure blood' of old aristocracy. The Buddhist idea of *karma* on the other hand, proved a boon for the old aristocracy, too. According to the theory of *karma*, well-being or misfortune is totally dependent on the individual's deeds. It converted the social order into a moral one in which differences in social rank were interpreted as just retribution for merit and demerit earned in the past life. It justified social inequalities and militated against any social change. It was regarded as impious to blame one's poverty on oppression or the evils of the social system. The attribution of one's own failure to *karma* means that it cannot be attributed to the alleged evils of the social order which, therefore, need not be changed. Hence, there could not be any point in raging against a system based on social inequalities. The doctrine of *karma*, the new and highly systematized view rationalizing their predominance in society was so good that the old aristocracy did not oppose the king's introduction of Buddhism. Buddhism, thus, was good enough to be a system which provided considerable theoretical background support to the king as well as the nobles of ancient Silla who wished to continue enjoying their privileged status.

The doctrine of *karma* influenced the *kolpum* system which conferred or withheld a variety of special privileges ranging from political preferment to advantages in everyday life in accordance with the degree of respect due to a person's bone-rank. It primarily regulated a person's politico-administrative status as well as marriage, size of residence, colour of costumes, cart, ware, etc. It was a class system evolved from the time of the tribal confederacy which was systematized at the time when Silla shaped its politico-governmental apparatus. The *kolpum* system did not emerge from any particular religious or philosophical idea. Nor did it emerge in any particular time frame. It emerged as the state structure started taking a concrete shape from its primitive tribal character. There are too many controversies with regard to the origin and its incipient social structure before the introduction of Buddhism for us to get involved in it. Nor is it feasible to describe its nature and its history in detail.[88] What we are, however, interested in tracing is the degree of its influence of Buddhism and on the development of its institutions. The main structure of the system after the introduction of Buddhism is as follows: two high *kols* or bone-ranks and six *tus* or head-ranks, viz., *songkols* or sacred-bone, *chinkols* or true-bone, six grades of head-ranks from *yuktupums* or head rank six down through *iltupums* or head-rank one.

How deeply did the Buddhist idea of social stratification influence the system? The reason for the evolution of *songkols* and *chinkols* within the Silla royal house of Kim into two high classes is not entirely clear. Kim Pusik, the author of the *Samguksagi*, the chronicle claiming to be the authority on the regime of Silla, maintains that the origin of *songkols* is from Hyokkose, the mythical figure who was supposed to be the founder of Silla, while monk Iryon, the author of *Samgukyusa,* attributes its beginnings to King Pop-hung who recognized Buddhism officially. Yet, it is generally maintained that the formation of rigid social classification definitely followed the cleavage of the Silla royal family in the process of a power struggle. The process came to possess a concrete structure in the period of the so-called middle antiquity of Silla (514-654). This was done at the time when Silla transformed the character of its state from clan confederacy to the monarchical system. The *kolpum,* thus, must have began to be a regular socio-legal institution by the time of the promulgation of the state law system by King Pop-hung in the year 520. It was systematized as a regular social institution with various procedures of development of the politico-governmental apparatus, viz., the establishment of departments in the government, consolidation of royal authority, recognition of Buddhism as state religion. So the development of the rigid social institution should be traced from the time of the consolidation of the royal class and corresponding political authority.

Such a classification is not directly derived from the Indian idea of the caste system for we cannot find any evidence of the basic ideas of caste-based classification that thrived on the idea of pollution and purity, restriction on marriage, commensality and so on in the Korean social system. Moreover, the *kolpum* system did not distinguish between the higher orders and the lower orders. The core of the *kolpum* system lies in social differentiation in the royal family in the matter of bureaucracy. The system mainly decides upon the members and groups eligible for the throne and grades of high offices. Kingship was a monopoly of the *songkols* while the various higher echelons of the bureaucracy were in the purview of the *chinkols.* However, no sharp exclusion of the lower class from the normal social order was ever witnessed. It did not project any idea of religious discrimination of the low-born. There are no details of peasants and artisans on whose revenues, tributes and manual work the higher orders lived. In the *kolpum* system, we do not have any instances of marital restrictions or taboo on food and drink, etc.

Buddhism indirectly influenced the establishment of the *kolpum* institution, based on rigid social difference in the so-called middle antiquity period of Silla. The firm establishment of the system was achieved through the concept of *songkols.* The idea of *song* or sacredness belonging to one group out of so many is the product of Korea's cultural contact with early India through Buddhism. Buddhists in Silla were quite aware of the 'myth of Kṣatriyas'. It is clearly illustrated in the monk Chajang episode on Mt. Odae in China in the year 636 recorded in the *Samgukyusa.*[89] Here the royal family of Silla is described as belonging to the Kṣatriya family of India and predestined by Buddhism. When a new thought makes an inroad into a new environment, everything associated with its founder seems appealing to the people. In this respect, the Kṣatriya chauvinism of the Buddha played a crucial role in determining social institutions in ancient Silla. The classification of the ruling elite according to the idea of sacred blood was used to denote their position and distance from the centre of power. Religion made it legitimate, and thus, acceptable to the people. In Silla, it was possible only in the period of the so-called middle antiquity, when the orthodox royal family succeeded in expanding royal power. In this period, they advocated their sovereign rights by calling the ruler an independent king and naming an independent era in the Chinese world order. In this manner, the royal family sanctified its lineage in order to differentiate itself from other noble families. It was the idea of the sacred lineage of the Kṣatriyas depicted in Buddhism that played a crucial role in establishing the *songkols* which, in turn, made the system rigid. This was done at the 'period of Buddhist titles for kings'[90] when, with the official recognition of Buddhism, an ethos permeated with Buddhism had become widely prevalent. The Buddhist world-view, the Buddhist idea of kingship and state including the idea of *cakravartin* and the myth of the Buddha-Land, Buddhist ideas on temple economy, religious rites, ceremonies and festivals in and around the temples, and so on occupied an important position in the people's everyday life. In this ethos, people's religious belief was strengthened and, along with it, the Buddhist idea of social stratification also got implanted in people's mind. Thus, one can argue that social stratification and the idea of sacredness became interwoven.

Yuktupums or head-rank six, the next *chinkols*, who seriously attacked the *kolpum* system and *chinkol's* exclusivism in the later Silla period were opposed to the theory of *karma.* Their stand is another good example of the *kolpum* system being interrelated with the theory of *karma.* Kang-su and Sol-ch'ong, the two prominent figures of this period, criticized the Buddhist world-view. They criticized the doctrine of *karma* and emphasized the importance of morality on earth. For them the morality of one's actions is the only criterion by which human beings should be judged. Kang-su maintained that the value of a human being should not be determined by his class but by his morals.[91] He protested against the social institution that prevented a man from marrying a girl from a family lower than his.[92] If such criteria was accepted, the *yuktupums* maintained that even royalty could not be an exception to it. The doctrine of *karma*, thus, was completely denied by the *yuktupums*, the middle high class in the *kolpum* system. Here, we should not fail to notice that the *yuktupums* too, belonged to a dominant social class and their attempt at reform was aimed at establishing themselves as the dominant class in society. In their attempted upward mobility they rejected the extreme conservative ideology associated with Buddhism and instead chose the comparatively less conservative ideology of Confucianism.

Nevertheless, the system of social stratification as prevalent in India was never fully transplanted into the Korean social fabric. The idea of an exclusive birth did not permeate the whole society but remained confined to the domain of the higher classes. Ideas about pollution-purity and of restriction on social and religious life due to religious discrimination did not find acceptance in Korea. Moreover, in early Korea status and power were never completely dissociated. We do not find any equivalent of the Brāhmaṇa-Kṣatriya relationship.[93] Buddhist kings were never dispossessed of religious prerogatives.

In any case, for the common masses neither the status-quoist doctrine of *karma* nor the morality-ability view of Confucianism promised any respite from their troubles. Instead, the concept of the 'next world', which is the other side of the doctrine of *karma*, emerged as the most influential idea among the masses. This resulted in the rise of the faith of 'Western Paradise'. The spirit of revolt against social rigidity based on the *kolpum* system also gave currency to the faith of 'Western Paradise'. Those who followed the faith were mostly exploited peasants and slaves. We have a good number of stories related to the people's faith in the 'Western Paradise'. The story of Uk-myon's slave girl,[94] who is said to have attained *nirvana* not after her death but in this world, and of the five monks[95] who were poor peasants and prayed for attaining the 'Western Paradise' in this world, witness the functional relation between the worst material conditions in which the masses had to exist and the trend of their faith. The people at the time were so oppressed by the heavy burden of taxes, labour and tolls for the expense of waging wars under despotic rulers that they could not lead an easy life. The expansion of territory by the unification of the three kingdoms brought the expansion of arable areas as well. The newly arisen ruling elite did not lose the chance to secure the larger plots of arable land and enjoyed various revenues from villages and larger districts. Large amounts of land were granted to high servants and Buddhist monasteries. Land, the chief means of subsistence for the people, thus, came mostly into the possession of a few members of the ruling class who elaborated a social mechanism through which the fruits of economic expansion since the seventh century could be cornered by a few members of the ruling class to the exclusion of peasants and artisans. We come across an endless number of landless peasants and labourers in our sources. These dispossesed classes found a way to overcome the difficulties created by their economic and social conditions in the faith of 'Western Paradise'. They dreamt of escaping from the bad conditions of this world in the name of Amitābha Buddha of the Western Paradise.

For the purposes of safety and cohesion, rulers generally encouraged religious toleration. Their patronage was not confined to one particular sect or religion. At the higher level the spirit of religious toleration appears as a marked feature. But one may notice below the surface, not only the dissensions among the various higher cults and sects, but also deeper tensions and conflict. The objection to the orthodox superior class within the fold of the state-religion suggests the tensions that prevailed in the circle of the privileged aristocracy. In such circumstances, the rulers of Silla supported the cult of Amitābha or Pure Land Buddhism for it did not promote the idea of social revolution and the establishment of an ideal society in this world but emphasized the vanity of this world and promised utopia in the next. Thus, it was expected to suppress the trend of popular unrest and help in the stabilization of society. In this respect, the rulers, in their own interest, encouraged the cult of Amitābha which, in any case, had a strong appeal to the people. The cult of Amitābha, therefore, paradoxically enough, resulted in granting indirect support to despotism, though its critical position was against the culture of the ruling classes.

The Buddhists never abandoned the doctrine of *karma* which in itself contained the idea of social stratification. As one Burmese monk put it, if complete equality—a classless society—were desirable or achievable, 'then why shouldn't the scorpion share his legs with the snake? There are two-legged, four-legged, and many legged animals. There is no equality in nature; it all depends on *karma*. If you want to establish a classless society, you are against *karma*.'[96]

NOTES

1. *SOB,* Ch. XI.
2. U.N. Ghoshal, *HIPI,* p. 65.
3. *Sut. Nip.*, II, 2. 2-10.
4. Celestine Bougle, *Essays on the Caste System* (Cambridge, 1971), p. 9.
5. *MN,* XCIII. 148.
6. *DN,* III. 78-9.
7. *Sut. Nip.*, III, 9. 8-26.
8. *Sut. Nip.*, II, 7.
9. *DP.* XXVI, 390-423; *Sut. Nip.*, I. 7.
10. *MN,* LXXXIV, 88.
11. Rhys Davids, *Dialogues of the Buddha,* SBB, pt. I, vol. II, p. 101.
12. G. C. Pande, *Śramana Tradition: Its History and Contribution to Indian Culture* (Ahmedabad, 1978), p. 54.
13. R. Fick, *The Social Organization in North-East India in Buddha's Time* (rpt., Delhi, 1972).
14. T.W. Rhys Davids, op. cit., pp. 140-1.
15. *MN,* XC, 128.
16. *SN,* 314-15
17. *Nakkhatta Jāt.*, no. 49.
18. *DN,* II, 100.
19. It does not indicate that the monks and nuns from the Śūdras and untouchables outnumber those from the Brāhmaṇas and Kṣatriyas. Cf. B.G. Gokhale's articles, 'The Early Buddhist Elite', *JIH,* XLIII, pt. ii. 1965, pp. 391ff; 'Early Buddhism and Brāhmaṇas', in *SHB,* pp. 67-80.
20. G.P. Malalasekera, *Dictionary of Pali Proper Names* (New Delhi, 1983, rpt.), i, 174.
21. *Sut. Nip.*, I, 7. 23-5.
22. A. Bose, Social a*nd Rural Economy of North India* (Calcutta, 1961), ii, p. 285 fn.1.
23. Calculated on the basis of the list given in B.C. Law, *History of Pali Literature* (rpt., Delhi, 1983), ii, 508-16.
24. *Vin., Cvg.*, IX, I. 4.
25. Romila Thapar, *CTEI,* p. 12.
26. Gokuldas De, *DEBS,* p. 20.
27. *Thāṇāṅga,* X, 712.
28. *Sūyagaḍam,* II, 2. 54.
29. Ibid., I, 7. 25.
30. *Vin., Mvg.*, I, 40. 1f.
31. R.S. Sharma, *SAI,* p. 149.
32. *DN,* I, 60-1.

33. R.S. Sharma, *SAI,* p. 150.
34. *DN,* I, 10-12.
35. R.S. Sharma, *SAI,* p. 150.
36. *Āpastamba Dharma Sūtra,* I, 7. 20. 15; *Vaśiṣṭha Dharma Sūtra,* II, 39.
37. *AN,* V; XVIII, 177.
38. *DN,* III, 191.
39. *Ācārāṅga Sūtta,* I, 2. 5. 1.
40. R.S. Sharma, *SAI,* pp. 151-2.
41. Romila Thapar, *AISH,* pp. 51-2.
42. *DN,* I, 3. 16.
43. D.P. Chattopadhyaya, *Lokāyata* (4th edn., New Delhi, 1978), pp. 466-7.
44. Ibid.
45. R. Fick, op.cit., p. 32.
46. *MN,* XC, 128-9.
47. Y. Krishnan 'Was there any conflict between the Brāhmaṇas and Buddhists', *IHQ,* vol. 30, no. 2, 1954, pp. 167-73.
48. *MS,* IX, 322.
49. *AS,* I, 9.
50. *HIL,* vol. II, p. 238.
51. *Nakkhatta Jāt.,* no. 49.
52. *Lal. Vis.,* III.
53. G.S.P. Misra, *The Age of Vinaya* (New Delhi, 1972), p. 129.
54. Richard F. Gombrich, *Pre. Prac.,* p. 307.
55. R.S. Sharma, *PSEHEI,* p. 239.
56. 'Feudalism', pp. 166ff.
57. Ibid., p. 174.
58. *Mahābhārata,* Anuśāsana Parva, 217. 13-15.
59. *Matsya Purāṇa,* 91. 23-32.
60. B.C. Law, *Heaven and Hell in Buddhist Perspective* (Calcutta and Simla, 1925), pp. 36-45.
61. *Vimuttimagga,* p. 36.
62. *Dāna,* p. 235.
63. *Mahābhārata,* Śānti Parva, 62. 13.
64. *Vajrasūci,* p. 21.
65. *MP,* 173.
66. Ibid., 358.
67. *MS,* V, 84.
68. Although the date of *Vajrasūci* is not certain, it does not seem to be the work of Aśvaghoṣa, the author of *Buddhacarita,* who lived in the post-Mauryan period. The work is ascribed to Dharmakīrti and was translated into Chinese between 973 and 981. For details, see *HIL,* vol. II, p. 255.
69. *Vajrasūci,* p. 5.
70. Ibid., p. 10.
71. Ibid., p. 7.
72. Ibid., p. 4.

73. H.C. Raychaudhri, *The Early History of the Vaisnava Sect* (Calcutta, 1920), p. 117.
74. *Bhāgavata Purāṇa*, V, 1. 35.
75. Ibid., III, 16. 6.
76. *Mahābhārata*, Anuśāsana Parva, 18. 81.
77. *Vāyu Purāṇa*, I, 30. 18
78. Ibid., II, 39, 352-4.
79. *I-tsing*, p. 82.
80. *MS*, V, 85.
81. *I-tsing*, pp. 35-7.
82. Ibid., pp. 107-8.
83. Ibid., pp. 107ff.
84. Ibid., p. 109.
85. *Sut. Nip.*, I, 7. 27.
86. *Yusa.*, III-iii, Nant'a Pyokche.
87. *Nipponshogi*, 19.
88. For details, see, Ki-dong Yi, *Silla Kolpum-je Sahoe-wa Hwarangdo* (Seoul, 1984).
89. *Yusa.*, III-iv, Hwangnyongsa Kuch'ungt'ap.
90. Ch'ol-jun Kim, op.cit., pp. 91-2.
91. Sagi, 46, Kang-su.
92. Ki-baek Yi, *SSY*, p. 217.
93. Louis Dumont, *Homo Hierarchichus* (Indian edn., Delhi, 1988), p. 215
94. *Yusa.*, V-vii, Uk-myon-pi Yombul Sosung.
95. *Yusa.*, V-viii, P'och'onsan O Pigu.
96. Melford E. Spiro, *BS*, pp. 439-40.

CHAPTER 6

Religious Ceremonies and Rites

Apotropaic Rituals

Originally Buddhism had little concern with the mundane affairs of everyday life. The doctrine that the Buddha preached was for each individual to internalize for himself. Its concern was with a soteriological goal such as *nirvāṇa.* It did not seek the aid of a supernatural being or saviour and as the Buddha pointed out repeatedly, salvation is achieved by the unaided efforts of the religious devotee. Neither the gods nor the Buddha, who was regarded as mortal, possessed any power to aid others. The exclusive soteriological concern, however, was unable to satisfy completely the needs of the masses for though it showed a way to cope with the sufferings of this world, its conception of suffering is rather limited being more philosophical and psychological than existential and physical. Most of all, the solution it offers is other-worldly.

The Buddha explained in his doctrine that attachment to the externals of religion such as rituals was one of the main hindrances to spiritual progress or the attainment of the supreme goal. He offered no respite from such immediate stresses as the bite of a poisonous snake, the illness of a loved one, the attack of a malevolent spirit and so on. Rather than treat symptoms, Buddhism attempts to root out the cause. Instead of providing temporary solutions for specific forms of misfortune, it offers an ultimate solution for the generic condition of suffering. The metaphysical analysis of the problem of suffering and the proposed solution for it have found little resonance among Buddhist masses. However sound it may be philosophically and however consistent it maybe logically, the analysis of one's present suffering through the doctrine of *karma,* i.e. the explanation that one's present suffering is determined entirely by *karma,* is emotionally frustrating. Not only does man seek an explanation for his sufferings but he wants to be able to do something about it. Moreover, though the Buddha converted hundreds of thousands of people, not all of them were competent to comprehend his abstruse doctrine and to follow his rigid spirituality. Most of all, the extreme soteriological doctrine provides little opportunity for escape from the seeming inevitability of present pain. Therefore, under pressure of need, various aspects of the doctrine of normative Buddhism have been modified or reinterpreted and a Buddhist theology and philosophy have been developed to satisfy it. It was in response to this strong pressure that apotropaic rituals were developed. Here, we use the term 'apotropaic' primarily to mean 'designed to avert evils'. In contrast to the soteriological aim of Buddhism, apotropaic rituals can never be related to the concept of *nirvāṇa* and/or better rebirth. The practise of the rituals cannot ever lead one to the final goal of religion. Melford E. Spiro, therefore, characterizes dimensions of apotropaic Buddhism as follows:

> its concern is with important matters in this present existence: health and illness, drought and rain, calamity and tranquillity. Second, it assumes that goals involved can be attained by specific magical acts which, unlike the ideology of soteriological Buddhism, either create immediate merit or enlist the assistance of supernatural beings and/or power. For apotropaic Buddhism, Buddhism as a whole—devotions, rituals, ethics, scripture—acts as a protective shield against the dangers of the present existence.[1]

In accordance with the needs of the time, its first ideological task was to modify the doctrine of *karma* so as to soften its harshness and allow for mutability in it. The modification is more properly interpreted as an attempt to legitimize a series of practises which clearly repudiate the implications of the doctrine. Prior to the ideological modification there had developed a host of rituals—recitation of spells, worship of images, performances of rites and so on—for protection against danger. The need for incantations, benedictions and blessings and for performing rituals had prevailed from very early times, growing out of Vedic *mantras,* especially those of the *Atharva Veda.* While in the *Ṛg Veda* we find elements of nature being propitiated by sacrifices, in the *Atharva Veda* different calamities are sought to be averted by mystic *mantras* of sorcery and witchcraft. Such deep-rooted apotropaic culture has played too great a part in the mind of the Indian people to be dispensed with easily.

The heresy was a survival from a primitive form of religion. It also satisfied some functional need of the people which is why these beliefs continued to be popular. Actually the ethos of the sixth century BC, when wrangling was the great vice of the age and the philosophic mind of the country was speculating on a thousand matters was most suitable for the growth of magical beliefs. The practise of magic was the regular profession of some Śramaṇas and Brāhmaṇas.

The Buddha was a product of his particular age and therefore he was not entirely free from the superstitious beliefs current in his time. In the *Vinaya Piṭaka* are recorded two stories which show how popular was the cultivation of magical powers amongst the Buddha's own disciples.[2] They not only practised magic but taught it to others as a regular art and charged fees for the tuition. Outside the pale of Vedic culture and religion, in Magadha, pre-Vedic and/or non-Vedic ideas and practises still survived and flourished. At this time religion and magic were inextricably blended together and the same person acted as both priest and magician to propitiate supernatural powers and perform impossible or difficult tasks in order to help in fulfilling the aim of his client. Those who were used to these primitive customs could not give up their traditional culture though they had converted to the new creed. It was through these people that apotropaic rituals were sustained. Subsequentely they made secret conclaves within the *saṃgha*, composed their own scriptures and managed to find sanctions for them by the clever manipulations of the words of the Buddha.

We find that there are contradictions in Buddhism at its incipient stage. It is said that this is simply because the Buddha taught in different ways to different people, according to their mentality and ability to understand. The Buddha clearly preached to his disciples that it was base to live by practising magic, fortune telling, uttering spells and so on. Such actions were forbidden strictly. The Buddha discouraged superstition and blind faith and encouraged the spirit of critical inquiry. In the *Brahmajāla Sutta* and *Kevaṭṭa Sutta*, the Buddha shows that he was not in favour of magical and superhuman feats and condemned magical arts as black, using the term *tiracchā na vijjā* or *micchājīva* to describe them. The Buddha was very much against disciples who attained supernatural powers (called *iddhi*) and then manifested them. The false declaration of this power is most serious offence, a *pārājika*, which can deprive a monk of his membership of the Buddhist community. In the *Cullavagga* of *Vinaya Piṭaka*, it is said that a monk who shows his miraculous powers to laymen for material gain is like a woman who trades her charms for money and is liable to a *dukkata* offence.[3]

At this time, the Brahmanical sacrificial cult, too, had become very popular due to the increase of agricultural surplus brought about by the later Vedic economy in the Ganga-Yamuna doab. This led to a separation between the religion of sacrifice and the cult of magic, with the latter being looked down upon as a lower craft as against the superior one of sacrifice. The Buddha, as a man in a society, was subject to his social ethos and it is alleged that sometimes he performed miracles to win people to his creed. B. Bhattacharya[4] maintains that being the clever organizer the Buddha was, he did not fail to notice the importance of magical practises amongst the masses, who were his favourite subjects. In an attempt to make his religion popular to all sections of society and to attract more adherents he did not forbid magical practises altogether. In fact, Parapariya, a monk who had studied under the Buddha, reveals in his lamenting verses the increase in healing activities carried on by monks in the years following the passing away of the Buddha.[5]

It was the power of deities, not their existence, that the Buddha denied. Thus, sacred Buddhist texts do not explicitly affirm that magic and the appeal to supernatural beings can never alter *karma.* It is expressly affirmed in sacred texts that all such beliefs are a hindrance to salvation and should be abandoned to attain *nirvāṇa.* Moreover, the lay masses, by virtue of their involvement in the social system, are incapable of attaining salvation in anyway; therefore practising or not practising apotropaic rituals makes little difference to their ultimate prospects. Although apotropaic rituals are doctrinally heretical, they are not intrinsically evil and practising them will not deprive the adherent of the secondary compensations of a happy rebirth or a period of relative bliss in heaven. Therefore, in order to make his religion acceptable, the founder had not only to satisfy the intelligentsia by giving them hopes for the next birth and promising a far-off salvation, but also those who had little interest in a distant emancipation or merits to be gained in the next birth but were eager to attain worldly prosperity in this very birth. It was to satisfy this second class of laity that the Buddha had to incorporate some sort of *parittas, dhāraṇis* and the like so that those wished to have prosperity in this birth would feel satisfied by practising them.

The improvization of *paritta* or *rakṣa mantras* and the like as protective chants in early Buddhism was undoubtedly due to the pressure of satisfying popular demand. It was the process through which the Śramaṇa tradition formed alliances with Brāhmaṇism and all kinds of primitive cults were perhaps mixed together. Not surprisingly, though the early Buddhists accepted the newrationalized creed, yet, like their predecessors, they could not overcome the sixteen fears which have been enumerated in the *Aṅguttara Nikāya.*[6] Such fears arise from the tyranny of the ruler, from thieves, robbers, malevolent spirits, stars, bad omens, fire, famine, disease and wild beasts, etc. The Buddhists, like other people, were naturally inclined to avail themselves of all possible means to avoid or overcome them. No religion would be acceptable to them if it could not assure them of its potency in overcoming these fears and inspire confidence that dangers would be averted.

Moreover, as other contending faiths entered the field and endeavoured to win people over to their side, they too were required to fulfil similar requirements by such means as they could devise. The Buddhists adopted the solemn chanting of *paritta* as one of the means. *Paritta* means protection. Curing disease by the chanting of the *paritta* is not mentioned in the Pali canon, but Nāgasena in the *Milindapañho*[7] maintains that it has been bequeathed by the Buddha himself. The essence of *parittas* was *saccakiriyā*, or effective expression of one's wish by an open declaration of truth. Through *parittas* the Buddhists tried to get rid of the objectionable features of Brahmanical rituals.[8] The aesthetic aspect was improved and the method was simplified.

Though the Buddha did not permit the use of *parittas, mantras* and the like, he himself not only performed some apotropaic rituals including miracles, which clearly went against his own teachings but recognized the supernatural powers of an *arhata.* He is alleged to have called *paritta* the protection against danger. Although not all *suttas* used as *paritta* were composed for that purpose, at least one of them, the *Khaṇḍa paritta,*[9] was (allegedly) composed as a spell by the Buddha himself. With only two exceptions, all other Suttas that comprise the classical collection (Pali, *mahāparitta*) must have been used as spells very early in the history of Theravada Buddhism.[10] According to a Vinaya source,[11] when the Buddha was informed that a certain monk had died of snakebite he said that this would not have happened had the monk '. . . let his love flow out over four royal breeds of serpents'—an end which can be achieved, he promised, by reciting the *paritta* which had been composed for the purpose. Moreover, one notices other esoteric elements with similar potentialities. In the *Majjhima Nikāya,* it is stated that the Buddha, in his early days, had stayed in a cemetery using bones as pillows. It is emphasized in the *Dīgha Nikāya* that the Buddha maintained *pañca-kāma-guṇa-diṭṭha-dhamma-nibbāṇa-vāda,* a philosophical view according to which the soul attains *nirvāṇa* through full indulgence in the pleasures of the five senses. The use of skulls as alms bowls by Buddhist monks, referred to in the *Cullavaga*, was evidently due to such influences.

Thus, the mind of early Buddhist monks as well as lay followers was not fully disabused of belief in the efficacy of apotropaic rituals. And whatever the original purpose of primitive collective magical performances might have been, subsequently they became the esoteric art of a class of people who made exorcism and sorcery a means of their livelihood, taking advantage of innocent people. The aesthetic aspect of early Buddhism changed as its teachings were simplified and the Buddha's followers took the easy way, the world of apotropaic religion, even while he was alive.

The Buddha, who never claimed to be more than a man, must have been aware of the uneradicable tendency in human nature to elevate saints and heroes to the position of gods. He, therefore, took pains to make his beloved disciple and cousin Ānanda understand that the truth embodied in *Dhamma* which he had taught was all that ought to take his place and represent him when he was gone. And for many years afterwards the only object of veneration allowed among early Buddhists was *Dhamma*. In time, however, the tendency to assimilate ideas and practises current in society led to Buddhism stepping down from its high pedestal of exclusiveness and abstruse ideals to appeal to the masses. It resulted in the formulation of a triple arrangement of venerated objects among Buddhists. Hence *triratna* came, first, to be held in honour and then a kind of personality was accorded to the three, as if the Brahmanic divine trinity was being replicated. Finally, there was an accretion of rituals in the form of *trisaraṇa*. The three articles of faith were encoded in the thrice uttered formula:

Buddhaṃ saraṇaṃ gacchāmi
Dhammaṃ saraṇaṃ gacchāmi
Saṃghaṃ saraṇaṃ gacchāmi
Buddhaṃ saraṇaṃ gacchāmi
Dhammaṃ saraṇaṃ gacchāmi
Saṃghaṃ saraṇaṃ gacchāmi
Buddhaṃ saraṇaṃ gacchāmi
Dhammaṃ saraṇaṃ gacchāmi
Saṃghaṃ saraṇaṃ gacchāmi

According to N. Dutt, *saraṇaṃ* means 'seeking protection' from evils and the protection that one seeks is not from worldly evils but from suffering to which a human being is destined.[12] The *triratna* came to be worshipped and its utterance was made compulsory for both monks and the laity and it was this utterance alone that transformed a non-Buddhist into a Buddhist. Moreover, a kind of personality was accorded to this *triratna*. Not only did the *triratna* serve as a means of popularizing religion it was also looked upon as *paritta* for protection from worldly evils or evil destiny. This story about Fa-hsien, though of a later time, gives us a good example of *triratna* working as *paritta* for protection; when Fa-hsien was on his way home and in great peril at sea, he committed himself to the protection of the *saṃgha* saying 'I have travelled far in search of Law. Let me, by your dread and supernatural power, return from my wanderings and reach my resting place.'[13] And again, on ending his travels, he gratefully acknowledged that he had been guarded in his perils by the dread power of the 'three precious ones' thus acknowledging the power of the Buddha as well as the Law and the Order.

In order to be protected one must fulfil certain conditions, as expounded in the *Milindapañho*:

> 'Just so, O king, is *pirit*[14] a protection to some and not to others. And there are three reasons for its failure—obstruction of *karma* and of sin and of unbelief. That *pirit* which is a protection to beings loses its protective power by acts done by those beings themselves.'[15] Nāgasena further continues '... this is only meant for those who have some portion of their life yet to run, who are of full age and restrain themselves from the evils of *karma*. And there is no ceremony or artificial means for prolonging the life of one whose allotted span of existence has come to an end.... All medicines in the world are useless ... but *pirit* is a protection and assistance to those who have a period yet to live, who are full of life, and restrain themselves from the evil of *karma*.'[16]

As the *Milindapañho* makes clear, it is for the protection of the people that *pirit* was appointed by the Blessed One.[17] Buddhists attributed the efficacy of *paritta* to the supernatural power released by the recitation of the text, for the words of the Buddha are powerful in themselves. Hence, although neither the Buddha nor any other being intervenes to help or protect, the power of the Buddha continues to reside in these words and protects when they are recited by a monk or somebody with authority. *Parittas* should be uttered to achieve a desired apotropaic goal by creating or harnessing magical power. They typically consist of scriptural passages ranging in length from a few sentences to an entire chapter. They may be recited either individually or collectively. Some or all may be recited as part of ordinary Buddhist devotions, serving as protection against generalized danger. More important, they are recited on special occasions to deal with a specifically known danger—either to remove it, if it has already appeared, or to prevent it, if it is imminent. The recitation of *parittas* affords defence against dangers of all kinds both, natural and supernatural. Although any *paritta* serves this protective function, each has a specialized function as well. One serves as a protection against the dangers of childbirth, another against snakebite and yet another against evil spirits, and so on.

Mora paritta is believed to be especially efficacious in protecting those in danger of arrest and in freeing those who have been arrested. According to one story, a monk informed the Buddha that he had broken his vow of chastity because he had seen a woman dressed in magnificent attire. Sympathetic, the Buddha said that even the holiest of men are tempted by and succumb to the seductive attraction of a woman. The spells are recited in the story by a peacock—the Buddha himself called it the *Mora paritta*. The *Dhajagga paritta* is believed to be efficacious in protecting those in fear, or those afflicted with panic and creeping of flesh in battle. The Buddha instructed his disciples that when they were frightened they should think of him and/or of the Law, and/or of the Order and at the same time they should recite verses which he then composed extolling the virtues of each of the *triratna*. The basis of *Ātānātiya paritta* running to five printed pages is an encounter between the Buddha and four kings who came to tell him that there were many demons in their land who, neither believing in the Buddha nor abiding by the Five Precepts, frightened and attacked his followers when they retired to lonely places for meditation. Moved by their complaint, the Buddha agreed that the *paritta* which they presented to him should be taught and used by all his followers. The *Aṅgulimāla paritta* is for difficult and dangerous childbirth. *Vattaka paritta* is especially efficacious as a protection against fire. *Bojjaṅga paritta* is recited for protection against illness. *Pubbaṇa paritta* is for protection from epidemics, especially for all dangers caused by the twelve planets.

The Buddhists were also believers in the efficacy of pronouncements of benediction by priests and other holy persons and in amulets and the like. In order to oust the vested interests of Brāhmaṇa from the field, the Buddhists had to introduce certain *maṅgalas*, claimed to be more efficacious. The Buddhists introduced the chanting of the *Maṅgala Sutta* laying much stress on the thirty-seven points of *maṅgala* or the moral condition of human welfare. From a Jātaka story it is clear that by '*maṅgalas*' the people of India understood the sighting of certain auspicious objects like the all-white chariot or the hearing of certain auspicious sounds and the touch of certain auspicious things.[18] In the *Maṅgala Sutta*, the Buddha teaches what he considers to be the best *maṅgalas*, omens of good luck, when requested by a *deva* to tell him what the 'highest the blessing' might be. The same spirit of a higher ethics permeates the remaining Suttas also. The *Ratna Sutta* is for protection from dangers especially those that are supernaturally caused. The *Tirokuḍḍa Sutta* is the earliest known Buddhist formula for offering oblations to departed spirits, a custom evidently taken from the Hindus. It is still devoted to the cult of the dead in Sri Lanka and Thailand. On a still higher plane is the *Nidhikaṇḍa Sutta* in which it is said that a treasure of good deeds is the best treasure that a Buddhist may collect. The *Mettā Sutta* is believed to be efficacious for protection from evil spirits. Whether the compilation of this *Khuddakapāṭha* is meant as a manual for a novice or as a prayer book remains an open question. Nevertheless, the five short Suttas through their formulae-like usages and refrains reveal themselves as serving liturgical purposes. These five Suttas are used even today at the time of the Buddhist *paritta* or *pirit* ceremony in Sri Lanka.

We have traced the origin of apotropaic rituals to early Buddhism. However, Pali scriptures as a whole pay little attention to this popular aspect of religion. It would seem that early Buddhists, who were responsible for the compilation of these texts, took a comparatively rationalistic view of the world and most probably intended to cover vain repetition of *parittas* and the like.

We find a similar trend in Aśoka's time in the third century BC. Under Aśoka, Buddhism extended its range and influence and enjoyed princely patronage and ease, losing its simple morality and agnostic idealism and becoming more metaphysical on the one hand and ritualistic on the other. And the Buddha was worshipped not so much for his agnostic idealism or the simplicity of his teaching or even for the touching renunciation of his high estate, beloved wife and child as for the magical powers which he was supposed to wield. Rituals became a part of the realm of religion and popular beliefs, grown out of lay devotees, came to be regarded as an indispensable part of Buddhism even though the Buddha himself had so vehemently opposed the practise of magic. However, Aśoka criticized vain and useless rituals. In Rock Edict IX, Aśoka says :

> People perform various rites in sickness, at marriages, on birth of sons, and on journeys. Rites for blessings[19] should undoubtedly be performed but a rite of this kind bears little fruit.

In the *Mahāvagga*, one such family-god (*natisalohiti devatā*) is recorded to have advised two businessmen, Tapussa and Bhallika, to serve the Buddha with *mantha* and *madhupiṇḍika* for it would bring happiness and fortune to them. From Vinaya, it is clear that gods and demigods were believed to be of a benevolent nature: they knew the minds of the people and tried to bring them on to the right track if they harboured any wrong and undesirable notions and heresies.

Irrespective of the emperor's attitude, the Buddhists in this period, just like the Brāhmaṇas who provided people with appropriate rituals for all domestic rites of householders, preached the performance of certain auspicious rites for the occasions mentioned above. In fact, the waning of Buddhist apotropaic rituals at the time of Aśoka was largely due to Aśoka's religious policy. Though his *dhamma* was not a narrow one, confined to Buddhism and he did not mean to preach only the Buddhist faith, he did make some dent in the way of life of the Brāhmaṇas. By moving away from orthodox Brahmanism, though not opposing it, and by giving open support to Buddhism and certain other sects such as the Ājīvikas, he was seeking the support of non-orthodox elements which may eventually have succeeded in weaning people away from orthodoxy and in the end making his own principles more acceptable to the populace.[20] For this purpose he was inclined towards laymen who were not welcomed by early Buddhism. He did not aim to rear orthodox and pious Buddhists who would stand out in society but to educate good and gentle citizens of empire. Aśoka sought support from lay Buddhists, having correctly evaluated their role in social and spiritual life. The similarity between the principles of *dhamma* in Aśoka's edicts and the rules of behaviour of a householder adhering to Buddhist teachings—*upāsakas,* as given in the Pali canon is obvious. Both rested on ethical rather than philosophical ideas and were determined by requirements of everyday life.[21] The common aim of both was the attainment of goodness and happiness here and the attainment of heaven (*svarga*) hereafter; the attainment of *nirvāṇa* or *mokṣa* was far beyond their scope. The chief interest of both centre round the three themes of *dāna* (charity), *sila* (virtue) and *sagga* (heaven), *dāna* and *sila* being the two means to the attainment of heaven.[22]

The spread of Buddhism in various regions of the sub-continent during Aśoka's time and his religious policy resulted in the rise of Buddhist sects whose number is usually given as eighteen. Out of these, the emergence, especially, of the sect of Mahāsāṅghikas, who advocated a more liberal interpretation of Vinaya rules gave more attention to laymen. Such attempts to take Buddhism to the masses led to the rise of Mahāyāna, which should not be depicted as simply a system of idealist philosophy. However eloquent sages may be on this issue, most ordinary people cannot help feeling that this kind of unworldliness is all very well, but for anyone who has to live in this world and on this earth it is quite unsuitable. Naturally, it insisted on the cultivation of easy virtues, i.e. *pāramitas.* Outside the Buddhist church and discipline the *bhakti* cult became very influential, specially among the Śaivas and Vaiṣṇavas. Keeping in mind this popular movement, Mahāyāna had to make a compromise with local cults. In this process Mahāyāna Buddhists transformed some of the *sūtras* into magical formulae, with their endless invocations to divine beings using mysterious words and syllables already so popular in the sacrificial mysticism of *Atharva Veda* and *Yajur Veda.*

Thus, once the process of compromising and assimilating local cults sets up, it multiplies and the development of the apotropaic rituals of Buddhism enters a new phase. According to N. Dutt, the growth of idealist philosophy and anti-worldly feeling, which was obviously connected with the emergence of a class-ridden society, evaporated in due course out of the mass culture but the popular elements remained as they were and there was no justification in calling them Buddhist.[23]

The spirit of mass-oriented Buddhism, authorising the orders of laymen resulted in the rise of Pure Land Buddhism. A passage in the Larger *Sukhāvatīvyūha* ('. . . and should not be strong in the knowledge of *dhāraṇis* . . .'[24]) shows that even the beings in the Sukhavati receive *dhāraṇis.* Before the composition of the *Larger Sukhāvatīvyūha sūtra* , there were the worshippers of Sakyamuni, of

Akṣobhya, of Amitābha and so on and finally the Pure Land of Amitābha became the most popular among the northern Buddhists. In the *Buddhāvataṃsaka Sūtra*, the Pure Land of Amitābha was regarded as the most inferior among many pure lands, the one nearest to the defiled and the mundane. This means that it was thought to be most accessible to common people with a cosmopolitan-commercial ethos and with the consciousness of living in the age of transition. And, it was for the sake of the welfare of the people that a *bodhisattva* needed to be reborn again and again in various professions—the central doctrine of the time, which is a good reflection of the flourishing urbanism of the times which sought material prosperity in this world.

In the literature of this period there is hardly any clear line of demarcation between *dhāraṇi* and *sūtra*. There are the *Mahāyāna sūtras* which are nothing but the recommendations of *dhāraṇis*. For instance, the *Aparimitāyuḥ Sūtra*, which we have not only in Sanskrit but in Chinese as well, is nothing more than the glorification of a *dhāraṇi*. The *Megha Sūtra* provides another good example of a *dhāraṇi* written for the fulfilment of worldly desires ranging from healing to prosperity. It begins, like the other *Mahāyāna sūtras*, with the words: 'Thus I have heard: once the Lord sojourned in the palace of the serpent princes Nanda and Upānanda.' Replying to the snake prince, the Buddha continues: 'O snake prince, you must use the *dhāraṇi* called *Sarvasukhānandalā* ('the all-hail-bringing'). This alleviates all the pains of all the snakes, brings torrents of rain down over India in due season and causes all grasses, shrubs, herbs and trees to grow, all seeds to sprout and all juices to flow forth.'[25] Already in *Divyāvadāna* occurs the most popular spell, '*Om maṇipadme huṃ*', of all the spells in apotropaic Buddhism. *Bhodhisattvabhūmi* also contains numerous spells and deals with the mystic aspect of syllables.

The very worldly character of the *dhāraṇi* supposedly expounded by the Buddha, which was also the source of their legitimization, shows that the cult of fertility which was a powerful force in Indian agrarian culture, got interwoven with the highly materialized Mahāyāna Buddhism. Thus, *dhāraṇis* consist of numerous invocations to female deities as holder, supporter, etc., and of the description of the magic rites which are to be performed with these *dhāraṇis*. The rites with *dhāraṇis* end with the assurance that in times of drought there is no better means of inducing rain than the use of this *sūtra*.

Finally, it must be pointed out that the *dhāraṇi* as a genre of the canon occupied an important position in Mahāyāna Buddhism, especially between the fourth and eighth centuries AD. It appears that in the post-Gupta period, under feudal influences and on account of numerous land-grants made to the monasteries, Buddhism transformed itself into Tantricism. In order to satisfy their lust of the basest type, feudal lords tried to cover their nefarious practises with the cloak of religion.[26] The burgeoning 'feudal' economy and polity had already permeated Buddhist organizations at various levels. A number of monastic centres developed with little or no organic relationship to the lay population surrounding them. Tantricism had begun to cast its lengthening shadow, comprising sublime mysticism on the one hand with gross magical ritual on the other.[27] The Gilgit manuscripts of the fifth and sixth centuries AD contain many *dhāraṇis*. *Pañcarakṣā* were collected and gained great popularity. These Five Protecting Spells are as follows:

(1) *Mahā-Pratisarā*, for protection against sin, disease and other evils;
(2) *Mahā-Sahasrapramardinī*, against evil spirits;
(3) *Mahā-Māyūrī*, against snake poison;
(4) *Mahā-Śītavatī*, against hostile planets, wild animals and poisonous insects; and
(5) *Mahā (raksa) mantranusarini*, against diseases.[28]

Of the extant *dhāraṇis*, reference should be made to the *Mahā-Māyūrī*, frequently entitled *Vidyārājñī*, 'Queen of Secret Sciences', translated into Chinese by Srimitra at the beginning of the fourth century and Kumārajīva in the fifth century AD. Most of the *parittas* were incorporated in this text.

Dharanis penetrated to a great extent into the ancient *Mahāyāna sūtras*. We have found them in Chapters XXI and XXVI, i.e. those chapters which were added at a later time, of the *Saddharmapuṇḍarīka*. The followers of the *Lotus Sūtra* extolled the practise of reciting *sūtras*. The custom of copying manuscripts of the *Lotus Sūtra* as a meritorious act was not prevalent when the earlier portion of the *sūtra* was composed, around the first century AD, but occurred in the process of enlarging the *sūtra*. *Dhāraṇis* were inserted later in the *sūtra*. In Chapters XXI and XXII, Bhaiṣajyarāja, the 'King of the Art of Healing' was worshipped as one who protects suffering people with magical formulas. In later days his worship came to the fore. *The Lotus Sūtra* speaks of the question of healing most directly in the parable of the physician, in which the physician must momentarily deceive his sons in order to make them take the medicine that will cure their illness. The physician's deception is compared with the Buddha's use of skilful means (*upāya*) to make doubters accept the law of Mahāyāna thus likening *dharma* to medicine. The further implication is that the teacher of the Law is a 'spiritual healer'.

We also find *dhāraṇis* in the last two chapters of the *Laṅkāvatāra*, chapters which are missing in the earliest Chinese translation of AD 443. The following passages of *Laṅkāvatāra Sūtra* attribute to the *mantras* it quotes the efficacy of dispelling evil spirits. Here the importance given to the *mantras*, and the fact that they are attributed to the Buddha himself, shows that Mahāyāna Buddhism was, by the fourth or fifth century AD, permeated with the ideas which were to lead to Vajrayāna:

> Then the Lord addressed the Great Being, the Bodhisattva Mahāmati thus:
>
> Mahāmati, hold to these magic syllables of the Laṅkāvatāra, recited . . . by all the Buddhas, past, present and future. Now I will repeat them, that those who proclaim the Law of Righteousness may keep them in mind:
>
> *Tuṭṭe tuṭṭe vuṭṭe paṭṭe paṭṭe kaṭṭe kaṭṭe amale amale vimale vimale nime nime hime hime vame vame kale kale kale kale aṭṭe maṭṭe vaṭṭe tuṭṭe jñeṭṭe spuṭṭe kaṭṭe kaṭṭe laṭṭe paṭṭe dime dime cale cale pace pace bandhe bandhe añce mañce dutāre dutāre patāre patāre arkke arkke sarkke sarkke cakre cakre dime dime hime hime ṭu ṭu ṭu ṭu ḍu ḍu ḍu ḍu ru ru ru ru phu phu phu phu svāhā.*
>
> If any women of good birth hold, retain, recite, and realize these magical syllables, nothing harmful shall come upon them—whether a god, a goddess, a serpent-spirit, a fairy, or a demon. . . . If anyone should be in the grip of misfortune, let him recite these one hundred and eight times, and the evil spirits, weeping and wailing, will go off in another direction.[29]

The *Prajñāpāramitā Sūtras* in their shortest form were used as *dhāraṇis*. Special mention should here be made of the *Prajñāpāramitā*, i.e. the '*mantra* which alleviates all pain'. Since the importance of *prajñā* in ancient Buddhism remained paramount 'the heart of *prajñāpāramitā*' retained its primacy and was used to meet the needs of the time in the new guise of *dhāraṇis*.

The *sūtras* lay greater emphasis on the cult of the female principle. In these texts, the goddess Prajñāpāramitā is conceived of as the Supreme Being and the mother of all *tathāgatas*. The *Kāraṇḍavyūha Sūtra*, an earlier Mahāyāna text, contains not only Tantric terminology and rituals as well as the concept of the female principle, but also some eminent Puranic deities who later became the chief objects of the Hindu Tantric cult. The *Suvarṇaprabhāsa Sūtra* which is, to a great extent Tantric in its contents, formulae, and rituals, mentions four *dhyānī* Buddhas, a few *bodhisattvas* and goddesses associated with the cult of the female principle. The *Bhaiṣajyaguruvaiḍūryaprabhāsa-pūrvapraṇidhāna viśeṣsavistara Sūtra* also shows remarkable Tantric influence. It specially mentions rituals of *ugra* or dread and fear.

By the seventh century, apotropaic rituals became an indispensable part of Buddhist life. Not only did the monks but lay devotees also practised them. As Mahāyāna Buddhists practised silent meditation, they received the texts with ease but without understanding their deep meaning. They lived strictly according to the rules and were experts, especially, in magical exorcisms.[30] A large number of *stotras* and *dhāraṇis* seem to have been composed during the post-Gupta period. Emperor Harṣa composed a morning prayer in praise of the Buddha, the *Suprobhāta Stotra.* In the eighth century the Kashmiri King Lalitaditya Muktāpīḍa was charmed by the magical practices of his Prime Minister Caṅkuṇa. At the former's request, Caṅkuṇa imparted the charms to the king and received in turn the great image of the Buddha which had been brought by Lalitāditya from Magadha. King Jayāpīḍa of Kashmir, who adopted the special name, Vinayāditya, 'the sun of discipline', patronized a 'Dravidian sorcerer' who performed miracles. Hsüan-tsang has recorded that the people in the territory which has been identified by A. Cunningham as Mandawa, near Bijnor, were practisal minded and 'well versed in magical arts'.

Tantrism laid down numerous magical rituals for the fulfilment of all kinds of material desires as well as for the achievement of enjoyment and even liberation. Buddhist apotropaic rituals served an important social purpose by prescribing numerous remedies, which were laid down not only as protection against diseases, injuries and attacks by ghosts, etc., but also for averting the adverse effects of planets, omens, etc. Though some aspects of the practise have changed in accordance with the material milieu of the time, the spirit of the tradition has persisted through millennia.

The circumstances of the times when the three kingdoms of ancient Korea were opposed to one another in a triangular contest were such that the need for the absolute power of kingship was felt but it could not be accomplished as long as the power of the old aristocrats continued.[31] The royal family, that had to achieve solid growth of the kingdom, desperately needed a new system or ideology which, above all, would break up the bondage of Shamanism, the source of the power of the old aristocrats. Though kingship moved from clan to clan it could not be claimed that old systems had been destroyed completely for the religious consciousness based on the idea of heavenly kingship derived from Shamanism still had its influence on the people. The people still considered Shamanism sacred as before. Shamanism is a religion which is mainly concerned with worldly matters like diseases, disasters, etc., and attributes them to evil gods or ghosts and suggets that therapies to them lie in cursing, threatening, pacifying and repelling the evils. Any new ideology like Buddhism would be expected, to adopt the main functions of Shamanism. Therefore, the rulers of ancient Korea were mainly concerned with the apotropaic aspect of Buddhism, which was thought to be more powerful and sacred enough in a rationalized system to replace the old ideology.

About the introduction of Buddhism into Korea, the *Samgukyusa* says:

At this time, the emperor of Liang China sent an envoy with clothing and incense to the king of Silla. However, nobody in the court knew what the incense was and how to use it. The king therefore sent a messenger to travel throughout the kingdom with the incense to see if he could find anyone who knew what it was. On hearing of it, Muk-ho-ja[32] said, 'They call it incense. It produces sweet fragrance when it is burnt, so that the devotion reaches the place of sacredness. As far as sacredness is concerned nothing is better than the Three Jewels, therefore if you pray with the incense burning, your wishes will definately be fulfilled.' At this time, the princess was seriously ill with a strange malady. Muk-ho-ja was summoned and as soon as he prayed with the incense burning, the princess rose from her bed and was completely recovered. Overjoyed, the king granted large rewards to Muk-ho-ja but he suddenly disappeared and nobody knew where he had gone.[33]

This story reveals some important facts. First, the incense must have been seen as coming from an advanced culture for it was brought from the royal court of China. Then, it turned out to be a smobol of Buddhism and Muk-ho-ja was its messenger. Muk-ho-ja emphasized the apotropaic aspect of Buddhism saying 'as far as sacredness is concerned, nothing is better than the three Jewels, therefore if you pray with this burning, your wishes will definitely be fulfilled'. Finally, Muk-ho-ja was the man who cured the strange malady after many Shamans had been tried, and it was Buddhism not Shamanism that accomplished the hard task. In short, Buddhism was accepted because it provided the best way to fulfil one's worldly desires, and could heal illness rather than because it showed the way to *nirvāṇa.* In this context, one recalls the words ascribed to the Buddha in the *Divyāvadāna,* 'A magical feat quickly wins over the minds of worldlings.'[34]

Shamanism was replaced by Buddhism in respect of social processes as well, as is demonstrated by the following story:

In the year 263, when king Mi-ch'u had been on the throne for two years, Ado[35] presented himself at court and asked permission to preach Buddhism to the people. But the courtiers, repelled by his strange appearance, not only denied his petition but even tried to kill him. So Ado bade farewell to the king and retreated to a hiding place. In the third year of the reign of the king, princess Song-guk contracted a strange illness, which neither medicine nor the sorcery of shamans could heal. Overworried, the king sent messengers throughout the country to seek a person who could heal the princess. Finally Ado made an appearance in the court and healed her disease completely. Highly pleased, the king said, 'My good monk, what's your wish? You shall have it.' Ado replied, 'I wish only that Your Majesty build a temple in Ch'onkyongnim where I may pray to the Buddha to send down blessings upon your kingdom.' The king, thus, allowed a temple to be built in the forest.[36]

Here, we find that the king admitted Buddhism because of its great apotropaic power, which was greater than that of Shamanism. And the Buddhist monk pleased the king by manifesting the purpose of Buddhism as being 'to send down blessings upon your kingdom'. As a matter of fact, some monks employed their healing powers as a means of spreading the *dharma* and converting non-believers. Certain monks from India and central Asia, who travelled to China between the second and fourth centuries AD, achieved great success in spreading the *dharma,* in part, by means of their gifted healing activities, especially within aristocratic circles.[37] This is how Buddhism spread in the kingdom of Paekche too. King A-shin of Paekche issued a royal decree ordering that respect and belief be accorded to Buddha's Law 'to seek blessings'.[38] The fact that they built a temple in Ch'onkyongnim, the holy place of Shamanism,[39] means Ado or the Buddhists, at the incipient stage in Korea, and king Mi-ch'u or the royal power at that time, tried to make Buddhism take the place of Shamanism.

The following story of monk Milbon shows us that the apotropaic aspect of Buddhism in the Three Kingdoms, some time after its introduction, was inclined towards Tantrism due to Korea's continuous contact with India through China or even directly.

Queen Son-dok (632-47) fell seriously ill. Pop-ch'ok, a monk from the temple Hungnyunsa was summoned to treat her but in vain and so the courtiers called on monk Mil-bon for his fame had spread wide all over the country. Mil-bon stood at the door of the Queen's chamber and chanted the *Bhaiṣajyaguru Sūtra*. As soon as he finished reading, his staff with six metal rings flew into the room and pierced an old fox and monk Pop-ch'ok and hurled them out into the garden. Immediately after that, the queen was healed. At this moment, a mystical five-coloured ray shone on the brow of Mil-bon and everybody was surprised at the sight.[40]

Here, we see that just as Shamanism was replaced by Mahāyāna Buddhism in the early stages, Mahāyāna Buddhism was replaced by Tantric Buddhism in respect of the function of religion in society. Here, the monk Pop-ch'ok, most probably a Mahāyāna Buddhist, was considered as wicked as a fox, the most wicked creature in Shamanism. It means that for Tantric Buddhists Mahāyāna Buddhism is no different from Shamanism, which has no efficacy at all, for they believe that their creed is the only legitimate one. A similar kind of assumption is found in the story of monk In-hye in our source[41] which shows the replacement of Tantric Buddhism with Mahāyāna Buddhism. In spite of the change of sect, however, the function of Buddhism has not changed. It still works as a means of fulfilling worldly desires, i.e. healing, protecting and the like.

It has been long established that the verbal component in a ritual is very important. According to E.R. Leach, 'ritual as one observes it in primitive communities is a complex of words and actions. . . . It is not the case that words are one thing and the rite another. The uttering of the words itself is a ritual.'[42] Word, power and deed are the essential elements of most ritual systems in which there is a reciprocal relation between the word and the deed. A healing ritual may emphasize words more whereas a collective rite, in which there is mass participation, may rely less on auditory communication and more on the display of conspicuous visible material symbols. The power lies in the words even though the words become effective only if uttered in the very special context of certain actions. It was not the man or his deed or anything else but the *sūtra*, the words ascribed to the Buddha, the *Bhaiṣajya Sūtra* in the above case, that radiated the magical power which ultimately cured the queen. The words uttered are referred to as the language of demons, as opposed to human language. The demonic language is consciously constructed to connote power and though largely unintelligible is nevertheless based on the theory of a language that the demons can understand. Thus, far from being nonsensical and indiscriminately concocted, the spells show a sophisticated logic. From the monks as well as the audience's point of view, the spells have power by virtue of their secrecy and their capacity to communicate with demons and thereby influence their actions.[43] Therefore, the monk in the above example did not have to enter the chamber and attend to the queen. What he had to do was to perform the ritual only. Though our source does not give any details of the ritual, we can reconstruct the details of the healing ritual with the help of anthropological studies. A Sinhalese healing ritual or exorcism ceremony exploits three main kinds of verbal forms which accompany other ritual acts (such as dance, mime, food offering, and manipulation of objects). They are called *mantra, kannalavva,* and *kaviya* and they are arranged in a progression of four sequences beginning and ending with the *mantra.* The *mantra* is muttered by the exorcist and must not be heard, for it constitutes secret knowledge. The ceremony begins with the recitation of the *mantra* which summons the demons responsible for the disease. These spells contain abbreviated allusions to myths and thus prepare the ground for the next sequence which is the *kannalavva,* which is chanted aloud in rhythmic prose composed of ordinary, intelligible language and is meant to be heard and understood by the participants. It makes a plea to the gods to come and bless the ceremony and to the demons to act benevolently and remove the disease. Typically, the pleas are accompanied by food offerings. The next in sequence are the *kavya.* They are nominally recorded in texts. From the point of view of the dramatic presentation of the ritual, it is important that they be sung loudly to the accompaniment of music and mime. The ceremony concludes with a *mantra* which enacts the expulsion of the demon itself.[44]

It seems a fair guess that the verses are of the same age as the rituals they accompany but unfortunately their origin is unknown. However, most of the offerings in the rites and ceremonies are accompanied by Pali verses. In fact, in India, no Buddhist songs are found in any of the sources of contemporary historical and archaeological nature. The life of the historical Buddha of the sixth century BC, chronicled in the *Lalitavistara,* is filled with musical imagery. While some texts such as those contained in the *Aṅguttara Nikāya,* stressed the sensual nature of singing and its distracting affect on monastic discipline, other texts recognized the use of sound to transcend individual consciousness for the development of *śrotra vijñāna* or aural knowledge. Monks were exhorted to practise *deva* hearing by becoming aware of the ritual sounds of the earth.

The language of the Buddha has been viewed not just as a means to refer to, or communicate with, the sacred realm but as an actual manifestation of sacred power. However, the language is regarded as sacred, not primarily because it is different from the vernacular but because it contains the teachings of revered figures from the past, such as gods, prophets, or ancestors.[45] *Hyang-ga*, literally meaning local song, is the best example of the sacred, not in Pali or in Sanskrit or even in Chinese but in the vernacular, i.e. Korean. On the first day of the fourth month of the nineteenth year of King Kyoung-dok, two suns turned up in the sky and continued to shine for ten days. The royal astrologer asked the king to find an ordained monk and ask him to make offerings of flowers, which repel the evil. The king ordered his servants to build an altar in front of the audience hall and proceeded to *Ch'ongyangnu* (Spring Pavilion) to await the coming of the ordained monk. Just then monk Wol-myoung was found walking along the road south of the palace. The king sent his man to the monk and asked him to compose a prayer. The monk replied 'I only know *hyang-ga* and I am not good at chanting Sanskrit verses.' The king said, 'Never mind. Since you are the ordained monk you may compose the song.'[46] Monk wol-myong then offered a song called the *Tosol-ga* or 'The Song of Tusita Heaven' which went as follows:

> Flowers, which I scatter here with a song of scattering flowers. Thou, obeyed by the decree of a strict mind serve Maitreya on his throne.[47]

Flowers, the commonest and most typical offerings, should be offered without leaf or stalk and each bloom should be laid down to face the image or Bo tree, etc. This is merely the kind of manners one shows to any superior, to whom one does not present one's feet or one's back.[48] What is important in the above illustration is not that the song is in Pali or Sanskrit. What mattered was that the verses in the ritual should be recited in order to repel the calamity.

The same stanzas recited in a flower offering ritual in Pali in Sri Lanka go as follows:

> *Vaṇṇa-gandha-guṇ-opetaṃ etaṃ kusuma-sanatiṃ*
> *Pūjyāmi Munindassa-sirīpāda-saroruhe*

Pūjemi Buddhaṃ Kusumena' nena
Puññena metena ca hotu mukkaṃ
Pupphaṃ milāyāti yathā idaṃ me
Kāyo tathā vū ti vinā sa-bhā vaṃ

The mass of flowers, fresh-hued, oderous and choice,
I offer at the sacred lotus-like feet of the Noble Sage.
With diverse flowers, the Buddha I adore, and through this merit may there be release or may I attain *moksa.* Even as these flowers must fade, so does my body reach a state of destruction.[49]

Notice the similarity between the song of monk Wol-myong and the first part of the Pali stanzas. The difference lies between 'Sage' and 'Maitreya'. The Korean song is dedicated to Maitreya due to contemporary trends in Buddhism in Korea. In spite of the long process of transmission the theme and structure of the song have not been changed. In other words, following the Buddhist tradition of reciting verses with flower offerings in an apotropaic ritual, Buddhist chanting was modified according to Korean requirements. Monks in ancient Korea are known to have performed sacred rites in a sacred language, often invented by themselves. We have a good number of *hyang-ga* used for ritual purposes which are faithful to the purpose and function of Buddhist *parittas, dhāraṇis, mantras,* etc.

Hyesong-ga (Song of the Comet), composed by monk Tung-ch'on goes as follows:

Watching Gandharva on the Eastern Coast, long ago.
'Japanese invaders!', people raising a torch on the border.
Hearing three *hwarangs* climb in sport.
The moon gives her light sincerely.
'Oh Comet!'
Watching a broom of a star, a man remarhed
Ah! the moon has sailed down over there.
What comet could there be![50]

Monks in ancient Korea did not play the role only of priests and sorcerers. Monk Yung-ch'on was deeply invloved in political affairs. In the *Song of the Comet,* surely the comet symbolizes Japanese pirates who retreated just after heairng the chant. Although our source does not give details, the monk surely performed a ritual according to the Buddhist tradition.

To-ch'onsugwanum-ga or 'The Song of Prayer to the Thousand Armed Avalokiteśvara' was dedicated to a child who became blind at the age of five. The child recovered his vision immediately after chanting the song. Here, it is not the monk but a child who chanted and achieved the healing. Therefore, one does not need to follow the norm that spells must be pronounced by a person who is initiated into the mysteries or endowed with supernatural powers and who is sexually, dietically and socially pure. Here is the song of the blind child:

> I fall on my knees and clasp both my hands
> To pray thee to have mercy on me. Oh bodhisattva Avalokiteśvara!
> Thou hast touched so many dark eyes with thy thousand arms
> And made them bright as daylight!
> Bestow me one eye for love and another for charity.
> If thou givest me mine eyes, I will sing thy great mercy.[51]

Other Buddhist *hyang-ga* extant are *Amin-ga* or 'The Song for a Peaceful Reign' composed and chanted by monk Ch'ung-dam by royal decree of King Kyong-dok, who tried to establish the centralization of royal power after unifying the three kingdoms. *Ujɔk-ga* or 'The Song for Repelling the Bandits' was composed by monk Yong-jae, who was on his way to the deep forest in order to spend the rest of his days as a reculse. And monk Wol-myong, the author of *Tosol-ga* composed another ritual song for his departed sister in her memorial sacrificial rite.

Ritual songs consist of words and rhythm. Words convey the power, while the rhythm enables a number of persons to join in the actions and perform them as a body. *Hyang-ga* was used as ritual song in Korea, sometimes in public and sometimes in private and the language was 'local', i.e. Korean whereas in the case of Theravāda Buddhist countries like Sri Lanka, Myanmar and Thailand the language used was Pali. Their function, however, has remained unchanged, following Buddhist tradition faithfully.

Another notable apotropaic ritual extant in ancient Korea was the *Mudrā* Rite, which was performed by monk Myong-rang when called upon by King Mun-mu, who was afraid of Chinese invaders. At the request of the king, the monk, with twelve eminent monks of *Yogācārin*, performed the *Mudrā* Rite in a make-shift temple made of various coloured silks where he installed grass pointing in the five directions. And soon after, a mighty typhoon arose and the angry waves swallowed Chinese invaders even before the troops could start the battle.[52] Though we do not know how Myong-rang performed the rite, the seventh volume of the Chinese tradition of the *Mahābhiṣeka mantra*[53] tells us '. . . if, the Buddha says, any diseases or fearful evils invade the people, imagine the Buddha, his disciples and bodhisattvas and the god of five directions as if you faced them clearly. Then the sick will be cured, the fearful recover peace and all evil spirits will be repelled'.[54] Myong-rang's performing the *Mudrā* Rite, which brought about the victory against the invaders, takes after that of *Amogavajra* and his feat against the An Lu-Shan rebellion and Tibetan invaders.

The ritual should be understood fully in the cosmological perspective. The ritual is seen as translation of a cosmology and the signs, symbols and other components of the ritual act as vehicles for expressing cosmological meaning. Cosmologies are classifications of the most encompassing scope. They are frameworks of concepts and relations which treat the universe or cosmos as an ordered system, describing it in terms of space, time, matter and motion, and peopling it with gods, humans, animals, spirits, demons and the like. The *Mudrā* Rites reveal much of their meaning when placed against the Buddhist cosmological scheme peopled with various beings such as gods, evil spirits, *bodhisattvas,* humans and Buddhas, etc.

Performing such apotropaic rites on a wider canvas, the *saṃgha* played a positive role in politics. Kings arranged rites on a grand scale in which specific *sūtras* were recited for the protection of the state from foreign invasion. The first instance of such a rite is recorded in the year 551 in the reign of King Chin-hung in which the *Inwangkyong* or 'The Sūtra of the Benevolent King' was recited. For the Korean kings, the most important portion was Section 5, entitled 'On the Protection of the State'. In this section the Buddha tells the assembled kings what they should do to protect their kingdoms against threats of internal and external danger. They should assemble a hundred images each of the Buddhas and the *bodhisattvas* and place them on elaborately decorated high seats. A hundred masters of the Law should be invited to recite and explain the *Inwangkyong*. This rite, called *Inwanghoew* or 'The Rite of Inwang' as well as *Paejwakanghoe* or 'The Rite of the Hundred Masters Reciting the Sūtra' together with the P'algwanhoe this was the most magnificent and prosperous rite in ancient Korea. If the *sūtra* were recited twice a day, all the spirits in the kingodm would come forth to protect the country. Not only does such a rite protect the country but it also brings blessings as well as wards off evils.

Due to the apotropaic character of rituals, the *saṃgha* came to be subordinated to the monarchy in a much more intensified way in

Korea. The *saṃgha* served as the religious arm of the monarchy. Since the main interest of the monks who were under the royal parasol lay in affairs of the state they gave up the first principle, i.e. renunciation of society. Instead of aloofness from secular affairs, they came to be deeply involved in politics. All the rites for the welfare of the state were supported by the royal treasury so that apotropaic rituals did not belong to the Buddhist community any more. This finally identified the *saṃgha* completely with the state.

Soteriological Rituals

Buddhism is properly characterized as 'the most radical form of striving for salvation conceivable'.[55] Ideationally, its conception of salvation is indeed a radical one. Sociologically, its charter for a soteriological community is equally radical; it is imperative that one abandon the material world. But physical retreat from the world is not sufficient; it is merely a necessary condition for yet another, a psychologically radical act: having abandoned the world, one must sever all ties with it and withdraw all attachment from it. Salvation can only be achieved by a total and radical rejection of the world in all its aspects.

The Buddhist salvation is the deliverance from suffering which, in effect, means release from the wheel of rebirth. And deliverance from suffering means permanent extinction. That it might, however, mean something other than extinction is implied by the many other metaphors and poetic images that are used to characterize *nirvāṇa*. Each of the following expressions is variously found in the canon: the blowing out of the flame or fire of life; the harbour of refuge; the cool cave; the island amidst floods; the place of bliss, emancipation, liberation, safety, the uncreated; the supreme and the transcendental.[56]

Consequent upon its message of salvation Buddhism rejects the world in all its forms, actual and conceivable; the world under any guise is an irreducible obstacle in the quest for salvation. Salvation can only be attained by the extinction of attachment to the world and all its vanities. Craving for and clinging to the world, in any of its manifestations must be totally uprooted. Therefore, the true Buddhist is the world rejector, the *bhikkhu* who has renounced the world. In the words of the canon:

> Full of hindrances is household life, a path leading to the dust of passion.

Free as the air is the life of him who has renounced all worldly things. How difficult is it for the man who dwells at home to live the higher life in all its fullness, in all its purity, in all its bright perfection. Let me then cut off my hair and beard, let me clothe myself in orange-coloured robes and let me go forth from household life into the homeless state.[57]

This is a tie, in this there is little happiness, little enjoyment, but more of pain; this is a fish-hook.[58]

Thus,

Having torn the ties, having broken the net like a fish in the water, like a fire that does not return to the place already burnt, let one wander alone like a rhinoceros.[59]

In the process of popularization, the radical soteriological ideology of Buddhism underwent important changes, which related to both the means and the goal of salvation. For the Buddhists, not only *upāsakas* but *bhikkhus*, not knowledge but merit is the goal of religious action, for merit is what can improve one's *karma*, and good *karma* is a prerequisite for their soteriological goal.

The Buddha finally entered *nirvāṇa* upon his death, but whatever the normative conception of *nirvāṇa* might be, it is a state to which life cannot apply. For all practisal purposes the Buddha is not alive, and one who is not alive cannot save others. If the Buddha is dead and neither God nor Saviour, what function, if any, does he carry out in the lives of men?[60] In the *Dhammapada* the Buddha is depicted as a preacher showing the way.[61] Therefore, although offerings to the Buddha, his relics and his symbols were certainly encouraged, they could in no way affect one's hope for *nirvāṇa*. They were simple expressions of *vandanā* or veneration and of *pūjā* or honour to the Buddha who had discovered the way.

The Buddha admonishes his disciple, Ānanda: 'Hinder not yourself, Ānanda, by honouring the remains of the Tathāgata.'[62] The confession of faith—*Buddhaṃ saraṇaṃ gacchāmi, Dhammaṃ saraṇaṃ gacchāmi, Saṃghaṃ saraṇaṃ gacchāmi*—is the one indispensable ritual of early Buddhism. All other ritual forms may be dispensed with. The confession of faith in the *triratna*, which functioned as the primary essence in the development of Buddhist soteriological ritual, shows us the transformation of the Buddha's character from a great man to an immortal god. Buddha's own adherents and disciples considered him to be a man of superhuman rank. And in the oldest Buddhist communities the Buddha was offered so much admiration and veneration that later ages inevitably placed him more and more into the supernatural sphere. The extraordinary importance of the founder is emphasized by asserting his pre-existence. In the Pali canon, the Buddha came to be conceived of as having had predecessors who are strictly schematic and entirely mythical. Typical of the Buddha's physical appearance are the thirty-two marks of beauty, with special importance being accorded to the foot prints of the Buddha.

In the *Mahāvastu*, the Buddha is said to have had five types of eyes. His spiritual powers, frequently listed in the Pali canon, are subsumed in the concept of omniscience. The enlightenment of the Buddha is something without effort, spontaneously achieved. By assigning omniscience to the Buddha, the Buddhists give him an attribute that in theistic religions is reserved for God alone. Thus the Buddha came to be placed on an equal footing with the cosmic lord. He is without anger or hate, full of compassion, always striving to protect all beings from what is unwholesome and to guide them toward the wholesome. The Buddha also became deeply entangled in legends. Such tendencies reached their full flowering in the *Saddharmapuṇḍarīka*, where the Buddha is a completely supernatural being who shows his powers by a multitude of miracles. His earthly existence as the historical *arhat* who entered *nirvāṇa* is but an illusion produced by him for the purpose of converting human beings. The historical Śākyamuni, thus, changed into the Buddha who would bring liberation to all beings for inconceivable periods of time. He looks after his believers and those who are oppressed by evil people. Now, he is the protector of men in need.

With such an enlargement the image of the Buddha, the cult naturally gains a meaning different from what it had for the early Buddhists. It is recorded in the *Mahāparinibbāna Sutta* that before passing away the Buddha instructed Ananda on how his corporal relics were to be treated after his cremation. Thus, traditionally, the erection of *dāgabas*, which is an interchangeable term for *stūpas* or *caityas* has the sanction of the Buddha himself. Eight simple ones were constructed after his death housing parts of his relics. With the popularization of Buddhism, huge *stūpas* began to be erected in compliance with the spiritual demands of mass believers. Following the worship of the relics of the Buddha and his disciples, the tumuli began to be built on sacred sites—at first as reliquaries, later as commemorative monuments. *Stūpas* often erected at ancient sacred sites, hills, trees, the confluence of streams—were, in many cases, sacred by virtue of non-Buddhist beliefs. They became associated with earth spirits and fertility deities. Thus, pre-Buddhist practises survived side by side and within Buddhist liturgy and belief. At this time also occurred the intensification of the devotional aspect of ritual and a greater degree of systematization as low and high traditions interacted. Monasteries near such sites assumed the role of shrine caretakers. Eventually, most monasteries became associated with *stūpas* marking the localities associated with the life of the Buddha as well as other ancient sacred sites. *Stūpas* eventually became sacred in themselves whether there was a relic in it or not. Chaples were built to contain the *caitya.* The *caitya* hall became the standard shrine room of the monastery: a stylized memorial tumulus built in stone or brick, housed in an apsidal hall with a processional for the ritual circumambulation. The *stūpa* represented the cosmic mountain at whose centre was found the *axis mundi* now represented by the Buddha's royal parasol.

I-tsing mentions *caitya-vandanā* or the worship of a *caitya* in his account. When the Great Teacher, the World-Honoured, entered into *nirvāṇa,* to burn his remains in the fire people brought all kinds of perfumes until they made a great pile, which was called *citi,* meaning piling. Derived from this we have afterwards the word *caitya.* But there are other explanations for this word. One is that it is called *caitya* because it was thought that all the virtues of the World-Honoured were deposited together here. Another is that because it was formed by piling up bricks or earth, it is called *caitya.* The meaning of this word has been, thus, clearly handed down.[63]

In India, at the time of I-tsing, *caitya* worship was performed by the priests late in the afternoon or in the evening, at twilight. All the assembled priests would come out of the gate of their monastery and walk three times round a *stūpa,* offering incense and flowers. They would all kneel down and one of them, who sang well, would begin to chant hymns describing the virtues of the Great Teacher in a melodious, pure and sonorous voice and continued to sing ten or twenty *ślokas.* Slowly, the monks would return to the place in the monastery where they usually assembled. When all of them had sat down, a *sūtra*-reciter, mounting the Lion-Seat, would read a short *sūtra.* The Lion-Seat, of well proportioned dimensions, would be placed near the head priest. Among the canons which are read on such occasions the 'service in the parts' is often used. This is a selection by the venerable Aśvaghoṣa. The first parts containing ten *ślokas,* consists of a hymn in praise of the *triratna*; the second part is a selection from some canons consisting of the Buddha's words. After the hymns and after reading the words of the Buddha, there is an additional hymn, as the third part of the service, of more than ten *ślokas,* being prayers that express the wish to bring one's good merit to maturity. After the recitation of these three sections all the assembled priests show appreciation of the recitor's speech by exclaiming 'well-spoken'. As soon as the *sūtra*-reciter ended his talk, the head priest would salute the Lion-seat and the seat of the saints. The priest second in rank, as well as the priest third in rank, would repeat the ceremony paying their respect to the head priest also. The remaining priests would salute the whole assembly at one and the same time.[64]

I-tsing saw the above-mentioned ceremony in Tāmralipti in eastern India. He also states that in the monastery at Nālandā he saw the same ceremony but in a different way. He describes further that everyday in Nālandā it was customary to send out one teacher to perform his devotional walk from one hall to another. He would go around in the company of lay-devotees and novices at twilight and also chant hymns in praise of the Great Teacher, i.e. the Buddha. Every time he sang three or five *ślokas* in a loud voice, some people would go to the temple in a small party to offer prayers with incense and flowers and they performed the three-fold salutation in this manner.[65]

I-tsing also gives an account of the ceremony of worship in a temple. He states, 'There is another posture to be adopted while looking on and praising a temple, i.e. bowing and worshipping with one's folded hands with both knees resting on the ground.' But Hsüan-tsang says that kneeling was not the only way to pay respect and to do worship. There were many ways of doing worship. From Hsüan-tsang's description of acts of salutation and reverence, we know that in India in his time, many people, who had a special request in mind circumambulated any object of reverential service or any object of worship, once or three times or as many times as they wished, depending on their feelings and their mental attitude.[66]

I-tsing also states that in India Buddhist monks and laymen worshipped earthen *caityas* or images of the Buddha on silk and paper. When they made images and *caityas* with gold, silver, copper, iron, earth, bricks and stone, they kept two kinds of *sarīras,* i.e. the relics of the Great Teacher and the *gāthā* of the chain of causation. The *gāthā* is as follows:

> All things arise from a cause.
> The Tathāgata has explained the cause.
> This cause of things has been finally destroyed;
> Such is the teaching of the Great Śramaṇa.[67]

I-tsing also refers to the rules of decorum in cleansing the sacred objects of worship. Washing the Buddha's image was another meritorious deed. It purified the mind and helped to give a chance of meeting with the Buddha in every birth. The Chinese traveller states that in his time in Indian monasteries the priest in charge, after announcing the time of the bathing the image of the Buddha, washed the holy image with scented and perfumed water. Such ceremonies were generally performed in the court of the monastery and a band of girls and musicians would play music at the time.[68]

Uposatha, too, was the product of this trend of cultural blending in the form of ritual. It was the custom for *bhikkhus* who lived in different rural areas to assemble on the sacred day.[69] The *uposatha* service had a strangely composite origin, with successive developments behind it. The Vedic people practised two sacrifices on the new and full moon days and the day preceding the sacrifice was preparatory, observed as a sanctified day with purificatory observances called *vrata,* such as fasting, rest from labour, abstinence from sexual pleasure and retirement at night into a room where a sacrificial fire was kept up all night. It was a holy day on which the auxiliary gods were supposed to dwell with the intending sacrificer. Hence, the *vrata* day was named the *upavastha* day. It was observed even in the wanderers' community who had no concern with sacrifices.[70]

The *vrata* rites had been prescribed for householders; they might be purificatory in the context of a householder's life but were by and large meaningless in relation to the wanderer's. Instead of these observances, the wanderer's *upavastha* took a form adapted to the ethos of the community: they were substituted by '*Dhamma*-rehearsal' in place of *vratas.* The *uposatha* days were given up by each sect to the study, rehearsal and public discussion of its own sacred texts, orally preserved. Thus, we find the rehearsal of the text of the Āraṇyakas and the Upaniṣads prescribed for the Brahmanical *saṃnyāsins.* The texts for *Dhamma*-rehearsal in the case of Buddhists would consist of Buddha-legends, *gāthās,* the Lord's sayings, etc.

The fortnightly *uposatha* service through the recital of the *pātimokkha* had become an established institution in the Buddhist monk community when the *āvāsa* shed its original character of a mere rain-retreat shelter. The *uposatha* rite was taken as the symbol and expression of the unitary character of a *saṃgha*. For this function, a complete gathering of all the residents at an *āvāsa* was required. If the gathering did not include the entire number, the function was not deemed to be valid. On the *uposatha* day, *bhikkhus* from some other *āvāsa* could be present for the function. The rule was that they were not to be excluded from the assembly but if they outnumbered the residents the function had to be held afresh.

The fortnightly *uposatha* day was for the monks a sacred one, for it involved the recital of the *pātimokkha* in an assembly. Aśoka, by an edict[71] placed these two days on his list of auspicious days when the killing or castration of animals was banned. Any ambiguity regarding the dates was removed by an additional elucidation and the service of *uposatha* was sought to be held lawfully by a complete congregation. Lay Buddhists observed the *uposatha* days as holy days but their observance was different from that of the monks for the *pātimokkha* was the monks' liturgy in which the laity could not participate. The lay observance of the *uposatha* consisted of the acceptance of the Eight Precepts of Morality. Hence it was called the '*uposatha* of the Eight Parts' (*Aṭṭhāṅgika uposatha*) and its aim and purpose is stated to be the 'purification of a soiled mind by a proper process'.[72] That it was essentially meant for laymen is made clear by the Buddha who said that the avowed purpose of this ceremony was to gain a passage to heaven and not the attainment of *nirvāṇa*.[73] The process invloved the taking of the Eight Vows (*Aṭṭhaśīla*) and of abstinence from eight specified disapproved acts. From *Panca uposatha Jātaka* we learn that *uposatha* was a very ancient observance which laymen kept to restrain the senses of *kama, krodha, lobha, moha, mada,* etc., and thereby acquire merit. In fact, the monks were enjoined not to attempt to expound to the unordained all the doctrines of the *Dhamma*.[74] Such separate embodiment in the canon was necessary because of the doctrine that prevailed among the monks that those who remain in the world are incapable of the higher reaches of spiritual attainments. The legends rubricated for householders are those that turn on ethical ideals and practise of morality—which is the way to the goal of heaven, not the goal of arhatship which is for monks alone.

From the time of early Mahāyāna Buddhism, the essence of

religion was sought in the life of the householder rather than in the life of the renouncer. Hence, lay Buddhism came to be advocated in the Mahāyāna as a religious ideal. The development of various cults and rituals should be explained in terms of such a change in the religion. However, the laity still remained outside the Buddhist fold and earned merit only by making gifts to the monks and offering worship to the *stūpas* and images of the Buddha. Their hopes were further strengthened by the cult of *pāramitās* and special texts were composed to show that perfection in the *pāramitās* assured one Buddhahood and that the practise of *pāramitās* was open to all, recluses or householders. The self-sacrifice of the *pāramitā* cult had a wide appeal. Evidently, it served a social function for it put the emphasis on insight into the world, rather than escape from it. It made participation in Buddhist ritual a social encounter rather than a private experience.

The emphasis in *saṃgha* life had evidently shifted in these centuries from Vinaya to cultivation of *bhakti* and its ritual expression in worship of the Buddha image and the *stūpa.* Naturally, it brought about the development of a Buddhist high liturgy. From the beginning of the Christian era, Buddhist liturgies became more complicated. The common rite is best represented by the litany of Avalokiteśvara, preserved in Buddhist literature and monuments. In its literary form, it is a solemn statement of the *bodhisattva's* capacity to save from peril those who call out his name. Another text, the *Triskandhaka* shows a unique, Mahāyāna aspect of the three-fold ritual: confession of sins, dedication of merit or formal rejoicing at the merit of others and request to all Buddhas and *bodhisattvas* that they remain in the world for the sake of suffering sentient beings. Here, the elements of merit-dedication and petition to celestial beings marked a link with the early non-literary tradition and the Buddhist tradition of the *triratna.* It shows an intimate connection between ritual and meditation, as it integrates—like many monastic manuals of meditation—the typical daily ritual cycle with a meditation session. The practise of meditation was, for Mahāyāna Buddhists, part of a ritual process beginning with the first feelings of compassion for other sentient beings, formulating the vow, including the expression of a strong desire to save all sentient beings and culminating in the dedication of these efforts to the salvation of others. In short, the *Triskandhaka* shows us the ritual practises to be expanded in the monastic tradition.

Pātimokkha developed in the wave of expansion of Buddhist monastic liturgy. The term *pātimokkha* means the onset of liberation or the commencement of virtuous nature. Observing the *pātimokkha* rite was a concession made by Buddhists to the public ethos of the time. The present ritual form of the *pātimokkha* was not its original form—the original was also the code of monastic discipline for monks and nuns. Thus, in contrast with ascetic practises, monastic rules are understood to foster seclusion of the mind insofar as the monk is restrained by his *pātimokkha* vow. In the *Mahāvagga* the word *pātimokkha* is explained thus: *ādimetaṃ mukhametaṃ pamukhametaṃ kusalānaṃ dhammānaṃ*, i.e. it is the beginning, it is the face, it is the supreme of all the good. Similarly in the *Cullavagga* the meaning of the term is given thus: *pātimokkhaṃ, atipāmukkhaṃ, atiseṭṭhaṃ, atiuttamaṃ iti attho* (the supreme, the excellent, the principal, i.e. the most important rules for the *saṃgha*). This word has also been used in the sense of 'strict observance of the *silas*'. For instance '*pātimokkhasaṃvarasaṃvutoviharati*' refers to one who is leading a life of strict observance of the *silas.*[75] Subsequently, this code became the basis of a congregational ritual and was re-edited for that purpose. It is laid down that it must be recited on the *uposatha* day. The Buddhist *bhikkhus* do not seem to have connected the *pātimokkha* in the beginning with the sacred day observance. In the *Mahāpadāna Sutta* they are reported as meeting together only once in six years to recite a hymn which constituted their *uposatha* service. But we are told that the *bhikkhus* afterwards adopted the custom of 'holy-day discourse' from other sects of *Parivrājakas*, and its later introduction into Buddhism is further evinced by the fact that we hear of 'ignorant, unlearned *bhikkhus* who neither know *uposatha* nor the recital of *pātimokkha*'.[76]

The incorporation of the concept of legal confession into the code was a necessity, as without it a large part of the code would remain inoperative and disciplinary proceedings could not be taken. Hence, emphasis is laid on the duty of confession; it is taken to be the root of monastic discipline and solemnity is imparted to it by prescribing the performance of this duty on ceremonially sacred days. The setting up of the confession ritual as a regular institution means that the *bhikkhus* had given up wandering and settled down to a life of the monastic community. It was the Buddhists alone among the *Parivrājakas* who developed coenobium in full. Among those who followed the eremitical ideal of an unsocial wandering life such a form of religious service would have little utility or purpose. Yet, interestingly enough, this practisal character of the confessional service evaporated afterwards and the original idea of a mere ceremonial observance reasserted itself. This was the very negation of the practisal character of the *uposatha* and an admission of its purely ritualistic character.

The *uposatha* became a colourful festival after the introduction of the ceremony of image worship. It lost its ancient simplicity and went back on the original purpose of monk-layman intercourse. I-tsing's account of the ceremonies with which the *uposatha* was attended shows that they centered mostly on the ritual worship of the Buddha and other deities. The monks were invited by laymen to officiate as priests, winding up the worship with offerings of flowers, chanting of hymns and recital of holy legends. And offerings of music such as of drums and stringed instruments, accompanied by songs, were made if the host desired.[77] This was followed by a sumptuous feast given by the host to the invited monks. According to I-tsing, the host approaches the priests and, after a salutation, invites them to the festival and the ceremony of feasting monks by a householder is observed on a scale so grand that all the trays and plates are full of the cakes and rice left over, and melted butter and cream can be partaken of to one's heart's content.[78] The good Chinese pilgrim enthusiastically describes the overflowing quantity and excellent quality of food provided and comments on the table manners observed by hosts and guests on the occasion.

As he travelled from the Pamir plateau to Pāṭaliputra, Fa-hsien participated in several great ceremonies and encountered many objects of Buddhist worship. In the state of Chieh-ch'a, probably in Kashmir, Fa-hsien witnessed a large congregation of Buddhist monks. This congregation was held once in five years, lasting from one to three months. At the end of the ceremony the king and his ministers granted great quantities of precious items and necessities to the monks. In addition to this big ceremony the king requested that monks congregate annually before the harvesting season. It is said that the ceremony could hasten the ripening of wheat, the only crop in the region.[79]

According to Fa-hsien, Buddhist rituals pervaded the whole society of Nāgarahāra, a state near Gandhāra. A skull bone of the Buddha was the centre of the ritual performance, and the king so feared losing the bone that he made the eight important families of the country guard it. Every morning they took the bone outside the monastery to a high platform, covered with a round plate made of the seven treasures. After the daily ceremony the bone was taken back into the monastery to its container, which was a small five foot high *stūpa* made of the seven treasures. Every morning peddlers met in front of the monastery to sell flowers and incense to worshippers. Kings from other countries also sent envoys to worship the bone. A tooth of the Buddha enjoyed similar veneration in the country. According to local tradition the ceremonies were efficacious for the summoning of rains in the country, which frequently suffered drought.[80]

The most extravagant Buddhist ceremony was the annual parade held in Pāṭaliputra. According to Fa-hsien, regularly every year on the eighth day of the second moon, a procession of images would be taken out. They make a five-storeyed, four-wheeled car by stacking bamboos together and the storeys are supported by posts in the form of crescent-bladed halberds. The car is over twenty feet in height and in form like a pagoda and it is draped with a kind of white cashmere, which is painted in various colours. They make images of *devas* ornamented with gold, silver, and brass, with silk banners and canopies overhead. At the four sides they make niches, each with a Buddha sitting inside and a *bodhisattva* in attendance. There may be some twenty cars, all beautifully ornamented and different from one another. In the procession were also singers and musicians who scattered flowers and incense. Monks and laity within the kingdom were invited to participate in the procession and the celebration lasted all through the night with lamps burning and music resounding.[81] While in Khotan, Fa-hsien witnessed a similar celebration and again gave a detailed description of the event. Streets in the city were swept clean beginning with the first day of the fourth month. Over the city gate was stretched a large awning with all kinds of ornamentation under which the king and queen and court ladies took their place. At a distance of three or four li from the city was made a four-wheeled image car, over thirty feet in height, looking like a movable 'Hall of the Buddha' and adorned with the *sapta ratna*, with streaming pennants and embroidered canopies. The image of the Buddha was placed in the middle of the car, with two attendant *bodhisattvas* and *devas* following behind. These were all beautifully carved with gold and silver and were suspended in the air. When the images entered the city the queen and court ladies, who were on the top of the gate, scattered far and wide all kinds of flowers which fluttered down and thus the splendour of decoration was offered up completely. The cars were all different; each monastery had a day for its own procession, beginning on the first day of the fourth moon and lasting until the fourteenth when the processions ended and the king and queen went back to the palace.[82]

In his descriptions Fa-hsien also remarks that various striking objects attracted many Buddhist worshippers. A big image of the Maitreya Buddha in a small state, Darada, in north-west India attracted the worship of kings. Big *stūpas* near Taxila enjoyed worship by both kings and the people. The *stūpa* built by Kaṇiṣka in Puruṣapura (modern Peshawar in Pakistan) was still the most magnificent and best decorated in the whole of India. And although the city of Śrāvasti was desolate, ritual performance in the Jetavana monastery, donated by Anāthapiṇḍika, never stopped.[83] These ritual performances derived and developed on the basis of the practise of giving donations and the accumulation of merit for the purpose of better future lives. Fa-hsien's accounts evince that numerous religious ceremonies and other ritual performances superseded donations as the main media through which both monks and laity sought and attained their soteriological goals.

Since the early-medieval period in Indian, there has been a strong trend to substitute a tangible and thus popular ritual for the earlier abstract meditations. Just as the Śaivas in the medieval ages set aside the ancient, abstract Vedic ritual in favour of their own richly decorative cult of the Supreme Being, Śiva enshrined in magnificent temples and celebrated through all the arts, so some Buddhists substituted a tangible, colourful, popular ritual for the old abstract meditations. And as in the case of Brahmanism, Buddhist Tantricism too laid dowm numerous soteriological rituals to achieve *mukti* or liberation as well as apotropaic rituals to avert the adverse effects of poisons, planets and diseases. In place of simple and temporary rituals, there developed a richly decorative cult of numerous celestial Buddhas and *bodhisattvas* represented in sculpture, personified or symbolically, with all the mythology of heaven, in permanent and magnificent temples. The Buddhists produced new rituals of their own, incorporating some of the popular forms as well as utilizing their own rich and ancient arts. This trend was totally different from the earlier performances and rituals which had developed in connection with the popularizing of Buddhism and as a means of propaganda.

In a ritual, doctrine is acted out in tangible form, not merely understood mentally. The *Mañjūśrimūla* supplies us with a great deal of information on ritual in its most tangible forms, with symbols and diagrams. The student is to observe virtue and meditation as preparation for the ritual. Then he is consecrated and taught the incantation by his teacher. Instructions in esoteric symbolism follow. After consecration *caryā*, the esoteric and secret ritual is performed. As an *Anuttarayoga* system the *Guhyasamāja* should operate through meditation only, namely the visualization of the Buddha as Vairocana with whom union is to be realized, accompanied by a circle of female *bodhisattvas*, a group of which constitutes a diagram. The ritualistic diagram is thus only to be imagined, it is transferred from concrete representation into pure meditation.

According to A.K. Warder the reason why it became desirable to make the doctrine visible was partly due to the material milieu of the early medieval period. He thought that an explanation might perhaps be sought in the history of the medieval temple, the main centre of the ritual and also the recipient of land-grants. He suggets that possibly the ritual was useful in making a suitable impression on the inhabitants of the lands in possession of the temple—the magnificent temple which replaced the simple community of monks seeking peace of mind and justifying donations to them by their teaching of the way to happiness. Such ideals and attitudes, offered to the rulers and the ruled, may have contributed significantly to social harmony and stability in a developing feudal order.[84] Thus, Buddhist soteriology was transformed from the *sūtra* and performing rituals of earlier times to esoteric rituals and conduct in Tantric Buddhism. From about the sixth century interesting and intriguing rituals were developed to replace abstract meditation or the passive thought of Amitābha, or the rather difficult exercise of imagining that un-happiness is imaginary and thinking oneself perfectly happy is the ultimate reality. Through ritual one could seek actively to realize supreme happiness and personal identity with the ultimate reality.[85]

Rites and Rituals: Their Socio-Economic Implications

Rites and ceremonies, the most essential function of the *saṃgha,* are not to be separated from other socio-economic activities. The devotee worshipped the Buddhas and the *bodhisattvas* and the monasteries provided him with various rites and ceremonies. The state also encouraged nationwide observance of some great festivities. Sometimes, for a festivity the suspension of state business was decreed. Such rites emanate from certain deeply embedded social traditions that run through all the members of the society from the king to the peasantry. In East Asia, the rite for the celebration of the Buddha's birthday is usually marked by a remarkable event, the procession of the Buddha's images which supplies us with useful insights. When images of the Buddha were paraded in China in 424, the emperor was present and enjoyed the spectacle and later the rite was celebrated with even greater enthusiasm and enjoyed by the populace. On the day before all images in the city, over a thousand in number, were first transported to the Ching-ming temple. On the next day they were carried through the streets of the capital in the direction of the imperial palace, where they were personally reviewed by the emperor. On this day, according to a contemporary observer,

> golden flowers sparkled in the sunlight, ornamented parasols floated about like clouds, the banners and pennants formed a forest, fumes from the incense resembled mist, music and chants resounded and shook heaven and earth. Joy and play were in full swing, with the dense crowd milling around everywhere; eminent monks and virtuous elders carrying their walking sticks formed groups while faithful laymen assembled, holding flowers in their hands. Carriages blocked all thoroughfares, causing a bewildering confusion in every place.[86]

Such events arose directly from the emphasis on mass salvation through merit-making rituals in Mahāyāna Buddhism. Every individual and all sectors of society took part in the rites and ceremonies to attain their respective soteriological goals.

The formulation and observance of the *uposatha* was a concession made by the Buddha to public ethos. It was one of the numerous concessions by the brotherhood to the religious and moral feelings of the people. Even though they betrayed the fundamental doctrines, the soteriological rituals of Buddhism played an important and crucial role in the social history of Buddhism in India and outside. The beliefs and ideas of culture have been formulated in the form of rituals more explicitly than through any other cultural trait. The religious history of ancient Korea centres round the triumph of Indian creeds over the local Shamanistic forms of worship and rituals.

The early Koreans believed in Shamanic cults and divinities and practised spirit worship. Magic and religion were inextricably intertwined at this stage. The former included choral singing and dancing as well as the drinking of intoxicating liquors in a great congregation. With the coming of Buddhism there occurred a revolutionary change and the ideas and rituals of the early Koreans were superseded by those of Buddhism. But we cannot say that all aspects of the older religious life were abandoned in favour of the new religion. Rather, we find that in due course of time most Shamanistic practises survived in the guise of Buddhist rites and ceremonies.

Just as Buddhism in India took over the religious traits of earlier religious even though many of these traits went radically against the fundamental doctrines of Buddhism, similarly outside India Buddhism became the instrument of assimilation of alien elements as well as a medium of cultural contact and internationalization. The rite of *P'algwanhoe* is a good example. Originally, in India, as described earlier, as a part of the *uposatha* rite, it was required that lay men and women receive and observe the eight precepts. However, the rite in Korea had no relationship at all with Buddhist contents. In Silla, the rite was held to pray for deceased soldiers and after the ceremony, prisoners were pardoned. In fact, pardoning prisoners was the main element of the harvest ceremony in ancient Korea before the advent of Buddhism. This explicitly points to the assimilation of Shamanic practises into those of Buddhism. We notice a good example of a similar phenomenon in the tenth century. In Koryo dynasty, the *P'algwanhoe* rite was meant to worship the heavenly god, mountain and river spirits, and the dragon god. It is rightly maintained that *P'algwanhoe,* though literally meaning 'Eight Precept Rite' is not the name of a Buddhist rite but simply a substitution of *Palgamhoe,* that is, the ancient Shamanic idea of sun-worship.[87]

The Lantern Festival, the rite that most attracted great throngs in ancient Korea, is another instance. This was the first festival on the annual calendar of Buddhist ceremonies. It was celebrated on the night of the first full-moon or the second full-moon night in a lunar year. Due to the paucity of sources we have to rely for the details of the ceremony on the customs prevalent in T'ang China, which were directly imported into Korea as well as on the materials of the Koryo dynasty in medieval times in Korea. It was the custom during T'ang times to have lighted lanterns in the temples and the streets of the cities during the three nights of the festival and to permit the populace to stay up through the night to revel in the festivities. During the three nights of the festival all ordinary restrictions headed by night curfew were lifted and inhabitants were permitted to roam around the city all through the night. It was also customary for monasteries to donate the oil necessary to keep the lanterns burning. The Lantern Festival in medieval Korea was so opulent that during lean periods the people had to appeal to the king to ban it keeping in mind the condition of the state economy. During the day the king would go to a temple to take part in the sacrifice for T'ae-jo, the founder of the Koryo dynasty and revel in the festivities drinking, dancing, listening to music and playing with all the ministers till night, which would be lit bright like the day. They worshipped not only the Buddha but also the Shamanic Heavenly-Earthly God for the welfare of the country and the royal family.

Most Buddhist rites, ceremonies and festivals fall at obvious transitional points of the agricultural year, i.e. the beginning or end of the rice cultivation cycle. In Korea the two greatest rites, the Lantern Festival and *P'algwanhoe* were held on the fifteenth day of the first or second month and on the fifteenth day of the tenth or eleventh month respectively. Kye-hyon Ahn maintains that the tenth month was nothing but the substitution of the Shamanic tenth month when most rites were performed.[88] We, however, insist that it is not merely the substitution of the time element. The tenth or eleventh month is the time when the harvest was ready. Buddhist and Shamanic rites were performed together at this post-harvest season. Therefore, it was in the eleventh month in Kaekyong, the capital city, and the tenth month in Sokyong, which has colder weather than Kaekyong, that the Buddhist rites were held on a grand national scale. This underlines the fact that the Buddhist rites were in tune with the cycle of rice cultivation in Korea. Meanwhile, the fifteenth day of the month and sometimes the thirtieth are the sacred days in India. The days of the full moon and new moon are regarded in India as auspicious days in Brahmanical reckoning from very early times.[89] Buddhist rites do not occur during the ploughing, transplanting or harvesting seasons. Here, it is to be noted that some rites follow the climatic calendar as well: the beginning or end of the monsoon in some countries which, unlike Korea, have a separate season of the monsoon. For instance in Myanmar Wa-zou, the Burmese Lantern Festival from the full moon of July through the full moon of October, is enhanced by the fact that it marks the beginning, not only of Lent, but of the rice production and monsoon seasons The villagers pass from an economically slow to an intensely busy period, planting and transplanting rice and the climate changes from the oppressive heat and drought of the dry months to the welcome rain and relative coolness of the monsoons.[90] The cycle of Buddhist temple rites, thus, is closely interwoven with the cycle of economic activities, especially the cycle of rice cultivation.

Rites and ceremonies were one of the main concessions by the Buddha and his brotherhood to the religious and moral feelings of the people. Even though they go against the fundamental doctrines, they played an important and crucial role in the social history of Buddhism in India and outside. The religious activities of monasteries, viz., the rites and ceremonies, the main function of the *saṃgha*, are not to be separated from other political and/or socio-economic activities.

With a complex ritual system, Buddhists participated in every facet of society including the socio-politico-economic activities of the people. Thus, Buddhist rites and ceremonies were not only a means to their religious goal but also channels for various kinds of social activities. Fa-hsien's account suggests that rites, ceremonies and the worship of objects provided the main fora for Buddhist preaching activities and constituted the main channel through which the Buddhist *saṃgha* maintained contact with its laity in the Gupta period.

The rationale by which the rituals functioned should be viewed in the context of the material formation of the society in question for that will reveal the actual social set-up in which they were formulated. At the local level of the feudal economy, rituals were the major channels through which the newly risen landlord class (from the fourth century in India and from the ninth century in Korea) as well as the state government sought to use priests to sanctify their status and authority. The monastery-based rites and ceremonies represent the monasteries' search for a dependable subsistence in their rural base. In both cases, that of India and Korea, rituals in ancient and early medieval times were the main representations by which all aspects of social and cultural motivations were identified. This was intensified by the soteriological character on the basis of merit-making ideology and practises and the apotropaic character attached to the mundane world. Every individual and all sectors of society took an active part in performing the rites and ceremonies mainly for the purpose of attaining their soteriological and apotropaic goals. Buddhist rituals, whatever their nature, are an expression of social unity. Their function is to recreate the social order by reaffirming and strengthening the sentiments on which social solidarity and social order depend. The rite of the *uposatha* procession of the Buddha's images, the Lantern Festival and so on are therefore regarded as arising from certain deeply embedded social traditions and prejudices amongst all the members of society, from the king to the peasantry. The king took an active part in the rite and the rite was celebrated with even greater enthusiasm and enjoyed by the people. The fact that all segments of society, right from the upper to the lower and from the king to the peasantry, believed in the power of the rites provided an ideological cementing bond. They served as a common link or as the chief cementing force which keeps society integrated. The performance of rites and ceremonies and their development into festivals was a clever device to keep the whole society together.

Maurice Bloch argues that the more institutionalized hierarchies a society has the more ritual there is, especially of the 'eternal return' type, which repeats past events. This is because rituals are highly limited codes of information that can be easily manipulated by the holders of power to falsify the sense of reality of the exploited classes. Therefore, ritual legitimizes social inequality and is greatest in those societies that are most politically differentiated.[91]

Economically speaking, rituals provided employment to many diverse craftsmen and artisans who made and repaired the chariot and its accessories, including the portable icons. The varied nature of work involved blacksmiths, painters and carpenters. Other artisans who helped to organize the festival included florists and garland-makers, oilmen, weavers and clothiers. In this respect, R.S. Sharma rightly points out the relationship between the state economy and the performance of rituals.[92] He states that if we believe Kauṭilya, the credulity of the people was cleverly exploited for promoting the interests of the state, internal as well as external. For augmenting the royal treasury the *Arthaśāstra* suggests several devices which play upon the superstitions of the people. On some nights the king may set up a god or a sacred shrine, or may point out an evil omen. Once the people are made aware of it and start making offerings, either for worshipping the god or for averting the calamity, he may appropriate the collections raised in this manner. Patañjali, who wrote a commentary on Pāṇini's grammar around 150 BC states that the images set up by the Maurya kings brought them income on account of their sale and provided livelihood through the offerings made to them. In addition to this, fairs were often arranged on such occasions, which gave an opportunity to local merchants and cottage industries to dispose of their goods locally and profitably. In East Asia, on such occasions, international trade in the form of tribute offerings to the Chinese emperor were often held on a large scale.

More attention has to be given to the crucial role of public ritual in sustaining the institution of monarchy. It is, of course, true that over much of early Indian history kings were perceived as secular, (or what Dumont[93] has called 'conventional'—in contrast to magico-religious) by Buddhists and Jainas. But the dominant conception of Brahmanic kingship continued to give fundamental significance to public ritual, as in the ancient horse sacrifice. As to 'magico-religious' kingship, south Indian historians have noted that sacrifice yielded to presentation as the characteristic form of kingly ritual.[94] The relationship between kingship and religious rituals was augmented by the celebration of the king's birthday in Buddhism. In East Asia, these were initiated by Hsüan-tsang, who ordered that vegetarian feasts be arranged in Buddhist temples for the occasion. Later, in Korea, all the temples in the country became the scene of the birthday ceremonies. Almost every vegetarian feast during a king's birthday celebrations was indeed a gigantic event attended by thousands of monks. On such occasions, the king, accompanied by the members of the royal family, participated in the rites held in the temple and donated large numbers of clothes to the monasteries. Though the service was performed in the Buddhist manner, with the worship of the Buddha, the chanting of Sanskrit hymns, the burning of incense, etc., the rite itself had nothing to do with Buddhism. It serves as an illustration of how closely identified Buddhist rite performances were with the ritual for sustaining the monarchical institution. 'Magico-religious' kingship, backed by Buddhist ritual, was fully established by the rite of the welcoming and worshipping of the Buddha's relics. The specimens of the Buddha's relics were regarded by the faithful as visual symbols of the Buddha and were therefore highly venerated. Thus, the king, of all the members of society, first welcomed the relics, followed in due course by rites in the royal palace chapel. The relic welcoming ceremony, commenced by the royal institution, played a significant role in the expression of sacred kingship. The rite of relics of the 'Dhammarājā' by kings and their courts followed by the royal decree and public ceremony was the major way in which sacred rule was expressed.

Ritual popularized the dry ideology of a limited number of renouncers, converting it into a mass-oriented system. Owing to the development of ritualism, Mahāyāna Buddhism succeeded in popularizing itself with the masses. It produced a body of doctrinaire literature that was acceptable to the common man as well as a system of rituals that led the non-flexible, philosophic Mahāyāna Buddhism towards a mass-oriented culture. The rituals attracted converts of a mediocre type and appreciably helped to establish the enlarged ecclesiastical body headed by priests. Around this body grew up a number of house-holders who, impressed by the saintly character of some of the monks as also by the simple ethical teachings of the religion and the rituals of *trisaraṇa* and other ecclesiastical functions like *pavārana* which required the services of laymen, avowed themselves as *upāsakas* and *upāsikās*. The rituals opened the way for lay society's participation in the religion. However, the religion did not yield to the wishes of the masses any further, and merely provided objects of worship in various rituals. The custom of monks and lay people coming together on the *uposatha* day helped to popularize religion and propagate it in the initial stage of its history. Moreover, the beliefs and ideas prevalent in different cultures at different times and places have been formulated in the form of rituals more explicitly than any other cultural trait.

The annual calendar of the Buddhist society in Korea was marked by a series of religious rites and ceremonies in which all the strata of society, from the king to the peasantry participated. Buddhist ceremonies were almost the only means which could bring together the king, the gentry, the rich, and the mass of peasantry. Thus, transactions between the Buddhist *saṃgha* and lay society in the performance of such luxurious rites and ceremonies also served a social function in this respect. Participation in Buddhist ritual led to the social encounter taking the form of reciprocity—donors gained merit through donations and donees returned the donations in the form of religious practises. Mahāyāna Buddhism, especially that of Western Paradise, was more responsive to the devotees' religious aspirations. The scope of rewards for devotion to the Buddha shifted from *nirvāṇa* to better prospects in future life-cycles and to material efficacy in this world.

As the value of gift items to the monasteries escalated, donors came to expect and to receive much more in return. In fact, competition between Buddhism and Brahmanism heightened the demand for luxury goods. Since these goods were related to religion, they often held a sacred meaning for the believers. Both donors and donees needed more and more sumptuous and luxurious ritual performances which were thought to supply reciprocal merits to both sides. The close relation between trade routes and the distribution of monasteries also suggests that the Buddhist *saṃgha* provided valuable services to the traders. As the monasteries were dependent on the donations of the itinerant merchants, they would have been inclined to assist their patrons. The monastery, thus, was the most important institution, purchasing clothes and other commodities for monks and retainers and costly materials for various rites and ceremonies.

Buddhist rituals, whose integral materials were luxury items for offerings, mainly from long-distance trade, turned out to be a means of exposing social disparity. The people of the upper classes sought rare goods within and outside their domain to mark themselves off from the lower classes. The practise of seeking genuine jewels for use in worship encouraged them to pay a high price for commodities brought from distant lands. They constantly strove for goods which could improve their status, which then provided the impetus for foreign trade in luxury goods. Thus, the various rituals of Buddhism through which people sought their soteriological goal of a better rebirth in the next life increased the prices of specific commodities in this life. Correspondingly, commodities demanded by the elite as signs of wealth and status could also become religious treasures. Once the precious items of secular purpose had gained a 'sacredness' owing to the reciprocal needs of monks and laity, religious practises further encouraged the demand for such rare commodities. Rituals backed by contemporary religious ideas motivated trading in such commodities, both through direct investment in another world by lay devotees and through its effect on secular consumption patterns. Thus, rituals which necessitated imported goods, especially various kinds of incenses, in some respect played a role in bringing intensification in social hierarchy. The rich tried their best to show off and stabilize their social status by offering incenses as varied as possible. But the poor people simply could not afford them. This finally led the poor people to make the purchase of expensive items for rituals their goal in life. In China, on the occasion of the ceremony of the Buddha's relic, all sorts of offerings such as medicines, foods and rice, rare fruits and flowers and different kinds of incense were presented to the Buddha. All these were spread out to be viewed by the public, who came in a huge stream to worship the sacred relics. The rich donated unlimited wealth to the monastery, while the common people vied with one another to make their offerings to the Buddha by giving up the earnings of a lifetime. In Korea, though we are not aware of the scale of such donations due to the lack of direct detailed data, the great scenery of ceremonies cannot be very different from what the Chinese practised. As a matter of fact, after the third century AD, the demand for Oriental incense and perfumes decreased in the Roman empire due to the puritanical attitude of the early Christians. Meanwhile, the demand in China seemed to have increased. Until the third century only royal families and their close social circle of nobles seemed to be able to enjoy these imported perfumes and incense. Following the propagation of Buddhism, the lower social orders also came to use incense because incense-burning was essential to Buddhist rituals. In addition to expensive perfumes and incense, other imported goods in China since Han times and in Korea since the last stage of the Three Kingdoms period were also enjoyed almost exclusively by the royal family. By the time the Northern Dynasties came to power, Buddhist followers had become the major buyers of these foreign goods. Such a trend in the social economy of China was never too different from that of ancient Korea, where luxurious foreign goods were in vogue when Buddhist monasteries became the centres of the economy of society.

NOTES

1. Melford E. Spiro, *BS*, p. 140
2. *Vin., Cvg.*, V, 8f.
3. Ibid., 8-9.
4. Benoytosh Bhattacharyya, *IBE*, p. 18.
5. Raoul Birnbaum, *The Healing Buddha* (revd. edn., Boston, 1979), p. 6.
6. *AN*, IV, XIII, 121f.
7. *MP*, IV, 2. 17.
8. B.C. Law, *IDETBJ*, p. 207.
9. *Vin., Cvg.*, V, 6.
10. Melford E. Spiro, *BS*, p. 144
11. *Vin., Cvg.*, V, 6. 1.
12. *IHQ*, vol. XXI, p. 247.
13. Fa-hsien, pp. 76-7.

14. Sinhalese equivalent of *paritta.*
15. *MP,* IV, 2. 19.
16. Ibid., IV, 2. 16.
17. Ibid.
18. *Mahā-Maṅgala Jāt.,* no. 453.
19. On this occasion, the *Maṅgala Sutta* mentioned above must be uttered.
20. Romila Thapar, *ADM,* p. 144.
21. N. Dutt, *Early Monastic Buddhism,* vol. 2, p. 207.
22. B.M. Barua, *Aśoka and His Inscriptions,* pt. 1 (3rd edn., Calcutta, 1968), p. 266.
23. 'Popular', pp. 218-19.
24. *Lg. SV,* p. 19.
25. *HIL,* vol. II, pp. 368-9.
26. R.S. Sharma, *PSEHEI,* pp. 238-9.
27. 'Buddhism', p. 129.
28. *HIL,* vol. II, p. 371.
29. *LS,* pp. 260-1.
30. *SBCI,* p. 13.
31. See Ch. 3.
32. Literally meaning 'dark complexion foreigner', it must have been used to denote an Indian monk.
33. *Yusa.,* III-iii, Adogira.
34. *Divya.,* p. 192.
35. It is maintained that Ado is not a proper name but a common noun, literally meaning 'bald head', denoting a Buddhist monk.
36. *Yusa.,* III-iii, Adogira.
37. Raoul Birnbaum, op.cit., p. 7.
38. *Yusa.,* III-iii, Nant'a Pyokche.
39. Ki-baek Yi, *SSY,* p. 29.
40. *Yusa.,* V-vi, Mil-bon ch'oesa.
41. Ibid.
42. E.R. Leach, 'Ritualization in man in relation to conceptual and social development', *Philosophical Transactions of the Royal Society of London,* series B, vol. 251, no. 722, p. 407.
43. S.J. Tambiah, 'The Magical Power of Words', *Man,* 3, no. 2, p. 178.
44. Ibid., pp. 177-8.
45. W.T. Wheelock, 'Sacred Language', *ER,* vol. 8, p. 441.
46. *Yusa.,* V-vii, Wol-myong-sa Tosolga.
47. Ibid.
48. Richard F. Gombrich, *Pre. Prac.,* p. 115.
49. L.A. de Silva, *Buddhism: Beliefs and Practices in Sri Lanka* (Sri Lanka, 1974), pp. 65-6.
50. *Yusa.,* V-vii, Yung-ch'on-sa Hyesongga.
51. *Yusa.,* III-iv, Punhwangsa Ch'onsu Taebi Maeng-a Tugan.
52. *Yusa.,* II-ii, Mun-ho-wang Pop-min.
53. Tae-wha Park, 'Silla Sidae-ui Milkyo Cholraego', *Cho myong-gi Paksa*

Hwangab Kinyom Pulkyosa Nonch'ong (Seoul, 1969), p. 73.
54. *Taisho*, vol. 21, p. 515.
55. Max Weber, *The Religion of India* (New York, 1958), p. 206.
56. T. W. Rhys Davids, *Early Buddhism* (London, 1908), pp. 71-2.
57. *DN*, II. 78.
58. *Sut. Nip.*, I. 3. 27.
59. Ibid.
60. Melford E. Spiro, *BS*, p. 34.
61. *DP*, XX, 274-6.
62. *DN*, II, 141.
63. I-tsing, p. 121.
64. Ibid., pp. 152-4.
65. Ibid., p. 155.
66. *OYCTI*, vol. I, p. 173.
67. I-tsing, pp. 150-1.
68. Ibid., pp. 147-9.
69. *BMMI*, p. 71.
70. Ibid., p. 73.
71. P.E., no. V.
72. *AN*, III, 7. 70. iv.
73. Gokuldas De, *DEBS*, p. 60.
74. *Vin.*, *Mvg.*, 13.1.
75. C.S. Upasak, *Dictionary of Early Buddhist Monastic Terms* (Varanasi, 1975), p. 152.
76. S. Dutt, *EBM*, p. 84.
77. I-tsing, pp. 41-2.
78. Ibid., pp. 35-40.
79. Fa-hsien, pp. 7-8.
80. Ibid., pp. 15-17.
81. Ibid., p. 47.
82. Ibid., pp. 5-6.
83. Ibid., pp. 9-14.
84. 'Feudalism', p. 174.
85. Ibid.
86. Hsua-chih Yang, *Lo-yang Chia-lan Chi*, 3; Taisho, 51, 1010b.
87. Kye-hyon Ahn, *P'algwanhoego*, Tongguk Sahak, vol. IV (Seoul, 1956), p. 37.
88. Ibid., p. 48.
89. S. Dutt, *EBM*, p. 82.
90. Melford E. Spiro, *BS*, p. 222.
91. Maurice Bloch, 'The Past and Present in the Present', *Man* (n.s.), 12 (August 1977), pp. 278-92.
92. R.S. Sharma, *PSEHEI*, p. 73.
93. Louis Dumont, 'Kingship in Ancient India', *CIS*, no. 6, December 1962.
94. Cf. Burton Stein, 'Mahānavami: Medieval and Modern Kingly Ritual in South India', in B.G. Gokhale (ed.), *Essays in Gupta Culture*, pp. 76-7.

CHAPTER 7

Conclusion

It is certain that whether direct or indirect, both Korea and India have had contacts with each other from early times. In historical times, there were definitely some contacts between the two countries but they do not seem to have been very close and rich. Direct contact between the two has certainly been very limited while Buddhism has played a crucial role in this respect. In this book, we have attempted to show that Buddhist ideas and rituals have produced variations in social realities in historical progress. The normative ideology of Buddhism, based on the tradition of renunciation, was not followed in its original formulation but fostered a variant set of traditions about the function of society. The complex philosophy of Buddhist thought was substituted with simplistic explanations both in India and Korea.

It is evident that kingship in Buddhist thought was an institution essential to the maintenance of order and a Buddhist king, therefore, was titled in three standard phrases as a *mahāsammata, khattiya* and *rājā*. He is the manifestation of incomparable perfection. He is the ideal character who, in his exalted capacity, maintains in human affairs as much of *dharma*, the ideal norm, that remains amid the general degradation of things. The Buddhist conception of *dharma* is an all encompassing norm for truth and cosmic law and the code of kingship embodying righteousness have their source in this concept of *dharma*. Warriorship was supposedly intrinsic to rulership, a fact further substantiated by the Ksatriya and *cakravartin* motifs in Brahmanical notions of kingship with which the Buddhist model has some apparent continuity. In fact, as a model of conduct for historical kings with Buddhistic inclinations, it is the policy of pacification after violence, that has been of great relevance. Thus, for the establishment of a powerful authority violence and benevolence were ranged together and overlapped in the name of religion. Immediately after the kings had fulfilled their political aims by using violence, they became devoted and religious and began to perform various religious deeds for purposes of merit-accumulation, mainly in order to evade a past dotted with evil deeds. This was the pattern of action which almost every Buddhist king in Asia exhibited and the Koreans were no exception albeit with some modifications. In this manner, the contradictions between the warrior king and the Buddhist ideal king were sought to be reconciled.

Moreover, the idea of the future Buddha as a *cakravartin* is a manifestation of utopian aspirations as well as of the profound political crisis in Buddhist society. No Buddhist king, whether he called himself a *cakravartin* or not, could get down to the business of performing meritorious deeds until the prior kingly, Ksatriya, business of securing the state had been accomplished. Here, it is interesting to note that the closer to violence or military conquest a king had been the more he devoted himself to religion, becoming more and more like a *bhikkhu* for instance. It became rather the standard and expected mode of governance by Korean Buddhist kings in the early centuries AD.

The organized system of Buddhist political ideas, ever since its introduction in Korea, was inextricably bound up with the concentration of political authority. Though, as K.M. Shrimali says, it would be an over-simplification to say that the Buddha's was an ideology of the Ksatriyas,[1] in respect of politics it defined the most favoured position for rulers in ancient Korea, achieved, mostly through terms related to Buddhist ideal figures like *cakravartin*, *bodhisattva* or the future Buddha or Aśoka. The idea simply was that Korea was the original home of the Buddha and *dhamma*. The myth of 'Buddha Land' was elaborated and played the role of a special charter in establishing powerful kingship in ancient Korea. Thus, kings tried to identify themselves with the myth that strengthened their claim to the royal throne, especially at times when a variety of groups were contending for the throne or fighting for supremacy. King Chin-hung and Kung-ye are good examples of figures in this category in ancient Korea. The attempt to legitimize political authority through the idea of the Buddhist ideal kingship was not peculiar only to Korea but occurred in every Buddhist country. At the same time, the purpose of kings who proclaimed that they ruled in accordance with *dhamma* lay not in their religious piety but in the ideology of political stability and security and social pacification. The *saṃgha*, originally an association of those who had renounced the world of politics, thus, became an alternative source of authority on politics. Organizing various artistic activities and rituals became an alternative way of seeking legitimacy by royal patrons. This mechanism has been widely inherent in Buddhist traditions.

The renouncer cannot be described simply as a religious leader since he accumulates in himself a complex interrelation of social signals. The *saṃgha*, thus, becomes the main channel through which the sect communicated with the rest of society. Donors gain and accumulate merit through donations and the *saṃgha* returns the donation in the form of religious activities such as rituals, ceremonies, preachings and so on. And with the shift in soteriological goal to the achievement of better rebirth rather than to its cessation, the aim of soteriological action became the improvement rather than the extinction of one's *karma*. And gifting to the *saṃgha* was regarded as much more effective in terms of *karma*. Making regular food offerings to the monks, giving them new robes and supplies, funding special ceremonies and festivals, building a new monastery or having a son or a daughter join the *saṃgha* were all typical lay acts of donation.

The monasteries in the Kuṣāṇa period augmented and accumulated properties such as *vihāras*, *stūpas*, images, currency and jewellery but not land. This institutional expansion of Buddhism was correlated to urban development and was largely due to the unprecedented increase in internal and foreign trade. The organization of guilds for craft, the extensive increase of metal currency and the inflow of large amounts of luxury goods such as gold from Rome and silk from China played a favourable role in the development of the merit-donation mechanism. This may have strengthened the donors in the urban culture ideologically and psychologically in pursuing their normal avocations. In Gupta India, however, Buddhism maintained its institutions by adding to its economic power, mainly by extension of landed property. Monasteries under the Guptas controlled currency and in order to earn interest on donations they were also involved in the enterprise of usury. The great and permanent value of land led the *saṃgha* to improve its economic position in a big and a more lasting way. It is worth noticing that accumulation of landed property by monasteries, both in the later Silla period and post-Gupta India, played a dominant role in introducing a feudal economy in both countries. The gift of land by kings impoverished the state, for a lasting source of revenue had been lost.

It was such a metamorphosed idea of merit as 'a single flower offered to him (the Buddha) yields the fruit of paradise (and even) final emancipation'[2] in an inscription at Ajanta that created an independent structure in Buddhist economies both in India and Korea in early times. Buddhist economy sustained Buddhism for a long time and was the major factor which kept up the intimate relationship between the laity and the *saṃgha.* It also meant a symbiosis of the *saṃgha*-monarchy relationship, ensuring powerful support in every aspect to the *saṃgha* from the patron. Without this patronage the Buddhist *saṃgha* may have gone the way of the Ājīvikas. What the *saṃgha* could offer in return was the legitimation of kingship or even the specific legitimation of a particular royal family as may have been the case with the Sillas. But paradoxically enough, it led to the collapse of Buddhism both in India and Korea due to the corruption inherent in the structure.

The profoundness of the doctrine of the Buddha on social distinction, which was so against the supremacy of the Brahmins, shows that it was mainly for the elite and not for the masses. Like the later medieval *bhakti* saints, the Buddha did not impose upon his followers the duty of looking upon caste as a social evil but only that they disregard it in their fellowship. Though Buddhist ideas and practices on social distinction undermined the Brahmins' clientele and led to some conflict of interests, it finally left the main structure of social inequalities intact. Monks could afford to stay in their monasteries and ignore the fight against social inequalities whereas the Brahmin had a family, and in general, closer ties with the people. Buddhism, therefore, succeeded in establishing an idealistic, equal society only in the *saṃgha* which was separated from society. Though Buddhism challenged the caste system, it could not transform it, for it did not wish to trouble the established social order. The Buddhists were far from trying to revamp the social structure of the unequal Brahmanical society and never ceased to draw on the same fund of ideas by which the unequal Brahmanical society existed. Buddhism did not produce a revolutionary set of new ideas, only traditional derivations. Buddhists, from the Buddha to the author of the *Vajrasūci,* maintained a conservative attitude, not willing to destabilize the existing social order. They did not try to reform society by eradicating social evils. This is the limitation of the Buddhist tradition on social transformation in the Indian scene.

Once Buddhism began to depend more and more on the financial and political support of royal authority, feudatory chiefs or nobles and wealthy patrons, it was obliged to follow the logic that he who pays the piper calls the tune. This was bound to lend powerful support to status-quoist forces. Introduced into ancient Korea, Buddhism, with its rationalized world-view, was most favourable to the royal authority and the aristocratic class. Kings were invested with sacred symbols and titles such as being called Ksatriyas by birth as exemplified in the 'myth of Ksatriya' in the *Samgukyusa.*[3] Moreover, the concept of the sacred lineage of Ksatriyas expounded in early Buddhist canonical literature led to the creation of a class of *songkols* who claimed that they, exclusively, had the right to the throne. It was Buddhism that legitimized such beliefs and made the ideology acceptable to the people. In turn, Buddhism made the *kolpum* system rigid. The notion of hereditary character and of privileged birth depicted in Buddhism contributed to the rigidity of social institutions and the *kolpum* system. It was aimed at the consolidation of the social authority of the aristocratic class.

Thus, at the time when dynasties were on the decline, *yuktupums,* in their attempted upward mobility, rejected the ideology of Buddhism and instead chose the ideology of Confucianism which disregarded the idea of making distinctions according to birth. The fight against the social rigidity of the *kolpum* system gave credence to the faith of 'Pure Land', whose followers were mostly poor peasants and slaves. They believed that the problems created by economic and social inequalities could be overcome in the faith of the Amitābha Buddha. They dreamt of an escape from the worst conditions of this world in the name of the tradition of Indian idealism. The rulers supported the cult, for such idealism did not foster social revolt. They emphasized instead the vanity of this world and the utopia available in the next world. It, thus, hoped to suppress the trend of popular unrest and so promote the stabilization of society.

The range of influence of the idea of social stratification coming from India was limited and minimal as far as Korea is concerned. The fundamental Indian social fabric was never fully transplanted. Social stratification based on birth applicable to all members of society, ideas of pollution and purity, of restriction on social and religious life due to religious disability and so forth were never introduced into Korea. Moreover, there was no equivalent of the Brahmin-Ksatriya relationship in early Korea, where status and power were never completely dissociated. Buddhist kings were never dispossessed of their religious prerogatives. What the Koreans acquired through their interaction with Buddhist was the two fold idea of Indian social stratification: the idea of the 'sacred' in addition to that of a 'classless society'. This paradoxical and ambiguous phenomenon was truly the result of Buddhism's two-sided view of social stratification. On the one hand, the Buddha attempted to obliterate the evil of caste distinctions but on the other, he never missed a chance to boast about the privileges of the Kṣatriya *varṇa* to which he belonged. It was this tradition which influenced to some extent the social formation of Buddhist society in early Korea.

Buddhism, in its incipient stage, was an ethic with absolute indifference to the question of whether there were gods and how they existed. Buddhism had no room for any saviour, prayer, rituals, etc. However, this radical soteriological ideology of Buddhism was one thing but its practice by the masses was another. Since the normative ideology was the creation of a religious virtuoso, the Buddha, its diffusion to the religiously unmusical masses necessarily entailed important transformations of the original message. If early Buddhism appealed primarily to a cultural stratum of the urban, world-weary intelligentsia, it could hardly have become the religion of an unsophisticated peasantry without undergoing important changes. Thus, in the process of becoming a popular religion promising mass salvation, the soteriological ideology of normative Buddhism had, indeed, to undergo important changes.

The idea of the *boddhisattva* as an ideal in place of *arhat* was a crucial point in the process of change. Instead of aiming straight away at total detachment and *nirvāṇa*, the idea of salvation from this world to the other became the dominant one. Thus, in practice, Buddhism for most Buddhists, not only *upāsakas* but also *bhikkhus*, became a means not so much for the extinction of desires as for its gratification, not so much for the cessation of rebirth as for a better rebirth. Not knowledge but merit became the goal of religious action, for merit alone improved one's *karma*, and good *karma* was a prerequisite for the soteriological aim, viz., a happy rebirth. As Buddhism developed, there came about an important shift from salvation through knowledge to salvation through works. Thus, in due course of time, Buddhism became a religion full of rites and ceremonies where salvation was no longer achieved through knowledge but through action. And actions bore fruit only in a future life. This doctrine formulated the main character of Buddhism as a religion of merit-making. Thus, the soteriology became the main theme for lay society which opened the doors to a sacramental, idolatrous and ritualistic culture. In this context, some rituals, which were of necessity associated with the worship of deities in monasteries, developed into major festivals which contained all the functions of society. *Uposatha,* entailing a procession of the Buddha's images, was one such rite through which can be seen reflected all aspects of the socio-economic, political and cultural values of the time.

Apotropaic ritualism in Buddhism as a potential religious force showed a strong utilitarian background and reflected the aspirations of the people from the time of the Buddha. The rituals were meant to fulfil all kinds of material desires of the people and obtain for them the elixir of life. This was one of the chief reasons why Buddhism succeeded in taking its root in the soil of Brahmanism and at the same time, paradoxically enough, faded out from the historical scene of its birth. As the product of a fusion between Brahmanical religion and tribal religion, it played an eminent role as a catalyst in integrating and restructuring various cults, including foreign and domestic ones, in all Buddhist countries.

In the case of Korea, on the one hand, owing to its systematic and rationalistic world-view in the apotropaic rituals, the new religion was welcomed by the mass of people who sought material prosperity and protection against diseases, evil spirits, natural calamities and the like. On the other hand, it also embraced the age-old world-view of the masses and incorporated their rituals into its mechanism. Therefore, it was acceptable to the people as it attempted religious reconciliation and integration rather than the accentuation of social and political conflict. In Korea Buddhism has developed into a ritualized religion which promotes a systematic and rationalistic belief in the efficacy of sacred words and deeds. However, unlike in India, in ancient Korea it was more the ideology of the ruling classes. Its rituals contributed greatly to the establishing of a powerful kingship at a time when there was a struggle for supremacy for they legitimized political and social inequality. Buddhism had a highly limited code of information that could easily be manipulated by holders of power to falsify the sense of reality of the exploited classes. When the Indian religion was introduced into Korea, the rulers of the Three Kingdoms were mainly interested in the materialistic and this-worldly aspect of the religion, which was considered to be sacred and powerful enough in a rationalized system to replace Shamanism. In turn, Buddhism was transformed into a state ideology under the parasol of royal authority. It was considered mainly to be a mechanism granting mystic power for the protection of the state, constructing a powerful government and a despotic kingship. In fact, in Sri Lanka King Duṭṭagāmaṇī exploited Buddhism in a similar vein. That he put a relic in his spear and made a statement of truth shows his understanding of the Buddha's relic as a magic amulet and His law as a spell. With this Buddhism had become severely distorted. Its anti-worldly doctrine had been transformed into a form of protective mechanism for worldly matters.

NOTES

1. 'Religion', p. 32.
2. G. Yazdani, *Ajanta* (London, 1930-55), p. 144.
3. *Yusa.*, III-iv, Hwangnyongsa Kuch'ungt'ap.

Bibliography

A. ORIGINAL SOURCES

Abhidharmakośa-bhāṣya, ed. by P. Pradhan (Patna, 1967); Hindi tr. by Narendradeva, pts. 1 and 2 (Allahabad, 1958, 1973).

Ācārāṅga Sūtra, tr. *Jaina Sutras*, by H. Jacobi, SBE, vol. XXII (Oxford, 1894).

Aṅguttara Nikāya, ed. by R. Morris and E. Hardy, 5 vols., PTS (London, 1885-1900); tr. *The Book of the Gradual Sayings*, vols. I, II and V by F.L. Woodward and III and IV by E.M. Hare, PTS (London, 1932-6).

Āpastamba Dharmasūtra, tr. by G. Buhler, SBE, II (rpt., Delhi, 1965).

Arthaśāstra, ed. and tr. by R.P. Kangle, 3 pts. (Bombay, 1975).

Buddhacarita, ed. and tr. *Acts of the Buddha*, by E.H. Johnston (Delhi, 1972).

Catuḥśataka, ed. by Hara Prasad Sastri, Memoirs of the Asiatic Society of Bengal, III, no. 8 (Calcutta, 1914).

Cūlavaṃsa, tr. by Wilhelm Geiger (rpt., New Delhi, 1992).

Cullavagga, ed. by Bhikkhu J. Kashyap, Nalanda Devanagari Pali Series (Nalanda, 1956); tr. *Vinaya Texts*, by T.W. Rhys Davids and Hermann Oldenberg, SBE, XVII and XX (rpt., Delhi, 1982).

Dhammapada, ed. by Bhikkhu J. Kashyap, Nalanda Devanagari Pali Series (Nalanda, 1959); tr. by Max Müller, SBE, X, pt. 1 (rpt., Delhi, 1988).

Dīgha Nikāya, ed. by T.W. Rhys Davids, and J.E. Carpenter, 3 vols., PTS (London, 1890-1); tr. *Dialogues of the Buddha* by T.W. Rhys Davids, 3 vols., SBB (London, 1899-1921).

Dīpavaṃsa, tr. by Hermann Oldenberg (rpt., New Delhi, 1982).

Divyāvadāna, ed. by P.L. Vaidya, Buddhist Sanskrit Texts, no. 20 (Darbhanga, 1959).

Giles, H.A. (tr.), *The Travels of Fa-hsien* (rpt., Delhi, 1972).

Jaiminiya Upaniṣad Brāhmaṇa, ed. by Rama Deva (Lahore, 1921).

Jātaka-Mālā, ed. by P.L. Vaidya, Buddhist Sanskrit Texts, no. 21 (Darbhanga, 1959); tr. by J.S. Speyer, 1895 (rpt. Delhi, 1971).

Jātakas, ed. by V. Fausboll, 6 vols. (London, 1877-98); tr. by E.B. Cowell (Cambridge, 1895-1913).

Khuddakapāṭha, tr. *The Minor Readings by Bhikkhu Nanamoil*, PTS, no. 32 (London, 1960).

Lahiri, Latika (tr.) *Chinese Monks in India* (Delhi, 1986).

Lalitavistara, ed. and tr. by R. Mitra, *Bibliotheca Indica*, New Series, no. 473 (Calcutta, 1877).

Laṅkāvatārasūtra, ed. by Bunyin Nanjio (Kyoto, 1923); tr. by D.T. Suzuki (London, 1932).

Mahābhārata, ed. by various hands (Poona, 1971-5); tr. by K.M. Ganguly, 12 vols. (3rd edn., Delhi, 1975).

Mahāvagga, ed. by Bhikkhu J. Kashyap, Nalanda Devanagari Pali Series (Nalanda, 1956); tr. by *Vinaya Texts*, by T.W. Rhys Davids and Hermann Oldenberg, SBE, XIII and XVII (rpt., Delhi, 1982).

Mahāvaṃsa, tr. by Wilhelm Geiger (rpt., New Delhi, 1986).

Mahāvastu, ed. by E. Senart, 3 vols. (Paris, 1882-97); tr. by J. J. Jones, 2 vols., SBB, vol. XVI (London, 1949, 1953, 1956).

Majjhima Nikāya, ed. by V. Trenckner and R. Chalmers, PTS, 3 vols. (London, 1886-96); tr. *The Collections of the Middle Length Sayings* by I.B. Horner, PTS, no. 29 (London, 1954).

Manusmṛti, ed. by V.N. Mandlik (Bombay, 1886); tr. *The Laws of Manu* by Wendy Doniger (rpt., New Delhi, 1992).

Matsya Purāṇa, ed. by Jivananda Vidyasagara (Calcutta, 1876).

Milindapañho, ed. by V. Trenckner (London, 1928); tr. *The Questions of King Milinda* by T.W. Rhys Davids, SBE, XXXV, XXXVI (rpt., Delhi, 1988).

Samguksagi, ed. and tr. by Yi Pyong-do (rpt., Seoul, 1988).

Samgukyusa, ed. and tr. by Yi Min-su (rpt., Seoul, 1987).

Samyutta Nikāya, ed. by Bhikkhu J. Kashyap, Nalanda Devanagari Pali Series (Nalanda, 1959); tr. *The Book of the Kindred Sayings* by Mrs. Rhys Davids, 5 vols. (London, 1950-6).

Saundarānanda, ed. and tr. by E.H. Johnston, 2 vols. (London, 1932).

Sukhāvatīvyūha, ed. by Max Müller (Oxford, 1881-4); tr. *Buddhist Mahāyāna texts* by Max Müller, SBE, vol. XXXXIX, pt. II (rpt., Delhi, 1985).

Sutta Nipāta, ed. by Bhikkhu J. Kashyap Nalanda Devanagari Pali Series (Nalanda, 1959); tr. by V. Fausboll, SBE, X, pt. 2. (rpt., Delhi, 1988).

Suvarṇaprabhasasūtra, ed. by S. Bagchi, Buddhist Sanskrit Text, no. 8 (Darbhanga, 1967); tr. *The Sūtra of Golden Light* by R.E. Emmerick (London, 1970).

Taisho Shinshu Daizokyo (Tokyo, 1924-8).

Takakusu, tr. *A Record of the Buddhist Religion as Practised in India and the Malay Archipelago* (2nd Indian edn., New Delhi, 1982).

Therāgāthā, tr. *Psalms of the Brethern* by Mrs. Rhys Davids, PTS (London, 1951).

Therīgāthā, tr. *Psalms of the Sisters* by Mrs. Rhys Davids, PTS (London, 1909).

Vajrasūci, ed. and tr. by Sujit Kumar Mukhopadhyaya (Santiniketan, 1950).

Vasiṣṭha Dharmasūtra, tr. by G. Buhler, SBE, XIV (rpt., Delhi, 1965).

Vāyu Purāṇa, ed. by R.L. Mitra, 2 vols., Bibliotheca Indica (Calcutta, 1880-8).

Vimuttimagga, tr. *The Path of Freedom* by Sona Thera (Colombo, 1961).
Vinaya Piṭaka, ed. by Hermann Oldenberg, 5 vols. (London, 1879-83); tr. *The Book of Discipline* by I.B. Horner, 5 pts., SBB (London, 1938-52).
Yang, Han-sung, *et al.*, tr., *The Hye Ch'o Diary: Memoir of the Pilgrimage to the Five Regions of India* (Berkeley and Seoul, 1987).
On Yuan Chwang's Travels in India, tr. by Thomas Watters, 2 vols. (rpt New Delhi, 1973).

B. Dictionaries and Reference Books

Brandon, Dines, *et al.*, *A Dictionary of Comparative Religion* (London, 1970).
Edgerton, F., *Buddhist Hybrid Sanskrit Dictionary* (Delhi, 1970).
Eliade, Mircea (ed.) *Encyclopedia of Religion* (New York, 1987).
Law, B.C., *History of Pali Literature* (rpt., Delhi, 1983).
Macdonell, A.A. and A.B. Keith, *Vedic Index of Names and Subjects*, 2 vols. (rpt., Delhi, 1982).
Malalasekera, G.P., *Dictionary of Pali Proper Names* (rpt., New Delhi, 1983).
Monier-Williams, M., *Sanskrit-English Dictionary* (2nd revd. edn., Delhi, 1981).
Rhys Davids, *et al.*, *Pali-English Dictionary* (rpt., New Delhi, 1975).
Upasak, C.S., *Dictionary of Early Buddhist Monastic Terms* (Varanasi, 1975).
Winternitz, M., *A History of Indian Literature*, 3 vols. (revd. edn., Delhi, 1983).

C. Secondary Works

Ahn, Kye-hyon, Palgwanhoego, *Tongguk Sahak*, vol. IV (Seoul, 1956).
Aiyangar, K.V.R., *Aspects of Ancient Indian Economic Thought* (Varanasi, 1965).
Allchin, F.R., 'Evidence of Early Distillation at Shaikhan Dheri', *South Asian Archaeology*, 1979.
Allen, Douglas, *Structure and Creativity in Religion, Hermeneutics in Mircea Eliade's Phenomenology and New Directions* (The Hague, 1978).
Ames, Michael M., 'Magical-animism and Buddhism: A Structural Analysis of the Sinhalese Religious System', *JAS*, XXIII, June, 1964.
Babb, Lawrence A., *The Divine Hierarchy: Popular Hinduism in Central India* (New York, 1975).
Bagchi, P.C., *India and China* (2nd revd. edn., Calcutta, 1981).
Bakker, Hans, 'The Rise of Ayodhya as a Place of Pilgrimage', *Indo-Iranian Journal*, vol. 24, 1982.
Barua, B.M., *Aśoka and His Inscriptions*, pt. 1 (3rd edn., Calcutta, 1968).
Barua, D.K., 'Buddha's Ethical Discourses to the Laity', *ME*, 1967.
Barua, P.R., 'Brhamin Doctrine of Sacrifice and Rituals in the Pali Canon', *JASP*, I, 1956, no. 1.
de Bary, W.M. Theodore, *et al.*, *Sources of Indian Tradition* (rpt., Delhi, 1988).

Beattie, J.H.M., 'Culture Contact and Social Change', *BJS*, vol. 12, 1961.

Beyer, Stephen, *Magic and Ritual in Tibet, The Cult of Tara* (Indian edn., Delhi, 1988).

Bhagat, M.G., *Ancient Indian Asceticism* (New Delhi, 1976).

Bhattacharyya, Benoytosh, *An Introduction to Buddhist Esoterism* (Indian rpt., Delhi, 1980).

Bhattacharyya, N.N., *The Indian Mother Goddess* (2nd edn., New Delhi, 1977).

———, *History of the Tantric Religion* (New Delhi, 1982).

———, *Indian Puberty Rites* (2nd revd. edn., New Delhi, 1980).

———, 'Popular Buddhism', *IHQ*, vol. XXI, 1945.

Bianchi, U., *et al.*, *Problems and Methods of the History of Religions* (Leiden, 1972).

Birnbaum, Raoul, *The Healing Buddha* (revd. edn., Boston, 1979).

Bloch, Maurice, *Ritual, History and Power,* Selected Papers in Anthropology (London, 1989).

Bongard-Levin, G.M., *A Complex Study of Ancient India* (Delhi, 1986).

———, *Mauryan India* (New Delhi, 1985)

Bose, A., *Social and Rural Economy of North India* (Calcutta, 1961).

Bougle, Celestine, *Essays on the Caste System* (Cambridge, 1971).

Burgges, S., *The Buddhist Stupas of Amaravati and Jaggayyapeta* (rpt., Varanasi, 1970).

Cannadine, David and Price, Simon, *Rituals of Royalty: Power and Ceremonial in Traditional Societies* (Cambridge, 1987).

Casson, L., *Ancient Trade and Society* (Detroit, 1984).

Champakalakshmi, R., 'Urbanisation in South India: The Role of Ideology and Polity', *PIHC*, 1986.

Chanana, D.R., *Slavery in Ancient India: As Depicted in Pali and Sanskrit Texts* (Delhi, 1960).

Chappell, David W., *Buddhist and Taoist Practice in Medieval Chinese Society* (Hawaii, 1987).

Chatterjee, Bhaskar, 'Religion and Policy in the Kushana Age', *JIH*, LIV, 1976.

Chattopadhyaya, B., *The Age of the Kushanas, A Numismatic Study* (Calcutta, 1967).

Chattopadhyaya, D.P., *Lokāyata* (4th edn., New Delhi, 1978).

———, *What is Living and What is Dead in Indian Philosophy* (2nd edn., New Delhi, 1977).

———, *Science and Society in Ancient India* (rpt., New Delhi, 1979).

Ch'en, Kenneth, K.S. *The Chinese Transformation of Buddhism* (Princeton, 1973).

———, *Buddhism in China, A Historical Survey* (2nd edn., Princeton, 1973).

Childe, G., *What Happened in History?* (London, 1942).

Choe, Nam-son (ed.), *Shinjong Samgukyusa* (Seoul, 1922).

Coedes, G., tr., H.M. Wright, *The Making of South East Asia* (rpt., London, 1966).

Cohn, Bernard S., *An Anthropologist among the Historians and Other Essays* (Delhi, 1987).

Das, Dipakranjan, *Economic History of Deccan* (Delhi, 1969).

De, Gokuldas, *Democracy in Early Buddhist Samgha* (Calcutta, 1955).

Desai, Santosh N., 'Rāmāyaṇa—An Instrument of Historical Contact and Cultural Transmission Between India and Asia', *JAS*, vol. 30, 1970-1.

Devahuti, D., Harsha, *A Political Study* (2nd edn., Delhi, 1983).

Dhammaratna, U., *Buddha and Caste System* (Shravasti Balrampur, 1969).

Dharma, P.C., 'Some Customs and Beliefs from the Ramayana', *PO*, II, 1937-8, pt. 2.

Drekmeier, C., *Kingship and Community in Early India* (Stanford, 1962).

Dumont, Louis, *Homo Hierarchichus* (Indian edn., Delhi, 1988).

———, 'Kingship in Ancient India', *CIS*, no. 6, December 1962.

Durkheim, E., *The Elementary Forms of the Religious Life* (London, 1915).

Dutt, N., *Early Monastic Buddhism*, 2 vols. (Calcutta, 1941).

———, *Mahāyāna Buddhism* (revd. edn., Delhi, 1978).

———, *Aspects of Mahāyāna Buddhism and its Relation to Hīnayāna* (London, 1930).

———, 'Popular Buddhism', *IHQ*, vol. XXI, 1945.

Dutt, S., *Buddhist Monks and Monasteries of India* (rpt., Delhi, 1988).

———, *Early Buddhist Monachism* (2nd edn., New Delhi, 1984).

Eliade, M., *Patterns in Comparative Religion* (London, 1958).

———, *Shamanism, Archaic Techniques of Ecstasy* (New York, 1964).

Evers, Hans-Dieter, *Monks, Priests and Peasants, A Study of Buddhism and Social Structure in Central Ceylon* (Leiden, 1972).

Fick, R., *The Social Organization in North-East India in Buddha's Time* (rpt., Delhi, 1972).

Frazer, J.G., *The Golden Bough: A Study in Magic and Religion* (London, 1954).

Getty, Alice, *The Gods of Northern Buddhism* (1st Indian edn., Delhi, 1978).

Ghoshal, U.N., *A History of Indian Political Ideas* (Oxford, 1959).

Ghurye, G.S., *Caste and Class in India* (Oxford, 1959).

Glasenapp, Helmuth Von, tr. by Irmgard Schloegl, *Buddhism—A Non-Theistic Religion* (London, 1954).

Gluckman, Max., *Politics Law and Ritual in Tribal Societies* (Oxford, 1977).

Gokhale, B.G., 'The Early Buddhist Elite', *JIH*, XLIII, pt. ii, 1965.

———, 'Dhammiko Dhammarāja: A Study in Buddhist Constitutional Concepts', *Indica*. Silver Jubilee Commemoration volume of the Indian Historical Research Institute (Bombay, 1953).

———, 'Early Buddhist Kingship', *JAS*, XXXI, 1, November 1966.

———, 'Brāhmaṇas in Early Buddhist Literature', *JIH*, XLVIII, 1970.

Gombrich, Richard F., *Precept and Practice: Traditional Buddhism in the Rural Highlands of Ceylon* (Oxford, 1971).

——— (ed.), *Indian Ritual and Its Exegesis* (Delhi, 1988).

Gonda, J., *Ancient Indian Kingship from the Religious Point of View* (Leiden, 1969).

———, *Change and Continuity in Indian Religion* (rpt., New Delhi, 1985).

Goody, Jack, 'Religion and Ritual: The Definitional Problem', *BJS*, vol. 12, 1961.

Gopal, Lallanji, 'India's Foreign Trade in the Ancient Period—Its Impact on Society', *QRHS*, V, 1965-6.

Goyal, S.R., *A History of Indian Buddhism* (Meerut, 1987).

Gunawardana, R.A.L.H., *Robe and Plough, Monasticism and Economic Interest in Early Medieval Sri Lanka* (Arizona, 1978).

Habib, Irfan, *Caste and Money in Indian History* (Bombay, 1987).

Hall, D.G.E., *A History of South-East Asia* (London, 1964).

Hardacre, Helen, 'The Transformation of Healing in the Japanese New Religion', *HR*, vol. 21, no. 4, May 1982.

Harper, Edward B., 'Ritual Pollution as an Integrator of Caste and Religion', *JAS*, XXIII, June 1964.

Hazra, Kanai Lal, *Buddhism in India as Described by the Chinese Pilgrims* (New Delhi, 1983).

Heesterman, J.C., 'The King's Order', *CIS* (n.s.), 20, 1, 1986.

———, 'Reflections on the Significance of the Daksina', *Indo-Iranian Journal*, III, 1959.

Holt, John Clifford, 'Ritual Expression in the Vinayapitaka: A Prolegomenon', *HR*, vol. 18, no. 1, August 1978.

Hwang, Su-yong, 'Koguryo Kumdong Pulsang-ui Shinnye Ijwa', Hankuk Pulsang-ui Yon-gu (Seoul, 1968).

Jain, J.C., *Life in Ancient India as Depicted in the Jain Canons* (Bombay, 1947).

Jaiswal, Suvira, *The Origin and Development of Vaiṣṇavism* (Delhi, 1967).

Jan, Yun-hwa, 'West India According to Hui-ch'ao's Record', *IHQ*, vol. 39, nos. 1 and 2, 1963.

———, 'South India in the VIII Century Hui-ch'ao's Description Re-examined', *Oriens Extremus*, XII, 1, 1968.

Jha, D.N., 'Early Indian Feudalism: A Historical Critique', *PHIC*, 1979.

Joshi, Lalmani, *Studies in the Buddhistic Culture of India* (rpt., 1987, Delhi).

Jung, C.G., *Psychology and Religion: West and East*, vol. II, tr. by Hull, R.F.C. (London, 1958).

Khosla, Sarla, *Aśvaghoṣa and His Times* (New Delhi, 1986).

Kim, Cheol-chun, 'Silla Sangdae Sahoe-ui Dual Organization', *Yoksahakpo*, no. 2, 1952.

Kim, Chong-hak, *Hankuk Sang-go-sa Yon-gu* (Seoul, 1990).

Kim, Mun-kyong, 'Samguk-kwa Silla Sidae-ui Sinang Kyolsa,' *Sahakchi*, vol. 10, 1976.

Kim, Sam-su, 'Po-ui Chon-gi-chok Chabon Kinung-e Kwanhan Chonggyo Sahoehak-chok Yon-gu', *Munhak Chongkyowa Kyongje* (Seoul, 1979).

Kim, Tae-shik, 'Kaya-ui Sahoe Palchon Tankye', *Hankuk Kodae Kukka-ui Hyongsong*, ed. by Hankuk Kodae Sahakhoe (Seoul, 1990).

Kim, Won-ryong, *Hankuk Minsulsa* (Seoul, 1968).

———, 'Samarquand Afraciab Kungjon Pyokhwa-ui Sajoltan', *Kogo Misul*, nos. 129 and 130 (Seoul, 1976).

Kim, Yeol-gyu, 'Mindam-ei Chonki-chok Yu-hyong', in *Hankuk Minsok-kwa Munhak Yon-gu* (2nd edn., Seoul, 1972).

Kim, Yong-tae, 'Silla Pulgukt'o Sasang', in *Hankuk Pulgyo Sasangsa* (Seoul, 1975).

Kirkland, J. Russel, 'The Spirit of the Mountain: Myth and State in pre-Buddhist Tibet', *HR*, vol. 20, no. 3, February 1982.

Ko, Byung-ik, 'Han-kuk-kwa So-yok', *Che O Hoe Kukche Haksul Kangyonhoe Nonmunchip* (Seoul, 1977).

Kosambi, D.D., *An Introduction to the Study of Indian History* (Bombay, 1975).

———, *The Culture and Civilization of Ancient India in Historical Outline* (rpt., Delhi, 1976).

———, *Myth and Reality: Study in the Formation of Indian Culture* (Bombay, 1962).

Krishna, K.B., *Political and Social Thought of the Buddhist Writers of the Early Christian Era* (Vijayawada, 1960).

Krishnan, Y., 'Was There Any Conflict Between the Brahmanas and Buddhists', *IHQ*, vol. 30, no. 2, 1954.

Lang Andrew, *Myth, Ritual and Religion* (4th edn., London, 1913).

Law, B.C., *Heaven and Hell in Buddhist Perspective* (Calcutta and Simla, 1925).

———, *India as Described in Early Texts of Buddhism and Jainism* (London, 1941).

———, *The Buddhist Conception of Spirits* (Delhi, 1988).

Law, N.N., *Aspects of Ancient Indian Polity* (Oxford, 1921).

Leach, E.R., 'Ritualization in Man in Relation to Conceptual and Social Development', *Philosophical Transactions of the Royal Society of London*, series B, vol. 251, no. 722.

———, *Dialectic in Practical Religion* (Cambridge, 1968).

Lubrun, G., 'Betel Chewing', *Journal of Oriental Research*, vol. XVII (1947-8).

Luders, H., 'A List of Brahmī Inscriptions from the Earliest Times to about AD 400 with the Exception of those of Aśoka', Appendix to *Epigraphia Indica* and *Record of the Archaeological Survey of India*, vol. I, X, 1909-19.

Mabbett, I.W., 'The Symbolism of Mount Meru', *HR*, vol. 23, no. 1, August 1983.

———, 'Varṇas in Angkor and the Indian Caste System', *JAS*, XXXVI, no. 3, May 1977.

Macdonell, A.A., *Vedic Mythology* (rpt., Delhi, 1981).

Majumdar, R.C., *India and South East Asia* (New Delhi, 1979).

———, *Corporate Life in Ancient India* (Calcutta, 1969).

——— (ed.), *The Age of Imperial Unity* (5th edn., Bombay, 1980).

——— (ed.), *The Classical Age* (4th edn., Bombay, 1988).

Malinowski, Bronislaw, *Magic, Science and Religion* (Glencoe, 1948)

Mallik, M.S., 'Brāhmaṇas as Depicted in Pali Canon', *Religion and Society in Ancient India,* S.C. Chattopadhyaya Commemorative Volume (Calcutta, 1984).

Maloney, C., 'The Effect of Early Costal Sea Traffic on the Development of Civilization in South India', Ph.D. thesis, unpublished (University of Pennsylvania, 1968).

Marasinghe, M.M.J., *Gods in Early Buddhism: A Study in their Social and Mythological Milieu as Depicted in the Nikāyas of the Pali Canon* (Sri Lanka, 1974).

Mauss, Marcel, *The Gift* (New York, 1967).

McCrindle, John W., *Ancient India as Described in Classical Literature* (1st Indian edn., New Delhi, 1979).

Mehta, R.N., *Excavations at Devnimori* (Baroda, 1966).

Miller, J.I., *The Spice Trade of the Roman Empire* (Oxford, 1969).

Misra, G.S.P., *The Age of Vinaya* (New Delhi, 1972).

Morgan, L.H., *Ancient Society* (Indian edn., Calcutta, 1982).

Nakamura, Hajime, *Indian Buddhism: A Survey with Bibliographical Notes* (1st Indian edn., Delhi, 1987).

Nandi, R.N., *Religious Institutions and Cults in the Deccan (c. AD 600-1000)* (Delhi, 1973).

———, *Social Roots of Religion in Ancient India* (Calcutta, 1986).

Narain, A.K. (ed.) *Studies in History of Buddhists* (Delhi, 1980).

Nath, Vijay, *Dāna: Gift System in Ancient India* (Delhi, 1987).

Needham, J., *Science and Civilization in China* (Chambridge and New York, 1954).

Noh, Tae-don, 'Tong-ilgi Kwijokui Kyongche Kiban', *Hankuksa* III.

Obeyesekere, Gananath, 'The Great Tradition and the Little in the Perspective of Sinhalese Buddhism', *JAS*, vol. 22, 1963.

O'Flaherty, Wendy Doniger (ed.), *Karma and Rebirth in Classical Indian Traditions* (1st Indian edn., Delhi, 1983).

Olivelle, Patrick, *The Origin and the Early Development of Buddhist Monachism* (Colombo, 1974).

Paek, Nam-woon, *Choson Sahoe Kyongchesa* (Tokyo, 1933).

Pande, G.C., *Śramaṇa Tradition: Its History and Contribution to Indian Culture* (Ahmedabad, 1978).

———, *Studies in the Origin of Buddhism* (3rd edn., Delhi, 1983).

———, *Foundations of Indian Culture*, vol. I, *Spiritual Vision and Symbolic Forms in Ancient India* (2nd edn., Delhi, 1990).

———, *Foudations of Indian Culture*, vol. II, *Dimensions of Ancient Indian Social History* (2nd edn., Delhi, 1990).

Pandeya, R.C. (ed.), *Buddhist Studies in India* (Delhi, 1975).

Pankhurst, R., *An Introduction to the Economic History of Ethiopia* (London, 1961).

Park, Tae-wha, 'Silla Sidae-ui Milkyo Cholraego', *Cho myong-gi Paksa Hwangab Kinyom Pulkyosa Nonch'ong* (Seoul, 1969).

Price, S.R.F., *Rituals and Power: The Roman Imperial Cult in Asia Minor* (Cambridge, 1984).

Przyluski, J., *The Legend of Emperor Aśoka in Indian and Chinese Texts*, tr. by D.K. Biswas (Calcutta, 1967).

———, 'Uposatha', *IHQ*, XII, no. 3, September 1936.

Puri, B.N., *India under the Kushanas* (Bombay, 1965).

Radcliffe Brown, A.R., *Structure and Function in Primitive Society* (London, 1952).

Rahula, Walpola, *History of Buddhism in Ceylon, the Anuradhapura Period Third Century BC–Tenth Century AD* (Colombo, 1956).

Rahula, Bhikkhu Telwatte, *A Critical Study of the Mahavastu* (Delhi, 1978).

Rapson, E.J., *The Cambridge History of India*, vol. I (London, 1921).

Raschke, M.G., 'New Studies in Roman Commerce with the East', *Aufsteig und Niedergang der Romischer Weit* (Berlin, 1978).

Rawlinson, H.G., *Intercourse Between India and the Western World: From the Earliest Times to the Fall of Rome* (rpt., Delhi, 1977).

Ray, Himanshu P., *Monastery and Guild: Commerce under the Satavahanas* (Delhi, 1986).

———, 'Early Trade in the Bay of Bengal', *IHR*, XIV, nos. 1-2 (July 1987 and January 1988).

Raychaudhri, H.C., *The Early History of the Vaiṣṇava Sect* (Calcutta, 1920).

Rea, A., *South Indian Buddhist Antiquities* (Madras, 1984).

Rhys Davids, T.W., *Early Buddhism* (London, 1908).

Ryan, Bryce, *Caste in Modern Ceylon, A System in Transition* (New Brunswick, 1953).

Saraswati, B.N., *Brahmanic Ritual Tradition* (Simla, 1977).

Sarkisyanz, E., *Buddhist Backgrounds of the Burmese Revolution* (The Hague, 1965).

Sen, Madhu (ed.), *Studies in Religion and Change* (New Delhi, 1983).

Sen, Mohit and M.B. Rao (eds.), *Das Kapital Centenary Volume* (Delhi, 1967).

Seneviratne, S., 'Social Base of Early Buddhism in South-east India and Sri Lanka', Ph.D. thesis (Jawaharlal Nehru University, 1985).

Sharma, Jagdish P. and Lee Siegel, *Dream Symbolism in the Sramanic Traditions* (Calcutta, 1980).

Sharma, R.S., *Indian Feudalism* (2nd edn., Delhi, 1980).

———, *Perspectives in Social and Economic History of Early India* (New Delhi, 1983).

———, *Aspects of Political Ideas and Institutions in Ancient India* (2nd edn., Delhi, 1968).

———, *Śūdras in Ancient India* (2nd revd edn., Delhi, 1980).

———, (ed.) *Indian Society: Historical Probings, In Memory of D.D. Kosambi* (3rd edn., New Delhi, 1984).

Shin, Chong-won, 'Silla-ui Pulkyo Chonrae-wa Ku Suyong Kwajong-e Tauhan Chaegomt'o', in *Paiksanhakpo,* vol. 22, 1977.

Shrimali, K.M., 'Religion, Ideology and Society', *pro.IHC,* 1988.

——— (ed.), *Essays in Indian Art, Religion and Society* (Delhi, 1987).

de Silva, L.A., *Buddhism: Beliefs and Practices in Sri Lanka* (Sri Lanka, 1974).

Singh, M. M., 'Dhamma of the Jātakas', *JBRS,* 1963.

———, 'The Early Jain Monastic Life', *IHQ,* XXXVI, 1960.

———, 'Life in the Buddhist Monastery during the Sixth Century BC', *JBRS,* XI, 1954.

Sircar, D.C., *Select Inscriptions,* vol. 1 (rpt., New Delhi, 1991).

———, *Inscriptions of Aśoka* (3rd edn., New Delhi).

——— (ed.), *Religious Life in Ancient India* (Calcutta, 1972).

——— (ed.), *Social Life in Ancient India* (Calcutta, 1972).

——— (ed.), *Early Indian Political and Administrative System* (Calcutta, 1972).

Slater, Robert Lawson, *Paradox and Nirvāṇa: A Study of Religious Ultimates with Special Reference to Burmese Buddhism* (Chicago, 1951).

Smith, Bardwell L., (ed.), *Religion and Legitimation of Power in Sri Lanka* (Chambersburg, 1978).

——— (ed.), *Essays on Gupta Culture* (Delhi, 1983).

Soni, R.L., 'Aspects of Dāna', *MB,* no. 65, 1957.

Spellman, John. W., *Political Theory of Ancient India* (Oxford, 1964).

Spiro, Melford E., *Buddhism and Society: A Great Tradition and Its Burmese Vicissitudes* (London, 1971).

Stcherbatsky, Thodore, *The Conception of Buddhist Nirvāṇa* (rpt., Delhi, 1989).

Strong, John S., *The Legend of King Aśoka* (1st Indian edn., Delhi, 1989).

Suzuki, D.T., *On Indian Mahāyāna Buddhism* (New York, 1968).

Swearer, Donald K., *Buddhism and Society in Southeast Asia* (Chambersburg, 1981).

Syed, A.J. (ed.), *D.D. Kosambi on History and Society; Problems of Interpretation* (Bombay, 1985).

Tambiah, S.J., *Culture, Thought, and Social Action* (Cambridge, 1985).

———, *World Conqueror and World Renouncer* (Cambridge, 1976).

Thakur, Upendra, 'Religion and Culture: A Study in Hindu Ethics', *Religion and Society in Ancient India*, S.C. Chattopadhyaya Commemoration Volume (Calcutta, 1984).

———, 'A Study in Barter and Exchange in Ancient India', *JESHO*, XIV, 1971.

Thapar, Romila, *Ancient Indian Social History: Some interpretations* (New Delhi, 1978).

———, *Cultural Transaction and Early India: Tradition and Patronage* (New Delhi, 1987).

———, 'Religion and the Social Order', *CIS* (n.s.), 21, 1, 1987.

Thomson, G., *Studies in Ancient Greek Society*, vol. I (London, 1949).

Varma, Viswanath Prasad, *Early Buddhism and Its Origins* (New Delhi, 1973).

Wagle, N., *Society at the Time of the Buddha* (Bombay, 1966).

Warder, A.K., *Indian Buddhism* (2nd revd. edn., Delhi, 1980).

Warren, Henry Clarke, *Buddhism in translations* (rpt., Delhi, 1987).

Weber, Max, *The Religion of India* (New York, 1958).

———, *The Sociology of Religion* (rpt., London, 1965).

Wells, Kenneth E., *Thai Buddhism: Its Rites and Activities* (Bangkok, 1960).

Yadava, B.N.S., *Society and Culture in Northern India in the Twelfth Century* (Allahabad, 1973).

Yalman, Nur, 'The Structure of Sinhalese Healing Rituals', *JAS*, special issue, 23.

Yazdani, G., *Ajanta* (London, 1930-55).

——— (ed.), *The Early History of the Deccan*, 2 vols. (Indian edn., New Delhi, 1982).

Yi, Ki-baek, *Silla Sasangsa Yonku* (2nd edn., Seoul, 1986).

Yi, Ki-baek and Yi, Ki-dong, *Hankuksa Kangjwa*, vol. I (Seoul, 1982).

Yi, Ki-dong, *Silla Kolpum-je Sahoe-wa Hwarangdo* (Seoul, 1984).

Yi, Woo-sung, 'Samukyusa Sojae Choyong Solhwa-ui I1 Punsok', *Kim Jae-won Paksa Hoegab Kinyom Nonch'ong* (Seoul, 1969).

Yi, Yong-bom, 'Ch'oyong Solhwa-ui Il Koch'al,' *Chindanhakpo*, vol. 32, 1969.

———, Yi, Yong-bom, 'Samkuksagi-e Poinun Islam Sangindul-ui Muyokp'um', *Yi Hongjik Paksa Hwangap Kinyom Nonmunjip* (Seoul, 1969).

Zimmer, Heinrich, *Myths and Symbols in Indian Art and Civilization* (New York, 1962).

Zurcher, E., *The Buddhist Conquest of China* (Leiden, 1959).

Index

रादशगीव् : द सुंबा वीर COLOR

विवेक कुमार पांडे शंभूनाथ

Made with ♥ on the Notion Press Platform
www.notionpress.com

- यह कहानी है लंकेश पति रावण की रादशगीवृ : द सुंबा वीर ।

रावण ने पहली बार सुंबा को जीतकर उस पर शासन किया । फिर लंका के नरेश बने रावण।

कहते हैं रावण के दस सिर थे। क्या सचमुच यह सही है? कुछ विद्वान मानते हैं कि रावण के दस सिर नहीं थे किंतु वह दस सिर होने का भ्रम पैदा कर देता था इसी कारण लोग उसे दशानन कहते थे। कुछ विद्वानों अनुसार रावण छह दर्शन और चारों वेद का ज्ञाता था इसीलिए उसे दसकंठी भी कहा जाता था। दसकंठी कहे जाने के कारण प्रचलन में उसके दस सिर मान लिए गए।

जैन शास्त्रों में उल्लेख है कि रावण के गले में बड़ी-बड़ी गोलाकार नौ मणियां होती थीं। उक्त नौ मणियों में उसका सिर दिखाई देता था जिसके कारण उसके दस सिर होने का भ्रम होता था।हालांकि ज्यादातर विद्वान और पुराणों अनुसार तो यही सही है कि रावण एक मायावी व्यक्ति था, जो अपनी माया के द्वारा दस सिर के होने का भ्रम पैदा कर सकता था। उसकी मायावी शक्ति और जादू के चर्चे जग प्रसिद्ध थे।र वण के दस सिर होने की चर्चा रामचरितमानस में आती है। वह कृष्णपक्ष की अमावस्या को युद्ध के लिए चला था तथा एक-एक दिन क्रमशः एक-एक सिर कटते थे। इस तरह दसवें दिन अर्थात् शुक्लपक्ष की दशमी को रावण का वध हुआ। इसीलिए दशमी के दिन रावण दहन किया जाता है।

रामचरितमानस में वर्णन आता है कि जिस सिर को राम अपने बाण से काट देते थे पुनः उसके स्थान पर दूसरा सिर उभर आता था। विचार करने की बात है कि क्या एक अंग के कट जाने पर वहाँ पुनः नया अंग उत्पन्न हो सकता है? वस्तुतः रावण के ये सिर कृत्रिम थे- आसुरी माया से बने हुए। मारीच का चांदी के बिन्दुओं से युक्त स्वर्ण मृग बन जाना, रावण का सीता के समक्ष राम का कटा हुआ सिर रखना आदि से सिद्ध होता है कि राक्षस मायावी थे। वे अनेक प्रकार के इन्द्रजाल (जादू) जानते थे। तो रावण के दस सिर और बीस हाथों को भी मायावी या कृत्रिम माना जा सकता है।

नाभि में जीवन : ऐसी मान्यता है कि रावण ने अमृत्व प्राप्ति के उद्देश्य से भगवान ब्रह्मा की घोर तपस्या कर वरदान माँगा, लेकिन ब्रह्मा ने उसके इस वरदान को न मानते हुए कहा कि तुम्हारा जीवन नाभि में स्थित रहेगा। रावण की अजर-अमर रहने की इच्छा रह ही गई। यही कारण था कि जब भगवान राम से रावण का युद्ध चल रहा था तो रावण और

उसकी सेना राम पर भारी पड़ने लगे थे। ऐसे में विभीषण ने राम को यह राज बताया कि रावण का जीवन उसकी नाभि में है। नाभि में ही अमृत है। तब राम ने रावण की नाभि में तीर मारा और रावण मारा गया।

रावण का परिवार : रावण ब्राह्मण पिता और राक्षस माता का पुत्र था। वाल्मीकि रामायण के अनुसार रावण पुलस्त्य मुनि का पोता था अर्थात् उनके पुत्र विश्वश्रवा का पुत्र था। विश्वश्रवा की वरवर्णिनी और कैकसी नामक दो पत्नियां थी। वरवर्णिनी के कुबेर को जन्म देने पर सौतिया डाह वश कैकसी ने अशुभ समय में गर्भ धारण किया। इसी कारण से उसके गर्भ से रावण तथा कुम्भकर्ण जैसे क्रूर स्वभाव वाले भयंकर राक्षस उत्पन्न हुए।

ऋषि विश्वश्रवा ने ऋषि भारद्वाज की पुत्री से विवाह किया था जिनसे कुबेर का जन्म हुआ। विश्वश्रवा की दूसरी पत्नी कैकसी से रावण, कुंभकरण, विभीषण और सूर्पणखा पैदा हुई थी। लक्ष्मण ने सूर्पणखा की नाक काट दी थी।

रावण का विवाह : कुबेर को बेदखल कर रावण के लंका में जम जाने के बाद उसने अपनी बहन शूर्पणखा का विवाह कालका के पुत्र दानवराज विद्युविह्वा के साथ कर दिया। उसने स्वयं दिति के पुत्र मय की कन्या मन्दोदरी से विवाह किया, जो हेमा नामक अप्सरा के गर्भ से उत्पन्न हुई थी। माना जाता है कि मंदोदरी राजस्थान के जोधपुर के निकट मन्डोर की थी।

विरोचनकुमार बलि की पुत्री वज्रज्वला से कुम्भकर्ण का और गन्धर्वराज महात्मा शैलूष की कन्या सरमा से विभीषण का विवाह हुआ। कुछ समय पश्चात् मन्दोदरी ने मेघनाद को जन्म दिया, जो इन्द्र को परास्त कर संसार में इन्द्रजीत के नाम से प्रसिद्ध हुआ।

मंदोदरी से रावण को पुत्र मिले- इंद्रजीत, मेघनाद, महोदर, प्रहस्त, विरुपाक्ष भीकम वीर। ऐसा माना जाता है कि राम-रावण के युद्ध एक मात्र विभिषण को छोड़कर उसके पूरे कुल का नाश हो गया था।

रावण का राज्य विस्तार : रावण ने सुंबा और बालीद्वीप को जीतकर अपने शासन का विस्तार करते हुए अंगद्वीप, मलयद्वीप, वराहद्वीप, शंखद्वीप, कुशद्वीप, यवद्वीप और आंध्रालय पर विजय प्राप्त की थी। इसके बाद रावण ने लंका को अपना लक्ष्य बनाया। लंका पर कुबेर का राज्य था।आज के युग अनुसार रावण का राज्य विस्तार, इंडोनेशिया,

मलेशिया, बर्मा, दक्षिण भारत के कुछ राज्य और श्रीलंका पर रावण का राज था।

दरअसल माली, सुमाली और माल्यवान नामक तीन दैत्यों द्वारा त्रिकुट सुबेल पर्वत पर बसाई लंकापुरी को देवों और यक्षों ने जीतकर कुबेर को लंकापति बना दिया था। रावण की माता कैकसी सुमाली की पुत्री थी। अपने नाना के उकसाने पर रावण ने अपनी सौतेली माता इलविल्ला के पुत्र कुबेर से युद्ध की ठानी, परंतु पिता ने लंका रावण को दिलासा दी तथा कुबेर को कैलाश पर्वत के आसपास के त्रिविष्टप (तिब्बत) क्षेत्र में रहने के लिए कह दिया। इसी तारतम्य में रावण ने कुबेर का पुष्पक विमान भी छीन लिया।

रावण ने रचा था नया संप्रदाय : आचार्य चतुरसेन द्वारा रचित बहुचर्चित उपन्यास 'वयम् रक्षामः' तथा पंडित मदन मोहन शर्मा शाही द्वारा तीन खंडों में रचित उपन्यास 'लंकेश्वर' के अनुसार रावण शिव का परम भक्त, यम और सूर्य तक को अपना प्रताप झेलने के लिए विवश कर देने वाला, प्रकांड विद्वान, सभी जातियों को समान मानते हुए भेदभावरहित समाज की स्थापना करने वाला था। सुरों के खिलाफ असुरों की ओर थे रावण। रावण ने आर्यों की भोग-विलास वाली 'यक्ष' संस्कृति से अलग सभी की रक्षा करने के लिए 'रक्ष' संस्कृति की स्थापना की थी। यही राक्षस थे।

शिव तांडव स्तोत्र : रावण ने शिव तांडव स्तोत्र की रचना करने के अलावा अन्य कई तंत्र ग्रंथों की रचना की। रावण ने कैलाश पर्वत ही उठा लिया था और जब पूरे पर्वत को ही लंका ले जाने लगा, तो भगवान शिव ने अपने अंगूठे से तनिक-सा जो दबाया तो कैलाश पर्वत फिर जहां था वहीं अवस्थित हो गया। इससे रावण का हाथ दब गया और वह क्षमा करते हुए कहने लगा- 'शंकर-शंकर'- अर्थात क्षमा करिए, क्षमा करिए और स्तुति करने लग गया। यह क्षमा याचना और स्तुति ही कालांतर में 'शिव तांडव स्तोत्र' कहलाया।

अरुण संहिता : संस्कृत के इस मूल ग्रंथ को अकसर 'लाल-किताब' के नाम से जाना जाता है। इस का अनुवाद कई भाषाओं में हो चुका है। मान्यता है कि इस का ज्ञान सूर्य के सार्थी अरुण ने लंकाधिपति रावण को दिया था। यह ग्रंथ जन्म कुण्डली, हस्त रेखा तथा सामुद्रिक शास्त्र का मिश्रण है।

रावण संहिता : रावण संहित जहां रावण के संपूर्ण जीवन के बारे में बताती है वहीं इसमें ज्योतिष की बेहतर जानकारियों का भंडार है।

रावण पर रचना : पुराणों सहित इतिहास ग्रंथ वाल्मीकि रामायण और रामचरित रामायण में तो रावण का वर्णन मिलता ही है किंतु आधुनिक काल में आचार्य चतुरसेन द्वारा रावण पर 'वयम् रक्षामः' नामक बहुचर्चित उपन्यास लिखा गया है। इसके अलावा पंडित मदनमोहन शर्मा शाही द्वारा तीन खंडों में 'लंकेश्वर' नामक उपन्यास भी पठनीय है।

लंका पुराण : माली, सुमाली और माल्यवान नामक तीन दैत्यों द्वारा त्रिकुट सुबेल पर्वत पर बसाई लंकापुरी को देवों और यक्षों ने जीतकर कुबेर को लंकापति बना दिया था। रावण की माता कैकसी सुमाली की पुत्री थी। अपने नाना के उकसाने पर रावण ने अपनी सौतेली माता इलविल्ला के पुत्र कुबेर से युद्ध की ठानी, परंतु पिता ने लंका रावण को दिला दी तथा कुबेर को कैलाश पर्वत के आसपास के त्रिविष्टप क्षेत्र (तिब्बत) में रहने के लिए कह दिया। इसी तारतम्य में रावण ने कुबेर का पुष्पक विमान भी छीन लिया था।

अन्य मत : कुबेर रावण का सौतेला भाई था। कुबेर धनपति था। कुबेर ने लंका पर राज कर उसका विस्तार किया था। रावण ने कुबेर से लंका को हड़पकर उस पर अपना शासन कायम किया। ऐसा माना जाता है कि लंका को भगवान शिव ने बसाया था। भगवान शिव ने पार्वती के लिए पूरी लंका को स्वर्णजड़ित बनवाया था।

शिवभक्त रावण : एक बार रावण जब अपने पुष्पक विमान से यात्रा कर रहे थे तो रास्ते में एक वनक्षेत्र से गुजर रहे थे। उस क्षेत्र के पहाड़ पर शिवजी ध्यानमग्न बैठे थे। शिव के गण नंदी ने रावण को रोकते हुए कहा कि इधर से गुजरना सभी के लिए निषिद्ध कर दिया गया है, क्योंकि भगवान तप में मगन हैं।रावण को यह सुनकर क्रोध उत्पन्न हुआ। उसने अपना विमान नीचे उतारकर नंदी के समक्ष खड़े होकर नंदी का अपमान किया और फिर जिस पर्वत पर शिव विराजमान थे उसे उठाने लगा। यह देख शिव ने अपने अँगूठे से पर्वत को दबा दिया जिस कारण रावण का हाथ भी दब गया और फिर वह शिव से प्रार्थना करने लगा की मुझे मुक्त कर दें। इस घटना के बाद वह शिव का भक्त बन गया।

रावण की विनम्रता : राम ने जब रामेश्वरम् में शिवलिंग की स्थापना की थी तब विद्वान पंडित की आवश्यकता थी। रावण ने इस आमंत्रण को स्वीकारा था। दूसरी और राम-रावण के युद्ध के दौरान रावण ने लंका के ख्यात आयुर्वेदाचार्य सुषेण द्वारा अनुमति मांगे जाने पर घायल लक्ष्मण की चिकित्सा करने की अनुमति सहर्ष प्रदान की थी। इस तरह रावण की विनम्रता और अच्छाई के किस्से भी कई है।रावण ने दो वर्ष सीता को अपने पास बंधक

बनाकर रखा था, लेकिन उसने भूलवश भी सीता को छूआ तक नहीं था। हालांकि इसके पीछे उसकी प्रतिज्ञा थी।

रावण का शव : अंतरिक्ष एजेंसी नासा का प्लेनेटेरियम सॉफ्टवेयर रामायणकालीन हर घटना की गणना कर सकता है। इसमें राम को वनवास हो, र म-रावण युद्ध हो या फिर अन्य कोई घटनाक्रम। इस सॉफ्टवेयर की गणना बताती है कि ईसा पूर्व 5076 साल पहले राम ने रावण का संहार किया था।

क्रम-सूची

क्रम-सूची

प्रस्तावना

रादशगीवृ : द सुंबा वीर एक अनोखी और महाकाव्य कहानी का उल्लेख किया गया है । इस किताब को लिखने के दौरान कोई भी धर्म या जाति और समाज एवम् किसी भी परिवार के सदस्य को नुक्सान नहीं पहुंचाया गया है। हम किसी को ठेस नहीं पहुंचाना चाहते हैं ।

भूमिका

लेखक जीवनी :

मेरा नाम विवेक कुमार पांडे है और मैं एक लेखक हु , में गुजरात के सुरत में निवास करता हूं.मेरा जन्म ३० सेप्टेंबर २००२ में हुआ था, और मुझे बचपन से एक्टर बनने का सोख रहा है और अभी भी है.। में कभी ये नहीं सोचता की लोग क्या कर रहे हैं में ये सोचता हूं कि में क्या कर रहा हूं, में आज सफल हूं तो अपने पापा की वजह से आज वो रहते तो उन्हें बहुत खुशी होती , वो सदा और हमेशा मेरे साथ रहेंगे.। मेरे रियल लाइफ के सुपरस्टार और सुपर हीरो मेरे प्यारे पापा है । आई लव यू पापा । पापा को मेरे हाथ कि चाय बहुत अच्छी लगती थी ।

जब उनका मन करता था चाय पीने के लिए तो वो कहते थे । मुझे चाय पीना है कौन बनाएगा मम्मी कहती में बना देती हूं लेकिन पापा कहते नहीं मेरा बेटा बनाएंगा । उसके हाथ कि चाय मुझे बहुत अच्छा लगता है । जब भी काम करके घर आने वाले होते हैं तब मुझे फोन करते है विवेक बेटा बोलो क्या खाओगे सेब ले लु । में कहता ठीक है पापा ले लिजिए । पापा कहते कितना लू एक किलो या 2 किलो । में कहता नहीं पापा सिर्फ में ही खाता हूं भईया और दीदी को फल अच्छा ही नहीं लगता है इसलिए 3 सेब ले लेना । लेकिन पापा मेरे लिए दो तीन किलो फल लेकर आ ही जाते थे । पहले ले लेते फिर मुझे फोन करते । हमेशा ऐसा ही करते थे ।

में ये नहीं कह रहा हूं कि मुझे बहुत ज्यादा प्यार और मानते थे । वो अपने तीनों संतानों को प्यार करते थे । सबसे छोटा तो में ही था घर में , मुझसे बड़ी मेरी बहन और मेरी बहन से भी बडे मेरे भईया । में आज भी वो दिन का इंतजार कर रहा हूं जब पापा मेरे लिए कुछ लेकर आएंगे । मेरे कान तरस रहे है वो आवाज़ सुनने के लिए । लेकिन कहते हैं जो चीज चली जाए वो कभी लौटकर नहीं आती है । आप सभी से निवेदन है आप अपने मम्मी और पापा का ध्यान रखें । दुनिया में एक ही भगवान है वो है माता ओर पिता ।

में बहुत ही शरारती था बचपन में । मुझे किताब लिखने का शोख बचपन से ही था । जब में तीसरी कक्षा में पढ़ता था । तब से ही किताब लिखता था में और मेरा दोस्त हम दोनों किताब लिखके सभी को दिखाते थे और कहते थे जिन्हें मेरा किताब अच्छा लगे तो अपना हस्ताक्षर कर दे । मेरे अंदर एक बहुत ही खास विशेषता है में किसी के चक्कर में नहीं रहता हूं । कौन क्या कर रहा है करने दो मुझे कुछ फर्क नहीं पड़ता है । मुझे सिर्फ अपने आप पर ध्यान देना है ।

क्योंकि दुनिया में ऐसे भी लोग हैं जो नहीं खुद कुछ करना चाहते हैं और नहीं दुसरो को कुछ करने देना चाहते हैं । एक बात ध्यान रखें अगर आप कोई भी नया काम करते हैं तो पहले लोग ताना मारते ही है । ये मत करो वो मत करो तुम्हारे बस कि बात नहीं है , तुम नहीं कर सकते हो . मुझे यह पता नहीं चलता लोग इतना सुझाव क्यों देते हैं । हमें जो करना है

हम वहीं करेंगे । कई लोग हैं जो दुसरो के कहने पर वही करते हैं लेकिन मैं आपसे कह रहा हूं आप जो करना चाहे वो करे किसी के कहने पर खाई में मत कुदे । आपकी जिंदगी आपके ही हाथों में है लोगों के हाथों में नहीं है ।

मेरा बस एक ही सपना है की में नाम कमाकर अपने पिताजी का अधुरा सपना पूरा करूं ।

1

शूर्पणखा

पंचवटी के अपने आश्रम में रामचन्द्र सीता के साथ सुखपूर्वक रहने लगे। एक दिन जब राम और लक्ष्मण वार्तालाप कर रहे थे तो वहाँ पर अकस्मात् रावण की बहन शूर्पणखा नामक राक्षसी आ पहुँची। वह राम के तेजस्वी मुखमण्डल, कमल-नयन तथा नीलाम्बुज सदृश शरीर की कान्ति को चकित होकर देख रही थी। राम का मुख सुन्दर था किन्तु शूर्पणखा का मुख अत्यन्त कुरूप था। राम का कटिप्रदेश एवं उदर क्षीण था किन्तु शूर्पणखा बेडौल लंबे पेट वाली थी। राम के नेत्र विशाल एवं मनोहर थे किन्तु शूर्पणखा की आँखें कुरूप तथा डरावनी थीं। राम की वाणी मधुर थी किन्तु शूर्पणखा भैरवनाद करने वाली थी। राम का रुप मनोहर था किन्तु शूर्पणखा का रूप वीभत्स एवं विकराल था।

उन्हें देख कर उसके हृदय में वासना का भाव जागृत हो उठा। इच्छानुसार रूप धारण करने वाली वह राक्षसी मनोहर रूप बनाकर राम के पास पहुँची और बोली, "तुम कौन हो? राक्षसों के इस देश में तुम कैसे आ गये? तुम्हारा वेश तो तपस्वियों जैसा है, किन्तु हाथों में धनुष बाण भी है। साथ में स्त्री भी है। ये बातें परस्पर विरोधी हैं। तुम मुझे अपना परिचय दो"

राम ने सरल भाव से कहा, "हे देवि! मैं अयोध्या के चक्रवर्ती नरेश महाराजा दशरथ का ज्येष्ठ पुत्र राम हूँ। मेरे साथ मेरा छोटा भाई लक्ष्मण और जन्कपुरी के महाराज जनक की राजकुमारी तथा मेरी पत्नी सीता हैं। पिताजी की आज्ञा से हम चौदह वर्ष के लिये वनों में निवास करने के लिये आये हैं। यही हमारा परिचय है। अब तुम अपना परिचय देकर मेरी इस जिज्ञासा को शान्त करो क्योंकि मुझे प्रतीत होता है कि तुम कोई इच्छानुसार रूप धारण करने वाली राक्षसी हो?"

राम के प्रश्न का उत्तर देते हुए वह राक्षसी बोली, "मेरा नाम शूर्पणखा है। मैं लंका के नरेश परम प्रतापी महाराज रावण की बहन हूँ। समस्त संसार में विख्यात विशालकाय कुम्भकरण और परम नीतिवान विभीषण भी मेरे भाई हैं। वे सब लंका में निवास करते हैं। पंचवटी के स्वामी अत्यन्त पराक्रमी खर और दूषण भी मेरे भाई हैं। संसार में शायद ही कोई वीर ऐसा होगा जो इन दोनों भाइयों के साथ समरभूमि में युद्ध करके उन्हें पराजित कर सके। मैं सर्व

प्रकार से सम्पन्न हूँ और अपनी इच्छा तथा शक्ति से समस्त लोकों में विचरण कर सकती हूँ। यह तुम्हारी पत्नी सीता मेरी दृष्टि में कुरूप, ओछी, विकृत मानवी है और तुम्हारे योग्य नहीं है। अतः तुम मेरे पति बन जाओ, मैं ही तुम्हारे अनुरूप हूँ। इस अबला सीता को लेकर तुम क्या करोगे। तुम्हारी भार्या बनने के पश्चात् मैं तुम्हारे भाई और सीता को खा जाऊँगी और तुम्हारे साथ विचरण करूँगी।"

उसके प्रस्ताव के उत्तर में राम मुसकाते हुए बोले, "भद्रे! तुम देख रही हो कि मैं विवाहित हूँ और मेरी पत्नी मेरे साथ है। हाँ, मेरा भाई लक्ष्मण यहाँ अकेला है। वह सुन्दर, शीलवान एवं बल-पराक्रम से सम्पन्न है। यदि तुम चाहो तो उसे सहमत करके उससे विवाह कर सकती हो।"

राम का उत्तर सुन शूर्पणखा ने लक्ष्मण के पास जाकर कहा, "हे राजकुमार! तुम सुन्दर हो और मैं युवा हूँ। तुम्हारे इस सुन्दर रूप के योग्य मैं ही हूँ, अतः मैं ही तुम्हारी परम सुन्दरी भार्य हो सकती हूँ। मुझे अंगीकार कर लेने पर तुम मेरे साथ इस दण्डकारण्य में सुखपूर्वक विचरण कर सकोगे।"

शूर्पणखा के इस विवाह प्रस्ताव को सुन कर वाक्-पटु लक्ष्मण ने कहा, "सुन्दरी! मैं राम का एक तुच्छ सा दास हूँ। मुझसे विवाह करके तुम केवल दासी कहलाओगी। अच्छा यही है कि तुम राम से ही विवाह कर के उनकी छोटी भार्या बन जाओ। तुम्हारा रूप-सौन्दर्य उन्हीं के योग्य है।"

लक्ष्मण के परिहास को न समझ कर शूर्पणखा ने उसे अपनी प्रशंसा समझा। वह पुनः राम के पास जा कर क्रोध से बोली, "हे राम! इस कुरूपा सीता के लिये तुम मेरा विवाह प्रस्ताव अस्वीकार कर के मेरा अपमान कर रहे हो। इसलिये पहले मैं इसे ही मार कर समाप्त किये देती हूँ। फिर तुम्हारे साथ विवाह कर के मैं अपना जीवन आनन्दपूर्वक व्यतीत करूँगी।"

इतना कह कर प्रचंड क्रोध करती हुई शूर्पणखा विद्युत वेग से सीता पर झपटी। राम ने उसके इस आकस्मिक आक्रमण को तत्परतापूर्वक रोका और लक्ष्मण से बोले, "हे वीर! इस दुष्टा राक्षसी से अधिक वाद-विवाद करना या इसके साथ हास्य विनोद करना उचित नहीं है। इसने तो जानकी की हत्या ही कर डाली होती। तुम्हें इस कुरूपा और कुलटा राक्षसी को उसके किसी अंग से विहीन कर देना चाहिये।"

राम की आज्ञा पाते ही लक्ष्मण ने तत्काल खड्ग निकाला और दुष्टा शूर्पणखा के नाक-कान काट डाले। पीड़ा और घोर अपमान के कारण रोती हुई शूर्पणखा अपने भाइयों, खर-दूषण, के पास पहुँची और घोर चीत्कार कर के उनके सामने गिर पड़ी।

2

खर-दूषण से युद्ध

शूर्पणखा का रक्त-रंजित मुखमण्डल देखकर वह क्रोध से काँपते हुये बोला, "बहन! मूर्छा और घबराहट छोड़ मुझे बताओ कि किसने तुम्हें रूपहीन बनाया है? किसने आज इस निद्रानिमग्न नागराज को छेड़ने की मूर्खता की है? किसके सिर पर काल नाच रहा है? मुझे शीघ्र उसका नाम बताओ, उस अपराधी को मेरे क्रोध से देवता, गन्धर्व, पिशाच और राक्षस कोई भी नहीं बचा सकता।"

खर के मुख से निकले इन वचनों सुन कर शूर्पणखा का कुछ धैर्य बँधा। उसने रोते-रोते खर से कहा, " राम और लक्ष्मण नामक दो राजकुमार, जो अयोध्या के राजा दशरथ के पुत्र हैं, इस वन में आये हुये हैं। उनके साथ राम की भार्या सीता भी है। वे दोनों ही बड़े सुन्दर, पराक्रमी और तपस्वी प्रतीत होते हैं। जब मैंने उनसे राम की पत्नी के विषय में पूछा तो वे चिढ़ गये और उनमें से एक ने मेरे नाक-कान काट लिये। भैया! तुम शीघ्र उन्हें परलोक भेज कर उनसे मेरे अपमान का प्रतिशोध लो। मेरे हृदय को शान्ति तभी मिलेगी जब मैं उन तीनों का गरम-गरम रुधिर पी लूँगी।"

तत्काल ही खर ने अपनी सेना के चौदह यमराज के समान भयंकर योद्धा एवं पराक्रमी राक्षसों को आज्ञा दी कि शूर्पणखा के साथ जा कर उन तीनों का वध करो। मेरी बहन को वहीं उनके शरीर का गरम-गरम रक्त पिला कर इसके अपमान कि ज्वाला को शान्त करो। खर की आज्ञा पाते ही वे राक्षस भयंकर अस्त्र-शस्त्रों से सुसज्जित होकर राम, लक्ष्मण तथा सीता का वध करने के लिये शूर्पणखा के साथ चल पड़े।

शूर्पणखा के साथ इस राक्षस दल को देखकर राम लक्ष्मण से बोले, "लक्ष्मण! तुम सीता के पास खड़े होकर उसकी रक्षा करो। मैं अभी इन राक्षसों को मार कर यमलोक भेजता हूँ।"

इसके पश्चात् राम धनुष पर प्रत्यंचा चढ़ा कर बाण सँभालकर उन राक्षसों से बोले, "दुष्टों! हम लोग तपस्वी धर्म का पालन कर रहे हैं और किसी निर्दोष पर कभी वार नहीं करते। तुम सब पापात्मा तथा ऋषियों का अपराध करने वाले हो। उन ऋषि-मुनियों की आज्ञा से ही मैं धनुष-बाण लेकर तुम लोगों का वध करने आया हूँ। तुम्हें यदि युद्ध से संतोष

प्राप्त होता हो तो यहाँ ही खड़े रहो अन्यथा लौट जाओ।"

उन राक्षसों ने एक साथ राम पर अपने शस्त्रों से आक्रमण कर दिया। प्रत्युत्तर में राम ने एक साथ चौदह बाण छोड़े जिन्होंने उनकी छातियों में घुस कर उनके प्राणों का हरण कर लिया। वे भूमि पर गिर कर तड़पने लगे और मृत्यु को प्राप्त हुये।

सभी राक्षसों के इस प्रकार मर जाने पर शूर्पणखा रोती-बिलखती खर के पास जाकर बोली, "उन सब राक्षसों को अकेले राम ने ही वध कर डाला। वे सब मिल कर भी उसका कुछ न कर सके। मुझे तो प्रतीत होता है कि तुम महासमर में सबल होने के बाद भी राम के सामने युद्ध में नहीं ठहर सकोगे। यदि तुम स्वयं को शूरवीर समझते हो तो तुम अपनी सम्पूर्ण शक्ति लगा कर उससे युद्ध करो। यदि तुमने शत्रुघाती राम का वध नहीं किया तो मैं तुम्हारे समक्ष ही आत्महत्या करके अपना प्राण त्याग दूँगी।"

शूर्पणखा के द्वारा इस प्रकार तिरस्कृत होने पर खर ने क्रोधित होकर कहा, "शूर्पणखे! तू व्यर्थ ही भयभीत हो कर आत्महत्या करने का प्रलाप कर रही है। मैं तत्काल जाकर उन दोनों भाइयों का वध कर डालूँगा। मेरे समक्ष उनका तेज वैसे ही है जैसे कि सूर्य के सामने जुगनू। तू अकारण चिंता करना त्याग दे।"

शूर्पणखा को सान्त्वना देकर खर अपनी विशाल सेना, जिसमें चौदह सहस्त्र विकट योद्धा थे, को साथ लेकर राम से संग्राम करने के लिये तीव्र गति से चला। विशाल सेना के साथ खर को आते देख कर राम ने लक्ष्मण से कहा, "महाबाहो! ऐसा प्रतीत होता है कि राक्षसराज अपने पूरे दल-बल के साथ चला आ रहा है। आज आर्य और अनार्य के मध्य संघर्ष होगा और निःसन्देह आर्य की विजय होगी। तुम सीता की रक्षा के लिये उसे साथ ले कर शीघ्र ही किसी गुफा में चले जाओ ताकि मैं निश्चिंत होकर युद्ध कर सकूँ।"

लक्ष्मण ने तत्काल अपने अग्रज की आज्ञा पालन किया। वे सीता को ले कर पर्वत की एक अँधेरी कन्दरा में चले गये। अभेद्य कवच धारण कर के राम युद्ध के लिये तैयार हो गये। देवता, यक्ष, किन्नर, गन्धर्व आदि सभी राम के विजय के लिये परमात्मा से इस प्रकार प्रार्थना करने लगे कि हे त्रिलोकीनाथ! वीर पराक्रमी रामचन्द्र को इतनी शक्ति प्रदान करो कि उनके हाथों गौ, ब्राह्मणों तथा ऋषि-मुनियों को अनेक प्रकार से कष्ट देने वाले राक्षसों का नाश हो सके। राक्षसों की सेना ने राम को चारों ओर से घेर लिया तथा आक्रमण की तैयारी करने लगे। राम ने भीषण विनाश करने वाली अग्नि बाण छोड़ दिया जिससे राक्षस हाहाकार करने लगे। राम तत्परता के साथ राक्षसों के द्वारा छोड़े गये बाणों को अपने बाणों से आकाश में ही काटने लगे।

इस पर राक्षसों ने अत्यन्त क्रोधित होकर एक साथ बाणों की वर्षा करना आरम्भ कर दिया और राम चारों ओर से उनके बाणों से आच्छादित हो गये। राम ने अपने धनुष को मण्डलाकार करके अद्भुत हस्त-लाघव का प्रदर्शन करते हुये बाणों को छोड़ना आरम्भ कर दिया जिससे राक्षसों के बाण कट-कट कर भूमि पर गिरने लगे। यह ज्ञात ही नहीं हो पाता था कि कब उन्होंने तरकस से बाण निकाला, कब प्रत्यंचा चढ़ाई और कब बाण छूटा। राम के

बाणों के लगने से राक्षसगण निष्प्राण होकर भूमि में लेटने लगे। अल्पकाल में ही राक्षसों की सेना उसी भाँति छिन्न-भिन्न हो गई जैसे आँधी आने पर बादल छिन्न-भिन्न हो जाते हैं। पूरा युद्धस्थल राक्षसों के कटे हुये अंगों से पट गया।

3

खर-दूषण वध

खर की सेना की दुर्दशा देख कर दूषण अपनी विशाल सेना को साथ ले कर राम के समक्ष आ डटा। कुछ ही काल में राम के बाणों से उसकी सेना की भी वैसी ही दशा हो गई जैसा कि खर की सेना की हुई थी। अपनी सेना की दुर्दशा देख कर क्रुद्ध दूषण ने मेघ के समान घोर गर्जना की और तीक्ष्ण बाणों की वर्षा आरम्भ कर दी। उसके इस आक्रमण से कुपित होकर राम ने चमकते खुर से दूषण के धनुष को काट डाला तथा एक साथ चार बाण छोड़ कर उसके रथ के चारों घोड़ों को बींध दिया जिससे चारों घोड़े निष्प्राण होकर भूमि पर गिर पड़े। पुनः राम ने एक अर्द्ध चन्द्राकार बाण छोड़कर दूषण के सारथी के सिर को धड़ से अलग कर दिया।

इस पर क्रोधित दूषण एक परिध उठा कर राम को मारने झपटा। राम ने भी पलक झपकते ही अपना खड्ग निकाल लिया और दूषण के दोनों हाथ काट डाले। पीड़ा से छटपटाता हुआ वह मूर्छित होकर धराशायी हो गया। दूषण की ऐसी दशा देख कर सैकड़ों राक्षसों ने एक साथ राम पर आक्रमण कर दिया। प्रत्युत्तर में रामचन्द्र ने स्वर्ण तथा वज्र से निर्मित तीक्ष्ण बाण छोड़ कर उन सभी राक्षसों का नाश कर दिया। इस प्रकार से दूषण सहित उसकी अपार सेना यमलोक पहुँच गई।

अब केवल दो लोग ही शेष रह गये थे – खर और उसका सेनापति त्रिशिरा। खर का मनोबल टूट चुका था। अतः उसे धैर्य बँधाते हुये त्रिशिरा ने कहा, "हे राक्षसराज! धैर्य धारण कीजिये। मैं अभी राम का वध करके अपने सैनिकों के वध का प्रतिशोध लेता हूँ। मैं प्रतिज्ञा करता हूँ कि मैं उस तपस्वी को अवश्य मारूँगा अन्यथा मैं युद्धभूमि में अपने प्राण त्याग दूँगा।"

खर को सान्त्वना दे कर वह राम की ओर द्रुत गति से झपटा। उसे अपनी ओर आते देख राम ने तत्परतापूर्वक बाण चलना आरम्भ कर दिया। राम के बाणों से त्रिशिरा के सारथी, घोड़े तथा ध्वजा कट गये। रथ तथा सारथी विहीन सेनापति हाथ में गदा ले कर राम की ओर दौड़ा, किन्तु पराक्रमी राम ने उसे अपने निकट पहुँचने के पहले ही तीक्ष्ण बाण छोड़ा जो उसके कवच को चीर कर हृदय तक पहुँच गया। हृदय में बाण लगते ही त्रिशिरा हतप्राण

होकर भूमि पर गिर गया। उस स्थान की सारी भूमि रक्त-रंजित हो गई।

सेनापति के वध हुआ देख कर क्रुद्ध खर राम पर अंधाधुंध बाणों की वर्षा करने लगा। उसके बाण वायुमण्डल में सभी दिशाओं में फैल गये। इस पर राम ने अग्निबाणों की बौछार करना आरम्भ कर दिया। और भी क्रुद्ध होकर खर ने एक बाण से रामचन्द्र के धनुष को काट दिया। खर के इस अद्भुत पराक्रम को देख कर यक्ष, गन्धर्व आदि भी आश्चर्यचकित रह गये, किन्तु अदम्य योद्धा राम तनिक भी विचलित नहीं हुये। उन्होंने अगस्त्य ऋषि के द्वारा दिया हुआ धनुष उठा कर क्षणमात्र में खर के घोड़ों को मार गिराया। रथहीन हो जाने पर अत्यन्त क्रोधित हो कर पराक्रमी खर हाथ में गदा ले राम को मारने के लिये दौड़ा। उसे अपनी ओर आता देख राघव बोले, "हे राक्षसराज! यदि सम्पूर्ण ब्रह्माण्ड का स्वामी भी निर्दोषों तथा सज्जनों को दुःख देता है तो उसे अन्त में अपने पापों का फल भोगना ही पड़ता है। तुझे भी निर्दोष ऋषि-मुनियों को भयंकर यातनाएँ देने का परिणाम भुगतना पड़ेगा। मैं तुझ जैसे अधर्मी, दुष्ट- दानवों का विनाश करने के लिये ही वन में आया हूँ। अब तेरा भी अन्तिम समय आ पहुँचा है। अब किसी भाँति तू बच नहीं सकता।"

राम के वचनों को सुन कर खर ने कहा, "हे अयोध्या के राजकुमार! तुमने स्वयं के मुख से स्वयं की प्रशंसा करके अपनी तुच्छता का ही परिचय दिया है। तुममें इतना सामर्थ्य नहीं है कि तुम मेरा वध कर सको। मेरी यह गदा आज यह तुम्हें चिरनिद्रा में सुला देगी।"

इतना कह कर खर ने अपनी शक्तिशाली गदा को राम के हृदय का लक्ष्य करके फेंका। राम ने एक ही बाण से उस गदा को काट दिया और एक साथ अनेक बाण छोड़ कर खर के शरीर को क्षत-विक्षत कर दिया। क्षत-विक्षत होने परे भी खर क्रुद्ध सर्प की भाँति राम की ओर झपटा। उसे अपनी ओर लपकते देख कर राम ने अगस्त्य मुनि द्वारा दिये गये एक ही बाण से खर का हृदय चीर डाला। भयानक चीत्कार करता हुआ खर विशाल पर्वत की भाँति धराशायी हो गया और उसकी इहलीला समाप्त हो गई।

राम के विजय पर ऋषि-मुनि, तपस्वी आदि उनकी जय-जयकार करते हुये उन पर पुष्प वर्षा करने लगे। उन्होंने राम की भूरि-भूरि प्रशंसा करते हुये कहा, "हे राघव! आपके इस महान उपकार को दण्डक वन के निवासी तपस्वी कभी न भुला सकेंगे। इन राक्षसों ने अपने विप्लव से हमारा जीवन, हमारी तपस्या, हमारी शान्ति सब कुछ नष्टप्राय कर दिये थे। आज से हम लोग आपकी कृपा से निर्भय और निश्चिन्त हो गये हैं। परमपिता परमात्मा आपका कल्याण करें। आशीर्वाद देकर वे अपने-अपने निवास स्थानों को लौट गये। लक्ष्मण भी सीता को गिरिकन्दरा से ले कर लौट आये। अपने महापराक्रमी पति की शौर्य गाथा सुन कर सीता का हृदय गद्-गद् हो गया।

4

रावण को सूचना

खर-दूषण का वध हो जाने पर खर के एक अकम्पन नामक सैनिक ने, जिसने किसी प्रकार से भागकर अपने प्राण बचा लिये थे, लंका में जाकर रावण को खर की सेना के नष्ट हो जाने की सूचना दी। रावण के समक्ष जाकर वह हाथ जोड़ कर बोला, "हे लंकेश! दण्डकारण्य स्थित आपके जनस्थान में रहने वाले आपके भाई खर और दूषण तथा उनके चौदह सहस्त्र सैनिकों का वध हो चुका है। किसी प्रकार से अपने प्राण बचाकर मैं आपको सूचना देने के लिये आया हूँ।"

यह सुन कर रावण को भारी क्रोध आया। उन्होंने कहा, "कौन है जिसने मेरे भाइयों का सेना सहित वध किया है? मैं अभी उसे नष्ट कर दूँगा। तुम मुझे पूरा वृत्तान्त बताओ।"

अकम्पन ने कहा, "हे लंकापति! अयोध्या के राजकुमार राम ने अपने पराक्रम से अकेले ही सभी राक्षस वीरों को मृत्यु के घाट उतार दिया।"

इस समाचार को सुनकर रावण को आश्चर्य हुआ और उसने पूछा, "खर को मारने के लिये क्या देवताओं ने राम की सहायता की है?"

अकम्पन ने उत्तर दिया, "नहीं प्रभो! देवताओं से राम को किसी प्रकार की सहायता नहीं मिली है, ऐसा उसने अकेले ही किया है। वास्तव में राम तेजस्वी, शक्तिवान और युद्धविद्या में पारंगत योद्धा है। खर जैसे रणबाँकुरे, जिसकी एक गर्जना से सारे देवता काँप जाते थे, को उनकी शक्तिशाली सेना सहित उसने खेल ही खेल में समाप्त कर दिया। उसका रणकौशल देख कर मुझे प्रतीत होता है कि आप अपनी सम्पूर्ण सेना के साथ युद्ध करके भी उसे परास्त नहीं कर सकेंगे। मेरे विचार से उस पर विजय पाने का एक ही उपाय है। उसके साथ उसकी अत्यन्त रूपवती, लावण्यमयी और सुकुमारी पत्नी भी है। राम उससे बहुत प्रेम करता है। वह अपनी पत्नी के बिना एक पल भी नहीं रह सकता। मेरा विश्वास है, यदि आप किसी प्रकार उसका अपहरण कर के ले आयें तो राम उसके वियोग में स्वयं ही मर जायेगा।"

लंकेश रावण को अकम्पन का यह प्रस्ताव सर्वथा उचित प्रतीत हुआ। तत्काल ही वह अपने दिव्य रथ पर सवार हो आकाश मार्ग से उड़ता हुआ अपने परम मित्र मारीच के पास

पहुँचा। बिना किसी पूर्व सूचना के रावण को अपने सम्मुख पाकर मारीच बोले, “हे लंकापति! आज अचानक ही आपके यहाँ आने का क्या कारण है? आपकी इतनी हड़बड़ी देखकर मेरे मन में नाना प्रकार की शंकाएँ उठ रही हैं। लंका में सब कुशल तो है?”

रावण ने कहा, “मैं एक विशेष कारण से ही यहाँ आया हूँ। अयोध्या के राजकुमार राम ने मेरे भाई खर और दूषण को उनकी सेना सहित मार डाला है। अब मैं चाहता हूँ कि राम की पत्नी का अपहरण कर लूँ और इसके लिये मुझे तुम्हारी सहायता की आवश्यक्ता है। सीता के वियोग में राम बिना युद्ध किये ही तड़प-तड़प कर मर जायेगा और मेरा प्रतिशोध पूरा हो जायेगा।”

रावण के वचनों को सुन कर मारीच बोला, “हे लंकापति! तुम्हारा यह विचार सर्वथा अनुचित है। जिस किसी ने भी तुम्हें सीता को हरने का सुझाव दिया है वह वास्तव में तुम्हारा मित्र नहीं शत्रु है। राम अत्यन्त बलशाली और पराक्रमी है और तुम उससे किसी प्रकार भी जीत सकते। राम के होते हुये तुम उससे सीता को नहीं छीन सकते। उसके अद्‌भुत पराक्रम के सम्मुख तुम एक क्षण भी नहीं टिक सकोगे। तुम्हारा हित इसी में है कि तुम इस विचार को भूलकर कर चुपचाप लंका में जा कर बैठ जाओ।”

5

रावण को शूर्पणखा का धिक्कार

रावण के मारीच के पास से लंका लौट आने के कुछ काल पश्चात् ही शूर्पणखा उसके पास आ पहुँची। उस समय रावण अपने मन्त्रियों से घिरा हुआ था। स्वर्ण-सिंहासन पर आरूढ़ रावण वैसे ही शोभा पा रहा था जैसे सोने के ईंटों से निर्मित यज्ञवेदी में घी के द्वारा प्रज्वलित अग्नि। समरभूमि में साक्षात् यमराज की भाँति दिखाई पड़ने वाले रावण ने देवता, गन्धर्व आदि सभी को जीत लिया था। राजोचित लक्षणों से सम्पन्न रावण ने वैदूर्यमणि (नीलम) तथा तपाये हुए सोने से निर्मित आभूषणों से अलंकृत हो रहा था। उसके अंगों पर विष्णु के चक्र तथा देवताओं के विविध आयुधों के अनेक प्रहार हुए थे किन्तु इन प्रहारों के बाद भी उसका कोई भी अंग खण्डित नहीं हुआ था।

वह रावण पर्वतशिखरों को तोड़कर फेंक देने वाला, देवताओं को रौंद डालने वाला, धर्म को जड़ से काट देने वाला, दूसरों की भार्याओं के सतीत्व का नाश करने वाला, यज्ञों में विघ्न डालने वाला तथा दिव्यास्त्रों का प्रयोग करने वाला था। उसने समुद्रों तथा पर्वतों पर विजय प्राप्त किया था, नागराज वासुकि को परास्त किया था, तक्षक की प्रिय पत्नी का हरण किया था, कुबेर पर विजय प्राप्त कर उससे पुष्पक विमान छीना था। इन्द्रादि समस्त देवता उससे भयभीत रहते थे, वायु देवता उस पर पंखा डुलाते थे, वरुण उसके यहाँ पानी भरता था और वह मृत्यु को भी परास्त करने की सामर्थ्य रखता था। उसने दस हजार वर्षों त घोर तपस्या करके तथा ब्रह्मा जी को अपने मस्तकों की बलि दे कर देवता, दानव, गन्धर्व, पिशाच, पक्षी और सर्पों से संग्राम में अभय प्राप्त कर लिया था। मनुष्य के सिवा अन्य किसी से भी उसे मृत्यु का भय नहीं रह गया था।

शूर्पणखा राम के द्वारा तिरस्कृत होकर अत्यन्त दुःखी हो रही थी। उसने रावण के पास आ कर क्रोध से फुँफकारते हुए कहा, "धिक्कार है तुम्हारे पराक्रम पर और तुम्हारे इन मन्त्रियों पर। तुम अपनी विलासिता में डूबे हुये हो। तुम सब तो सुरा और सुन्दरियों में व्यस्त रहते हो। हे नीतिवान रावण! क्या अब मुझे तुमको यह भी बताना पड़ेगा कि समय पर उचित

कार्य न करने वाले और अपने देश की रक्षा के प्रति असावधान रहने वाले राजा के राज्य के नष्ट हो जाने में क्षणमात्र भी देर नहीं लगती। तुम्हें ज्ञात होना चाहिये कि वृक्ष से गिरे हुये पत्ते और राज्य से च्युत राजा का कोई मूल्य नहीं होता। प्रजा उसी राजा की पूजा करती है जो स्थूल आँखों से सोता है किन्तु नीति की आँखों से जागता है, जिसका क्रोध प्रलयंकर और प्रसन्नता सुखदायिनी है।

जिस राजा के गुप्तचर सक्रिय और सतर्क नहीं रहते वह राज्य करने योग्य नहीं होता। तुम्हारे गुप्तचर तो मूर्ख, अयोग्य और आलसी हैं। तुम्हारी बुद्धि दूषित है और मन्त्री भी सर्वथा अयोग्य हैं। उन्हें अभी तक यह पता नहीं कि उनके राज्य दण्डकारण्य में कितनी भयंकर घटना घट चुकी है। मेरे वीर भ्राताओं खर-दूषण का चौदह सहस्त्र राक्षसों सहित संहार हो चुका है। जो ऋषि-मुनि कल तुम्हारे नाम से थर-थर काँपते थे वे आज सिर उठा कर निर्भय हो घूम रहे हैं। तुम तो राम द्वारा किये गये भीषण हत्याकाण्ड से अभी तक अपरिचित हो।"

शूर्पणखा के कटु वचनों से कुपित होकर रावण बोला, "शूर्पणखे! मुझे बताओ कि राम कौन है? उसका बल और पराक्रम कितना है? दुष्कर दण्डकवन में में उसने किसलिये प्रवेश किया है? उसके पास ऐसा कौन सा अस्त्र है जिससे उसने खर, दूषण और त्रिशिरा का सेना सहित संहार कर दिया? उसने तुझ जैसी सुन्दर अंगों वाली को क्यों कुरूप बना दिया?"

रावण के प्रश्नों का उत्तर देते हुए शूर्पणखा ने कहा, "हे भाई! महाबली राम अयोध्या नरेश दशरथ के पुत्र हैं। वे अत्यन्त निपुण धनुर्धारी हैं। वे अकेले और पैदल थे तो भी उन्होंने मात्र डेढ़ मुहूर्त (तीन घड़ी) में समस्त राक्षसों का संहार कर डाला। मैंने राम के बाणों की वर्षा से राक्षसों को मरते हुए तो देखा किन्तु यह नहीं देख पाई कि कब राम ने धनुष खींचा और कब बाण छोड़ा। स्त्री होने के कारण राम ने मेरा वध नहीं किया और केवल अपमानित करके छोड़ दिया। राम के समान ही पराक्रमी उसका भाई लक्ष्मण और अत्यन्त सुन्दरी उसकी पत्नी सीता भी उसके साथ है। इस भूतल पर मैंने आज तक सीता के समान रूपवती अन्य कोई स्त्री नहीं देखा है। जब मैं सीता को तुम्हारी भार्या बनाने के लिये लाने के लिये उद्यत हुई तो लक्ष्मण ने मुझे कुरूप बना दिया। सीता तुम्हारी ही भार्या बनने योग्य है अतः तुम उसे शीघ्रातिशीघ्र हर लाओ।"

शूर्पणखा का कथन सुनने तथा अपने मन्त्रियों से विचार विमर्ष करने के पश्चात् रावण ने सीता को हर लाने का निश्चय कर लिया। तत्काल उसने अपना रथ तैयार करवाया और उस पर सवार हो अपने मित्र मारीच के पास पहुँच गया।

मारीच ने रावण का समुचित सत्कार करके पूछा, "राजन्! लंका में सब कुशल तो है ना? आप इतनी जल्दी पुनः कैसे लौट आये?"

रावण बोला, "हे मारीच! क्रूर और मूर्ख राम ने अपने बल का आश्रय लेकर मेरे भाई खर और दूषण सेनासहित त्रिशिरा का वध कर दिया है। उसने मेरी बहन शूर्पणखा को भी कुरूप बना दिया है। तुम मेरे मित्र हो। मित्र ही संकट के समय मित्र की सहायता करता है। मैं जानता हूँ कि मेरे मित्रों और शुभचिन्तकों में तुमसे बढ़ कर बलवान, नीतिवान और मुझसे सच्चा

स्नेह करने वाला और कोई नहीं है। अतः हे मारीच! मैं चाहता हूँ कि तुम रजत बिन्दुओं वाला स्वर्णमृग बन कर राम के आश्रम के सामने जाओ। तुम्हें देख कर सीता अवश्य राम-लक्ष्मण को तुम्हें पकड़ने के लिये भेजेगी। उन दोनों के चले जाने पर मैं अकेली सीता का अपहरण कर के ले जाऊँगा। राम को सीता का वियोग असह्य होगा और विरह की उस अवस्था में राम को मार डालना मेरे लिये कठिन नहीं होगा।"

रावण के वचन सुनकर मारीच बोला, "हे लंकापति! जैसे कि मैं मैं पहले भी कह चुका हूँ कि ऐसा करना तुम्हारे लिये उचित नहीं होगा। यह कार्य तुम्हारे जीवन के लिये काल बन जायेगा। आश्चर्य की बात है कि वेद-शास्त्रों के ज्ञाता होते हुये भी तुम परस्त्री हरण जैसा भयंकर पाप करने जा रहे हो। तुम्हें ज्ञात होना चाहिये कि राम के क्रोध से तुम बच नहीं सकोगे।"

मारीच के इस उत्तर से क्रुद्ध हो हाथ में खड्ग ले कर रावण बोला, "मारीच! मैं तुझे अपना मित्र समझ कर तेरे पास आया था। तेरा अनर्गल प्रलाप सुनने के लिये नहीं। तेरी कायरतापूर्ण युक्तियों को सुन कर मैं अपना विचार नहीं बदल सकता। सीता का हरण मैं अवश्य ही करूँगा और तू मेरे आज्ञा का पालन भी करेगा। यदि तू मेरी आज्ञा मान कर मेरे इस कार्य में सहायता नहीं करेगा तो राम-लक्ष्मण से पहले मैं तेरा वध करूँगा।"

रावण के क्रोध से भयभीत होकर मारीच ने अपनी सहमति दे दी। उसकी सहमति से प्रसन्न हो कर रावण बोला, "अब सिद्ध हो गया कि तू मेरा परम मित्र है।"

रावण उसे ले कर दण्डक वन में पहुँच राम के आश्रम की खोज करने लगा। जब आश्रम मिल गया तो मारीच ने रावण के निर्देशानुसार मृग का रूप धारण किया और आश्रम के निकट विचरण करने लगा। इस अद्भुत स्वर्णिम मृग की शोभा देख कर सीता आश्चर्यचकित रह गई और विस्मित हो कर उसके पास पहुँची। मायावी मारीच ने अपनी मृग-सुलभ क्रीड़ाओं से सीता का मन मुग्ध कर लिया।

6

स्वर्णमृग

सीता की इच्छा इस अद्भुत मृग को पकड़ कर आश्रम में रखने की हुई। अतः वे राम को पुकारते हुए बोलीं, "हे आर्यपुत्र! आप और लक्ष्मण शीघ्र आइये देखिये, कितना सुन्दर और अद्भुत स्वर्णमृग यहाँ विचरण कर रहा है। उस माया मृग को देख कर लक्ष्मण को सन्देह हुआ और उन्होंने राम से कहा, "तात! मुझे ऐसा प्रतीत होता है कि हमें छलने के लिये इस मृग के रूप में स्वेच्छारूपधारी मारीच ही आया है। हे जगत्पति! इस भूतल पर कहीं भी ऐसा विचित्र रत्नमय मृग नहीं है, अतः निःसन्देह यह माया ही है।"

लक्ष्मण को बीच में ही रोकते हुए सीता राम से बोली, "हे नाथ! यह मृग अत्यन्त सुन्दर है, इसने मेरे मन को मोह लिया है। आप अवश्य ही इसे पकड़ कर लाइये। जब हम वनवास समाप्त कर के अयोध्या लौटेंगे तो यह हमारे प्रासाद की शोभा बढ़ायेगा। यदि यह जीवित न पकड़ा जा सके तो इसे मार कर मृगछाला ही ले आइये। मैं उस पर आपके साथ बैठना चाहती हूँ।"

सीता के आग्रह को देख कर राम लक्ष्मण से बोले, "हे लक्ष्मण! निःसन्देह इस मृग का रूप अत्यंत मनोहर एवं आकर्षक है। यदि यह पकड़ा नहीं भी गया तो मारा तो अवश्य ही जायेगा। इसमें भी सन्देह नहीं है कि इसकी मृगछाला मनोहारी होगी। सीता का आग्रह पूर्ण करने के लिये इसे अवश्य ही पकड़ना चाहिये। तुम्हारी शंका के अनुसार यदि यह राक्षसी माया है तो भी इस राक्षस को मारना उचित ही होगा। तुम सीता की रक्षा करो। मैं इसे जीवित पकड़ने या मारने के लिये जाता हूँ।"

इतना कह कर राम अपने शस्त्रास्त्र धारण कर मायावी मृग के पीछे चल पड़े। राम को अपनी ओर आता देख मृग भी उछलता कूदता गहन वन के भीतर चला गया। वह विविध वृक्षों, झाड़ियों के बीच कभी छिपता और कभी प्रकट होता कभी धीमी तो कभी द्रुत गति से भागने लगा। उसका पीछा करते-करते रामचन्द्र आश्रम से बहुत दूर निकल गये। अन्ततः मृग के दृष्टिगत होते ही क्रुद्ध हो कर राम ने एक तीक्ष्ण बाण छोड़ा जो मारीच के हृदय तक पहुँच गया। बाण लगते ही मारीच अपने असली वेश में धराशायी हो गया और राम के स्वर

में 'हा सीते! हा लक्ष्मण! चीत्कार करते हुए मर गया।

उस राक्षस के मृत शरीर को तथा उसका अपने स्वर में चीत्कार करना देख कर राम को लक्ष्मण का कथन स्मरण हो आया। वास्तव में यह मारीच की माया ही निकली। उन्हें चिन्ता होने लगी कि मेरे स्वर में किये गये चीत्कार को सुन कर सीता की क्या दशा होगी। उन्हे किसी अनिष्ट की आशंका होने लगी और वे द्रुत गति से आश्रम की ओर लौट पड़े।

इधर जब सीता ने अपने पति के स्वर में 'हा सीते! हा लक्ष्मण!' सुना तो उन्होंने व्याकुल हो कर लक्ष्मण से कहा, "हे लक्ष्मण! प्रतीत होता है कि तुम्हारे भैया अवश्य ही किसी संकट में पड़ गये हैं। तुम शीघ्र जा कर उनकी सहायता करो। उनके दुःख भरे शब्द सुनकर मेरा हृदय चिन्ता से बहुत घबरा रहा है।"

आशंका से आतुर सीता के वचन सुन कर लक्ष्मण बोले, "हे आर्ये! इस प्रकार मैं आप को अकेला छोड़ कर नहीं जा सकता। भैया ने आपकी रक्षा का भार मुझे सौंपा है। आप धैर्य धारण करें, भैया अभी आते ही होंगे।"

दुःखी हो कर सीता बोलीं, "लक्ष्मण! ऐसा प्रतीत होता है कि तुम भाई के रूप में उनके शत्रु हो। इसीलिये उनके ऐसे आर्त स्वर सुन कर भी उनकी सहायता के लिये नहीं जाना चाहते। जब उनको ही कुछ हो गया तो मेरी रक्षा से क्या लाभ?"

इस प्रकार कहते हुये उनके नेत्रों से अश्रुधारा बहने लगी। सीता की यह दशा देख कर लक्ष्मण हाथ जोड़ कर बोले, "देवि! आप व्यर्थ दुःखी न हों। संसार में ऐसा कोई भी देवता, दानव, मनुष्य, गन्धर्व नहीं है जो भैया के पराक्रम का सामना कर सके। मायावी राक्षस नाना प्रकार के रूप धारण करते हैं और विविध प्रकार की बोलियाँ बोलते हैं, अतः आपको चिन्ता करने की आवश्यकता नहीं है। आप तनिक प्रतीक्षा करें, वे आते ही होंगे।"

लक्ष्मण के तर्कयुक्त वचनों ने सीता के क्रोध को और बढ़ा दिया। वे बोलीं, "लक्ष्मण! मैं तुम्हारे मनोभावों को भली-भाँति समझ रही हूँ। तुम राम के न रहने पर मुझे पा लेने की लालसा लेकर ही वन में चले आये हो। मैं तुम्हारी दुष्ट इच्छा को कभी पूरा नहीं होने दूँगी। राम के वियोग में मैं अपने प्राण त्याग दूँगी।"

सीता के ये वचन सुन कर लक्ष्मण का हृदय विदीर्ण हो उठा। वे बोले, "देवि! मैं आपकी बातों का कोई उत्तर नहीं दे सकता। स्त्रियों के द्वारा ऐसी अनुचित और प्रतिकूल बातें मुँह से निकालना कोई आश्चर्य की बात नहीं है क्योंकि संसार में नारियों का ऐसा स्वभाव प्रायः देखा जाता है। आज आप की बुद्धि भ्रष्ट हो गई है जो अपने अग्रज की आज्ञा पालन करने वाले अनुज पर ऐसा दुष्टतापूर्ण लांछन लगा रही हैं। मुझे संशय हो रहा है कि आज आप पर अवश्य कोई संकट आने वाला है। वन के समस्त देवता आपकी रक्षा करें। वन के देवता इसके साक्षी हैं कि मैं आपके द्वारा बलात् भेजा जा रहा हूँ।"

लक्ष्मण के वचन सुनकर सीता के नेत्रों से अश्रुधारा बहने लगे और लक्ष्मण उस ओर चल दिये जिधर राम गये थे।

7

सीता हरण

(रावण की पहली गलती थी। सीता हरण ,उसने यह सब कुछ अपने बहन के लिए किया उसे नहीं पता था की गलती शूर्पणखा का ही था।)

लक्ष्मण के जाने के पश्चात् रावण को अवसर मिल गया। वह ब्राह्मण भिक्षुक का वेष धारण कर रावण सीता के पास आया और बोला, "हे सुन्दरी! तुम कोई वन देवी हो या लक्ष्मी अथवा कामदेव की प्रिया स्वयं रति हो? इस पृथ्वी पर तो मैंने तुम्हारे जैसी रूपवती, लावण्यमयी युवती मैंने आज तक इस संसार में नहीं देखा है। तुम कौन हो? किसकी कन्या हो? और इस वन में किस लिये निवास कर रही हो? कहाँ यह तुम्हारा तीनों लोकों में सबसे सुन्दर रूप, तुम्हारी सुकुमारता और कहाँ इस दुर्गम वन में निवास? यह स्थान तो इच्छानुसार रूप धारण करनेवाले भयंकर राक्षसों का निवासस्थान है। तुम यहाँ से चली जाओ, तुम यहाँ रहने योग्य नहीं हो।"

सीता ने कहा, "हे ब्राह्मण! मेरा नाम सीता है। मैं मिथिलानरेश जनक की पुत्री और अयोध्यापति दशरथ के ज्येष्ठ पुत्र श्री रामचन्द्र की पत्नी हूँ। पिता की आज्ञा से मेरे पति अपने भाई भरत को अयोध्या का राज्य दे कर चौदह वर्ष के लिये वनवास कर रहे हैं। उन पराक्रमी सत्यपरायण वीर के साथ मेरे तेजस्वी देवर लक्ष्मण भी हैं। आप अतिथि हैं अतः इस आसन पर बैठ कर यह जल और फल ग्रहण कीजिये। मेरे पति अभी आते ही होंगे। अब आप बताइये महात्मन्! आप कौन हैं और यहाँ किस उद्देश्य से पधारे है?"

सीता का प्रश्न सुन कर रावण गरज कर बोला, "हे सीते! मैं तीनों लोकों, चौदह भुवनों का विजेता महाप्रतापी लंकापति रावण हूँ जिसके नाम से देवता, दानव, यक्ष, किन्नर, गन्धर्व, मुनि सभी भयभीत रहते हैं। इन्द्र, वरुण, कुबेर जैसे देवता जिसकी सेवा कर के अपने आप को धन्य समझते हैं। मैं तुम्हारे लावण्यमय सौन्दर्य को देख कर अपनी सुन्दर रानियों को भी भूल गया हूँ और मैं तुम्हें ले जा कर अपनी भार्या बनाना चाहता हूँ। हे मृगलोचने! तुम मेरे साथ चल कर नाना देशों से आई हुई मेरी अत्यन्त सुन्दर रानियों पर पटरानी बन कर शासन करो। मेरी नगरी लंका की सुन्दरता को देख कर तुम इस वन के कष्टों को भूल जाओगी।

इसलिये मेरे साथ चलने को तैयार हो जाओ।"

रावण का नीचतापूर्ण प्रस्ताव सुन कर सीता क्रुद्ध स्वर में बोली, "हे अधम राक्षस! तुम परम तेजस्वी, अद्भुत पराक्रमी और महान योद्धा रामचन्द्र के पराक्रम को नहीं जानते इसीलिये तुम मेरे सम्मुख यह कुत्सित प्रस्ताव रखने का दुःसाहस कर रहे हो। अरे मूर्ख! क्या तू वनराज सिंह के मुख में से उसके दाँत उखाड़ना चाहता है? तेरे सिर पर काल नाच रहा है इसीलिये तू यह घृणित प्रस्ताव ले कर यहाँ आया है। तेरी मृत्यु ही तुझे यहाँ ले कर आई है।"

सीता के ये अपमानजनक वाक्य सुन कर रावण के अत्यन्त कुपति हो गया। आँखें लाल करते हुये उसने कहा, "सीते! तू मेरे बल और प्रताप को नहीं जानती। मैं आकाश में खड़ा हो कर पृथ्वी को गेंद की भाँति उठा सकता हूँ। अथाह समुद्र को एक चुल्लू में भर कर पी सकता हूँ। मैं तुझे लेने के लिये आया हूँ और ले कर ही जाऊँगा।"

यह कह कर रावण ने अपने ब्राह्मण वेश को त्याग कर विकराल रूप धारण कर लिया और दोनों हाथों से सीता को उठा कर अपने कंधे पर बिठा निकटवर्ती खड़े विमान पर जा सवार हुआ। इस प्रकार अप्रत्यशित रूप से पकड़े जाने पर सीता ने 'हा राम! हा राम!!' कहते हुये स्वयं को रावण के हाथों से छुड़ाने का प्रयास किया। परन्तु बलवान रावण के सामने उनकी एक न चली। उसने उन्हें बाँध कर विमान में एक ओर डाल दिया और तीव्र गति से लंका की ओर चल पड़ा। सीता निरन्तर विलाप किये जा रही थी, "हा राम! पापी रावण मुझे लिये जा रहा है। हे लक्ष्मण! तुम कहाँ हो? तुम्हारी बलवान भुजाएँ इस समय इस दुष्ट से मेरी रक्षा क्यों नहीं करतीं? हाय! आज कैकेयी की मनोकामना पूरी हुई।"

इस प्रकार विलाप करती हुई सीता ने मार्ग में खड़े जटायु को देखा। जटायु को देखते ही सीता चिल्लाई, "हे आर्य जटायु! देखो, लंका का यह दुष्ट राजा रावण मेरा अपहरण कर के लिये जा रहा है। इस नराधम से आप मेरी रक्षा करने में आप असमर्थ हैं क्योंकि यह बलवान है और अनेक युद्धों में विजय पाने के कारण इसका दुस्साहस बढ़ा हुआ है। आप रावण द्वारा मेरे हर लिये जाने का यह वृत्तान्त मेरे पति से तो अवश्य ही कह देना।"

8

जटायु वध

सीता की करुण पुकार सुन कर जटायु ने उस ओर देखा तथा रावण को सीता सहित विमान में जाते देख बोले, "अरे रावण! तू एक पर-स्त्री का अपहरण कर के ले जा रहा है। अरे लंकेश! यह महाप्रतापी श्री रामचन्द्र जी की भार्या है। एक राजा होकर तू ऐसा निन्दनीय कर्म कैसे कर रहा है? राजा का धर्म तो पर-स्त्री की रक्षा करना है। तू काम के वशीभूत हो कर अपना विवेक खो बैठा है। छोड़ दे राम की पत्नी को। हे रावण! मेरे समक्ष तू सीता को नहीं ले जा सकता। प्राण रहते तक मैं सीता की रक्षा करूँगा। ठहर! मैं अभी आता हूँ तुझसे युद्ध करने।"

जटायु के इन कठोर अपमानजनक शब्दों को सुन कर रावण उसकी ओर झपटा जो सीता को मुक्त कराने के लिये विमान की ओर तेजी से बढ़ रहा था। विशालाकार दो पर्वतों की भाँति वे एक दूसरे से टकराये। क्रुद्ध जटायु ने अपने पराक्रम से दो बार रावण के धनुष को तोड़ डाला, उसके रथ को तहस-नहस कर डाला और रावण के सारथि का वध कर डाला। उन्होंने मार-मार कर रावण को घायल कर दिया। घायल होने के बाद भी, रावण वृद्ध और दुर्बल जटायु से अधिक शक्तिशाली था। अवसर पा कर उसने जटायु की दोनों भुजायें काट दीं। पीड़ा से व्याकुल हो कर मूर्छित हो वह पृथ्वी पर गिर पड़ा।

जटायु को भूमि पर गिरते देख जानकी "हा राम! हा लक्ष्मण!!" कह कर विलाप करने लगीं। रावण ने सीता को उसके केश पकड़ कर उठा लिया और आकाशमार्ग से लंका की ओर उड़ने लगा। उस समय उन्नत भाल वाली, सुन्दर कृष्ण केशों वाली, गौरवर्णा, मृगनयनी जानकी का सुन्दर मुख रावण की गोद में पड़ा ऐसा प्रतीत हो रहा था जैसे पूर्णमासी का चन्द्रमा नीले बादलों को चीर कर चमक रहा हो। सीता का क्रन्दन सुन कर वन के सिंह, बाघ, मृग आदि रावण से कुपित हो कर उसके विमान के नीचे उसके पीछे पीछे दौड़ने लगे। पर्वतों से गिरते हुये जल-प्रपात ऐसे प्रतीत हो रहे थे मानों वे भी सीता के दुःख से दुःखी हो कर करुण क्रन्दन करते हुये अश्रु बहा रहे हों। श्वेत बादल से आच्छादित सूर्य भी ऐसा प्रतीत हो रहा था जैसे अपनी कुलवधू की दुर्दशा देख कर उसका मुख श्रीहीन हो गया हो। सब सीता के दुःख से दुःखी हो रहे थे।

दुष्ट रावण से मुक्ति का कोई उपाय न देखकर सीता दीनतापूर्वक परमात्मा से प्रार्थना करने लगी, "हे परमपिता परमात्मा! हे प्रभो! मेरी रक्षा करो, रक्षा करो! हे सर्वशक्तिमान! इस समय मेरी रक्षा करने वाला तुम्हारे अतिरिक्त और कोई नहीं है। हे दयामय! मेरे सतीत्व की रक्षा करने वाले केवल तुम ही हो।"

मार्ग में सीता ने नीचे एक पर्वत पर पाँच वानरों को बैठे देखा। उनको देख कर सीता ने, यह सोचकर कि शायद ये राम को मेरा समाचार बता सकें, अपने सुनहरे रंग की रेशमी चादर में वस्त्र-आभूषण बाँधकर उसे उन वानरों के बीच गिरा दिया। तीव्र गति से उड़ने में व्यस्त रावण को सीता के इस कार्य का बोध नहीं हो पाया।

वनों, पर्वतों और सागर को पार करता हुआ रावण सीता सहित लंकापुरी में पहुँचा। वहाँ उसने सीता को मय दानव द्वारा निर्मित सुन्दर महल में रखा और क्रूर राक्षसियों को बुला कर आज्ञा दी, "मेरी आज्ञा के बिना कोई भी इस स्त्री से मिलने न पावे। यह जो भी वस्त्र, आभूषण, खाद्यपदार्थ माँगे, वह तत्काल इसे दिया जाय। इसे किसी भी प्रकार का कष्ट नहीं होना चाहिये और न कोई इसका तिरस्कार करे। अवज्ञा करने वालों को दण्ड मिलेगा।"

इस प्रकार राक्षसनियों को आदेश दे कर अपने महल में पहुँचा। वहाँ उसने अपने आठ शूरवीर सेनापतियों को बुला कर आज्ञा दी, "तुम लोग जा कर दण्डक वन में रहो। हमारे जनस्थान को राम लक्ष्मण नामक दो तपस्वियों ने उजाड़ दिया है। तुम वहाँ रह कर उनकी गतिविधियों पर दृष्टि रखो और उनकी सूचना मुझे यथाशीघ्र देते रहो। अवसर पा कर उन दोनों की हत्या कर डालो। मैं तुम्हारे पराक्रम से भली-भाँति परिचित हूँ इसीलिये उन्हें मारने का दायित्व तुम्हें सौंप रहा हूँ।"

उन्हें इस प्रकार आदेश दे कर वह कामी राक्षस वासना से पीड़ित हो कर सीता से मिलने के लिये चल पड़ा।

9

रावण-सीता संवाद

दुःख से कातर और राम के वियोग में अश्रु बहाती हुई सीता के पास जा कर रावण बोला, "शोभने! अब उस राज्य से च्युत, दीन, तपस्वी राम के लिये अश्रु बहाना व्यर्थ है। राम में इतनी शक्ति कहाँ है कि यहाँ तक आने का मनोरथ भी कर सके। तू उसे विस्मृत कर दे। विशाललोचने! तू मुझे पति के रूप में अंगीकार ले। समुद्र से घिरे सौ योजन विस्तार वाले अपने इस राज्य को मैं तुझे अर्पित कर दूँगा। मैं, जो तीनों लोकों का स्वामी हूँ, तेरे चरणों का दास बन कर रहूँगा। मेरी समस्त सुन्दर रानियाँ तेरी दासी बन कर रहेंगीं समस्त देव, दानव, नर, किन्नर जो मेरे दास हैं, तेरे दास बन कर रहेंगे।

तेरे पहले के दुष्कर्म तुझे वनवास का कष्ट देकर समाप्त हो चुके हैं और अब तेरा पुण्यकर्म ही शेष रह गया है। अब मेरे साथ यहाँ रह कर समस्त प्रकार के पुष्पहार, दिव्य गंध और श्रेष्ठ आभूषण आदि का सेवन कर। सुमुखि! तेरा यह कमल के समान सुन्दर, निर्मल और मनोहर मुख शोक से पीड़ित होकर शोभाहीन हो गया है, मुझे स्वीकार करके उसे पुनः शोभायमान कर। धर्म और लोकलाज का भय निर्मूल है, यह सब मात्र तेरे मिथ्या विचार हैं। किसी सुन्दरी का युद्ध में हरण कर के उसके साथ विवाह करना भी तो वैदिक रीति का ही एक अंग है। इसलिये तू निःशंक हो कर मेरी बन जा। मैं तेरे इन कोमल चरणों पर अपने ये दसों मस्तक रख रहा हूँ, मुझ पर शीघ्र कृपा कर।"

रावण के इन वचनों को सुन कर शोक से कष्ट पाती हुई वैदेही, अपने और रावण के बीच में तिनके का ओट करके, बोली, "हे नराधम! परम पराक्रमी धर्मपरायण एवं सत्यप्रतिज्ञ दशरथनन्दन श्री रामचन्द्र जी ही मेरे पति हैं। मैं उनके अतिरिक्त किसी अन्य की ओर दृष्टि तक भी नहीं कर सकती। यदि तूने मुझे बलपूर्वक मेरा अपहरण किया होता तो अपने भाई खर की तरह जनस्थान के युद्धस्थल पर ही मारा गया होता किन्तु तू कायरों की तरह मुझे चुरा लाया है। तेरे इस अनर्गल प्रलाप से ऐसा प्रतीत होता है कि अब लंका सहित तेरे विनाश का समय आ गया है। तू इस भ्रम में मत रह कि यदि देवता और राक्षस तेरा कुछ नहीं बिगाड़ सके तो राम भी तुझे नहीं मार सकेंगे। उनके हाथों से ही तेरी मृत्यु निश्चित

है। अब तेरा जीवनकाल समाप्तप्राय हो चुका है। तेरे तेज, बल और बुद्धि तो पहले ही नष्ट हो चुके हैं। और जिसकी बुद्धि नष्ट हो चुकी होती है, उसका विनाश-काल दूर नहीं होता। अरे राक्षसाधम! तू महापापी है इसलिये मेरा स्पर्श नहीं कर सकता। तूने कभी सोचा भी है कि कमलों में विहार करने वाली हंसिनी क्या कभी कुक्कुट के साथ रह सकती है? तू मेरे इस संज्ञाशून्य जड़ शरीर को बाँध कर रख ले या काट डाल पर मैं कलंक देने वाला कोई भी निन्दनीय कार्य नहीं कर सकती।"

सीता के कठोर एवं अपमानजनक वाक्य सुन कर रावण कुपित हो कर बोला, "हे मनोहर हास्य वाली भामिनी! मैं तुझे बारह माह का समय देता हूँ। यदि एक वर्ष के अन्दर तू स्वेच्छापूर्वक मेरे पास नहीं आई तो मैं तेरे टुकड़े-टुकड़े कर दूँगा।"

फिर वह राक्षसनियों से बोला, "तुम इसे यहाँ से अशोक वाटिका में ले जा कर रखो और जितना भय और कष्ट दे सकती हो, दो।"

लंकापति रावण की आज्ञा पाकर राक्षसनियाँ सीता को अशोक वाटिका में ले गईं। अशोक वाटिका एक रमणीय स्थल था किन्तु पति वियोग और निशाचरी दुर्व्यवहार के कारण सीता वहाँ अत्यन्त दुःखी थीं।

सीता का अशोकवाटिका में प्रवेश जानकर पितामह ब्रह्मा देवराज इन्द्र के पास आये और बोले, "सदा सुख में पली हुई पतिव्रता महाभागा सीता पति के चरणों के दर्शन से वंचित होने के कारण दुःख और चिन्ताओं से सन्तप्त हो गई हैं और प्राणयात्रा (भोजन) नहीं कर रही हैं। ऐसी दशा में निःसन्देह वे अपना प्राणत्याग कर देंगी। अतः तुम शीघ्र लंकापुरी में प्रवेश करके उन्हें उत्तम हविष्य प्रदान करो।"

ब्रह्मा जी के आज्ञानुसार इन्द्र तत्काल लंकापुरी पहुँचे। उन्होंने निद्रादेवी की सहायता से समस्त राक्षसों को मोहित कर दिया। फिर वे सीता के पास जाकर बोले, "हे देवि! आप शोक न करें। मैं, शचीपति इन्द्र, राम की सहायता करूँगा। मेरे प्रसाद से वे विशाल सेना लेकर समुद्र पार करके यहाँ आयेंगे। अतः तुम इस हविष्य को स्वीकार करो। इसे खा लेने पर तुम्हें हजारों वर्षों तक भूख और प्यास सन्तप्त नहीं कर पायेंगे।"

शंकित सीता ने उनसे कहा, "मुझे कैसे विश्वास हो कि आप देवराज इन्द्र ही हैं?"

इस पर देवराज इन्द्र ने समस्त देवोचित लक्षणों का प्रदर्शन करके सीता की शंका का निवारण कर दिया।

विश्वास हो जाने पर सीता बोलीं, "यह मेरा सौभाग्य है कि आज आपके मुख से मुझे अपने पति का नाम सुनने को मिला। आप मेरे लिये मेरे श्वसुर दशरथ और पिता जनक के तुल्य हैं। मैं आपके हाथों से इस पायसरूप हविष्य (दूध से बनी हुई खीर) को स्वीकार करती हूँ। यह रघुकुल की वृद्धि करने वाला हो।"

इस प्रकार से इन्द्र द्वारा प्रदत्त हविष्य को खाकर जानकी भूख-प्यास के कष्ट से मुक्त हो गईं और देवराज इन्द्र, राक्षसों को मोहित करने वाली निद्रा के साथ, देवलोक को चले गये।

10

राम की वापसी और विलाप

मारीच का वध कर के राम आश्रम की ओर लौट रहे थे तो पीछे से एक मादा सियार ने बड़े कठोर स्वर में चीत्कार किया। वन के मृग एवं पक्षी उनके बायों ओर चलने और उड़ने लगे। इन अपशकुनों को देखकर राम का हृदय आशंकित हो उठा। उन्हें सीता के अशुभ की चिन्ता सन्तप्त करने लगी। इतने में ही उन्होंने मार्ग में लक्ष्मण को आते देखा। लक्ष्मण को देख कर उन्हें ऐसा प्रतीत हुआ कि किसी राक्षसी षड़यंत्र के फलस्वरूप सीता किसी कठिनाई में फँस गई है।

चिन्तित हो कर उन्होंने लक्ष्मण से पूछा, “लक्ष्मण! सीता कहाँ है? मैंने तुम्हें आदेश दिया था कि तुम सीता की रक्षा करना तो तुम उसे अकेली कैसे छोड़ आये? वह किसी विपत्ति में तो नहीं फँस गई? वह जीवित होगी कि नहीं? शीघ्र बताओ उसे क्या हुआ है? यदि वह जीवित नहीं होगी तो मैं भी अपने प्राण त्याग दूँगा। कहीं ऐसा तो नहीं है कि उस मायावी राक्षस ने हा ‘लक्ष्मण!’ कह कर तुम्हें भी भ्रम में डाल दिया है और तुम सीता को अकेली छोड़ कर यहा दौड़ आये हो? अथवा सीता ने ही भ्रमित हो कर तुम्हें यहाँ आने को विवश किया हो। ऐसा प्रतीत होता है कि राक्षसों ने अपने प्रतिशोध लेने के लिये यह चाल चली है और तुम इसमें फँस गये हो। खर और दूषण की मृत्यु का बदला लेने के लिये उन्होंने सीता का वध कर डाला होगा।”

राम के इन वचनों से व्यथित लक्ष्मण बोले, “भैया! मैं उन्हें स्वयं अपनी इच्छा से छोड़ कर नहीं आया हूँ। मैंने उन्हें अनेक प्रकार से समझाया किन्तु वे चेतना मोह से ग्रसित होकर मुझसे कहने लगीं कि तुम्हारे मन में पापपूर्ण भाव भरा हुआ है, तुम अपने भाई के दुश्मन हो और उनकी मृत्यु के पश्चात् मुझे प्राप्त करना चाहते हो। उनके इस प्रकार से कहने पर मैं रोष से भर उठा और आश्रम से निकल आया। इस प्रकार से उन्होंने ही कठोर वचन कह कह कर मुझे यहाँ आने के लिये विवश कर दिया।”

लक्ष्मण के वचनों को सुनकर राम ने कहा, “सौम्य! तुम सीता को छोड़ कर चले आये यह तुमने अच्छा नहीं किया। सीता तो क्रोध में विक्षिप्त हो रही थी और क्रोध में भरी हुई नारी

के मुख से कठोर वचन निकलना आश्चर्य की बात नहीं है। किन्तु तुम तो समझदार हो। मेरे आदेश की अवहेलना कर तुम्हारा इस प्रकार से चले आना अनुचित है।"

चिन्तित राम और लक्ष्मण जब अपने आश्रम पहुँचे तो। उन्हें सीता कहीं दिखाई नहीं दी। उन्होंने समस्त पर्णशालाओं को देख डाला किन्तु वे सभी सभी सूनी मिलीं। जैसे हेमन्त ऋतु के हिम से ध्वस्त होकर कमलिनी श्रीहीन हो जाती है उसी प्रकार से पर्णशालाएँ शोभाशून्य थीं। आश्रम के वृक्ष और पत्ते भी वायु में सन-सना कर दुःख से रो रहे प्रतीत होते थे। मृगछाला और कुश इधर-उधर बिखरे पड़े थे, आसन औंधे पड़े थे, वृक्षों के फूल-पत्ते तथा कहीं-कहीं टहनियाँ टूटी या अधटूटी पड़ी थीं।

आश्रम का अस्त-व्यस्त दृष्य देख कर राम विचार करने लगे। सीता का किसी ने हरण कर लिया, अथवा किसी दुष्ट राक्षस ने उसे अपना आहार बना लिया। कहीं वह फूल चुनने तो नहीं गई या जल लाने नदी पर तो नहीं चली गई। जब सब ओर खोजने पर भी उन्हें सीता कहीं दिखाई न दी तो शोक के कारण उनकी आँखें लाल हो गईं। नदी-नालों, पर्वत-कन्दराओं में जा-जा कर वे उन्मत्त की भाँति आवाज दे-दे कर सीता की खोज करने लगे। अन्त में उनकी उन्मत्तता इतनी बढ़ गई कि वे कभी कदम्ब के वृक्ष के पास जाकर कहते, "हे कदम्ब! मेरी सीता को तेरे पुष्पों से बहुत स्नेह था। तू ही बता वह कहाँ है?" कभी विल्व के पास जा कर उससे पूछते, "हे विल्व विटप! क्या तुमने पीतवस्त्रधारिणी सीता को कहीं देखा है?" इस प्रकार वे कभी किसी वृक्ष से, कभी किसी लता से और कभी पुष्प समूहों से सीता का पता पूछते। कभी अशोक वृक्ष के पास जा कर कहते, "अरे अशोक विटप! तेरा तो नाम ही अशोक है, फिर तू सीता से मेरी भेंट करा कर मेरे शोक का हरण क्यों नहीं करता?" फिर ताड़ के वृक्ष से कहते, "तू तो सब वृक्षों से ऊँचा है। तू दूर-दूर की वस्तुएँ देख सकता है। देख कर बता क्या तुझे सीता कहीं दिखाई दे रही है। चुपचाप खड़ा न रह। यदि तू देखना चाहेगा तो तुझे वह अवश्य दिखाई देगी।"

इस प्रकार नाना प्रकार के वृक्षों से पूछ-पूछ कर रामचन्द्र विलाप करने लगे, "हे प्राणवल्लभे जानकी! तू कहाँ छिप गई? यदि तू वृक्षों की ओट में छिप कर हँसी कर रही है तो मैं तुझसे प्रार्थना करता हूँ, तू प्रकट हो जा। देख, मैं तेरे बिना कितना व्याकुल हो रहा हूँ। अब बहुत हँसी हो चुकी। मैं हार मानता हूँ। मैं तुझे नहीं ढूँढ पा रहा हूँ। या तू सचमुच मुझसे रूठ गई है। हा सीते! बोल, जल्दी बोल, तू कहाँ है? इधर देख, तेरे साथ खेलने वाले मृग शावक भी तेरे वियोग में अश्रु बहा रहे हैं। सीते! तेरे बिना मैं जीवित नहीं रह सकता। मैं चाहता हूँ, अभी तेरे वियोग में अपने प्राण त्याग दूँ किन्तु पिता की आज्ञा से विवश हूँ। मुझे स्वर्ग में पा कर वे धिक्करेंगे और कहेंगे 'तू मेरी आज्ञा की अवहेलना कर के – चौदह वर्ष की वनवास की अवधि पूरी किये बिना ही – स्वर्ग में कैसे चला आया।' हा! मैं कितना अभागा हूँ, जो तुम्हारे विरह में मर भी नहीं सकता। हाय जानकी! तुम ही बताओ, तुम्हारे बिना मैं क्या करूं?"

बड़े भाई को विलाप करते देख लक्ष्मण ने उन्हें धैर्य बँधाते हुये कहा, "हे नरोत्तम! रोने और धैर्य खोने से कोई लाभ नहीं होगा। आइये, आश्रम से बाहर चल कर वनों और गिरि-

कन्दराओं में भाभी की खोज करें। उन्हें वनों तथा पर्वतों में भ्रमण करने का चाव था। सम्भव है, वहीं कहीं भ्रमण कर रही हों। यह भी सम्भव है कि गोदावरी के तट पर बैठी मछलियों की जलक्रीड़ा देख रहीं हों या किसी भय की आशंका से भयभीत हो कर किसी लता कुँज में बैठी हों। इसलिये हमारे लिये यही उचित है कि हम विषाद और चिन्ता को छोड़ कर उनकी खोज करें।"

लक्ष्मण के युक्तियुक्त वचन सुन कर राम उसके साथ वनों, लताओं, गिरि-कन्दराओं आदि में खोज करने के लिये चले। उन दोनों ने समस्त वन, पर्वत-कन्दरा आदि में खोज डाला, किन्तु सीता उन्हें कहीं नहीं मिली।

अन्त में राम निराश हो कर बोले, "सौमित्र! यहाँ तो कोई ऐसा स्थान शेष नहीं बचा जहाँ हमने जानकी की खोज न की हो, परन्तु हमें सर्वत्र निराशा ही हाथ लगी। अब ऐसा प्रतीत होता है कि मेरी सीता मुझे कभी नहीं मिलेगी। मैं वनवास की अवधि बिता कर जब अयोध्या लौटूँगा और माता कौसल्या पूछेंगी कि सीता कहाँ है तो मैं उन्हें क्या उत्तर दूँगा? मिथिलापति जनक को क्या मुँह दिखाउँगा।"

वे जोर-जोर से विलाप करने लगे, "हे सीते! मैं तुम्हें कहाँ ढूँढू? हे वनों के मृगों! क्या तुमने कहीं मृगनयनी सीता को देखा है? हे वनों की कोकिलों! क्या तुमने कहीं कोकिलाकण्ठी जानकी को देखा है? कोई तो कुछ बताओ। क्या सभी मेरे लिये निर्मोही हो गये हो? कोई नहीं बोलता, कोई नहीं बताता। कोई भी मुझसे बात करना नहीं चाहता। मैं नपुंसक हूँ, कायर हूँ जो अपनी भार्या की रक्षा न कर सका।"

थोड़ी देर मौन रहने के पश्चात् वे फिर लक्ष्मण से बोले, "हे सौमित्र! अब सीता के बिना मैं किसी को मुख दिखाने के लायक नहीं रहा। मैं अवधि पूर्ण होने पर भी अयोध्या नहीं जाउँगा। तुम अब अयोध्या लौट जाओ। भरत से कह देना अब तुम ही अयोध्या का राज्य सँभालो। मैं कभी नहीं लौटूँगा। माता कौसल्या से कहना कि किस प्रकार सीता का अपहरण हो गया और उसकी विरह-व्यथा को न सह सकने के कारण राम ने आत्महत्या कर ली।

अब तुम्हारे जाते ही मैं गोदावरी नदी में डूब कर अपने प्रण त्याग दूँगा। मैं इस संसार में सबसे बड़ा पापी हूँ। इसीलिये तो मुझे एक के पश्चात् एक अनेक दुःख मिलते चले जा रहे हैं। पहले पिताजी का स्वर्गवास हुआ और अब सीता भी मुझे छोड़ कर जाने कहाँ चली गई। घर बार और सम्बंधी तो पहले ही छूट गये थे। मुझे रह-रह कर यह ध्यान आता है कि सीता राक्षसों के चंगुल में फँस गई है। वह भी रो-रो कर अपने प्राण विसर्जित कर रही होगी। तुम कहते हो कि वन में या गोदावरी के तट पर गई होगी। ये सब मुझे बहलाने की बातें हैं। जो वनवास की इतनी लम्बी अवधि में एक बार भी आश्रम से अकेली बाहर नहीं निकली, वह आज ही कैसे जा सकती है? अवश्य ही राक्षसों ने उसका अपहरण कर लिया है अथवा उसे अपना आहार बना लिया है। इन वृक्षों, पशुओं आदि से इतना सामीप्य होते हुये भी कोई मुझे सीता का पता नहीं बताता। हा सीते। हा प्राणवल्लभे! तू ही बता मैं तुझे कहाँ ढूँढू? कहाँ जा कर खोजूँ?"

11

जटायु की मृत्यु

राम को इस प्रकार दुःख से कातर और शोक सन्तप्त देख लक्ष्मण ने उन्हें धैर्य बँधाते हुये कहा, "भैया! आप तो सदैव मृदु स्वभाव वाले और जितेन्द्रिय रहे हैं। शोक के वशीभूत होकरआप अपने स्वभाव का परित्याग मत कीजिये। हे रघुकुलभूषण! कितने ही महान कर्म, अनुष्ठान और तपस्या करके हमारे पिता महाराज दशरथ ने आपको प्राप्त किया है। आपसे वियोग हो जाने के कारण ही उन्होंने अपने प्राण त्याग दिये। आप धैर्य धारण करें। संसार में प्रत्येक प्राणी पर विपत्तियाँ आतीं हैं किन्तु विपत्तियाँ हमेशा नहीं रहतीं, कुछ काल पश्चात् उनका अन्त हो जाता है। हमारे गुरु वसिष्ठ जी के सौ पुत्रों का एक ही दिन में गुरु विश्वामित्र ने वध कर दिया था। देवता तक भी प्रारब्ध की मार से नहीं बच पाते फिर देहधारी प्राणी कैसे बच सकते हैं? आप तो स्वयं महान विद्वान हैं मै भला आपको क्या शिक्षा दे सकता हूँ। आप परिस्थितियों पर विचार कर के धैर्य धारण करें। इस जनस्थान में खोजने से कहीं न कहीं हमें जानकी जी अवश्य मिल जायेंगी।"

लक्ष्मण के सारगर्भित उत्तम वचनों को सुन कर राम ने प्रयासपूर्वक धैर्य धारण किया और लक्ष्मण के साथ सीता की खोज करने के लिये खर-दूषण के जनस्थान की ओर चले। मार्ग में उन्होंने विशाल पर्वताकार शरीर वाले जटायु को देखा। उसे देख कर उन्होंने लक्ष्मण से कहा, "भैया! मुझे ऐसा प्रतीत होता है कि इसी जटायु ने सीता को खा डाला है। मैं अभी इसे यमलोक भेजता हूँ।"

ऐसा कह कर अत्यन्त क्रोधित राम ने अपने धनुष पर प्रत्यंचा चढ़ाई और जटायु को मारने के लिये आगे बढ़े। राम को अपनी ओर आते देख जटायु बोला, "आयुष्मान्! अच्छा हुआ कि तुम आ गये। सीता को लंका का राजा हर कर दक्षिण दिशा की ओर ले गया है और उसी ने मेरे पंखों को काट कर मुझे बुरी तरह से घायल कर दिया है। सीता की पुकार सुन कर मैंनें उसकी सहायता के लिये रावण से युद्ध भी किया। ये मेरे द्वारा तोड़े हुए रावण के धनुष उसके बाण हैं। इधर उसके विमान का टूटा हुआ भाग भी पड़ा है। यह रावण का सारथि भी मरा हुआ पड़ा है। परन्तु उस महाबली राक्षस ने मुझे मार-मार कर मेरी यह दशा कर दी। वह

रावण विश्रवा का पुत्र और कुबेर का भाई है।"

इतना कह कर जटायु का गला रुँध गया, आँखें पथरा गईं और उसके प्राण पखेरू उड़ गये।

जटायु के प्राणहीन रक्तरंजित शरीर को देख कर राम अत्यन्त दुःखी हुए और लक्ष्मण से बोले, "भैया! मैं कितना अभागा हूँ। राज्य छिन गया, घर से निर्वासित हुआ, पिता का स्वर्गवास हो गया, सीता का अपहरण हुआ और आज पिता के मित्र जटायु का भी मेरे कारण निधन हुआ। मेरे ही कारण इन्होंने अपने शरीर की बलि चढ़ा दी। इनकी मृत्यु का मुझे बड़ा दुःख है। तुम जा कर लकड़ियाँ एकत्रित करो। ये मेरे पिता तुल्य थे इसलिये मैं अपने हाथों से इनका दाह-संस्कार करूँगा।"

राम की आज्ञा पाकर लक्ष्मण ने लकड़ियाँ एकत्रित कीं। दोनों ने मिल कर चिता का निर्माण किया। राम ने पत्थरों को रगड़ कर अग्नि निकाली। फिर द्विज जटायु के शरीर को चिता पर रख कर बोले, "हे पूज्य गृद्धराज! जिस लोक में यज्ञ एवं अग्निहोत्र करने वाले, समरांगण में लड़ कर प्राण देने वाले और धर्मात्मा व्यक्ति जाते हैं, उसी लोक को आप प्रस्थान करें। आपकी कीर्ति इस संसार में सदैव बनी रहेगी।"

यह कह कर उन्होंने चिता में अग्नि प्रज्वलित कर दी। थोड़ी ही देर में जटायु का नश्वर शरीर पंचभूतों में मिल गया। इसके पश्चात् दोनों भाइयों ने गोदावरी के तट पर जा कर दिवंगत जटायु को जलांजलि दी।

12

कबन्ध का वध

इस प्रकार पक्षिराज जटायु के लिये जलांजलि दान कर के वे दोनों रघुवंशी बन्धु सीता की खोज में दक्षिण दिशा की ओर चले। कुछ दूर आगे चल कर वे एक ऐसे वन में पहुँचे जो बहुत से वृक्षों, झाड़ियों एवं लता बेलों द्वारा सभी ओर से घिरा हुआ था तथा अत्यन्त दुर्गम, गहन और दुर्गम था। उसे पार कर वे क्रौंचारण्य नामक वन, जो कि जनस्थान से तीन कोस दूरी पर स्थित था, के भीतर पहुँचे। वह वन भी सघन अनेक मेघों के समूह के सदृश श्याम प्रतीत होता था किन्तु विविध रंग के सुन्दर फूलों से सुशोभित होने का कारण हर्षोत्फुल्ल सा भी जान पड़ता था। उसके भीतर अनेक पशु-पक्षी निवास करते थे। वहाँ पर उन्होंने सीता को खोजना आरम्भ किया किन्तु बहुत खोजने पर भी जब कोई परिणाम नहीं निकला तो वे और आगे चले। इस वन को पार कर के मतंग मुनि के आश्रम ले पास जा पहुँचे। वय वन भी भयानक और हिंसक पशुओं से परिपूर्ण था। घूमते-घूमते वे ऐसी पर्वत कन्दरा पर पहुँचे तो पाताल की भाँति गहरी तथा सदा अन्धकार से आवर्त रहती थी।

उस विशाल कन्दरा के मुख पर एक अत्यन्त मलिन, लम्बे पेट वाली, बड़े-बड़े दाँतों और बिखरे केश वाली, मलिनमुखी विकराल राक्षसी बैठी हुई हड्डी चबा रही थी। राम लक्ष्मण को देख कर वह अट्टहास करती हुई दौड़ी और लक्ष्मण से लिपट कर बोली, "आओ हम दोनों रमण करें। मेरा नाम अयोमुखी है। तुम मुझे पतिरूप में मिले हो और मैं अब तुम्हारी भार्या हूँ।"

उसकी इस कुचेष्टा से क्रुद्ध हो कर लक्ष्मण ने अपनी म्यान से तलवार निकाली और उसके नाक, कान तथा स्तन काट डाले। उसके सारे शरीर पर रक्त की धाराएँ बहने लगीं और वह चीत्कार करती हुई वहाँ से भाग गई।

अयोमुखी के भाग जाने के पश्चात् दोनों भाई थोड़ी दूर गये थे कि वन में भयंकर आँधी चलने लगी। उन्हें एक भयंकर स्वर सुनाई दिया जिसकी गर्जना से सम्पूर्ण वनप्रान्त गूँज उठा। सावधान हो कर दोनों भाइयों ने तलवार निकाल कर उस दिशा में पग बढ़ाये जिधर से वह भयंकर गर्जना आ रही थी। कुछ ही दूर जाने पर उन्होंने गज के आकार वाले बिना गर्दन

के कबन्ध (धड़मात्र) राक्षस को देखा। उसका न तो गर्दन था और न ही मस्तक। उसके पेट में ही उसका मुँह बना हुआ था और छाती में ललाट था जिसमें अंगारे के समान दहकती हुई एक ही आँख थी। वह दोनों मुट्ठियों में वन के जन्तुओं को पकड़े इनका मार्ग रोके खड़ा था। राम-लक्ष्मण को देखते ही उसने लपक कर दोनों को एक साथ ही बलपूर्वक तथा पीड़ा देते हुए पकड़ लिया और बोला, "बड़े भाग्य से आज ऐसा सुन्दर भोजन मिला है। तुम दोनों को खा कर मैं अपनी क्षुधा शान्त करूँगा।"

इस आकस्मिक आक्रमण से लक्ष्मण किंकर्तव्यविमूढ़ हो गये, परन्तु रामचन्द्र ने बड़ी फुर्ती से उस राक्षस की दाहिनी भुजा काट डाली। लक्ष्मण ने भी क्रोधित होकर उसकी बाँयी भुजा को काट दिया। वह चीत्कार करता हुआ पृथ्वी पर गिर पड़ा।

पृथ्वी पर गिर कर उसने पूछा, "वीरों! आप दोनों कौन हैं?"

उसके इस प्रकार पूछने पर लक्ष्मण ने उसे दोनों भाइयों का परिचय दिया।

उनका परिचय सुनकर कबन्ध ने राम से कहा, "महाबाहु राम! पूर्वकाल में मैं अत्यन्त पराक्रमी था किन्तु पराक्रमी होते हुए भी राक्षस रूप धारण कर ऋषियों को डराया करता था। एक बार क्रोधित होकर स्थूलशिरा नामक महर्षि ने मुझे राक्षस हो जाने का शाप दे दिया। शापमुक्ति के लिये मेरे द्वारा प्रार्थना करने पर उन्होंने बताया कि जब राम तुम्हारी भुजाओं को काट देगा तो तुम्हारी मुक्ति हो जायेगी। हे पुरुष श्रेष्ठ! आपने राक्षस योनि से मुझे मुक्ति दिला कर मेरा बड़ा उपकार किया है। अब आप मुझ पर इतनी कृपा और करना कि अपने हाथों से मेरा दाह-संस्कार कर देना।"

कबन्ध की प्रार्थना सुन कर राम बोले, "हे राक्षसराज! मैं तुम्हारी इच्छा अवश्य पूरी करूँगा। मैं तुमसे कुछ सूचना प्राप्त करना चाहता हूँ। आशा है अवश्य दोगे। दण्डक वन से मेरी अनुपस्थिति में लंकापति रावण मेरी पत्नी का अपहरण कर के ले गया है। मैं उसके बल, पराक्रम, स्थान आदि के विषय में तुमसे पूरी जानकारी चाहता हूँ। यदि जानते हो तो बताओ।"

राम का प्रश्न सुन कर कबन्ध बोला, "हे रघुनन्दन! रावण बड़ा बलवान और शक्तिशाली नरेश है। उससे देव-दानव सभी भयभीत रहते हैं। उस पर विजय प्राप्त करने के लिये आपको नीति का सहारा लेना होगा। आप यहाँ से पम्पा सरोवर चले जाइये। वहाँ ऋष्यमूक पर्वत पर वानरों का राजा सुग्रीव अपने चार वीर वानरों के साथ निवास करता है। वह अत्यन्त वीर, पराक्रमी, तेजस्वी, बुद्धिमान, धीर और नीतिनिपुण है।

उसके पास एक विशाल पराक्रमी सेना भी है जिसकी सहायता से आप रावण पर विजय प्राप्त कर सकते हैं। उसके ज्येष्ठ भ्राता बालि ने उसके राज्य और उसकी पत्नी का अपहरण कर लिया है। यदि आप उसे मित्र बना सकें तो आपका कार्य सिद्ध हो जायेगा। वह राक्षसों के सब स्थानों को जानता और उनकी मायावी चालों को भी समझता है। उसे भी इस समय एक सच्चे पराक्रमी मित्र की आवश्यकता है। आपका मित्र बन जाने पर वह अपने वानरों को भेज कर सीता की खोज करा देगा। साथ ही सीता को वापस दिलाने में भी आपकी सहायता

करेगा।"

इतना कह कर कबन्ध ने अपने प्राण त्याग दिये। रामचन्द्र उसका अन्तिम संस्कार कर के लक्ष्मण सहित पम्पासर की ओर चले। पम्पासर के निकट उन्होंने एक सुन्दर सरोवर देखा जिसमें दोनों भाइयों ने स्नान किया।

13

लंका में सीता की खोज

इस प्रकार से सुग्रीव का हित करने वाले कपिराज हनुमान जी ने लंकापुरी में प्रवेश कर मानो शत्रुओं के सिर पर अपना बायाँ पैर रख दिया। वे राजमार्ग का आश्रय ले उस रमणीय लंकापुरी की और चले। वहाँ पर स्वर्ण निर्मित विशाल भवनों में दीपक जगमगा रहे थे। कहीं नृत्य हो रहा था और कहीं सुरा पी कर मस्त हुये राक्षस अनर्गल प्रलाप कर रहे थे। हनुमान जी ने देखा कि बहुत से राक्षस मन्त्रों का जाप करते हुए स्वाध्याय में तत्पर थे। कोई जटा बढ़ाये तो कोई मूड़ मुड़ाये रावण के अनेक गुप्तचर भी उन्हें दृष्टिगत हुए।

हनुमान जी ने नगर के सब भवनों तथा एकान्त स्थानों को छान डाला, परन्तु कहीं सीता दिखाई नहीं दीं। अन्त में उन्होंने सब ओर से निराश हो कर रावण के उस राजप्रासाद में प्रवेश किया जिसमें लंका के मन्त्री, सचिव एवं प्रमुख सभासद निवास करते थे। उन सब का भली-भाँति निरीक्षण करने के पश्चात् वे रावण के अत्यन्त प्रिय बृहत्शाला की ओर चले। वहाँ की सीढ़ियाँ रत्नजटित थीं। स्वर्ण निर्मित वातायन दीपों के प्रकाश से जगमगा रही थीं। स्थान-स्थान पर हाथी दाँत का काम किया हुआ था। छतें और स्तम्भ मणियों तथा रत्नों से जड़े हुये थे। इन्द्र के भवन से भी अधिक सुसज्जित इस भव्य शाला को देख कर हनुमान चकित रह गये। उन्होंने एक ओर स्फटिक के सुन्दर पलंग पर रावण को हुए मदिरा के मद में पड़े देखा जो कि अनिंद्य सुन्दरियों से घिरे हए था। उसके नेत्र अद्र्धनिमीलित हो रहे थे। अनेक रमणियों के वस्त्राभूषण अस्त-व्यस्त हो रहे थे और वे सुरा के प्रभाव से अछूती भी नहीं थीं। वहाँ भी सीता को न पा कर पवनसुत बाहर निकल आये।

फिर हनुमान जी ने रावण के अन्य निकट सम्बंधियों के निवास स्थानों में सीता की खोज की किन्तु वहाँ भी उन्हें असफलता ही मिली। तत्पश्चात् हनुमान ने रावण की पटरानी मन्दोदरी के भवन में प्रवेश किया। अपने शयनागार में मन्दोदरी एक स्फटिक से श्वेत पलंग पर सो रही थी। उसके शय्या के चारों ओर रंग-बिरंगी सुवासित पुष्पमालायें झूल रही थीं। उसके अद्‌भुत रूप, लावण्य, सौन्दर्य एवं यौवन को देख कर हनुमान के मन में विचार आया, सम्भवतः यही जनकनन्दिनी सीता हैं, परन्तु उसी क्षण उनके मन में एक और विचार उठा

कि ये सीता नहीं हो सकतीं क्योंकि रामचन्द्र जी के वियोग में पतिव्रता सीता न तो सो सकती हैं और न इस प्रकार आभूषण आदि पहन कर श्रृंगार ही कर सकती हैं। अतएव यह स्त्री अनुपम लावण्यमयी होते हुये भी सीता कदापि नहीं है। यह सोच कर वे उदास हो गये और मन्दोदरी के कक्ष से बाहर निक आये।

अकस्मात् वे सोचने लगे कि आज मैंने पराई स्त्रियों को अस्त-व्यस्त वेष में सोते हुये देख कर भारी पाप किया है। वे इस पर पश्चाताप करने लगे। फिर यह विचार कर उन्होंने अपने मन को शान्ति दी कि उन्हें देख कर मेरे मन में कोई विकार उत्पन्न नहीं हुआ इसलिये यह पाप नहीं है। फिर जिस उद्देश्य के लिये मुझे भेजा गया है, उसकी पूर्ति के लिये मुझे अनिवार्य रूप से स्त्रियों का अवलोकन करना पड़ेगा। इसके बिना मैं अपना कार्य कैसे पूरा कर सकूँगा। फिर वे सोचने लगे मुझे सीता जी कहीं नहीं मिलीं। रावण ने उन्हें मार तो नहीं डाला? यदि ऐसा है तो मेरा सारा परिश्रम व्यर्थ गया।

नहीं, मुझे यह नहीं सोचना चाहिये। जब तक मैं लंका का कोना-कोना न छान मारूँ, तब तक मुझे निराश नहीं होना चाहिये। यह सोच कर अब उन्होंने ऐसे-ऐसे स्थानों की खोज आरम्भ की, जहाँ तनिक भी असावधानी उन्हें यमलोक तक पहुँचा सकती थी। उन स्थानों में उन्होंने रावण द्वारा हरी गई अनुपम सुन्दर नागकन्याओं एवं किन्नरियों को भी देखा, परन्तु सीता कहीं नहीं मिलीं। सब ओर से निराश हो कर उन्होंने सोचा, मैं बिना सीता जी का समाचार लिये लौट कर किसी को मुख नहीं दिखा सकता। इसलिये यहीं रह कर उनकी खोज करता रहूँगा, अथवा अपने प्राण दे दूँगा। यह सोच कर भी उन्होंने सीता को खोजने का कार्य बन्द नहीं किया।

14

रावण-सीता संवाद

इस प्रकार फूले हुए वृक्षों से सुशोभित उस वन की शोभा देखते और विदेहनन्दिनी का अनुसंधान करते हुए हनुमान जी की वह सारी रात प्रायः व्यतीत हो चली। रात्रि जब मात्र एक प्रहर बाकी रही तो रात के उस पिछले प्रहर में छहों अंगोंसहित सम्पूर्ण वेदों के विद्वान तथा श्रेष्ठ यज्ञों द्वारा यजन करने वाले ब्रह्म-राक्षसों के घर में वेदपाठ की ध्वनि होने लगी जिसे हनुमान जी ने सुना।

तदन्तर मंगल वाद्यों तथा श्रवण-सुखद शब्दों द्वारा महाबाहु दशमुख रावण को जगाया गया। जागने पर महाभागी एवं प्रतापी राक्षसराज रावण ने सबसे पहले विदेहनन्दिनी सीता का चिन्तन किया। सीता के प्रति आसक्त एवं काम से प्रेरित रावण ने सब प्रकार के आभूषण धारण कर तथा परम उत्तम शोभा से सम्पन्न हो अशोकवाटिका में प्रवेश किया। पुलस्त्यनन्दन रावण के पीछे-पीछे लगभग एक सौ सुन्दरियाँ भी थीं। काम के आधीन एवं मन में सीता की आस लगाये मन्दगति से आगे बढ़ता रावण अद्भुत शोभा पा रहा था। काम, दर्प और मद से युक्त अचिन्त्य बल-पौरुष से सम्पन्न रावण के अशोकवाटिका के द्वार तक पहुँचने पर कपिवर हुनमान जी ने उसे देखा। यद्यपि मतिमान् हनुमान जी अत्यन्त उग्रतेजस्वी थे, तथापि रावण के तेज से तिरस्कृत-से होकर सघन पत्तो में घुसकर छिप गये।

अनिंद्य सुन्दरी राजकुमारी सीता ने जब उत्तमोत्तम आभूषणों से विभूषित तथा रूप-यौवन से सम्पन्न राक्षसराज रावण को आते देखा तो वे प्रचण्ड हवा में हिलने वाली कदली के समान भय के मारे थर-थर काँपने लगीं। सुन्दर कान्ति वाली विशाललोचना जानकी ने अपने जंघाओं से पेट और दोनों भुजाओं से स्तन छिपा लिये और रुदन करने लगीं। निशाचरियों से घिरी आसन रहित भूमि पर शोक-विह्वल दीन सीता को रावण ने ध्यानपूर्वक देखा जो दृष्टि नीची किये एकटक पृथ्वी की ओर देख रही थी।

ऐसी दुःखी जानकी के पास आकर लंकापति रावण हँसता हुआ बोले, "हे मृगनयनी! मुझे देख कर तू अपने शरीर को छिपाने का प्रयत्न क्यों कर रही है। स्मरण रख, तेरी इच्छा के बिना मैं कदापि तेरा स्पर्श नहीं करूँगा। तू मुझ पर और मेरे कथन पर विश्वास रख और इस

प्रकार दुःखी हो कर अश्रु मत बहा। तेरी यह मलिन, आभूषणरहित वेश-भूषा देख कर मुझे अत्यधिक पीड़ा होती है। तू संसार की सुन्दरियों में शिरोमणि है। अपने इस सौन्दर्य तथा यौवन को व्यर्थ नष्ट मत होने दे। यदि एक बार यह यौवन नष्ट हो गया तो फिर लौट कर नहीं आयेगा। मैं फिर कहता हूँ, तू विश्व की अनुपम सुन्दरी है विधाता की अद्वितीय सृष्टि है। तेरे निर्माण में ब्रह्मा ने अपना सारा कौशल और चतुराई लगा दी। इसीलिये तेरी रचना में उसने किसी प्रकार की कोई कमी नहीं रखी है। तेरे किस-किस अंग की मैं सराहना करूँ।

जिस अंग पर दृष्टि पड़ती है, उसी पर अटक कर रह जाती है। मैं तुझे पूरे हृदय से अपनाना चाहता हूँ। मैं तेरे प्रत्येक अंग का रसास्वादन करना चाहता हूँ। इसी लिये तुझसे कहता हूँ, तू राम का मोह छोड़ दे। मैं तुझे अपनी पटरानी बनाउँगा। मेरी सब रानियाँ तो तेरी चरणों की दासी बनेंगी ही, मैं भी तेरा दास बन कर रहूँगा। अपने भुजबल से अर्जित सम्पूर्ण सम्पत्ति तेरे चरणों में अर्पित कर दूँगा। जीते हुये समस्त राज्य तेरे पिता जनक को दे दूँगा। तू वास्तव में इतनी सुन्दर है कि तुझे देख कर तो तुझे बनाने वाला स्वयं विधाता कामवश हो जायेगा, मेरी तो बात ही क्या है? इसलिये तू मेरी बात स्वीकार कर ले। राम से भयभीत होने की आवश्यकता कोई नहीं है। संसार में कोई भी मुझसे लोहा नहीं ले सकता। चल, उठ कर खड़ी हो जा और सुन्दर वस्त्राभूषण धारण कर के मेरे साथ रमण कर। हे कल्याणी! चल कर तू मेरे ऐश्वर्य को देख और उस कंगाल वनवासी को भूल जा। तू ही सोच, राम के पास न राज्य है, न धन है, न कोई दास है, न सेना है और न कोई साधन है। फिर यह भी क्या पता है कि वह अभी जीता है या मर गया। यदि जीवित भी हो तो भी न तो तू उसके पास पहुँच सकती है और न वह स्वयं ही यहाँ आ सकता है। अतएव चिन्ता का परित्याग कर के निश्चिन्त हो कर मेरे साथ रमण कर।"

रावण के नीच वचनों को सुन कर मध्य में तृण रख कर जानकी बोलीं, "हे लंकेश! तुम्हारे जैसे विद्वान के लिये यह उचित होगा कि तुम अपनी मर्यादाओं का उल्लंघन न करो और मुझसे अपना मन हटा कर अपनी रानियों से प्रेम करो। स्मरण रखो, पापी और नीच भावना रखने वाले पुरुषों को अपने उद्देश्य में कभी सफलता नहीं मिलती। मैं उत्तम कुल में जन्म लेने वाली पतिपरायणा पत्नी हूँ, तुम मुझे मेरे सतीत्व से कदापि विचलित नहीं कर सकते। अपने प्राण रहते मैं तुम्हारे नीचता से परिपूर्ण प्रस्ताव को किसी भी दशा में स्वीकार नहीं कर सकती। यदि तुममें तनिक भी न्याय-बुद्धि होती तो तुम अन्य स्त्रियों के धर्म की उसी प्रकार रक्षा करते जिस प्रकार अपनी रानियों के सतीत्व की करते हो। क्या इस लंका में ऐसा कोई समझदार व्यक्ति नहीं है जो तुम्हें इस साधारण सी बात का बोध कराये? तुम तो नीतिवान बनते हो, फिर नीति का यह वाक्य कैसे भूल गये कि जिस राजा की इन्द्रियाँ उसके वश में नहीं रहतीं, वह चाहे कितना ही ऐश्वर्यवान हो, अन्त में रसातल को जाता है, उसका सर्वस्व नष्ट हो जाता है। हे दुर्बुद्धे! तूने अभी तक मुझे पहचाना नहीं है।

मैं तेरे ऐश्वर्य, राज्य, धन-सम्पत्ति के लोभ में नहीं फँस सकती। तेरा यह कहना भी एक व्यर्थ का प्रलाप है कि मैं रघुकुलमणि रामचन्द्र जी से नहीं मिल सकती। अरे मूर्ख! वे तो सदैव

मेरे हृदय में निवास करते हैं। मुझे कोई उनसे अलग नहीं कर सकता। मेरा उनका ऐसा अटूट सम्बंध है जैसा कि सूर्य का उसकी प्रभा से। इसलिये मैं उनकी हूँ और सदा ही उनकी रहूँगी। यदि तू सोच-समझ कर यह मान ले कि तूने मेरा अपहरण कर के एक भयंकर अपराध किया है और इसलिये मुझे लौटाते हुये तुझे भय लगता है तो मैं तुझे अभयदान देते हुये वचन देती हूँ कि तू मुझे उनके पास पहुँचा दे, मैं तुझे उनसे क्षमा करा दूँगी। यदि तुम अब भी अपनी हठ पर अड़े रहे तो विश्वास करो कि तुम्हारी मृत्य निश्चित है और तुम्हें उनके बाणों से कोई नहीं बचा सकता। इसलिये मैं फिर कहती हूँ कि सावधान हो जाओ। अपने साथ लंका और लंकावासियों का नाश मत करो। इसी में तुम्हारा और तुम्हारे राक्षसकुल का कल्याण है।"

सीता के ये कठोर वचन सुनकर राक्षसराज रावण ने उन प्रियदर्शना सीता को यह अप्रिय उत्तर दिया, "लोक में पुरुष जैसे-जैसे अनुनय-विनय करता है, वैसे-वैसे ही वह उनका प्रिय होता जाता है किन्तु मैं तुमसे ज्यों-ज्यों मीठे वचन बोलता हूँ त्यों-त्यों तुम मेरा तिरस्कार करती जाती हो। तुम्हारे प्रति जो मेरा प्रेम उत्पन्न हो गया है, वही मेरे क्रोध को रोक रहा है। हे समुखि! यही कारण है कि वध और तिरस्कार के योग्य होने पर भी मैं तुम्हारा वध नहीं कर रहा हूँ। मिथिलेशकुमारी! तुम मुझसे जैसी कठोर बातें कह रही हो, उनके प्रतिकार में तुम्हें कठोर प्राणदण्ड देना ही उचित है। हे सुन्दरि! मैंने तुम्हारे लिये जो अवधि नियुक्त की है उसके अनुसार मुझे दो महीने और प्रतीक्षा करनी है। तत्पश्चात् तुम्हें मेरी शय्या पर आना ही होगा। स्मरण रखो यदि दो महीने बाद तुमने अपना पति स्वीकार नहीं करोगी तो मेरे रसोइये मेरे कलेवे के लिये तुम्हारे टुकड़े-टुकड़े कर डालेंगे।"

राक्षसराज रावण के इन वचनों को सुनकर पातिव्रत्य और पति के शौर्य के अभिमान से परिपूर्ण सीता ने कहा, "निश्चय ही इस नगर में तेरा भला चहने वाला कोई भी ऐसा पुरुष नहीं है जो तुझे इस निन्दित कर्म से रोके। नीच राक्षस! तूने अमित तेजस्वी श्री राम की भार्या से जो पाप की बात कही है, उसके परिणामस्वरूप दण्ड से तू कहाँ जाकर छुटकारा पायेगा? मैं धर्मात्मा श्री राम की धर्मपत्नी और महाराज दशरथ की पुत्रवधू हूँ। दशमुख रावण! मेरा तेज ही तुझे भस्म कर डालने के लिये पर्याप्त है। केवल श्रीराम की आज्ञा न होने से और अपनी तपस्या को सुरक्षि रखने के विचार से मैं तुझे भस्म नहीं कर रही हूँ। निःसन्देह तेरे वध के लिये ही विधाता ने यह विधा रच दिया है। तू कितना वीर और पराक्रमी है इसका पता तो मुझे उसी दिन चल गया था, जब तेरे पास इतनी विशाल सेना, बल और तेज होते हुये भी तू मुझे चोरों की भाँति मेरे पति की अनुपस्थिति में चुरा लाया था। क्या इससे तेरी कायरता का पता नहीं चलता।"

सीता के मुख से ऐसे अप्रत्याशित एवं अपमानजनक वचन सुनकर रावण का सम्पूर्ण शरीर क्रोध से थर-थर काँपने लगा। उसके नेत्रों से अंगारे बरसाने लगे। वह दहाड़ता हुआ बोला, "अन्यायी और निर्धन मनुष्य का अनुसरण करने वाली नारी! जैसे सूर्यदेव अपने तेज से प्रातःकालिक संध्या के अन्धकार को नष्ट कर देते हैं उसी प्रकार मैं तेरा तत्काल विनाश किये देता हूँ।"

तत्पश्चात् रावण ने एकाक्षी (एक आँख वाली), एककर्णा (एक कान वाली), अश्वपदी (घोड़े के समान पैर वाली), सिंहमुखी (सिंह के समान मुख वाली) आदि विकराल दिखायी देनेवाली राक्षसियों को सम्बोधित करते हुए कहा, "जिस प्रकार भी हो, सीता को मेरे वश में होने के लिये विवश करो। यदि वह प्रेम से न माने तो इसे मनचाहा दण्ड दो ताकि यह हाथ जोड़ कर गिड़गिड़ाती तुई मुझसे प्रार्थाना करे और मुझे अपना पति स्वीकार करे।"

राक्षसियों को इस प्रकार आज्ञा देकर काम और क्रोध से व्याकुल हुआ राक्षसराज रावण सीता की ओर देखकर गर्जना करने लगा। रावण को अत्यन्त क्रोधित देखकर मन्दोदरी और धान्यमालिनी नाम की एक अन्य राक्षस-कन्या शीघ्र रावण के पास आयीं और उसका आलिंगन कर बोलीं, "हे प्राणनाथ! आप इस कुरूप सीता के लिये क्यों इतने व्याकुल होते हैं? भला इसके फीके पतले अधरों, अनाकर्षक कान्ति और छोटे भद्दे आकार में क्या आकर्षण है? आप चल कर मेरे साथ विहार कीजिये। इस अभागी को मरने दीजिये। इसके ऐसे भाग्य कहाँ जो आप जैसे अपूर्व बलिष्ठ, अद्भुत पराक्रमी, तीनों लोकों के विजेता के साथ रमण-सुख प्राप्त कर सके। नाथ! जो स्त्री आपको नहीं चाहती, उसके पीछे उन्मत्त की भाँति दौड़ने से क्या लाभ? इससे तो व्यर्थ ही मन को दुःख होता है।"

जब उन राक्षसियों ने ऐसा कहा और उसे दूसरी ओर हटा ले गयीं तो मेघ के समान काला और बलवान राक्षस रावण जोर-जोर से हँसता हुआ अपने भव्य प्रासाद की ओर चल पड़ा।

15

जानकी राक्षसी घेरे में

राक्षसराज रावण के चले जाने के बार भयानक रूप वाली राक्षसियों ने सीता को घेर लिया और उन्हें अनेक प्रकार से डराने धमकाने लगीं। वे सीता की भर्त्सना करते हुए कहने लगीं, "हे मूर्ख अभागिन! हे नीच नारी! तीनों लोकों और चौदह भुवनों को अपने पराक्रम से पराजित करने वाले परम तेजस्वी राक्षसराज की शैया प्रत्येक को नहीं मिलती। यह तो तुम्हारा परम सौभाग्य है कि स्वयं लंकापति तुम्हें अपनी अंकशायिनी बनाना चाहते हैं।

तनिक विचार कर देखो, कहाँ अगाध ऐश्‍वर्य, स्वर्णपुरी तथा अतुल सम्पत्ति का एकछत्र स्वामी और कहाँ वह राज्य से निकाला हुआ, कंगालों की भाँति वन-वन में भटकने वाला, हतभाग्य साधारण सा मनुष्य! सोच-समझ कर निर्णय करो और महाप्रतापी लंकाधिपति रावण को पति के रूप में स्वीकार करो। उसकी अद्‌र्धांगिनी बनने में ही तुम्हारा कल्याण है। अन्यथा राम के वियोग में तड़प-तड़प कर मरोगी या राक्षसराज के हाथों मारी जाओगी। तुम्हारा यह कोमल शरीर इस प्रकार नष्ट होने के लिये नहीं है। महाराज रावण के साथ विलास भवन में जा कर रमण करो। महाराज तुम्हें इतना विलासमय सुख देंगे जिसकी तुमने उस कंगाल वनवासी के साथ रहते कल्पना भी नहीं की होगी।"

राक्षसियों की ये बातें सुनकर कमलनयनी सीता ने अश्रुपूर्ण नेत्रों से उनकी ओर देख कर कहा, "तुम सब का यह लोक-विरुद्‌ध एवं पापपूर्ण प्रस्ताव मेरे हृदय में क्षणमात्र को भी ठहर नहीं पाता। एक मानवकन्या किसी राक्षस की भार्या नहीं हो सकती। तुम सब लोग भले ही मुझे खा जाओ किन्तु मैं तुम्हारी बात नहीं मान सकती। मेरे पति दीन हों अथवा राज्यहीन, वे ही मेरे स्वामी हैं और मैं सदा उन्हीं में अनुरक्त हूँ तथा आगे भी रहूँगी। जैसे सुवर्चला सूर्य में, महाभागा शची इन्द्र में, अरुन्धती महर्षि वसिष्ठ में, रोहिणि चन्द्र में, सुकन्या च्यवन में, सावित्री सत्यवान में, श्रीमती कपिल में, मदयन्ती सौदास में, केशिनी सगर में और दमयन्ती नल में अनुराग रखती हैं वैसे ही मैं भी अपने पति इक्ष्वाकुवंशशिरोमणि श्री राम में अनुरक्त हूँ।

सीता के वचन सुन कर राक्षसियों के क्रोध की सीमा न रही। वे रावण की आज्ञानुसार कठोर वचनों द्वारा उन्हें धमकाने लगीं। अशोकवृक्ष में चुपचाप छिपे बैठे हुए हनुमान जी सीता को फटकारती हुई राक्षसियों की बाते सुनते रहे। वे सब राक्षसियाँ कुपित होकर काँपती हुई सीता पर चारों ओर से टूट पड़ीं। उनका क्रोध बहुत बढ़ा हुआ था। राक्षसियों के बारम्बार धमकाने पर सर्वांगसुन्दरी कल्याणी सीता अपने आँसू पोंछती हुई उसी अशोकवृक्ष के नीचे चली आईं जिस पर हनुमान जी छिपे बैठे थे। शोकसागर में डूबी हुईं विशाललोचना वैदेही वहाँ चुपचाप बैठ गईं। वे अत्यन्त दीन व दुर्बल हो गई थीं तथा उनके वस्त्र मलिन हो चुके थे। विकराल राक्षसियाँ फिर उन्हें घेरकर तरह-तरह से धमकाने लगीं।

विकराल रूप वाली राक्षसियों के द्वारा इस प्रकार से धमकाये जाने पर देवकन्या के समान सुन्दरी सीता धैर्य छोड़ कर रोने लगीं। विलाप करते हुए वे कहने लगीं, "हे भगवान! अब यह विपत्ति नहीं सही जाती। प्रभो! मुझे इस विपत्ति से छुटकारा दिलाओ, या मुझे इस पृथ्वी से उठा लो। बड़े लोगों ने सच कहा है कि समय से पहले मृत्यु भी नहीं आती। आज मेरी कैसी दयनीय दशा हो गई है। कहाँ अयोध्या का वह राजप्रासाद जहाँ मैं अपने परिजनों तथा पति के साथ अलौकिक सुख भोगती थे और कहाँ यह दुर्दिन जब मैं पति से विमुख छल द्वारा हरी गई इन राक्षसों के फंदों में फँस कर निरीह हिरणी की भाँति दुःखी हो रही हूँ। आज अपने प्राणेश्वर के बिना मैं जल से निकाली गई मछली की भाँति तड़प रही हूँ।

इतनी भायंकर वेदना सह कर भी मेरे प्राण नहीं निकल रहे हैं। आश्चर्य यह है कि मर्मान्तक पीड़ा सह कर भी मेरा हृदय टुकड़े-टुकड़े नहीं हो गया। मुझ जैसी अभागिनी कौन होगी जो अपने प्राणाधिक प्रियतम से बिछुड़ कर भी अपने प्राणों को सँजोये बैठी है। अभी न जाने कौन-कौन से दुःख मेरे भाग्य में लिखे हैं। न जाने वह दुष्ट रावण मेरी कैसी दुर्गति करेगा। चाहे कुछ भी हो, मैं उस महापातकी को अपने बायें पैर से भी स्पर्श न करूँगी, उसके इंगित पर आत्म समर्पण करना तो दूर की बात है। यह मेरा दुर्भाग्य ही है किस एक परमप्रतापी वीर की भार्या हो कर भी दुष्ट रावण के हाथों सताई जा रही हूँ और वे मेरी रक्षा करने के लिये अभी तक यहाँ नहीं पहुँचे। मेरा तो भाग्य ही उल्टा चल रहा है।

यदि परोपकारी जटायुराज इस नीच के हाथों न मारे जाते तो वे अवश्य राघव को मेरा पता बता देते और वे आ कर रावण का विनाश करके मुझे इस भयानक यातना से मुक्ति दिलाते। परन्तु मेरा मन कह रहा है दि दुश्चरित्र रावण के पापों का घड़ा भरने वाला है। अब उसका अन्त अधिक दूर नहीं है। वह अवश्य ही मेरे पति के हाथों मारा जायेगा। उनके तीक्ष्ण बाण लंका को लम्पट राक्षसों के आधिपत्य से मुक्त करके अवश्य मेरा उद्धार करेंगे।

किन्तु उनकी प्रतीक्षा करते-करते मुझे इतने दिन हो गये और वे अभी तक नहीं आये। कहीं ऐसा तो नहीं है कि उन्होंने मुझे मरा हुआ समझ लिया हो और इसलिये अब वे मेरी खोज खबर ही न ले रहे हों। यह भी तो हो सकता है कि दुष्ट मायावी रावण ने जिस प्रकार छल से मेरा हरण किया, उसी प्रकार उसने छल से उन दोनों भाइयों का वध कर डाला हो। उस दुष्ट के लिये कोई भी नीच कार्य अकरणीय नहीं है। दोनों दशाओं में मेरे जीवित रहने

का प्रयोजन नहीं है। यदि उन्होंने मुझे मरा हुआ समझ लिया है या इस दुष्ट ने उन दोनों का वध कर दिया है तो भी मेरा और उनका मिलन जअब असम्भव हो गया है। जब मैं अपने प्राणेश्वर से नहीं मिल सकती तो मेरा जीवित रहना व्यर्थ है। मैं अभी इसी समय अपने प्राणों का उत्सर्ग करूँगी।"

सीता के इन निराशा भरे वचनों को सुन कर पवनपुत्र हनुमान अपने मन में विचार करने लगे कि अब इस बात में कोई सन्देह नहीं है कि यह ही जनकनन्दिनी जानकी हैं जो अपने पति के वियोग में व्यकुल हो रही हैं। यही वह समय है, जब इन्हें धैर्य की सबसे अधिक आवश्यकता है।

16

समुद्र पार करने की चिन्ता

हनुमान के मुख से सीता का समाचार पाकर रामचन्द्र जी अत्यन्त प्रसन्न हुये और कहने लगे, "हनुमान ने बहुत भारी कार्य किया है भूतल पर ऐसा कार्य होना कठिन है। इस महासागर को लाँघ सकने की क्षमता गरुड़, वायु और हनुमान को छोड़कर किसी दूसरे में नहीं है। देवताओं, राक्षसों, यक्षों, गन्धर्वों तथा दैत्यों द्वारा रक्षित लंका में प्रवेश करके उसमें से सुरक्षित निकल आना केवल हनुमान के लिये ही सम्भव है। इन्होंने समुद्र-लंघन आदि कार्यों के द्वारा अपने पराक्रम के अनुरूप बल प्रकट कर के एक सच्चे सेवक के योग्य सुग्रीव का बहुत बड़ा कार्य सम्पन्न किया है।

स्वामी द्वारा दिये गये कार्य को सेवक उत्साह तथा लगन से पूरा करे तो वह श्रेष्ठ होता है। जो सेवक कार्य तो पूर्ण कर दे, किन्तु बिना किसी उत्साह के पूरा करे, वह मध्यम होता है और आज्ञा पाकर भी कार्य न करने वाला सेवक अधम कहलाता है। हनुमान ने स्वामी के एक कार्य में नियुक्त होकर उसके साथ ही दूसरे महत्वपूर्ण कार्यों को भी पूरा किया है और सुग्रीव को पूर्णतः सन्तुष्ट कर दिया है। आज मेरे पास पुरस्कार देने योग्य वस्तु का अभाव है। यह बात मेरे मन कसक उत्पन्न कर रही है कि यहाँ जिसने मुझे ऐसा प्रिय संवाद सुनाया, उसका मैं कोई वैसा ही प्रिय कार्य नहीं कर पा रहा हूँ। अतः इस समय मैं इन महात्मा हनुमान को केवल अपना प्रगाढ़ आलिंगन प्रदान अपना सर्वस्व इसे समर्पित करता हूँ।"

ऐसा कहते-कहते श्री रामचन्द्र जी के अंग-प्रत्यंग प्रेम से पुलकित हो गये और उन्होंने अपनी आज्ञा के पालन में सफलता पाकर लौटे हुए पवित्रात्मा हनुमान जी को हृदय से लगा लिया।

फिर थोड़ी देर तक विचार करके रामचन्द्र जी ने सुग्रीव से कहा, "हे वानरराज! जानकी की खोज का कार्य तो सुचारुरूप से सम्पन्न हो गया किन्तु समुद्र की दुस्तरता का विचार करके मेरे मन का उत्साह पुनः नष्ट हो रहा है। महान जलराधि से परिपूर्ण समुद्र को पार करना अत्यन्त कठिन है। यह कार्य कैसे हो पायेगा?"

राम को इस प्रकार चिन्तित देख सुग्रीव ने कहा, “वीरवर! आप दूसरे साधारण मनुष्यों की भाँति क्यों सन्ताप कर रहे हैं? जैसे कृतघ्न पुरुष सौहार्द्र को त्याग देता है उसी प्रकार से आप भी इस सन्ताप को त्याग दें। जब सीता जी का पता लग गया है तो मुझे आपके इस दुःख और चिन्ता का कोई कारण नहीं दिखाई देता। मेरी वानर सेना की वीरता और पराक्रम के सामने यह समुद्र बाधा बन कर खड़ा नहीं हो सकता। हम समुद्र पर पुल बना कर उसे पार करेंगे। परिश्रम और उद्योग से कौन सा कार्य सिद्ध नहीं हो सकता? हमें कायरों की भाँति समुद्र को बाधा मान निराश होकर नहीं बैठना चाहिये।”

सुग्रीव के उत्साहपूर्ण शब्दों से सन्तुष्ट होकर राघव हनुमान से बोले, “हे वीर हनुमान! कपिराज सुग्रीव की पुल बनाने की योजना से मैं सहमत हूँ। यह कार्य शीघ्र आरम्भ हो जाये, ऐसी व्यवस्था तो सुग्रीव कर ही देंगे। इस बीच तुम मुझे रावण की सेना, उसकी शक्ति, युद्ध कौशल, दुर्गों आदि के विषय में विस्तृत जानकारी दो। मुझे विश्वास है कि तुमने इन सारी बातों का अवश्य ही विस्तारपूर्वक अध्ययन किया होगा। तुम्हारी विश्लेषण क्षमता पर मुझे पूर्ण विश्वास है।”

रघुनाथ जी का आदेश पाकर पवनपुत्र हनुमान ने कहा, “हे सीतापते! लंका जितनी ऐश्वर्य तथा समृद्धि से युक्त है, उतनी ही वह विलासिता में डूबी हुई भी है। सैनिक शक्ति उसकी महत्वपूर्ण है। उसमें असंख्य उन्मत्त हाथी, रथ और घोड़े हैं। बड़े-बड़े पराक्रमी योद्धा सावधानी से लंकापुरी की रक्षा करते हैं। उस विशाल नगरी के चार बड़े-बड़े द्वार हैं। प्रत्येक द्वार पर ऐसे शक्तिशाली यन्त्र लगे हुये हैं जो लाखों की संख्या में आक्रमण करने वाले शत्रु सैनिकों को भी द्वार से दूर रखने की क्षमता रखते हैं। इसके अतिरिक्त प्रत्येक द्वार पर अनेक बड़ी-बड़ी शतघनी (तोप) रखी हुई हैं जो विशाल गोले छोड़ कर अपनी अग्नि से समुद्र जैसी विशाल सेना को नष्ट करने की सामर्थ्य रखती है।

लंका को और भी अधिक सुरक्षित रखने के लिये उसके चारों ओर अभेद्य स्वर्ण का परकोटा खींचा गया है। परकोटे के साथ-साथ गहरी खाइयाँ खुदी हुई हैं जो अगाध जल से भरी हुई हैं। उस जल में नक्र, मकर जैसे भयानक हिंसक जल-जीव निवास करते हैं। परकोटे पर थोड़े-थोड़े अन्तर से बुर्ज बने हुये हैं। उन पर विभिन्न प्रकार के विचित्र किन्तु शक्तिशाली यन्त्र रखे हुये हैं। यदि किसी प्रकार से शत्रु के सैनिक परकोटे पर चढ़ने में सफल हो भी जायें तो ये यन्त्र अपनी चमत्कारिक शक्ति से उन्हें खाई में धकेल देते हैं।

लंका के पूर्वी द्वार पर दस सहस्त्र पराक्रमी योद्धा शूल तथा खड्ग लिये सतर्कतापूर्वक पहरा देते हैं। दक्षिण द्वार पर एक लाख योद्धा अस्त्र-शस्त्रों से सुसज्जित होकर सदैव सावधानी की मुद्रा में खड़े रहते हैं। उत्तर और पश्चिम के द्वारों पर भी सुरक्षा की ऐसी ही व्यवस्था है। इतना सब कुछ होते हुये भी आपकी कृपा से मैंने उनकी शक्ति काफी क्षीण कर दी है क्योंकि जब रावण ने मेरी पूँछ में कपड़ा लपेट कर आग लगवा दी थी तो मैंने उसी जलती हुई पूँछ से लंका के दुर्गों को या तो समूल नष्ट कर दिया या उन्हें अपार क्षति पहुँचाई है। अनेक यन्त्रों की दुर्दशा कर दी है और कई बड़े-बड़े सेनापतियों को यमलोक भेज दिया है।

अब तो केवल सागर पर सेतु बाँधने की देर है, फिर तो राक्षसों का विनाश होते अधिक देर नहीं लगेगी।"

17

वानर सेना का प्रस्थान

हनुमान के मुख से लंका का यह विशद वर्णन सुन कर रामचन्द्र बोले, "हनुमान! तुमने भयानक राक्षस रावण की जिस लंकापुरी का वर्णन किया है, उसे मैं शीघ्र ही नष्ट कर डालूँगा। सुग्रीव! अभी विजय नामक मुहूर्त है और इस मुहूर्त में प्रस्थान करना अत्यन्त उपयुक्त है। अतः तुम तत्काल प्रस्थान की तैयारी करो। आज उत्तराफाल्गुनी नामक नक्षत्र है। कल चन्द्रमा का हस्त नक्षत्र से योग होगा। इसलिये हे सुग्रीव! हम लोगों का आज ही सारी सेनाओं के साथ यात्रा आरम्भ कर देना ही उचित है। इस समय जो शकुन प्रकट हो रहे हैं उन्हें देखकर यह विश्वास होता है कि मैं अवश्य ही रावण का वध कर के जनकनन्दिनी सीता को ले आऊँगा।"

रघुनाथ जी के वचन सुनकर महापराक्रमी वानरशिरोमणि सुग्रीव ने वानर सेनापतियों को यथोचित आज्ञा दी और समस्त महाबली वानरगण अपनी गुफाओं और शिखरों से शीघ्र ही निकल कर उछलते-कूदते हुए चलने लगे। उनमें से कुछ वानर उस सेना की रक्षा के लिये उछलते-कूदते चारों ओर चक्कर लगाते थे, कुछ मार्गशोधन के लिये कूदते-फाँदते आगे बढ़ते जाते थे, कुछ वानर मेघों के समान गर्जते, कुछ सिंहों के समान दहाड़ते और कुछ किलकारियाँ भरते हुए दक्षिण दिशा की ओर अग्रसर हो रहे थे। इस प्रकार से लाखों और करोड़ों वानर आगे-आगे श्री रामचन्द्र, लक्ष्मण और सुग्रीव को ले कर जयजयकार करते हुये सागर तट की ओर चल पड़े। 'श्री रामचन्द्र की जय' और 'रावण की क्षय' की घोषणाओं से दसों दिशाएँ गूँजने लगीं। कुछ वानर बारी-बारी से दोनों भाइयों को अपनी पीठ पर चढ़ाये लिये जा रहे थे। उनको अपनी-अपनी पीठ पर चढ़ाने के लिये वे एक दूसरे से प्रतिस्पर्धा करने लगे। उनकी तीव्र गति के कारण समस्त वातावरण धूलि-धूसरित हो रहा था।

अम्बर धूमिल हो गया था और आकाश में चमकता हुआ सूर्य भी फीका पड़ गया था। जब वह सेना नदी नालों को पार करती तो उनके प्रवाह भी उसके कारण परिवर्तित हो जाते थे। चारों ओर वानर ही वानर दिखाई देते थे। वे मार्ग में कहीं विश्राम लेने के लिये भी एक क्षण को नहीं ठहरते थे। उनके मन मस्तिष्क पर केवल रावण छाया हुआ था। वे सोचते थे कि कब

लंका पहुँचें और कब राक्षसों का संहार करें। इस प्रकार राक्षसों के संहार की कल्पना में लीन यह विशाल वानर सेना समुद्र तट पर जा पहुँची। अब वे उस क्षण की कल्पना करने लगे जब वे समुद्र पार करके दुष्ट रावण की लंका में प्रवेश करके अपने अद्भुत पराक्रम का प्रदर्शन करेंगे।

सागर के तट पर एक स्वच्छ शिला पर बैठ राम सुग्रीव से बोले, "हे सुग्रीव! हम सागर के तट तक तो पहुँच गये। अब यहाँ मन में फिर वही चिन्ता उत्पन्न हो गई कि इस विशाल सागर को कैसे पार किया जाय। अपनी सेना की छावनी यहीं डाल कर हमें इस समुद्र को पार करने का उपाय सोचना चाहिये। इधर जब तक हम इसका उपाय ढूँढें, तुम अपने गुप्तचरों को सावधान कर दो कि वे शत्रु की गतिविधियों के प्रति सचेष्ट रहें। कोई वानर अपने छावनी से अकारण बाहर भी न जाये क्योंकि इस क्षेत्रमें लंकेश के गुप्तचर अवश्य सक्रिय होंगे।

रामचन्द्र जी के निर्देशानुसार समुद्र तट पर छावनी डाल दी गई। समुद्र की उत्तुंग तरंगें आकाश का चुम्बन कर अपने विराट रूप का प्रदर्शन कर रहा था। सम्पूर्ण वातावरण जलमय प्रतीत होता था। आकाश में चमकने वाला नक्षत्र समुदाय सागर में प्रतिबिंबित होकर समुद्र को ही आकाश का प्रतिरूप बना रहा था। वानर समुदाय समुद्र की छवि को आश्चर्य, कौतुक और आशंका से देख रहा था।

18

लंका में राक्षसी मन्त्रणा

इन्द्रतुल्य पराक्रमी हनुमान जी ने लंका में जो अत्यन्त भयावह घोर कर्म किया था, उसे देखकर राक्षसराज रावण को बड़ी लज्जा और ग्लानि हुई। उसने समस्त प्रमुख राक्षसों को बुला कर कहा, "निशाचरों! एकमात्र वानर हनुमान अकेला इस दुधुर्ष पुरी में घुस आया। उसने इसे तहस-नहस कर डाला और जनककुमारी सीता से भेंट भी कर लिया। सूचना मिली है कि राम सहस्त्रों धीरवीर वानरों के साथ हमारी लंकापुरी पर आक्रमण करने के लिये आ रहे हैं। यह बात भी भलीभाँति स्पष्ट हो चुकी है कि वे रघुवंशी राम अपने समुचित बल के द्वारा भाई, सेना और सेवकों सहित सुखपूर्वक समुद्र को पार कर लेंगे। ऐसी स्थिति में वानरों से विरोध आ पड़ने पर नगर और सेना के लिये जो भी हितकर हो, वैसे सलाह आप लोग दीजिये।"

राक्षस बलवान तो बहुत थे किन्तु न तो उन्हें नीति का ज्ञान था और न ही वे शत्रुपक्ष के बलाबल को समझते थे। इसलिये वे कहने लगे, "राजन्! आप व्यर्थ ही भयभीत हो रहे हैं। आपने नागों और गन्धर्वों को भी युद्ध में परास्त कर दिया है, दानवराज मय ने आपसे भयभीत होकर अपनी कन्या आपको समर्पित कर दी थी, मधु नामक दैत्य को आपने जीता है। आपके पुत्र मेघनाद ने देवताओं के अधिपति इन्द्र पर विजय प्राप्त करके इन्द्रजित की उपाधि प्राप्त की है। साधारण नर और वानरों से प्राप्त हुई इस आपत्ति के विषय में चिन्ता करना आपके लिये उचित नहीं है। आप सहज ही राम का वध कर डालेंगे।"

रावण के समक्ष प्रहस्त, दुर्मुख, वज्रदंष्ट्र, निकुम्भ, वज्रहनु आदि प्रमुख राक्षसों शत्रुसेना को मार गिराने के लिये अत्यन्त उत्साह दिखाया। उनके उत्साहवर्धक वचन सुनकर रावण अत्यन्त प्रसन्न हुआ और उनकी हाँ में हाँ मिलाने लगा।

मन्त्रियों को रावण की हाँ में हाँ मिलाते देख विभीषण ने हाथ जोड़कर कहा, "हे तात! जो मनोरथ साम (मेल मिलाप), दान (प्रलोभन) और भेद (शत्रु पक्ष में फूट डालना) से सिद्ध न हो सके, उसकी प्राप्ति के लिये नीतिशास्त्र का आश्रय लेना चाहिये। हे रावण! अस्थिर बुद्धि, व्याधिग्रस्त आदि लोगों पर बल का प्रयोग करके कार्य सिद्ध करना चाहिये, परन्तु राम न

तो अस्थिर बुद्धि है और न व्याधिग्रस्त। वह तो दृढ़ निश्चय के साथ आपसे युद्ध करने के लिये आया है, इसलिये उस पर विजय प्राप्त करना सरल नहीं है।

क्या हम जानते थे कि एक छोटा सा वानर हनुमान इतना विशाल सागर पार करके लंका में घुस आयेगा? परन्तु वह केवल आया ही नहीं, लंका को भी विध्वंस कर गया। इस एक घटना से हमें राम की शक्ति का अनुमान लगा लेना चाहिये। उस सेना में हनुमान जैसे लाखों वानर हैं जो राम के लिये अपने प्राणों की भी बलि चढ़ा सकते हैं। इसलिये मेरी सम्मति है कि आप राम को सीता लौटा दें और लंका को भारी संकट से बचा लें। यदि ऐसा न किया गया तो मुझे भय है कि लंका का सर्वनाथ हो जायेगा। राम-लक्ष्मण के तीक्ष्ण बाणों से लंका का एक भी नागरिक जीवित नहीं बचेगा। आप मेरे प्रस्ताव पर गम्भीरता से विचार करें। यह मेरा निवेदन है।”

19
विभीषण का निष्कासन

दूसरे दिन महान मेघों की गर्जना के समान घरघराहट पैदा करने वाले मणियों से अलंकृत चार घोड़ों से युक्त स्वर्ण-रथ पर आरूढ़ हो रावण अपने सभा भवन की ओर चला। भाँति-भाँति के अस्त्र-शस्त्रों से सुसज्जित राक्षस सैनिक उसके आगे-पीछे उसकी जयजयकार करते हुये चले। मार्ग में लोग शंखों और नगाड़ों के तुमुलनाद से सम्पूर्ण वातावरण को गुँजायमान कर रहे थे। सड़कों पर सहस्त्रों नागरिक खड़े होकर उसका अभिवादन कर रहे थे जिससे उसका मस्तक गर्व से उन्नत हो रहा था। इस समय वह अपनी वैभव की तुलना देवराज इन्द्र से कर रहा था। सभा भवन में पहुँच कर वह अपने मणिमय स्वर्ण-सिंहासन पर जाकर बैठ गया। उसके सिंहासनासीन होने पर अन्य दरबारियों अवं मन्त्रियों ने भी अपने-अपने आसन ग्रहण किये।

शत्रुविजयी रावण ने उस समपूर्ण सभा की ओर दृष्टिपात करके कहा, "सभासदों! मैं दण्डकारण्य से राम की प्रिय रानी जनकदुलारी सीता को हर लाया हूँ। किन्तु वह मेरी शय्या पर आरूढ़ होना नहीं चाहती है। मेरी दृष्टि में तीनों लोकों के भीतर सीता के समान सुन्दरी अन्य कोई स्त्री नहीं है। उसे देखने के बाद मेरा मन मेरे वश में नहीं रह गया है। काम ने मुझे आधीन कर लिया है।"

कामातुर रावण का यह प्रलाप सुनकर कुम्भकर्ण ने क्रोधित होकर कहा, "महाराज! तुमने जो यह छलपूर्वक छिपकर परस्त्री-हरण का कार्य किया है, यह तुम्हारे लिये बहुत अनुचित है। इस पापकर्म को करने से पहले आपको हमसे परामर्श कर लेना चाहिये था। यद्यपि तुमने अनुचित कर्म किया है तथापि तुम्हारे शत्रुओं का संहार करूँगा।"

कुम्भकर्ण के वचन सुनकर रावण को क्रोधित होते देख महापार्श्व ने हाथ जोड़कर कहा, "शत्रुसूदन महाराज! आप तो स्वयं ही ईश्वर हैं! आप विदेहकुमारी सीता के साथ उसकी इच्छा की परवाह न कर रमण कीजिये। आपके जो भी शत्रु आयेंगे, उन्हें हम लोग अपने शस्त्रों के प्रताप से जीत लेंगे।"

महापार्श्व के ऐसा कहने पर लंकाधिपति रावण ने उसकी प्रशंसा करते हुए कहा, "महापार्श्व! पूर्वकाल में मैंने एक बार आकाश में अग्नि-पुञ्ज के समान प्रकाशित होती हुई पुञ्जिकस्थला नाम की अप्सरा से बलात् सम्भोग किया था। मेरे इस कृत्य से अप्रसन्न होकर मुझे शाप दे दिया था कि आज के बाद यदि किसी दूसरी नारी के साथ बलपूर्वक समागम करेगा तो तेरे मस्तक के सौ टुकड़े हो जायेंगे। उस शाप से भयभीत होने के कारण मैं विदेहकुमारी से बलात् समागम नहीं कर सकता।"

फिर अपने शूरवीर सेनानायकों एवं मन्त्रियों को सम्बोधित करते हुये वह बोला, "हे बुद्धमान और वीर सभासदों! आज हम लोगों को अपने भावी कार्यक्रम पर विचार करना है। राम सुग्रीव की वानर सेना लेकर समुद्र के उस पार आ पहुँचा है। हमें उसके साथ किस नीति का अनुसरण करना है, इसके विषय में तुम लोग सोच-विचार कर अपनी सम्मति दो क्योंकि तुम सभी बुद्धिमान, नीतिनिपुण और अनुभवी हो।"

रावण की बात सुन कर लगभग सभी राक्षसों ने उत्साहित होकर उसे वानर सेना से युद्ध करने का परामर्श दिया। उनका मत था कि हमारे अपार बल के आगे ये छोटे-छोटे वानर ठहर नहीं सकेंगे। प्रत्येक दशा में विजय हमारी होगी।

अन्य सभी राक्षसों के सम्मति दे चुकने पर विभीषण ने खड़े होकर कहा, "हे तात! सीता का जो अपहरण आपने किया है, वह अत्यन्त अनुचित है। सीता वास्तव में एक विषैली नागिन है जो आपके गले में आकर लिपट गई है। उसके उन्नत उरोज भयंकर फन हैं, उसका चिन्तन मारक विष है और उसकी मुस्कान तीक्ष्ण दाढ़ें हैं। उसकी पाँचों अँगुलियाँ उसके पाँच सिर हैं। यह आपके प्राणों को अपना निशाना बना कर बैठी है। इसलिये मैं आपसे कहता हूँ कि यदि आपने इस नागिन से छुटकारा नहीं पाया तो राम के बाण राक्षसों के सिर काटने में तनिक भी संकोच न करेंगे। इसलिये सबका कल्याण इसी में है कि सीता को तत्काल लौटा कर राम से संधि कर ली जाय।"

विभीषण के वचन सुन कर प्रहस्त ने कहा, "विभीषण! हमने युद्ध में देवताओं, राक्षसों तथा दानवों को पराजित किया है, फिर एक साधारण मानव से भयभीत होने की क्या आवश्याकता है?"

प्रहस्त का प्रश्न सुनकर विभीषण ने उत्तर दिया, "हे मन्त्रिवर! राम कोई साधारण मानव नहीं हैं। उनका वध करना वैसा ही असम्भव है जैसा बिना नौका के सागर को पार करना। मैं उनकी शक्ति को जानता हूँ, हमारी सम्पूर्ण दानवीय शक्ति भी उनके सम्मुख नहीं ठहर सकतीं। राक्षस ही क्या देव, गन्धर्व और किन्नर भी उनसे जीत नहीं सकते।"

फिर विभीषण ने रावण को सम्बोधित करते हुए कहा, "हे राक्षसराज! आप काम के वशीभूत होकर अनुचित कार्य करने जा रहे हैं और ये मन्त्रिगण केवल चाटुकारिता में आपकी हाँ में हाँ मिला रहे हैं। ये आपके हित की सच्ची बात नहीं कह रहे हैं। मैं फिर आपसे कहता हूँ कि सीता को लौटाकर राम से संधि कर लेने में ही आपका, लंका का और सम्पूर्ण राक्षस समुदाय का कल्याण है।"

विभीषण की बातों से चिढ़ कर मेघनाद बोला, "चाचा जी! आप सदा कायरों की भाँति निरुत्साहित करने वाली बातें किया करते हैं। आपने अपनी कायरता से पुलस्त्य वंश को कलंकित किया है। क्षमा करें, इस कुल में आज तक कोई ऐसा भीरु और निर्वीर्य व्यक्ति ने जन्म नहीं लिया।"

मेघनाद के मुख से ये अपमानजनक शब्द सुनकर भी विभीषण ने अपने ऊपर संयम रखते हुये कहा, "मेघनाद! तुम अभी बालक हो। तुम में दूरदर्शिता का अभाव है। इसीलिये तुम ऐसी बात कर रहे हो। मैं फिर कहता हूँ कि राघव से क्षमा माँग कर सीता को लौटाने में ही हमारा कल्याण है।"

विभीषण को बार-बार सीता को लौटाने की बात करते देख रावण ने क्रुद्ध होकर कहा, "बुद्धिमान लोगों ने ठीक ही कहा है कि चाहे शत्रु के साथ निवास करें, सर्प के साथ रहें, परन्तु शत्रु का हित चाहने वाले मित्र के साथ कदापि न रहें। ऐसे लोग मित्र के वेश में घोर शत्रु होते हैं। विभीषण! तुम हमारे सबसे बड़े शत्रु हो जो राम की सराहना करके हमारा मनोबल गिराने का प्रयत्न करते हो। मैं जानता हूँ कि तुम मुख से मेरे हित की बात करते हो परन्तु हृदय से मेरे ऐश्वर्य, वैभव तथा लोकप्रियता से ईर्ष्या करते हो। यदि तुम मेरे भाई न होते तो सबसे पहले मैं तुम्हारा वध करता। यदि वध न करता तो भी कम से कम तुम्हारी जीभ अवश्य खिंचवा लेता। मेरे सामने से दूर हो जा देशद्रोही! और फिर अपना मुख मुझे कभी मत दिखाना।"

रावण से अपमानित होकर विभीषण उठ खड़ा हुआ और बोला, "मैं समझ गया हूँ, तुम्हारे सिर पर काल मँडरा रहा है। इसलिये तुम मित्र और शत्रु में भेद नहीं कर सकते। मैं जाता हूँ। फिर तुम्हें मुख नहीं दिखाउँगा।"

इतना कह कर विभीषण वहाँ से चल दिया।

20

सेतु बन्धन

वानरसेना के समक्ष विशाल समुद्र लहरें मार रहा था और उसे पार करना एक बहुत बड़ी समस्या थी। राम के क्रोध से भयभीत होकर समुद्र ने स्वयं वहाँ आकर बताया कि सुग्रीव की सेना में नल और नील कुशल शिल्पी हैं। उनके नेतृत्व में समुद्र पर सेतु बाँधना सम्भव हो सकेगा। इतना बताकर समुद्र वापस चले गये।

समुद्र की बात सुनकर वानर नल ने श्री राम से कहा, "प्रभो, मैं विश्वकर्मा का औरस पुत्र हूँ और गुण में उन्हीं के समान हूँ। मैं महासागर पर पुल बाँधने में सर्वथा समर्थ हूँ इसलिये मैं समुद्र पर सेतु का निर्माण करूँगा।

नल-नील असंख्य वानरों को लेकर सेतु निर्माण के कार्य में जुट गये। उनके आदेश के अनुसार वानर सेना बड़े-बड़े वृक्षों को उखाड़ कर समुद्र तट पर एकत्रित करने लगे। देखते-देखते वहाँ साल, अश्वकर्ण, धब, बाँस, कुटज, अर्जुन, कर्णिकार, जामुन, अशोक आदि वृक्षों का एक विशाल गगनचुम्बी ढेर लग गया। इस प्रकार सागर के किनारे वृक्षों तथा शिलाओं के दो विशाल पर्वत बन गये। इसके पश्चात् उन्होंने बड़े-बड़े शिलाखण्डों को समुद्र में नल-नील के निर्देशानुसार डालना आरम्भ किया। उन शिलाखण्डों एवं वृक्षों को शिल्पकला में चतुर नल-नील सेतु का रूप देते जा रहे थे। इस प्रकार उन्होंने अधिक परिश्रम करके पहले ही दिन छप्पन कोस लम्बा पुल बना दिया। दूसरे दिन उन्होंने और भी अधिक फुर्ती दिखाई और चौरासी कोस लम्बा पुल बनाया। फिर अतुल परिश्रम से तीसरे दिन बानबे कोस लम्बा सेतु बनाया। इस प्रकार निरन्तर परिश्रम करके उन्होंने चार सौ कोस लम्बा पुल बना डाला। अब नल-नील के प्रयत्नों से चालीस कोस चौड़ा और चार सौ कोस लम्बा मजबूत पुल बन कर तैयार हो गया।

समुद्र पर सेतु बन जाने के पश्चात् श्री रामचन्द्र जी ने हनुमान की पीठ पर और लक्ष्मण ने अंगद की पीठ पर बैठ कर सेतु पर होते हुये विशाल सागर पार किया। उनके पीछे-पीछे सम्पूर्ण वानर सेना भी सुग्रीव के नेतृत्व में समुद्र को पार कर लंका में पहुँच गई। इस सेना के लंका में पहुँचते ही राक्षसों में भयानक हलचल मच गई। वे लंका दहन की घटना को स्मरण

कर भयभीत होने लगे।

उधर रावण ने शुक और सारण नामक मन्त्रियों को बुला कर उन्से कहा, "हे चतुर मन्त्रियों! अब राम ने वानरों की सहायता से अगाध समुद्र पर सेतु बाँध कर उसे पार कर लिया है और वह लंका के द्वार पर आ पहुँचा है। तुम दोनों वानरों का वेश बना कर राम की सेना में प्रवेश करो और यह पता लगाओ कि शत्रु सेना में कुल कितने वानर हैं, उनके पास अस्त्र-शस्त्र कितने और किस प्रकार के हैं तथा मुख्य-मुख्य वानर नायकों के नाम क्या हैं।"

रावण की आज्ञा पाकर दोनों कूटनीतिज्ञ मायावी राक्षस वानरों का वेश बना कर वानरोंसेना में घुस गये, परन्तु वे विभीषण की तीक्ष्ण दृष्टि से बच न सके। विभीषण ने उन दोनों को पकड़ कर राम के सम्मुख करते हुये कहा, "हे राघव! ये दोनों गुप्तचर रावण के मन्त्री शुक और सारण हैं जो हमारे कटक में गुप्तचरी करते पकड़े गये हैं।"

राम के सामने जाकर दोनों राक्षस थर-थर काँपते हुये बोले, "हे राजन्! हम राक्षसराज रावण के सेवक हैं। उन्हीं की आज्ञा से आपके बल का पता लगाने के लिये आये थे। हम उनकी आज्ञा के दास हैं, इसलिये उनका आदेश पालन करने के लिये विवश हैं। राजभक्ति के कारण हमें ऐसा करना पड़ा है। इसमें हमारा कोई दोष नहीं है।"

उनके ये निश्चल वचन सुन कर रामचन्द्र बोले, "हे मन्त्रियों! हम तुम्हारे सत्य भाषण से बहुत प्रसन्न हैं। तुमने यदि हमारी शक्ति देख ली है, तो जाओ। यदि अभी कुछ और देखना शेष हो तो भली-भाँति देख लो। हम तुम्हें कोई दण्ड नहीं देंगे। आर्य लोग शस्त्रहीन व्यक्ति पर वार नहीं करते। अतएव तुम अपना कार्य पूरा करके निर्भय हो लंका को लौट जाओ। तुम साधारण गुप्तचर नहीं, रावण के मन्त्री हो। इसलिये उससे कहना, जिस बल के भरोसे पर तुमने मेरी सीता का हरण किया है, उस बल का परिचय अपने भाइयों, पुत्रों तथा सेना के साथ हमें रणभूमि में देना। कल सूर्योदय होते ही अन्धकार की भाँति तुम्हारी सेना का विनाश भी आरम्भ हो जायेगा।"

श्री रामचन्द्र जी के वचनों से भयरहित हो उनका जयजयकार करते हुये शुक तथा सारण लंका में पहुँचे और रावण के सम्मुख उपस्थित होकर बोले, "हे स्वामिन्! हमारे वानर सेना में प्रवेश करते ही विभीषण ने हमें पहचान कर राम के सम्मुख उपस्थित कर दिया, परन्तु राम ने हमें निःशस्त्र दूत समझ कर छोड़ दिया। अब रही वानरों के बल की बात, उसका पता लगाना सम्भव नहीं है, क्योंकि उनमें प्रत्येक के मन में आपके विरुद्ध क्रोध तथा घृणा की ज्वाला धधक रही है। उनसे बात करना ही सम्भव नहीं है, किसी बात का पता लगाना तो बहुत कठिन है। राम ने कहलवाया है कि सूर्योदय होते ही वह राक्षस सेना का विनाश आरम्भ कर देगा। अब आप जैसा उचित समझें वैसा करें।"

दोनों मन्त्रियों के ये वचन सुनकर रावण क्रोध से उबलते हुये बोला, "चाहे कुछ भी हो जाय, मैं किसी भी दशा में सीता को वापिस नहीं करूँगा। मुझे विश्वास है, राम अपनी सेना सहित युद्ध भूमि में मेरे हाथों से अवश्य मारा जायेगा।"

मन्त्रियों के उत्तर से सन्तुष्ट न होकर रावण ने कुछ अन्य गुप्तचरों को छद्म वेश में वानर सेना में भेजा। उन्होंने बड़ी चतुराई से सम्पूर्ण जानकारी प्राप्त करके रावण को बतलाया कि राम ने अपना सैनिक शिविर सुवेल पर्वत पर लगाया है। उनमें जाम्बवन्त नामक ऋक्ष सबसे दुर्धुर्ष एवं तेजस्वी है। उसके अतिरिक्त तीन वानर सबसे अधिक बलवान और पराक्रमी हैं। उनके नाम सुमुख, दुर्मुख तथा वेगदर्शी हैं। नल-नील उस सैनिक टुकड़ी के अध्यक्ष हैं जिसने समुद्र पर सेतु बाँधा है। अंगद अपने पिता वालि से भी अधिक तेजस्वी एवं बलवान है। उसके अतिरिक्त सहस्त्रों अद्भुत शक्तिसम्पन्न पराक्रमी वानर हैं। राम और लक्ष्मण तो जनस्थान को नष्ट करके अपने बल का परिचय आपको दे ही चुके हैं।

21

सीता के साथ छल

जब रावण के गुप्तचरों ने बताया कि श्री रामचन्द्र जी की सेना सुवेल पर्वत पर आकर ठहरी है और उस पर विजय पाना असम्भव है तब वह उद्वेलित हो गया। उसने महाबली, महामायावी, मायाविशारद राक्षस विधुज्जिह्व को बुलाकर आदेश दिया कि वह शीघ्र श्री रामचन्द्र जी का मायानिर्मित मस्तक बनाकर लाये। रावण की आज्ञा पाकर वह शीघ्र ही श्री राम का सिर बना लाया जो रक्त से लथपथ था। उसे देखकर कोई नहीं कह सकता था कि ये वास्तव में राम का मस्तक नहीं है। उस मस्तक को बाण की नोक पर रखकर वह अशोकवाटिका में जाकर सीता से बोला, “हे सीते! तूने राम की शक्ति पर अगाध विश्वास करके मेरा कहना नहीं माना। देख, राम युद्धभूमि में मारा गया। ले, अपने पति के मरने का समाचार सुन और इस सिर को देखकर अपने अभिमान पर आँसू बहा। वह अभिमानी वानरों के भरोसे मुझसे युद्ध करने आया था।

रात्रि को जब वानर सेना सहित राम और लक्ष्मण दोनों सो रहे थे, तब मेरे सेनापति प्रहस्त ने एक विशाल सेना लेकर उस पर आक्रमण कर दिया और अपने भयंकर हथियारों से मारकाट मचा दी। बहुत सी सेना मारी गई और जो बचे, वे प्राण लेकर भाग गये। तब प्रहस्त ने सोते हुये राम के सिर को काट डाला। इस आक्रमण में विभीषण भी मारा गया। तुझे प्राप्त करने के लिये मुझे ऐसा भयंकर संहार करना पड़ा। अब तेरा कोई आश्रय नहीं रह गया है, इसलिये अब तुझे चाहिये कि तू मुझे पति रूप में स्वीकार कर ले।”

इतना कह कर रावण ने उस मायारचित सिर को सीता के समक्ष रख दिया।

जब सीता ने उन दोनों मस्तकों को देखा जो सब प्रकार से आकृति, मुद्रा आदि में राम से मिलता था तो वह बिलख-बिलख कर रो पड़ी और नाना प्रकार से विलाप करती हुई कैकेयी को कोसने लगी, “हा! आज कैकेयी की मनोकामना पूरी हो गई। हा नागिन! आज तुम्हारी इच्छा पूरी हुई। अब तुम्हारा भरत निष्कंटक होकर राज करेगा। तुमने अपने स्वार्थ के पीछे रघुकुल का नाश कर दिया।”

इस प्रकार विलाप करती हुई वे मूर्च्छित होकर पृथ्वी पर गिर पड़ीं। जब चेतना लौटी तो वे फिर विलाप करने लगीं, "हा नाथ! यह सब क्या हो गया? आज मैं विधवा हो गई। आप मुझे यहाँ किसके भरोसे पर छोड़ गये। मुझसे ऐसा क्या अपराध हो गया है कि मैं रो-रो कर मर रही हूँ और आप चुपचाप देख रहे हैं।

मुझसे सान्त्वना का एक शब्द भी नहीं कह रहे। ऐसे निर्मोही तो आप कभी नहीं थे। वन चलते समय आपने वचन दिया था कि तेरा साथ कभी नहीं छोड़ूँगा, परन्तु आज आप मुझे अकेला छोड़ कर चल दिये। आपकी प्रतीक्षा में आँखें बिछाये कौसल्या जब ये समाचार सुनेंगीं तो उनकी क्या दशा होगी? कौन उनके आँसू पोंछेगा? हा! आज मैं ही आप दोनों कि मृत्यु का कारण बन गई। हे नीच रावण! तूने दोनों भाइयों की हत्या तो करा ही दी अब मेरा शीश भी काटकर अपनी कृपाण की प्यास बुझा ले। मेरे पति स्वर्ग में मेंरी प्रतीक्षा कर रहे हैं। अब मैं इस संसार में एक क्षण भी रहना नहीं चाहती। उठा तलवार, कर अपना काम।"

जब सीता इस प्रकार विलाप कर रही थी तभी एक राक्षस ने आकर रावण को सूचना दी कि मन्त्री प्रहस्त अत्यन्त आवश्यक कार्य से इसी समय आपके दर्शन करना चाहते हैं। यह सुनते ही रावण तत्काल उस सिर को लेकर वहाँ से चला गया। उस समय तक सीता पुनः मूर्च्छित हो चुकी थीं।

विभीषण की स्त्री इस घटना की सूचना पा कर अशोकवाटिका में आई। वह सीता की मूर्छा दूर करके उन्हें समझाने लगी, "रावण ने तुमसे जो कुछ कहा है, वह झूठ है। राम न तो मारे गये हैं और न ये दुष्ट उन्हें मार ही सकते हैं। ये सिर माया से बनाया गया हैं। तुम इसके छल में पड़कर यह भी भूल गईं कि लक्ष्मण दिन रात राघव की सेवा में रहते हैं और वे रात को कभी नहीं सोते। फिर सोते में उनके सिर कैसे काटे जा सकते हैं? तनिक कान लगाकर सुनो। रण की तैयारी करती हुई राक्षस सेना की गर्जना की ध्वनि स्पष्ट सुनाई दे रही है। यदि राम-लक्ष्मण वानरों सहित मारे जाते तो फिर यह तैयारी किसलिये होती?"

ये तर्कयुक्त वचन सुनकर सीता इस बात पर विचार करने लगी।

22

अंगद रावण दरबार में

सुवेल पर्वत पर श्री रामचन्द्र जी ने लंका का निरीक्षण करने के पश्चात् वे अपने सेनपतियों, विभीषण तथा वानरों आदि को लेकर लंका के मुख्य द्वार के निकट पहुँचे। यही लंका का सबसे विशाल मुख्य द्वार था। उन्होंने वहाँ पर एक दर्भेद्य व्यूह की रचना की। उस विशाल द्वार पर लक्ष्मण सहित राम धनुष धारण कर खड़े हो गये। पूर्व द्वार पर सेनापति नल, नील, मैंद तथा द्विविद असंख्य पराक्रमी वीरों के साथ खड़े हुये। दक्षिण द्वार पर अंगद, ऋषभ, गज, गवय तथा गवाक्ष नामक तेजस्वी सेनापति एकत्रित हुये। पश्चिम द्वार से आक्रमण का भार हनुमान, प्रजंघ, तरस आदि अद्वतीय पराक्रमी सेनानायकों को सौंपा गया। उन सबके मध्य में एक दुर्भेद्य व्यूह बनाकर वानरराज सुग्रीव चुने हुये वानरों के साथ खड़े हो गये। रामचन्द्र और सुग्रीव दोनों के बीच में विशाल सेना लेकर जाम्बवन्त तथा सुषेण खड़े हुये।

इस प्रकार की व्यूह रचना करके राम ने राजधर्म का विचार करते हुए वालिपुत्र अंगद को बुला कर बोले, "सौम्य! कपिवर! तुम तेजस्वी, बलवान तथा वाक्-पटु हो। इस लिये तुम रावण से जाकर कहो कि तुम चोरों की भाँति एकान्त से सीता को चुरा लाये थे। अब रणभूमि में आकर अपना रणकौशल दिखाओ। हम तुम्हें एक अवसर और देते हैं। यदि तुम सीता को लेकर दाँतों में तृण दबाकर हमसे अपने अपराध के लिये क्षमायाचना करोगे तो हम तुम्हें अब भी क्षमा कर देंगे, अन्यथा कल प्रातःकाल से युद्ध होगा जिसमें तुम समस्त राक्षसों के साथ मारे जाओगे।"

रामचन्द्र की आज्ञा पाकर वालिसुत अंगद छलांग लगाकर लंका के परकोटे को पार कर रावण के दरबार में पहुँचे। उन्होंने कहा, "मैं वालि का पुत्र और श्री रामचन्द्र जी का दूत अंगद हूँ। श्री रामचन्द्र जी ने कहलाया है किस तुमने सीता को चुरा कर जो जघन्य अपराध किया है, उसके लिये मैं परिवार सहित तुम्हारा और तुम्हारे वंश का नाश करूँगा। यदि अब भी तुम अपनी कुशल चाहते हो तो सीता को आगे करके मुख में तृण रखकर क्षमायाचना करो, तुमको क्षमा कर दिया जायेगा तुम देवता, दानवों, यक्ष, गन्धर्व सबके शत्रु हो, इसलिये तुम्हारा

विनाश करना ही श्रेयस्कर है। मैं श्री रामचन्द्र जी की ओर से तुम्हें एक बार फिर समझाता हूँ, यदि तुमने उनसे क्षमा नहीं माँगी तो तुम मारे जाओगे और लंका का राज्य तथा ऐश्वर्य तुम्हारा भाई विभीषण भोगेगा।"

अंगद के कठोर वचन सुनकर क्रुद्ध हो रावण ने अपने सैनिकों को आज्ञा दी, "इस दुर्बुद्धि वानर को पकड़ कर मौत के घाट उतार दो।"

रावण की आज्ञा पाते ही चार राक्षसों ने अंगद को पकड़ लिया। पकड़े जाने पर उन्होंने एक धक्का देकर उन्हें भूमि पर गिरा दिया और स्वयं छलांग लगाकर छत पर पहुँच गये। क्रोध से जब उन्होंने छत पर अपना पैर पटका तो एक ही आघात से छत ध्वस्त हो कर नीचे आ गिरी। फिर विजय गर्जना करते हुये अपने कटक को लौट गये।

इसी समय गुप्तचरों ने आकर रावण को सूचना दी कि वानरों ने लंका को चारों ओर से घेर लिया है। उसने स्वयं छत पर चढ़कर चारों ओर वानरों की विशाल सेना को व्यूह बनाये देखा तो एक बार उसका हृदय भी भय और आशंका व्याप्त हो उठा।

उधर अंगद के पहुँचने के पश्चात् रामचन्द्र जी ने अपनी सेना को लंका का विध्वंस करने तथा राक्षसों का वध करने की आज्ञा दी। आज्ञा पाते ही वानर सेना बड़े-बड़े वृक्षों एवं शिलाखण्डों को लेकर लंका पर चढ़ दौड़ी। वे वृक्षों, पत्थरों, लात-घूसों से परकोटे और उसके द्वारों को तोड़ने और विशाल खाई को पाटने लगे। थोड़ी ही देर में उन्होंने भयंकर आघातों से नगर के चारों फाटक चूर-चूर कर दिया। परकोटे में बड़े-बड़े छेद हो गये। जब पुरी के द्वार और परकोटे नष्ट-भ्रष्ट हो गये तो रावण ने राक्षस योद्धाओं को बाहर निकल कर युद्ध करने का आदेश दिया।

आदेश मिलते ही राक्षस सेना हाथियों, घोड़ों, रथों आदि पर सवार होकर अपनी पैदल सेना के साथ पूरे वेग से वानरों पर टूट पड़ी। दोनों ओर के सैनिक अपने प्राणों का मोह त्याग कर भयानक युद्ध करने लगे। हाथी, घोड़ों की चिंघाड़ तथा हिनहिनाहट से, तलवारों की झंकार और सैनिकों के ललकार भरे जयजयकार से सारा वातावरण गूँज उठा। नाना प्रकार के वाद्यवृनद तथा रणभेरियाँ योद्धाओं के उत्साह को द्विगुणित कर रही थीं। वानरों का उत्साह राक्षसों से कई गुणा अधिक था। उनके वृक्षों, शिलाओं, नखों तथा दाँतों के प्रहार ने राक्षसों की सेना में भयंकर मार-काट मचा दी अस्ख्य राक्षस मर-मर कर गिरने लगे। समुद्र तट से लंका के द्वार तक भूमि मृत एवं घयल सैनिकों से पटी दिखाई देती थी।

23

राम लक्ष्मण बन्धन में

इस प्रकार से युद्ध चल ही रहा था कि सूर्यदेव अस्त हो गये तथा प्राणों का संहार करने वाली रात्रि का आगमन हो गया। दोनों पक्ष के योद्धा बड़े भयंकर थे तथा अपनी-अपनी विजय चाहते थे; अतः उनके मध्य रात्रियुद्ध होने लगा। दोनों पक्ष के मध्य घनघोर युद्ध मच गया, 'मारो-मारो', 'काटो-काटो' शब्दों से समस्त समरभूमि गुंजायमान हो गई और रक्त की नदियाँ बहने लगीं। घायल होकर कराहते हुए राक्षसों तथा शस्त्रों से क्षत-विक्षत हुए वानरों का आर्तनाद बड़ा भयंकर प्रतीत होने लगा। वानरों और राक्षसों का संहार करने वाली वह भयंकर रजनी कालरात्रि के समान समस्त प्राणियों के दुर्लंघ्य हो गई थी।

श्री रामचन्द्र जी ने अग्निज्वाला के समान छः भयानक बाणों से निमिष मात्र में दुर्धुर्ष वीर यज्ञशत्रु, महापार्श्व, महोदर, महाकाय, वज्रदंष्ट्र, शुक और सारण को घायल कर दिया। वे छहों राक्षस श्री रामचन्द्र जी के बाणसमूहों से अपने मर्मस्थान में चोट खाने पर युद्ध छोड़ कर भाग गये; इसीलिये उनके प्राण बच गये और उनकी आयु शेष रह गई महारथी श्री राम ने अग्नि-शिखा के समान प्रज्वलित भयंकर बाणों द्वारा समस्त दिशाओं में प्रकाश कर दिया। उनके समक्ष जो भी राक्षसवीर आते थे वे उसी प्रकार से नष्ट होते जाते थे जिस प्रकार से आग में पड़कर पतिंगे जल जाते हैं।

राक्षस सेना की यह दुर्दशा देखकर रावण के पुत्र मेघनाद के तन-बदन में आग लग गई। उसने शीघ्र ही नाग बाणों की फाँस बना कर राम-लक्ष्मण दोनों को उसमें बाँध लिया। नाग फाँस में बँधने पर दोनों भाई मूर्छित हो गये।

श्री राम के मूर्छित होकर पृथ्वी पर गिरते ही मेघनाद ने हर्षोन्मत्त होकर दसों दिशाओं को गुँजाने वाली गर्जना की। राक्षस सेना में फिर से नवजीवन आ गया और वह मेघनाद की जयजयकार करती हुई बड़े उत्साह से वानर सेना पर टूट पड़ी। मेघनाद उनके उत्साह को बढ़ाते हुये कह रहा था, "जिनके कारण आज शोणित की सरिता बह रही है, वे ही दोनों भाई नागपाश कें बँधे पृथ्वी पर मूर्छित पड़े हैं। अब देव, नर, किन्नर किसी में इतनी सामर्थ्य नहीं है जो इन्हें नागपाश से मुक्त कर सके। अब युद्ध समाप्त हो गया, लंकापति की विजय

हुई।"

इस प्रकार विजयघोष करता हुआ मेघनाद लंका को लौट गया।

राम-लक्ष्मण के मूर्छित हो जाने से सम्पूर्ण वानर सेना में शोक छा गया। सुग्रीव, अंगद, हनुमान, जाम्बवन्त आदि सभी सेनाध्यक्ष किंकर्तव्यविमूढ़ होकर दोनों भाइयों को घेर कर खड़े हो गये और इस विपत्ति से त्राण पाने का उपाय खोजने लगे। तभी विभीषण ने उन्हें धैर्य बँधाते हुये कहा, "हे वीरों! भयभीत होने की आवश्यकता नहीं है। यह नागपाश इन दोनों भाइयों का कुछ नहीं बिगाड़ सकती और न वे मर ही सकते हैं। इसलिये तुम इनकी चिन्ता छोड़कर अपने-अपने मोर्चों पर जाकर युद्ध करो। इन दोनों भाइयों को तुम मेरे ऊपर छोड़ दो।"

उधर जब रावण ने मेघनाद के मुख से राम-लक्ष्मण के नागपाश में बँधकर मूर्छित होने का समाचार सुना तो उसके हर्ष का पारावार न रहा। उसने सीता की रक्षा पर नियुक्त राक्षस नारियों को बुलाकर आदेश दिया, "तुम लोग सीता को पुष्पक विमान पर चढ़ाकर युद्ध भूमि में ले जाओ और उन्हें ले जाकर राम-लक्ष्मण को दिखाओ जो पृथ्वी पर मरे पड़े हैं।"

रावण की आज्ञा पाते ही राक्षसनियाँ जानकी को विमान में चढ़ाकर युद्धभूमि में ले गईं जहाँ राम-लक्ष्मण मूर्छित अवस्था में पड़े थे। सीता ने देखा राक्षस सेना जयजयनाद कर रही है और वानर सेना शोक में डूबी हुई निराश खड़ी है। दोनों भाइयों को इस प्रकार पृथ्वी पर पड़ा देखकर सीता के धैर्य का बाँध टूट गया और वे फूट-फूट कर रोने लगी, "हाय! आज मैं विधवा हो गई। बड़े-बड़े ज्योतिषियों की यह भविष्वाणी मिथ्या हो गई कि मैं आजीवन सधवा रहूँगी, पुत्रवती बनूँगी। हे नाथ! आपने तो कहा था कि मैं अयोध्या लौटकर अश्वमेघ यज्ञ करूँगा। अब उस कथन का क्या होगा! जो विश्व को जीतने की शक्ति रखते थे, आज वे कैसे मौन पड़े हैं! हा विधाता! तेरी यह क्या लीला है? हे त्रिजटे! तू मेरे सती होने का प्रबन्ध करा दे। अब मैं इस संसार में अपने प्रिय राम के बिना नहीं रहूँगी। अब मेरा जीना व्यर्थ है।"

सीता को इस प्रकार विलाप करते देख त्रिजटा ने कहा, "हे जानकी! तुम व्यर्थ में विलाप करके जी छोटा मत करो। मेरा विश्वास है, राम-लक्ष्मण दोनों जीवित हैं, केवल मूर्छित हो गये हैं। यह देखो वानर सेना फिर युद्ध के लिये लौट रही है। सुग्रीव और विभीषण उनके चेतन होने की प्रतीक्षा कर रहे हैं। मेरा अनुमान मिथ्या नहीं है। वे उठकर फिर युद्ध करेंगे और रावण का वध करके तुम्हें अवश्य ले जायेंगे, तुम धैर्य धारण करो।"

इस प्रकार सीता को समझा-बुझा कर त्रिजटा सीता सहित विमान को पुनः अशोकवाटिका में ले आई।

नागपाश में बँधे राम और लक्ष्मण काफी देर तक भूमि पर पड़े रहे। तभी अकस्मात् जोर से आँधी चलने लगी, आकाश में घने बादल छा गये। इतने में ही आकाशमार्ग से विनिता का पुत्र गरुड़ उड़ता हुआ आया। उसने दोनों भाइयों के पास बैठकर उनके शरीर का स्पर्श किया। गरुड़ के स्पर्श करते ही समस्त नाग भयभीत होकर पृथ्वी में छिप गये। नागों के बन्धन से मुक्त होने पर राम और लक्ष्मण ने अपने नेत्र खोले। उनके पीले पड़े हुये मुखमण्डल फर

नवीन आभा से चमकने लगे। चैतन्य होकर राम ने गरुड़ को धन्यवाद देते हुये कहा, "हे वैनतेश! तुम्हारे अनुग्रह से हम दोनों भाई इस बन्धन से मुन्त हुये हैं। हम तुम्हारा कैसे आभार प्रदर्शन कर लकते हैं?"

राम की यह विनम्र वाणी सुनकर गरुड़ ने उत्तर दिया, "हे रघव! मैं तुम्हारा मित्र हूँ। वन में विचरण करते हुये मैंने सुना था कि मेघनाद ने तुम्हें इस नागपाश में बाँध लिया है जिसे देवता, राक्षस, यक्ष, गन्धर्व कोई भी नहीं खोल सकते। इसलिये मैं मित्र धर्म के नाते यहाँ आ पहुँचा और मैंने तुम्हें नागपाश से मुक्त करा दिया। भविष्य में अधिक सतर्क रहकर युद्ध करना क्योंकि ये राक्षस बड़े कपटी तथा मायावी हैं।"

इतना कहकर गरुड़ ने उनसे विदा ली।

राम और लक्ष्मण को पूर्णतया स्वस्थ पाकर वानर सेना के आनन्द का पारावार न रहा। वे रघुवीर की जयजयकार करके बाजे-नगाड़े, रणभेरी आदि बजाकर राक्षसों को भयभीत करने लगे।

24

धूम्राक्ष और वज्रदंष्ट्र का वध

जब हर्षोन्मत्त वानरों का तुमुलनाद सुन कर रावण को आश्चर्य हुआ और आशंका ने उसे आ घेरा। उसने तत्काल मन्त्रियों से कहा, "वानरसेना में इतना उत्साह कैसे आ गया? मेघनाद ने तो राम और लक्ष्मण का वध कर दिया था। शीघ्र पता लगाकर बताओ, इसका क्या कारण है? कहीं भरत तो अयोध्या से विशाल सेना लेकर नहीं आ गया? आखिर ऐसी कौन सी बात हुई है जो वानर सेना राम की मुत्यु का दुःख भी भूलकार गर्जना कर रही है।"

तभी एक गुप्तचर ने आकर सूचना दी कि राम और लक्ष्मण मरे नहीं हैं, वे नागपाश से मुक्त होकर युद्ध की तैयारी कर रहे हैं।

यह सुनते ही रावण का मुख फीका पड़ गया। उसने क्रोधित होकर पराक्रमी धूम्राक्ष को आज्ञा दी, "हे वीरश्रेष्ठ धूम्राक्ष! तुमने अब तक अनेक बार अद्भुत पराक्रम प्रदर्शित किया है। तुम सहस्त्रों वीरों को अकेले मार सकते हो। एक विशाल सेना लेकर जाओ और राम-लक्ष्मण सहित शत्रु सेना का वध करो।"

रावण की आज्ञा पाते ही शूल, गदा, तोमर, भाले, पट्टिश आदि शस्त्रों से युक्त राक्षसों की विशाल सेना लेकर धूम्राक्ष रणभूमि में जा पहुँचा। इस विशाल वाहिनी को देख कर वानर सेना घोर गर्जना करती हुई उस पर टूट पड़ी। धूम्राक्ष कंकपत्रों वाले तीक्ष्ण बाणों से वानरों को घायल करने लगा। वे भी राक्षसों के वार बचाकर बड़े-बड़े शिलाखण्ड ले आकाश में उड़ कर उन पर फेंकने लगे। आकाश को उद्यत राक्षसी सेना को अपने प्राण बचाने कठिन हो गये। फिर भी राक्षस सेना का एक भाग अपने प्राणों की चिन्ता न करके बाणों, त्रिशूलों आदि से वानरों का लहू बहा रहा था। चारों ओर रक्त की नदियाँ बहने लगीं। जिधर देखो उधर ही राक्षसों और वानरों के रुण्ड-मुण्ड दिखाई देते थे। कानों के पर्दों को फाड़ने वाला चीत्कार और हाहाकार सुनाई दे रहा था। रणोन्मत्त धूम्राक्ष हताहत वीरों के शरीरों को रौंदता हुआ अपने अग्नि बाणों से वानर सेना को भस्मीभूत कर रहा था। उसके आक्रमण की ताव न लाकर वानर सेना इधर-उधर भागने लगी।

अपनी सेना की यह दुर्दशा देख कर हनुमान ने क्रोध से भरकर एक विशाल शिला उखाड़ी और लक्ष्य तानकर धूम्राक्ष की ओर फेंक दी। उस शिला को अपनी ओर आते देख वह फुर्ती से रथ से कूद पड़ा। इस बीच में रथ चूर-चूर हो चुका था और घोड़े तथा सारथी मर चुके थे। राक्षस सेनापति को इस प्रकार बचता देख हनुमान का क्रोध और भी भड़क उठा। उन्होंने दाँतों, नाखूनों से उनके और धूम्राक्ष के बीच में आने वाले राक्षस समुदाय का विनाश करके मार्ग साफ कर लिया। जब उसने हनुमान को भयंकर रूप से अपनी ओर आते देखा तो लोहे के काँटों से भरी हुई गदा उठाकर उनके सिर पर दे मारी। हनुमान ने वार बचा कर एक भारी शिला उठाई और आकाश में उड़ कर धूम्राक्ष को दे मारी। इससे उसके शरीर की समस्त हड्डियाँ टूट गईं और वह पृथ्वी पर गिरकर यमलोक सिधार गया। उसके मरते ही राक्षस भी भाग छूटे।

रावण ने जब धूम्राक्ष की मृत्यु का समाचार सुना तो वह क्रोध से पागल हो गया। उसके नेत्रों से चिंगारियाँ निकलने लगीं। उसने वज्रदंष्ट्र को बुलाकर आज्ञा दी कि वह राम-लक्ष्मण तथा हनुमान सहित वानरसेना का वध करके अपने शौर्य का परिचय दे। वज्रदंष्ट्र जितना वीर था, उससे अधिक मायावी था। वह अपनी भीमकर्मा पराक्रमी सेना लेकर दक्षिण द्वार से चला। युद्धभूमि में पहुँचते ही उसने अपने सम्मुख अंगद को पाया जो अपनी सेना के साथ उससे युद्ध करने के लिये तत्पर खड़ा था।

वज्रदंष्ट्र को देखते ही वानर सेना किचकिचा कर राक्षसों पर टूट पड़ी। दोनों ओर से भयंकर मारकाट मच गई। सम्पूर्ण युद्धभूमि रुण्ड-मुण्डों, हताहत सैनिकों तथा रक्त के नालों एवं सरिताओं से भर गई। रक्त सरिताओं में नाना प्रकार के शस्त्र-शस्त्र, कटे हुये हाथ तथा मस्तक छोटे-छोटे द्वीपों की भाँति दिखाई देने लगे। अंगद तथा वानर सेनापतियों द्वारा बार-बार की जाने वाली सिंहगर्जना ने राक्षस सैनिकों का मनोबल तोड़ दिया। जब उन्हें अपने चारों ओर राक्षसों के कटे हुये अंग दिखाई देने लगे तो वह अपने प्राणों के मोह से रणभूमि से पलायन करने लगे।

अपनी सेना को मरते-कटते और कायरों की तरह भागते देख वज्रदंष्ट्र दोगुने पराक्रम और क्रोध से युद्ध करने लगा। उसने तीक्ष्णतर बाणों का प्रयोग करके वानरों को घायल करना आरम्भ कर दिया। क्रुद्ध वज्रदंष्ट्र के भयानक आक्रमण से पीड़ित होकर वानर सेना भी इधर-उधर छिपने लगी। उनकी यह दशा देखकर अंगद ने उस राक्षस सेनापति को ललकारा, "वज्रदंष्ट्र! तूने बहुत मारकाट कर ली। तेरा अंत समय आ गया है अब मैं तुझे धूम्राक्ष के पास भेजता हूँ।" यह कहकर अंगद उससे जाकर भिड़ गये। दोनों महान योद्धा मस्त हाथियों की भाँति एक दूसरे पर प्रहार करने लगे। दोनों ही रक्त से लथपथ हो गये। फिर अवसर पाकर अंगद ने तलवार से वज्रदंष्ट्र का सिर काट डाला। अपने सेनापति के मरते ही राक्षस सेना मैदान से भाग खड़ी हुई।

25

अकम्पन का वध

वालिपुत्र अंगद के हाथ से वज्रदंष्ट्र के वध का समाचार सुनकर रावण ने सेनापति अकम्पन को उसके शौर्य एवं पराक्रम की प्रशंसा करते हुये राम-लक्ष्मण के विरुद्ध युद्ध करने के लिये भेजा। महापराक्रमी अकम्पन सोने के रथ में बैठकर असंख्य चुने हुये भयानक नेत्रोंवाले भयंकर राक्षस सैनिकों के साथ नगर से बाहर निकला। महासमर में देवता भी उसे कम्पित नहीं कर सकते थे, इसीलिये वह अकम्पन नाम से विख्यात था। रणभूमि में पहुँचते ही उसने दसों दिशाओं को कँपाने वाला सिंहनाद दिया। उसके सिंहनाद से अविचल वीर वानर सेना राक्षस दल पर टूट पड़ी। एक बार फिर अभूतपरूर्व युद्ध आरम्भ हो गया। उन सबके ललकारने और गरजने के स्वर के सामने सागर की गर्जना भी फीकी प्रतीत होने लगी।

परस्पर युद्ध करते हुए वानरों और राक्षसों के द्वारा उड़ाई गई लाल रंग के धूल ने दसों दिशाओं को आच्छादित कर दिया और सम्पूर्ण वातावरण अन्धकारमय हो गया। उस महाअन्धकार में योद्धा अपने तथा विपक्षी दल के सैनिकों में भेद न कर सके। वानर वानरों को और राक्षस राक्षसों को मारने लगे। इस युद्ध में वीर वानर कुमुद, नल, मैन्द और द्विविद ने कुपित हो अपना उत्तम वेग प्रकट किया तथा उनके इस वेग से उत्साहित वानरों ने क्रुद्ध होकर वृक्षों, शिलाओं, दाँतों तथा नाखूनों से रिपुदल में भयंकर मारकाट मचा दी जिससे उसके पाँव उखड़ने लगे।

अपनी सेना के पैर उखड़ते देख अकम्पन मेघों के समान गर्जना करके अग्नि बाणों से वानर दल को जलाने लगा। वानर सेना को इस प्रकार अग्नि में भस्म होते देख परम तेजस्वी पवनपुत्र हनुमान ने आगे बढ़कर अकम्पन को ललकारा। जब अन्य वानरों ने हनुमान का रौद्ररूप देखा तो वे भी उनके साथ फिर फुर्ती से युद्ध करने लगे। उधर हनुमान को देखकर अकम्पन भी गरजा। उसने अपने तरकस से तीक्ष्ण बाण निकालकर हनुमान को अपने लक्ष्य बनाया। उन्होंने वार बचाकर एक विशाल शिला अकम्पन की ओर फेंकी।

जब तक वह शिला अकम्पन तक पहुँचती तब कर उसने अर्द्धचन्द्राकार बाण छोड़कर उस शिला को चूर-चूर कर दिया। इस प्रकार शिला के नष्ट होने पर हनुमान ने कर्णिकार का

वृक्ष उखाड़कर अकम्पन की ओर फेंका। अकम्पन ने अपने एक बाण से उस वृक्ष को भी नष्ट किया और एक साथ चौदह बाण छोड़कर हनुमान के शरीर को रक्तरंजित कर दिया। इससे हनुमान के क्रोध की सीमा न रही। उन्होंने एक विशाल वृक्ष उखाड़कर अकम्पन के सिर पर दे मारा। इससे वह प्राणहीन होकर भूमि पर गिर पड़ा। अकम्पन के मरते ही सारे राक्षस सिर पर पैर रख कर भागे। वानरों ने उन भागते हुये शत्रुओं को पेड़ों तथा पत्थरों से वहीं कुचल दिया। जो शेष बचे, उन्होंने रावण को अकम्पन के मरने की सूचना सुनाई।

26

प्रहस्त का वध

रावण अकम्पन को अदम्य समझता था इसलिये उसकी मृत्यु से रावण को भारी आघात पहुँचा। वह गहन शोक में डूब गया। रात्रि को वह शान्ति से विश्राम भी न कर सका। दूसरे दिन उसने मन्त्रियों को बुलाकर कहा, "वानरों की सेना हमारी कल्पना से भी अधिक शक्तिशाली और पराक्रमी सिद्ध हुई है। पिछले चार दिनों में हमारी बहुत सी सेना मारी जा चुकी है। सैनिकों का मनोबल टूटने लगा है। नागरिकों को शत्रु के घेरे के कारण बाहर से उपलब्ध होने वाली खाद्य सामग्री प्राप्त नहीं हो रही है।

वे अत्यन्त दुःखी हो रहे हैं। चार दिन के युद्ध को देखकर मैं इस निष्कर्ष पर पहुँचा हूँ कि शत्रु पर विजय प्राप्त करना साधारण राक्षसों के लिये सम्भव नहीं है। इसलिये हे वीर प्रहस्त! मुझे ऐसा प्रतीत होता है कि शत्रु को परास्त करने के लिये कुम्भकर्ण को, मेघनाद को, तुम्हें अथवा मुझे ही आगे आना पड़ेगा। अतः आज युद्ध का नेतृत्व तुम करो। तुम युद्ध कला विशारद हो। ये वानर चंचल और वीर तो हैं, परन्तु प्रशिक्षित नहीं हैं। तुम युद्ध नीति से उन पर विजय प्राप्त कर सकते हो। इसलिये हे वीर! तुम शीघ्र जाकर राम-लक्ष्मण सहित समस्त शत्रुओं का संहार कर मुझे निश्चिंत करो।"

अपने ऊपर इस प्रकार का विश्वास व्यक्त करते देख प्रहस्त ने कहा, "आज मैं अपने अतुल पराक्रम से शत्रु सेना का विनाश करके आप को निश्चिंत कर दूँगा। आज मेरे कृपाण के शौर्य से मैं रणचण्डी को प्रसन्न करके चील, कौवों, गीदड़ों आदि को शत्रु का माँस खिलाकर तृप्त करूँगा।"

इतना कहकर वह भयानक राक्षसों की सेना को लेकर युद्धस्थल की ओर चल दिया।

इस विशालकाय सेनापति को सदल-बल आते देख रामचन्द्र जी ने विभीषण से पूछा, "हे लंकापति! यह विशाल देह वाला सेनापति कौन है? क्या शूरवीर है?"

विभीषण ने उत्तर दिया, "हे रघुकुलतिलक! यह रावण का मन्त्री और वीर सेनापति प्रहस्त है। लंका की सेना का तीसरा भाग इसके अधिकार में है। यह बड़ा बलवान, पराक्रमी तथा युद्धकला विशारद है।"

यह सुनकर श्रीराम ने सुग्रीव से कहा, "हे वानराधिपति! ऐसा प्रतीत होता है कि रावण को इस पर बहुत विश्वास है। तुम इसे मारकर रावण का विश्वास भंग करो। इसके मरने पर रावण का मनोबल गिर जायेगा।"

राम का निर्देश पाते ही सुग्रीव ने श्रेष्ठ वानर सेनापतियों को यथोचित आज्ञा दी, जो बड़े वेग से राक्षसों पर टूट पड़े। राक्षस भी तोमर, त्रिशूल, गदा, तीर-कमान आदि से वानर सेना पर आक्रमण करने लगे। प्रहस्त ने स्वयं और उसके सेनानायकों ने अपने अप्रतिम रण कौशल से भयंकर दृश्य उपस्थित कर दिया और सहस्त्रों वानरों का सफाया करके रणभूमि को शवागार बना दिया। यह देख अनेक महारथी वानर अपनी पूरी शक्ति से राक्षसों से जूझने लगे।

उन्होंने भी भयानक प्रतिशोध लेकर सहस्त्रों राक्षसों को सदा के लिये समरभूमि में सुला दिया। एक ओर राक्षसों की तलवार से कट-कट कर सैकड़ों वानर भूमि पर धराशायी हो रहे थे तो दूसरी ओर वानरों के घूँसों और थप्पड़ों की मार से सहस्त्रों राक्षस रक्त की उल्टियाँ कर रहे थे। कभी वीरों की गर्जना से भूमि काँप उठती और कभी आहतों के चीत्कार से आकाश थर्रा उठता। ऐसा प्रतीत होता था कि रक्त की सरिता में बाढ़ आ गई है और उसने सागर का रूप धारण कर लिया है।

जब वानर वीर द्विविद ने महावीर नरात्तक के हाथों अपने सैनिकों की दुर्गति होती देखी तो एक भारी शिला का वार करके उसका प्राणान्त कर दिया। द्विविद के इस शौर्य से उत्साहित होकर दुर्मुख ने प्रहस्त के प्रमुख सेनापति समुन्नत को मार गिराया। उधर जाम्बवन्त ने एक भारी शिला से प्रहार करके महानाद का अन्त कर दिया। फिर तारा नामक वानर ने अपने नाखूनों से कम्भानु का पेट चीरकर उसे यमलोक भेज दिया।

कुछ ही क्षणों में इन चार सेनानायकों को मरते देख प्रहस्त ने क्रोध करके चारों दिशाओं में बाण छोड़ने आरम्भ कर दिये। इस आकस्मिक आक्रमण से अत्यधिक क्रुद्ध होकर वानर सेना अपने प्राणों का मोह छोड़कर शत्रुओं पर पिल पड़ी। उधर सेनापति नील पर्वत का एक टीला उठाकर प्रहस्त को मारने के लिये दौड़ा। मार्ग में ही प्रहस्त ने अपने बाणों से उस टीले की धज्जियाँ उड़ा दीं। इस पर नील ने एक दूसरा टीला उठाकर उसके रथ पर दे मारा जिससे उसका रथ टूट गया और घोड़े मर गये। रथ के टूटते ही प्रहस्त हाथ में मूसल लेकर नील को मारने के लिये दौड़ा। नील भी कम न था। दोनों परस्पर भिड़ गये।

अवसर पाकर प्रहस्त ने मूसल नील के सिर पर दे मारा जिससे उसका सिर फट गया और रक्त बहने लगा। इससे नील को और भी क्रोध आ गया। उसते फुर्ती से एक शिला उठाकर प्रहस्त के सिर पर पूरे वेग से दे मारा जिससे उसका सिर चूर-चूर हो गया और वह मर गया। प्रहस्त के मरते ही उसकी सेना ने पलायन कर दिया।

27
रावण कुम्भकर्ण संवाद

अग्निपुत्र नील के हाथों प्रहस्त के वध का समाचार सुनते ही रावण क्रोध से तमतमा उठा; किन्तु थोड़ी ही देर में उसका चित्त उसके लिये शोक से व्याकुल हो गया। उसके मन में भय उत्पन्न होने लगा। वह मन्त्रियों से बोला, "शत्रुओं को नगण्य समझकर मैं उनकी अवहेलना करता रहा इसी का परिणाम है प्रहस्त भी मारा गया। अब मैं समझता हूँ कि मुझे परमवीर कुम्भकर्ण को जगाकर रणभूमि में भेजना होगा। केवल वही ऐसा पराक्रमी है जो देखते-देखते शत्रु की सम्पूर्ण सेना का संहार कर सकता है।"

रावण की आज्ञा पाकर उसके मन्त्री ब्रह्मा के शाप के कारण सोये हुये कुम्भकर्ण के पास जाकर उसे जगाने लगे। जब वह चीखने-चिल्लाने और झकझोरने से भी न उठा तो वे लाठियों और मूसलों से मार-मार उसे उठाने लगे। साथ ही ढोल, नगाड़े तथा तुरहियों को बजाकर भारी शोर करने लगे, किन्तु उसकी नींद न खुली। अन्त में तोपों को दागकर, उसकी नाक में डोरी डालकर बड़ी कठिनाई से उसे जगाया गया। जब उसकी नींद टूटी तो माँस-मदिरा का असाधारण कलेवा करके वह बोला, "तुम लोगों ने मुझे कच्ची नींद से क्यों जगा दिया? सब कुशल तो है?"

कुम्भकर्ण का प्रश्न सुनकर मन्त्री यूपाक्ष ने हाथ जोड़कर निवेदन किया, "हे राक्षस शिरोमणि! लंका पर वानरों ने आक्रमण कर दिया है। अब तक हमारे बहुत से पराक्रमी वीरों तथा असंख्य राक्षस सैनिकों का संहार हो चुका है। मारे जाने वालों में खर-दूषण, प्रहस्त आदि महारथी सम्मिलित हैं। लंका भी जला दी गई है। ये सब वानर अयोध्या के राजकुमार राम की ओर से युद्ध कर रहे हैं। इस भयंकर परिस्थिति के कारण ही महाराज ने आपको जगाने की आज्ञा दी है। अब आप जाकर उन्हें धैर्य बँधायें।"

यह समाचार सुनकर कुम्भकर्ण स्नानादि से निवृत होकर राजसभा में रावण के पास पहुँचा। उसके चरणस्पर्श करके बोले, "महाराज! आपने मुझे किसलिये स्मरण किया है?"

कुम्भकर्ण को देखकर रावण प्रसन्न हुआ। वह बोला, "महाबली वीर! दीर्घकाल तक सोते रहने के कारण तुम्हें यहाँ के विषय में कोई जानकारी नहीं है। अयोध्या के राजकुमार राम

और लक्ष्मण वानरों की सेना को लेकर लंका का विनाश कर रहे हैं। उन्होंने समुद्र पर पुल बाँधकर उसे पार कर लिया है। इस समय लंका के चारों ओर वानर ही वानर दिखाई देते हैं। प्रहस्त, खर, दूषण आदि असंख्य वीर राक्षस सेना के साथ मारे जा चुके हैं। लंका में भय से त्राहि-त्राहि मच रही है। तुम पर मुझे पूर्ण विश्वास है। तुमने देवासुर संग्राम में देवताओं को खदेड़ कर जो अद्भुत वीरता दिखाई थी, वह मुझे आज भी स्मरण है। इसलिये तुम वानर सेना सहित दोनों भाइयों का संहार करके लंका को बचाओ।"

इसके अतिरिक्त रावण ने विभीषण के निष्कासन आदि की बातें भी उसे विस्तारपूर्वक बताईं।

यह सुनकर कुम्भकर्ण ने पहले तो रावण को नीति सम्बंधी बहुत सी बातें कहते हुए रावण को उपालम्भ दिया। फिर वह बोले, "भैया! आप भाभी मन्दोदरी और भैया विभीषण द्वारा दी हुई सम्मति के अनुसार कार्य करते तो आज लंका की यह दुर्दशा न होती। आपने मूर्ख मन्त्रियों के कहने में आकर स्वयं दुर्दिन को आमन्त्रण दिया है। परन्तु अब जो हो गया सो हो गया। उस पर पश्चाताप करने से क्या लाभ? अब आप के अनुचित कर्मों के फलस्वरूप उत्पन्न भय को मैं दूर करूँगा। मैं उन दोनों भाइयों का वध करूँगा और दुःखी राक्षसों के आँसू पोछूँगा। आप शोक न करें। मैं शीघ्र ही राम-लक्ष्मण का सिर आपके चरणों में रखूँगा।"

28

कुम्भकर्ण वध

शोकमग्न रावण को धैर्य बँधाकर कुम्भकर्ण युद्धभूमि में पहुँचा। स्वर्ण कवच से सुसज्जित कुम्भकर्ण ने हाथों में विद्युत के सदृश प्रकाशित भयंकर शूल उठा रखा था। लाखों चुने हुये सैनिकों को लेकर रणभूमि में पहुँचते ही उसने पृथ्वी को कँपा देने वाली भयंकर गर्जना की जिससे अनेक वानर मूर्छित होकर पृथ्वी पर गिर पड़े। इस विशाल पर्वताकार पराक्रमी राक्षस को देखकर साधारण वानरों की तो बात ही क्या; नल, नील, गवाक्ष तथा कुमुद जैसे पराक्रमी योद्धा भी भयभीत होकर रणभूमि से पलायन करने लगे। असंख्य वानर सैनिकों ने भी अपने इन सेनानायकों का अनुसरण किया।

अपनी सेना को इस प्रकार प्राणों के भय से भागते देख युवराज अंगद ने ललकार कर कहा, "हे वानरों! क्या इस प्रकार शत्रु को पीठ दिखाना तुम्हें शोभा देता है? तुम जैसे वीरों को भी प्राणों का मोह सताने लगा? धिक्कार है तुम्हें और तुम्हारी वीरता को! जिस कुम्भकर्ण को देखकर तुम भाग रहे हो, क्या वह कोई असाधारण योद्धा है? माँस मदिरा का सेवन करके उसका शरीर फूल गया है। वह तो बड़ी सरलता से मारा जायेगा। क्या रामचन्द्र जी के तेज के सम्मुख यह ठहर सकता है? आओ, लौटकर युद्ध करो। भागकर संसार में अपयश के भागी मत बनो।

अंगद के उत्साह भरे वचन सुनकर वानर सेना पुनः रणभूमि में लौट आई। वे प्राणों का मोह छोड़कर कुम्भकर्ण और उसकी सेना पर आक्रमण करने लगे। कुम्भकर्ण भी अपनी विशाल गदा के प्रहार से वानर सेना को मार-मार कर ढेर लगाने लगा। फिर भी शेष वानर वृक्षों तथा शिलाओं से राक्षस सेना का विनाश करने में जुटे रहे। कुम्भकर्ण उस समय साक्षात् यमराज प्रतीत हो रहा था। वह वानरों को गाजर मूली की भाँति काटकर ढेर लगाता जा रहा था। उसके चारों ओर हताहत वानरों के शरीर ही शरीर दिखाई दे रहे थे। क्रुद्ध होकर द्विविद ने एक पर्वत के टीले को उठाकर आकाश से कुम्भकर्ण के सिर पर मारा। कुम्भकर्ण तो उस वार से बच गया, किन्तु बहुत से राक्षस उसके नीचे दबकर मर गये।

राक्षसों की इतनी भारी क्षति से उत्साहित होकर वानरों ने दूने बल से राक्षस सेना का संहार आरम्भ किया जिससे सम्पूर्ण समरभूमि में रक्त की नदियाँ बहने लगीं। अब कुम्भकर्ण पर हनुमान भी आकाश मार्ग से पत्थरों की वर्षा करने लगे, परन्तु उस पर इसका कोई प्रभाव नहीं पड़ा। वह अपने शूल से पत्थरों के टुकड़े करके इधर-उधर छितराता रहा। इस प्रकार अपने वार खाली जाते देख हनुमान ने एक नुकीला वृक्ष उठाकर कुम्भकर्ण पर वार किया और उसका शरीर लहूलुहान कर दिया। उसने जब अपने शरीर से शोणित बहता देखा तो उसने वज्र के सदृश एक शूल पवनकुमार के मारकर उनकी छाती चीर दी। उसकी पीड़ा से वे व्याकुल हो गये। उनके मुख से रक्त बहने लगा हनुमान की यह दशा देखकर राक्षस सेना ने जयनाद किया और वे तीव्र वेग से मारकाट मचाने लगे।

हनुमान को घायल होता देख गन्धमादन, नील, ऋषभ, शरभ तथा गवाक्ष, पाँचों पराक्रमी सेनानायक एक साथ कुम्भकर्ण पर टूट पड़े। इस संयुक्त आक्रमण का भी उस पर कोई विशेष प्रभाव नहीं पड़ा। उसने पाँचों को पकड़कर इस प्रकार मसला कि वे नूर्छित होकर पृथ्वी पर गिर पड़े। अपने सेनानायकों को इस प्रकार मूर्छित होते देख वानर सेना एक साथ कुम्भकर्ण से चिपट गई। वह इससे भी विचलित नहीं हुआ और मुक्कों से मार-मार कर उनका सफाया करने लगा। सैकड़ों को उसने पूँछ पकड़-पकड़ कर फेंक दिया और बहुत से वानरों को पैरों के तले रौंद डाला।

जब उसके सम्मुख हनुमान, अंगद, नील, द्विविद, सुग्रीव जैसे वीर भी न ठहर सके और वानरों का अभूतपूर्व विनाश होने लगा तो सेना में भगदड़ मच गई। उन्होंने रामचन्द्र जी के पास जाकर गुहार की, "हे रघुवीर! कुम्भकर्ण ने हमारी सेना को तहस-नहस कर दिया है। हमारे बड़े-बड़े सेनापति घायल हो गये हैं। वह यमराज की भाँति हमारी सेना का घोर विनाश कर रहा है। ऐसा प्रतीत होता है कि वह हमारी सम्पूर्ण सेना को नष्ट कर डालेगा। इसलिये हम आपकी शरण में आये हैं। अब आप ही कुछ कीजिये, अन्यथा आज हमारी सेना का नामोनिशान नहीं बचेगा।

अपनी सेना की दुर्दशा का वृत्तान्त सुनकर लक्ष्मण का मुख क्रोध से रक्तवर्ण हो गया। वे राम की अनुमति लेकर कुम्भकर्ण से युद्ध करने के लिये चले। उनके पीछे-पीछे वानर सेनापति भी जयघोष करते हुये चले। अपने सम्मुख लक्ष्मण को देखकर कुम्भकर्ण ने हर्षनाद करते हुये कहा, "लक्ष्मण! मुझसे युद्ध करने का तुम्हारा साहस देखकर मैं प्रसन्न हुआ। तुम अभी बालक हो और मैं तुम्हारा वध नहीं करना चाहता। तुम लौट जावो और राम को भेजो, मैं उसका ही वध करूँगा।

इस प्रकार से लक्ष्मण का निरादर करके कुम्भकर्ण उस ओर दौड़ा जहाँ राम खड़े थे। कुम्भकर्ण को अपनी ओर आते देख वे उस पर रौद्र अस्त्रों से प्रहार करने लगे। जब इन अस्त्रों का उस पर कोई प्रभाव न पड़ा तो उन्होंने मयूर पंखों से सुसज्जित तीक्ष्ण बाण छोड़कर उसकी छाती फाड़ दी। इसकी पीड़ा से वह व्याकुल हो गया। उसके हाथों से गदा तथा अन्य अस्त्र छूटकर पृथ्वी पर गिर पड़े। जब रामचन्द्र जी के आगे उसकी एक न चली तो वह

खिसियाकर मुक्कों, लातों और थप्पड़ों से वानरों को मारने लगा। इस पर श्री राम ने उसे फिर ललकारा और तीक्ष्ण बाणों से उसके शरीर को छलनी कर दिया।

तब कुपित होकर कुम्भकर्ण ने पृथ्वी से एक भारी शिला उठाकर रामचन्द्र जी पर फेंकी जिसे उन्होंने सात बाण मारकर चूर-चूर कर दिया। फिर तीक्ष्ण नोक वाले तीन बाण छोड़कर उसका कवच तोड़ डाला। कवच के टूटते ही वानरों ने फिर उस पर धावा बोल दिया। उनसे घायल होकर वह क्रोध में इतना पागल हो गया कि उसे अपने और पराये का भी ज्ञान न रहा। उसने वानरों और राक्षसों सभी को मारना आरम्भ कर दिया। कुम्भकर्ण की यह दशा देखकर राम ने उसे फिर ललकार कर कहा, "अरे राक्षस! उन सैनिकों से क्या उलझ रहा है? इधर आकर मुझसे युद्ध कर।

राम की ललकार सुनते ही कुम्भकर्ण सामने आकर बोला, "हे राम! बहुत समय से मैं तुम्हारा वध करना चाहता था। आज सौभाग्य से तुम मेरे सम्मुख आये हो। मैं खर, दूषण, विराध या कबन्ध नहीं हूँ; मैं कुम्भकर्ण हूँ। मुझे अपने बल का परिचय दो।

कुम्भकर्ण की ललकार सुनकर रामचन्द्र जी ने अनेक अग्निबाण एक साथ छोड़े, परन्तु उन्हें कुम्भकर्ण ने मार्ग में ही नष्ट कर दिया। इस पर उन्होंने वायव्य बाण छोड़कर उसकी एक भुजा काट डाली। भुजा कटने पर क्रोध और पीड़ा से गर्जता हुआ भी वह वानरों का संहार करने लगा। इस भीषण मारकाट से भयभीत होकर वानर त्राहिमाम्-त्राहिमाम् कहते हुये रामचन्द्र जी के पीछे जाकर खड़े हो गये। तब रामचन्द्र जी ने ऐन्द्र नामक बाण से उसकी दूसरी भुजा भी काट डाली। फिर उन्होंने अद्र्धचन्द्राकार बाणों से उसके दोनों पैर काट डाले।

इससे वह भयंकर शब्द करता हुआ पृथ्वी पर गिर पड़ा। तब उन्होंने इन्द्र द्वारा दिया हुआ सूर्य की किरण की भाँति जाज्वल्यमान ब्रह्मदण्ड नामक बाण छोड़ा जो कुण्डलों से युक्त कुम्भकर्ण के मस्तक को काटकर आकाश में उड़ा और फिर उसे पृथ्वी पर गिरा दिया। कुम्भकर्ण के मरते ही वानर सेना में हर्ष की लहर दौड़ गई। उनके जयनाद ने सम्पूर्ण लंकापुरी को थर्रा दिया। कुम्भकर्ण के मरने के पश्चात् राक्षसों ने रावण को जाकर दुःखद संवाद सुनाया।

कुम्भकर्ण की मृत्यु का समाचार सुनकर रावण मूर्छित हो पृथ्वी पर गिर पड़ा। नरान्तक, देवान्तक, त्रिशिरा आदि राक्षस भी अपने चाचा की मृत्यु का समाचार सुनकर रोने लगे। जब रावण की मूर्छा भंग हुई तो वह विलाप करके रोने लगा। "हाय! आज मैं भाई को खोकर बिल्कुल असहाय हो गया। जिस कुम्भकर्ण के नाम से देव-दानव तक थर्राते थे, वह वीर आज मनुष्य और वानरों के हाथों मारा गया। तुम्हारे बिना आज यह राज्य मेरे किस काम का? तुमने ठीक ही कहा था कि मैंने विभीषण की बात न मानकर भूल की थी। हा कुम्भकर्ण! तुम मुझे अकेला क्यों छोड़ गये? बिना भाई के यह जीवन भी कोई जीवन है? मैं तुम्हारे बिना अब किस के भरोसे जिऊँगा?" इस प्रकार विलाप करते हुये वह फिर मूर्छित हो गया।

जब रावण को फिर सुधि आई तो त्रिशिरा ने उसे धैर्य बँधाते हुये कहा, "पिताजी! चाचाजी के मरने का आप इतना शोक क्यों करते हैं? उन्होंने तो शत्रु के छक्के छुड़ाने के पश्चात्

ही वीर गति प्राप्त की है। अभी आपको निराश होने की क्या आवश्यकता है, आपके पास तो ब्रह्मा की दी हुई शक्ति है। उसी से आप सेना सहित राम का नाश कीजिये। हम सब भी आपके साथ चलेंगे। आप अभी शोकाकुल हैं विश्राम कीजिये। हमें रणभूमि में जाने की अनुमति दीजिये।"

त्रिशिरा के इन वचनों को सुनकर रावण को कुछ धैर्य बँधा और उसने अपने पुत्रों को युद्ध में जाने की अनुमति दे दी।

29

त्रिशिरा, अतिकाय आदि का वध

लंकेश रावण के आज्ञानुसार उसके चार पुत्र त्रिशिरा, अतिकाय, देवान्तक तथा नरान्तक अपने दो चाचाओं महोदर एवं महापार्श्व के साथ युद्ध करने के लिये चले। उनके पीछे हाथियों, घुड़सवारों, रथों की एवं पैदल सेना थी। युद्धभूमि में उनका सामना करने के लिये वानरों की अपार सेना पत्थरों, शिलाओं तथा बड़े-बड़े वृक्षों को लिये तैयार खड़ी थी। राक्षस सेना को देखते ही उन्होंने भयंकर गर्जना की और वे शत्रुओं पर टूट पड़ी। वानरों के पत्थरों एवं वृक्षों द्वारा किये जाने वाले आक्रमण के प्रतिउत्तर में राक्षस बाणों, लौह-मुद्गरों तथा अन्य शस्त्रों से वार करने लगे।

इस भयंकर युद्ध के परिणामस्वरूप थोड़ी ही देर में सम्पूर्ण रणभूमि रक्त-रंजित हो गई। राक्षस सेनानायकों ने इतनी भीषण मारकाट मचाई कि चारों ओर वानरों के हताहत शरीर दिखाई देने लगे। राक्षस सैनिकों की भी ऐसी ही दशा थी। उनके घायल शरीर वानरों के शरीरों के साथ मिलकर एक वीभत्स दृष्य उत्पन्न कर रहे थे। जिनके अस्त्र-शस्त्र समाप्त हो जाते थे या नष्ट हो जाते थे, वे परस्पर भिड़कर लात-घूँसों का प्रयोग करने लगते थे। राक्षस वानरों की पूँछ पकड़कर उन्हीं से अन्य वानरों को मारते थे तो वानर राक्षसों की टाँगें पकड़कर उन्हें घमाते हुये अन्य राक्षसों पर वार करते थे। उस समय दोनों दल के पराक्रमी सैनिक निर्भय होकर शत्रुओं का विनाश करने में जुटे हुये थे।

जब वानर सेनानायकों ने राक्षसों को भारी संख्या में मार डाला तो रावण के पुत्र नरान्तक ने क्रोध में भरकर अपने रणकौशल का प्रदर्शन करते हुये थोड़ी ही देर में सहस्त्रों वानरों को मार गिराया। इससे वानर सेना में हाहाकार मच गया। यह हाहाकार सुन अंगद ने क्रोधित होकर नरान्तक को ललकारा।

अंगद की ललकार सुनकर नरान्तक ने गरजते हुये उसके वक्ष पर प्रास का वार किया किन्तु अंगद ने फुर्ती से प्रास को तोड़कर नरान्तक के रथ पर ऐसी लात जमाई कि उसका रथ पृथ्वी पर लुढ़क गया और उसके चारों घोड़े गिरकर मर गये। नरान्तक रथ से कूद पड़ा

और अंगद के सिर पर घूँसे ही घूँसे बरसाने लगा। तब अंगद ने भी बड़े जोर से उसकी छाती में घूँसा मारा जिससे उसकी आँखों की पुतलियाँ फिर गईं। वह रक्त वमन करता हुआ पृथ्वी पर ऐसा गिरा कि फिर वह कभी जीवित नहीं उठ सका। नरान्तक के मरते ही वानर सेना ने हर्षनाद किया।

नरान्तक के वध होते ही हाथी पर सवार रावण का भाई महोदर अंगद की ओर बढ़ा। भाई की मृत्यु का प्रतिशोध लेने के लिये देवान्तक और त्रिशिरा भी अपने-अपने रथ दौड़ाते हुये अंगद को मारने के लिये झपटे। तीनों महारथी एक साथ अंगद पर बाण छोड़ने लगे। तीनों के आक्रमणों का मुकाबला करते हुये अंगद ने सबसे पहले महोदर के हाथी को एक ऐसी लात जमाई कि वह गम्भीर गर्जना करता हुआ मैदान से भाग निकला। अंगद ने भागते हुये हाथी के दाँत उखाड़कर उनसे ही शत्रु का संहार करना आरम्भ कर दिया। जब हनुमान ने अंगद को तीन महारथियों से घिरा देखा तो उन्होंने लपककर देवान्तक की छाती में इतने जोर का मुक्का मारा कि वह वहीं तड़पकर ठंडा हो गया। अपनी आँखों के सामने देवान्तक को इस प्रकार मरते देखकर त्रिशिरा और महोदर के नेत्रों से ज्वाला फूटने लगी।

उन दोनों ने भयंकर बाणों की मार से अंगद, हनुमान सहित अनेक सेनानायकों को व्याकुल कर दिया। नील ने अपने वीरों को इस प्रकार घायल होते देख किलकिलाकर एक बहुत भारी शिलाखण्ड उखाड़ा। फिर उसे महोदर के सिर पर दे मारा। उसके नीचे महोदर पिस कर मर गया। इसके मरने पर त्रिशिरा ने वानर सेना पर एक साथ अनेक बाण छोड़े, किन्तु इस समय वानर सेना का साहस बढ़ा हुआ था और नरान्तक देवान्तक तथा महोदर जैसे सेनापतियों के मारे जाने के कारण राक्षस सेना के पैर उखड़ने लगे थे। अवसर पाकर हनुमान ने कूदकर त्रिशिरा का सिर धड़ से अलग कर दिया।

इस प्रकार चार महारथियों के मारे जाने पर महापार्श्व ने क्रोध से उन्मत्त होकर लोहे की भारी गदा से वानरों पर वार करना आरम्भ कर दिया। देखते ही देखते बीसियों वानर उसकी क्रोधाग्नि में जलकर स्वाहा हो गये। उस समय उसकी रक्तरंजित गदा प्रलयंकर अग्नि की भाँति वानरों को अपना ग्रास बना रही थी। इस पर ऋषभ नानक तेजस्वी वानर योद्धा ने क्रुद्ध होकर महापार्श्व को बड़ी जोर से लात मारी। उस आघात को न सह सकने के कारण महापार्श्व पृथ्वी पर गिर पड़ा। उसके गिरते ही वानर सेना ने चारों ओर से उसे घेरकर उसका शरीर नखों और दाँतों से फाड़ डाला जिससे वह तड़प-तड़प कर मर गया।

इन पाँचों महारथियों की मृत्यु से सेनापति अतिकाय को बड़ा क्रोध और क्षोभ हुआ। वह अपना विशाल रथ लेकर वानर सेना में घुस आया। उसे अपने बल पर बड़ा गर्व था क्योंकि वह अनेक बार देवताओं और दानवों को लोहे के चने चबवा चुका था। उसके भयंकर संहार से त्रस्त वानर सैनिक त्राहि-त्राहि करते हुये रामचन्द्र जी के पास पहुँचे। उसके विराट रूप और अद्भुत रणकौशल को देखकर उन्होंने विभीषण से पूछा, “हे विभीषण! यह पर्वताकार अद्भुत वीर सेनानी कौन है जो वानर सेना का प्रलयंकर विनाश कर रहा है?”

विभीषण ने बताया, "यह रावण का पुत्र अतिकाय है। मन्दोदरी इसकी माता है। साहस और पराक्रम में यह रावण से किसी भी प्रकार कम नहीं है। इसने अपनी तपस्या के बल पर दिव्य कवच तथा रथ प्राप्त किये हैं। सहस्त्रों बार इसने देवताओं और दानवों को परास्त किया है। इसलिये आप इसे मारने का शीघ्र ही उपाय करें, अन्यथा यह हमारी सम्पूर्ण सेना का विनाश कर देगा।"

इतने में वानर सेना में अभूतपूर्व मारकाट मचाता हुआ अतिकाय रामचन्द्र जी के पास अपना रथ दौड़ाता आ पहुँचा और उनसे क्रोध तथा गर्वपूर्वक बोला, "हे तुच्छ मनुष्यों! तुम दोनों भाई मेरे हाथों से क्यों इन बेचारे वानरों का नाश कराते हो? इन्हें मारने में न तो मेरा पराक्रम है और न मेरी कीर्ति ही है। इसलिये मैं तुमसे कहता हूँ कि यदि तुममें युद्ध करने की क्षमता और साहस हो तो मेरे साथ युद्ध करो अन्यथा लौट जाओ और वानर सेना से युद्ध बन्द करने के लिये कह दो।"

अतिकाय के दर्प भरे इन वचनों को सुन कर लक्ष्मण बोले, "अरे राक्षस! तू बढ़-चढ़ जितनी बातें बना रहा है, उतना वीर तो तू दिखाई नहीं देता। तेरा सिर तेरे धड़ से मैं उसी प्रकार अलग कर दूँगा जिस प्रकार आँधी पके हुये ताड़ के फल को गिरा देती है। संभाल अपने अस्त्र-शस्त्र और देख, मेरे बाण तेरे वक्ष का कैसे रक्तपान करते हैं। लक्ष्मण के ये कठोर वचन सुनकर अतिकाय ने क्रुद्ध हो एक जलता हुआ बाण उन पर छोड़ा।

लक्ष्मण ने उस सर्पाकार बाण को अपने अर्द्धचन्द्राकार बाण से काटकर दूसरा अग्निबान उसके मस्तक को लक्ष्य करके छोड़ा जो सीधा उसके मस्तक में घुस गया जिससे रक्त का फौवारा छूट निकला। एक बार तो वह थर्रा गया, किन्तु शीघ्र ही संभलकर वह फिर आक्रमण करने लगा। दोनों ही वीर अपनी-अपनी रक्षा करते हुये अद्भुत रणकौशल का परिचय देने लगे। अतिकाय बार-बार सिंह गर्जना करके लक्ष्मण को आतंकित करना चाहता था, किन्तु इस गर्जना का उन पर उल्टा ही प्रभाव पड़ रहा था। जितना ही वह अधिक जोर से गरजता, उतने ही अधिक कौशल और स्फूर्ति से लक्ष्मण बाणों की वर्षा करते। जब अतिकाय का हस्तलाघव क्षीण होता दिखाई नहीं दिया तो लक्ष्मण ने क्रुद्ध होकर उस पर ब्रह्मशक्ति छोड़ी। अतिकाय ने उसे प्रत्याक्रमण करके रोकने का निष्फल प्रयास किया। उस ब्रह्मशक्ति ने अतिकाय का सिर काटकर उड़ा दिया। उसके मरते ही राक्षस सेना निराश होकर मैदान छोड़ गई।

30

मायासीता का वध

युद्ध में चार पराक्रमी पुत्रों और दो भाइयों के मारे जाने का समाचार सुनकर रावण को बहुत अधिक दुःख और रोष हुआ। हताश होकर वह सोचने लगा कि इस शत्रु से कैसे त्राण पाया जाये। अत्यधिक चिन्तन करने पर पर भी उसे कोई मुक्ति नहीं सूझ रही थी। अन्त में उसने मेघनाद को बुलाकर कहा, "हे पुत्र! शत्रुओं ने अपनी सेना के सभी श्रेष्ठ योद्धाओं को एक-एक करके मार डाला है। अब मुझे लंका में ऐसा कोई महावीर दिखाई नहीं देता जो राम-लक्ष्मण सहित वानर सेना का विनाश कर सके। अतः मेरी आशा तुम्हारे ऊपर ही टिकी हुई है। इसलिये अब तुम ही रणभूमि में जाकर दुर्दमनीय शत्रुओं का नाश करके लंका की रक्षा करो। तुमने महापराक्रमी इन्द्र को भी परास्त किया है तथा तुम सब प्रकार की युद्ध कला में प्रवीण भी हो। इसलिये तुम्हीं उनका विनाश कर सकते हो।"

पिता की आज्ञा के अनुसार मेघनाद दिव्य रथ में आरूढ़ हो विशाल राक्षसी सेना के साथ युद्धभूमि की ओर चला। मार्ग में वह विचार करने लगा कि राम और लक्ष्मण बड़े शक्तिशाली योद्धा हैं जिन्होंने प्रहस्त, कुम्भकर्ण, महोदर तथा अतिकाय जैसे पराक्रमी योद्धाओं का वध कर डाला। यदि किसी प्रकार इनका मनोबल टूट जाय तो इन पर विजय प्राप्त करना सरल हो जायेगा। इस प्रकार विचार करते हुये उसके मस्तिष्क में एक युक्ति आई। उसने अपनी माया के बल से सीता की आकृति का निर्माण किया और उसे रथ में रख लिया। इसके पश्चात् वह सिंह गर्जना करता हुआ वानर सेना के सम्मुख जा पहुँचा। मेघनाद सहित शत्रु सेना को सामने देखकर वानर शिला और वृक्ष लेकर उस पर टूट पड़े।

हनुमान भी एक भारी शिला उखाड़कर मेघनाद पर झपटे, परन्तु रथ में दीन-मलिन, दुर्बल सीता को देखकर ठिठक गये। फिर उन्होंने सीता को बचाकर मेघनाद पर वार करना आरम्भ कर दिया। हनुमान को लगातार अपने ऊपर वार करते देख वह एक हाथ से तलवार खींचकर दूसरे हाथ से मायानिर्मित सीता के केश पकड़ उसे झकझोरने लगा। सीता की यह दुर्दशा देखकर क्रोध और सन्ताप से विदीर्ण हुये पनवपुत्र बोले, "अरे नीच! ब्राह्मण की सन्तान होते हुये तुझे स्त्री पर हाथ उठाते लज्जा नहीं आती? धिक्कार है तेरी बुद्धि और बल

पर। एक अबला को मारकर अपनी वीरता को कलंकित करते हुये तुझे संकोच नहीं होता? रे दुष्ट! तू जानकी की हत्या करके कभी जीवित नहीं बच सकेगा।"

इतना कहकर हनुमान और वानर सेना पत्थर बरसाते हुये उसे मारने के लिये दौड़े, किन्तु मेघनाद और उसके सैनिकों ने उन्हें रथ तक नहीं पहुँचने दिया। उनके सारे प्रयत्नों को निष्फल कर दिया।

तब घोर गर्जना करता हुआ मेघनाद बोला, "हनुमान! स्त्री पर हाथ डालना यद्यपि धर्म के विरुद्ध है, किन्तु शत्रु को प्रत्येक प्रकार से पीड़ा पहुँचाना नीति के विरुद्ध नहीं है। इसलिये तेरे सामने ही मैं सीता का वध करूँगा। सीता ही सारे दुःखों की जड़ है। उसके मरने के बाद ही लंका में सुख-शान्ति स्थापित होगी।"

यह कहकर उसने माया से बनी सीता का सिर काट दिया। सिर कटते ही वानर सेना में निराशा फैल गई। वह दुःख के सागर में डूबकर किंकर्तव्यविमूढ़ सी खड़ी रह गई। इस दशा का लाभ उठाकर राक्षस बड़ी मात्रा में वानरों का विनाश करने लगे। उधर हनुमान ने दुःखी होकर रामचन्द्र जी को समाचार दिया कि मेघनाद ने हमारे सामने सीता जी का सिर तलवार से काट दिया और वे "हा राम! हा राम!!" कहती हुई स्वर्ग सिधार गईं। यह समाचार सुनते ही राम मूर्छित होकर पृथ्वी पर गिर पड़े। कुछ वानर उन्हें घेरकर चैतन्य करने का प्रयत्न करने लगे। लक्ष्मण भी शोकातुर होकर विलाप करने लगे। साथ ही वे अपने बड़े भाई को होश में लाने की चेष्टा भी करते जाते थे।

जब विभीषण ने यह संवाद सुना तो उसने आकर बड़ी कठिनाई से रामचन्द्र को सचेत किया और समझाते हुये कहा, "हे रघुनन्दन! हनुमान ने जो कुछ आपसे कहा है, वह सत्य नहीं है। सीता का वध किसी भी दशा में सम्भव नहीं है। रावण ऐसा कभी नहीं करेगा और न किसी को उन्हें स्पर्श करने देगा।

इसमें सन्देह नहीं कि मेघनाद ने आपके साथ छल किया है। इस समय वह रणभूमि में भी नहीं है। मेरी सूचना के अनुसार वह निकुम्मिला देवी के मन्दिर में यज्ञ करने के लिये गया है। इस यज्ञ के सम्पन्न हो जाने पर वह अपराजेय हो जायेगा। इसलिये आप तत्काल सेना सहित लक्ष्मण को उस मन्दिर में भेजकर यज्ञ को पूरा न होने दें और वहीं मेघनाद का वध करा दें। आप लक्ष्मण को आज्ञा दें। मैं भी उनके साथ जाऊँगा। आज यज्ञ पूर्ण होने से पहले मेघनाद का वध होना ही चाहिये।"

31
लक्ष्मण मेघनाद युद्ध

विभीषण की सम्मति के अनुसार रामचन्द्र जी ने लक्ष्मण जी को आज्ञा दी कि वे अपने पराक्रम का परिचय देकर मेघनाद का वध करें। अपने अग्रज की आज्ञा पाते ही लक्ष्मण कवच पहन, हाथ में धनुष बाण ले राम के चरणस्पर्श कर मेघनाद का वध करने के लिये चल पड़े। लक्ष्मण के पीछे-पीछे विभीषण, सुग्रीव, हनुमान, जाम्बवन्त तथा वानरों की विशाल सेना चली। निकुम्मिला देवी के मन्दिर के निकट मेघनाद के रक्षक के रूप में असंख्य पराक्रमी राक्षस हाथी, घोड़ों एवं रथों पर सवार युद्ध के लिये सन्नद्ध खड़े थे। लक्ष्मण को सेना सहित आते देख उन्होंने भयंकर हुंकार की।

हुंकार कि चिन्ता न कर लक्ष्मण तथा अंगद मारकाट मचाते हुये राक्षस सेना में घुस गये। शेष वानर सेना ने भी उनका अनुसरण किया और वृक्षों, पत्थरों तथा शिलाओं की मार से राक्षसों का विनाश करने लगे। बदले में वे भी तीर, भालों, तलवारों तथा गदाओं से वानरों पर प्रति आक्रमण करने लगे। दोनों ओर से होने वाली गर्जनाओं से सम्पूर्ण लंकापुरी गूँज उठी। दोनों ओर भयंकर कारकाट मच रही थी. सैनिकों के मस्तक, धड़, हाथ-पैर आदि कट-कट कर शोणित की सरिता में बह रहे थे। मृत शरीरों का एकत्रित ढेर रुधिर सरिता में द्वीप की भाँति प्रतीत हो रहा था।

अंगद, हनुमान और लक्ष्मण की भयंकर मार से राक्षस सेना त्राहि-त्राहि कर उठी और उनका आर्तनाद सुनकर मेघनाद यज्ञ पूरा किये बिना ही क्रुद्ध होकर युद्ध करने के लिये मन्दिर से निकल पड़ा। जब उसने लक्ष्मण के साथ विभीषण को भी देखा तो क्रोध से उसका मुख तमतमा गया। वह भ्रकुटि चढ़ाकर उससे बोला, "हे राक्षसकुलकलंक! तुम परम तेजस्वी पुलस्त्य वंश पर कलंक हो जिसने अपने सहोदर भाई के साथ विश्वासघात करके शत्रु का साथ दिया है। राम न तो हमारे वंश का है, न हमारा मित्र है और न कोई धर्मपरायण व्यक्ति ही है। फिर तुम उसका साथ क्यों दे रहे हो? यह मत भूलो कि अपना अपना होता है और पराया पराया ही होता है। धिक्कार है तुम्हारी बुद्धि पर जो तुम स्वयं दास बनकर सम्पूर्ण राक्षस जाति को एक विदेशी का दास बनाने के उद्यत हो गये। तुम याद रखना कि राम कभी

तुम्हारा सगा नहीं बनेगा। वह यह करकर तुम्हें मरवा देगा कि जो अपने सगे भाई का नहीं हुआ, वह हमारा क्या होगा?"

मेघनाद के कठोर वचन सुनकर विभीषण ने उत्तर दिया, "हे दुर्बुद्धे! तुझे प्रलाप करते समय यह भी ध्यान नहीं रहा कि मैं तेरे पिता का भ्राता हूँ। इसलिये तुझे मेरे साथ सम्मानपूर्वक वार्तालाप करना चाहिये। स्मरण रख, राक्षस कुल में जन्म लेकर भी मैं क्रूर व्यक्तियों की संगति से सदा बचता रहा हूँ। मैंने तुम्हारे पिता को भी उचित सम्मति दी थी, परन्तु उसे मानना तो एक ओर, उन्होंने भरी सभा में मेरा घोर अपमान किया। तुम लोग नीतिवान होने का दम्भ करके भी इस साधारण सी बात को भूल गये कि पराई स्त्री का हरण करना, पराया धन बलात् लेना और मित्र पर विश्वास न करना, तीनों ही विनाश के कारण बनते हैं। ये तीनों दुर्गुण तेरे पिता में आ गये हैं, इसलिये अब राक्षस वंश का नाश होने जा रहा है।"

विभीषण के इन शब्दों ने मेघनाद की क्रोधाग्नि और भी भड़का दिया और वह क्रोधित होकर अपने तीक्ष्ण बाणों से वानरों का संहार करने लगा। यह देख लक्ष्मण के क्रोध का पारावार न रहा। उन्होंने मेघनाद को ललकार कर उसके रथ को अपने बाणों से आच्छादित कर दिया। मेघनाद ने इन बाणों को काटकर अनेक बाण एक साथ छोड़े। दोनों में से कोई किसी से पीछे नहीं रहना चाहता था। वे गरज-गरज कर रणोन्मत्त सिंहों की भाँति युद्ध कर रहे थे। मेघनाद की गति जब मन्द पड़ने लगी तो वानर सेना ने उत्साहित होकर लक्ष्मण का जयघोष किया।

इससे मेघनाद को बहुत क्रोध आया। उसने एक साथ असंख्य बाण छोड़कर वानर सेना को पीछे धकेल दिया। तब लक्ष्मण ने तीक्ष्ण नोक वाले सात बाण छोड़कर उसका दुर्भेद्य कवच तोड़ डाला जिससे वह टुकड़े-टुकड़े होकर पृथ्वी पर बिखर गया। फिर तो मेघनाद के कवचहीन शरीर में नुकीले तीर घुसकर उसके शरीर को छलनी करने लगे।

इस भयंकर वार से विचलित हो गया और उसने एक हजार बाण मारकर लक्ष्मण के कवच के भी टुकड़े-टुकड़े कर डाले। अब दोनों मतवाले वीर बिना कवच के युद्ध करने लगे। दोनों के शरीरों में एक दूसरे के तीक्ष्ण बाण घुसकर शोणित की धाराएँ प्रवाहित करने लगे। साथ ही उनके बाण एक दूसरे के बाणों को काटकर चिनगारी भी उगलते जाते थे। उनके रक्तरंजित शरीर ऐसे प्रतीत हो रहे थे मानो वन में टेसू और सेमल के फूल खिल रहे हों। दोनों सेनाएँ इन वीर महारथियों का पराक्रम देखकर विस्मित हो रही थीं जो युद्ध से न हटते थे और न थकते थे।

32

मेघनाद वध

विभीषण ने क्रोध करके अग्नि के समान बाणों की बौछार करके राक्षस सेना का विनाश करना आरम्भ कर दिया। विभीषण की बाणवर्षा से प्रोत्साहित होकर वानर सेना पूरे बल से हनुमान के नेतृत्व में शिला और वृक्ष मारकर राक्षसों को यमलोक भेजने लगी। इस महायुद्ध को देखकर देवता-दानव सबके हृदय दहल गये। पृथ्वी पर शवों के अतिरिक्त वृक्षों एवं शिलाओं के समूह से गगनचुम्बी पर्वत बन गये। वहाँ लक्ष्मण और मेघनाद के बाणों से दसों दिशाएँ आच्छादित हो गईं, उनके बाणों से सूर्य छिप गया और चारों ओर अन्धकार छा गया। तभी सुमित्रानन्दन ने मेघनाद के रथ के चारों घोड़ों को मारकर सारथि का सिर काट डाला। यह देखकर राक्षसों के उत्साह पर पाला पड़ गया और वानर सेना में फिर से नवजीवन का संचार हो गया। तभी मेघनाद लपक कर दूसरे रथ पर चढ़ गया और उस पर से बाणों वर्षा करने लगा।

मेघनाद ने जब दूसरे रथ पर चढ़कर युद्ध करना आरम्भ किया तो विभीषण को बहुत क्रोध आया। उसने पूरे वेग से गदा का वार करके उसके रथ को चूर-चूर कर दिया और सारथि को मार डाला। अपने चाचा द्वारा किये गये इस विनाशकारी आक्रमण से मेघनाद जलभुन गया और उसने एक साथ दस बाण विभीषण को मारने के लिये छोड़े। मेघनाद के लक्ष्य को दृष्टि में रखकर लक्ष्मण ने अपने तीक्ष्ण बाणों से उन बाणों को मार्ग में ही नष्ट कर दिया।

अपना वार इस प्रकार खाली जाते देख मेघनाद क्रोध से उन्मत्त हो गया और उसने विभीषण को मारने के लिये वह शक्तिशाली बाण छोड़ा जो उसे यमराज से प्राप्त हुआ था। वह एक अद्भुत बाण था जिसे इन्द्र आदि देवता भी नहीं काट सकते थे और जिसके वार को तीनों लोकों में भी कोई सहन नहीं कर सकता था। इस यम बाण को अपनी ओर आता देख लक्ष्मण ने भी वह अप्रमेय शक्ति वाला बाण निकाला जो उन्हें कुबेर ने दिया था। उन बाणों के छूटने से सम्पूर्ण आकाश प्रकाश से जगमगा उठा।

वे दोनों एक दूसरे से टकराये जिससे भयानक अग्नि उत्पन्न हुई और दोनों बाण जलकर भस्म हो गये। अपने बाण को व्यर्थ जाता देख लक्ष्मण ने मेघनाद पर वरुणास्त्र छोड़ा। उस प्रलयंकारी अस्त्र का निवारण करने के लिये इन्द्रजित ने आग्नेय बाण छोड़ा। इसके परिणामस्वरूप लक्ष्मण का वरुणास्त्र निरस्त होकर पृथ्वी पर गिर पड़ा। लगभग उसी समय मेघनाद ने लक्ष्मण के प्राण लेने के लिये आसुरास्त्र नामक बाण छोड़ा। उसके छूटते ही सम्पूर्ण वातावरण में अन्धकार छा गया और कुछ भी देखना सम्भव नहीं रह गया। अपने इस सफलता पर मेघनाद ने बड़े जोर की गर्जना की, किन्तु दूसरे ही क्षण लक्ष्मण ने सूर्यास्त्र छोड़कर उस अन्धकार को दूर कर दिया जिससे पृथ्वी, आकाश एव सभी दिशाएँ पूर्ववत् चमकने लगीं।

उसी के साथ उन्होंने एक अद्वितीय बाण प्रत्यंचा पर चढ़ाते हुये यह कहकर कि 'यदि रघुवंशमणि महात्मा राम परम सत्यवादी, धर्मपरायण तथा दृढ़व्रती हैं तो हे बाण! तू शीघ्र जाकर दुष्ट मेघनाद को यमलोक पहुँचा' वेदमन्त्रों का उच्चारण करते हुये उन्होंने वह बाण छोड़ दिया। तीनों लोकों का क्षय करने की सामर्थ्य वाला वह अजेय बाण सम्पूर्ण वातावरण को प्रकाशित करता हुआ मेघनाद को लगा और उसका मस्तक उड़ाकर आकाश में बहुत दूर तक ले गया।

मेघनाद का मस्तकविहीन धड़ बड़े जोर का धमाका करता हुआ पृथ्वी पर गिरा। इन्द्र को भी समरभूमि में पराजित करने वाले, सम्पूर्ण देवताओं एवं दानवों को अपने नाम से ही भयभीत करने वाले इस परम पराक्रमी मेघनाद का सुमित्रानन्दन के हाथों वध होता देख वानर सेना के आनन्द की सीमा न रही। वे बड़े जोर से हर्षध्वनि और सिंह गर्जना करते हुये राक्षसों को चुन-चुन कर मारने लगे। लंका के महत्वपूर्ण स्तम्भ तथा राक्षसकुल के परम तेजस्वी युवराज को इस प्रकार मरते देख राक्षस सेना का मनोबल टूट गया।

उनके पैर उखड़ गये। कुछ साहसी राक्षस आधे मन से लड़ते रहे और शेष प्राण बचाकर लंका की ओर दौड़े। वानर सेना उस समय विजयोन्माद से उन्मत्त हो रही थी। उसने भागते हुये राक्षसों को भी न छोड़ा और उन पर निरन्तर पत्थरों से आक्रमण करते रहे। जो उनकी पकड़ में आ गये, उन्हें नाखूनों और दाँतों से चीर डाला। एक ओर राक्षस हाहाकार करते हुये भागे जा रहे थे तो दूसरी ओर ऋक्ष एवं वानर राम-लक्ष्मण की जयजयकार करते हुये उन्हें खदेड़ रहे थे। देवताओं एवं ऋषि-मुनियों के भयंकर शत्रु के मर जाने पर सब लोग प्रसन्न हो हर्षनाद कर रहे थे।

33

लक्ष्मण मूर्छित

इस भयंकर युद्ध में लक्ष्मण ने रावण की ध्वजा काटकर उसके सारथि का वध कर डाला और रावण के धनुष को काट डाला। साथ ही विभीषण ने भी अपनी गदा से रावण के रथ के घोड़ों को मार डाला। विभीषण के इस कृत्य से रावण को इतना क्रोध आया कि उसने विभीषण पर एक प्रज्वलित शक्ति चलाई किन्तु विभीषण के पास आने के पहले ही लक्ष्मण ने उस शक्ति को अपने बाणों से नष्ट कर दिया।

इस पर अत्यन्त क्रोधित होकर रावण ने विभीषण पर ऐसी अमोघ शक्ति चलाई जिसका वेग काल भी न सह सकता था। विभीषण के प्राण संकट में देख लक्ष्मण स्वयं आगे बढ़कर शक्ति के सामने खड़े हो गये। वज्र और अशनि के समान गड़गड़ाहट उत्पन्न करने वाली तथा विषधर सर्प के समान वह भयंकर महातेजस्वी शक्ति लक्ष्मण आकर लगी। उस नागराज वासुकी की जिह्वा के समान देदीप्यमान शक्ति ने लक्ष्मण के वक्ष को विदीर्ण कर दिया और वे रक्त से लथपथ होकर मूर्छित हो पृथ्वी पर गिर पड़े।

वानरों ने उस शक्ति को लक्ष्मण के शरीर में से निकालने का भरसक प्रयत्न किया, किन्तु सफल न हो सके। अन्त में श्री राम ने पूरी शक्ति लगा कर दोनों हाथों से खींचकर उसे बाहर निकाला और तोड़कर भूमि पर फेंक दिया। जब तक राम शक्ति को खींचकर निकालते रहे रावण निरन्तर बाणों की वर्षा करके उन्हें घायल करता रहा। शक्ति निकाल कर उन्होंने शीघ्र ही रावण को मार डालने की प्रतिज्ञा की। फिर वे रावण के साथ भयानक युद्ध करने लगे। जब रावण उनके बाणों को न सह सका तो वह घायल होकर रणभूमि से भाग गया।

श्रीराम लक्ष्मण के पास बैठकर नाना प्रकार से विलाप करने लगे। उनके विलाप से दुःखी सारी वानर सेना रोने लगी। तभी सुषेण ने कहा, "हे वीरशिरोमणि! आप दुःखी न हों। ये जीवित हैं, इनकी हृदयगति चल रही है।"

फिर हनुमान से कहा, "तुम शीघ्र ही महोदय पर्वत पर जाकर विशल्यकरणी, सावण्यकरणी, संजीवकरणी तथा संधानी नामक औषधियाँ ले आओ। उनसे लक्ष्मण के प्राणों की रक्षा हो सकेगी।" सुषेण के निर्देशानुसार हनुमान तत्काल महोदय गिरि पर जा

पहुँचे, परन्तु इन औषधियों की पहचान न होने के कारण उस शिखर को ही उखाड़ लाये जिस पर अनेक प्रकार की औषधियों के वृक्ष उग रहे थे। सुषेण ने इनमें से औषधियों को पहचानकर उनको कूट-पीस कर लक्ष्मण को सुँघाया। इससे वे थोड़ी ही देर में स्वस्थ होकर उठ खड़े हुये।

34

रावण वध

उधर रावण रथारूढ़ हो फिर युद्ध करने के लिये लौट आया। राम पृथ्वी पर खड़े होकर रथ में सवार रावण से युद्ध करने लगे तो देवराज इन्द्र ने उनके पास अपना रथ भिजवाकर प्रार्थना की कि वे उस पर सवार होकर युद्ध करें। दोनों ही पराक्रमी वीर रथों पर सवार होकर भीषण युद्ध करने लगे। उनके अद्भुत रण-कौशल को देखकर दिग्गज वीरों भी रोमांचित होने लगे। इधर रावण ने नागास्त्र छोड़ा तो उधर श्रीराम ने गरुड़ास्त्र।

रावण ने इन्द्र के रथ की ध्वजा काट डाली और घोड़ों को घायल कर दिया। रावण के बाणों से बार-बार आहत होने के कारण श्रीराम अपने बाणों को प्रत्यंचा पर नहीं चढ़ा पा रहे थे। जब रावण ने उन पर शूल नामक महाभयंकर शक्ति छोड़ी तो राम ने क्रोधपूर्वक इन्द्र द्वारा दी हुई शक्ति छोड़कर उस शूल को नष्ट कर दिया। फिर उन्होंने लगातार बाण वर्षा करके रावण को बुरी तरह घायल कर दिया। रावण की यह दशा देखकर उसका सारथी उसे रणभूमि से बाहर ले गया। अपने सारथी के इस कार्य से रावण को बहुत क्रोध आया और उस फटकार कर उसने रथ को पुनः रणभूमि में ले चलने आज्ञा दी।

श्रीराम के सम्मुख पहुँचकर वह फिर उन पर बाणों की वर्षा करने लगा। दोनों महावीर महारथियों के बीच फिर ऐसा भयंकर युद्ध आरम्भ हुआ कि वानरों और राक्षसों की विशाल सेनाएँ और पराक्रमी वीर अपने हाथों में हथियार होते हुये भी निश्चेष्ट होकर उनका रणकौशल देखने लगे। राक्षसों की दृष्टि रावण के पराक्रम पर अटकी हुई थी तो वानरों की श्रीराम के शौर्य पर। श्रीराम को अपनी विजय पर पूर्ण विश्वास था और परिस्थितियों को देखते हुये रावण समझ गया था कि उसकी मृत्यु निश्चित है। यह सोचकर दोनों रणकेसरी अपनी पूरी शक्ति से युद्ध करने लगे। पहले रामचन्द्र जी ने रावण के रथ की ध्वजा को एक ही बाण से काट गिराया। इससे क्रोधित होकर रावण चारों ओर गदा, चक्र, परिध, मूसल, शूल तथा माया निर्मित शस्त्रों की वर्षा करने लगा। दोनों ओर से भयानक घात-प्रतिघात होने लगे।

युद्ध विषयक प्रवृति और निवृति में दोनों ही रणपण्डित अपना-अपना अद्भुत कौशल दिखाने लगे। सनसनाते बाणों के घटाटोप से सूर्य की प्रभा लुप्त हो गई और वायु की गति भी मन्द पड़ गई। देव, गन्धर्व, किन्नर, यक्ष, सिद्ध, महर्षि सभी चिन्ता में पड़ गये। तभी अवसर पाकर महाबाहु राम ने एक विषधर समान बाण छोड़कर रावण का मस्तक काट डाला, परन्तु उसके स्थान पर रावण का वैसा ही दूसरा नया सिर उत्पन्न हो गया। जब श्रीराम ने उसे भी काट डाला तो वहाँ तीसरा शीश प्रकट हो गया। इस प्रकार बार-बार शीश कटने पर भी उसका अन्त नहीं हो रहा था।

यह दशा देखकर इन्द्र के सारथी मातलि ने कहा, "प्रभो! आप इसे मारने के ब्रह्मास्त्र का प्रयोग कीजिये। अब उसके विनाश का समय आ पहुँचा है। मातलि की बात सुनकर रघुनाथ जी को ब्रह्मा के उस बाण का स्मरण हो आया जो उन्हें अगस्त्य मुनि ने दिया था। उन्होंने रावण की छाती को लक्ष्य करके वह बाण पूरे वेग के साथ छोड़ दिया जिसने रावण के हृदय को विदीर्ण कर दिया। इससे रावण के प्राण पखेरू उड़ गये। रावण को मारकर वह बाण पृथ्वी में समा गया और पुनः स्वच्छ होकर श्रीराम के तरकस में लौट आया। रावण के विनाश और श्रीराम की विजय से समस्त लोकों में हर्ष की लहर दौड़ गई। चारों ओर श्रीराम की जयजयकार होने लगी। वानर सेना में आनन्द का पारावार न रहा। प्रत्येक सैनिक विजय गर्व से फूला न समाता था।

पराजित और मरे हुये भाई को देखकर विभीषण अपने आँसुओं को न रोक सका और वह फूट-फूट कर विलाप करने लगा और कहने लगा, "हे भाई! अहंकार के वशीभूत होकर तुमने मेरी, प्रहस्त, कुम्भकर्ण, इन्द्रजित, नरान्तक आदि किसी की भी बात न मानी। उसी का फल यह सामने आया। तुम्हारे मरने से नीति पर चलने वाले लोगों की मर्यादा टूट गई, धर्म का मूर्तिवान विग्रह चला गया, सूर्य पृथ्वी पर गिर पड़ा, चन्द्रमा अन्धेरे में डूब गया और जलती अग्नि शिखा बुझ गई।"

विभीषण को इस प्रकार विलाप करते देख श्रीराम ने उसे समझाया, "हे विभीषण! तुम्हें इस प्रकार शोक नहीं करना चाहिये। रावण असमर्थ होकर नहीं मरा है। उसने प्रचण्ड पराक्रम का प्रदर्शन किया है। इस प्रकार क्षत्रिय धर्म का पालन करते हुये मरने वालों के लिये शोक नहीं करना चाहिये। युद्ध में सदा विजय ही विजय मिले, ऐसा पहले भी कभी नहीं हुआ है। यह सोचकर उठो और संयत मन से प्रेत कर्म करो। मैं इसमें तुम्हें पूरा सहयोग दूँगा। बैर जीवनकाल तक ही रहता है। मरने के बाद उस बैर का अन्त हो जाता है। इसलिये यह जैसा तुम्हारा स्नेहपात्र है, उसी तरह मेरा भी है।"

35

मन्दोदरी का विलाप और रावण की अन्त्येष्टि

रावण की मृत्यु का समाचार सुनकर मन्दोदरी सहित उसकी सभी रानियाँ शोकाकुल होकर अन्तःपुर से निकल पड़ीं। वे चीख-चीख कर विलाप करने लगीं। 'हा आर्यपुत्र! हा नाथ!' पुकारते हुये वे कटी हुई लताओं की भाँति रावण के मृत शरीर पर गिर कर हाहाकार करने लगीं, "हाय! असुर, देवता और नाग जिसके भय से काँपा करते थे, आज उन्हीं की एक मनुष्य ने यह दशा कर दी। आपके प्रिय भाई विभीषण ने आपके हित की बात कही थी, उसे ही आपने निकाल बाहर किया। राक्षसशिरोमणे! ऐसी बात नहीं है कि आपके स्वेच्छाचार से हमारा विनाश हुआ है, दैव ही सब कुछ कराता है।"

मन्दोदरी बिलख-बिलख कर कह रही थी, "नाथ! पहले आपने इन्द्रियों को जीतकर ही तीनों लोकों पर विजय पाई थी, उस बैर का प्रतिशोध लेकर इन्द्रियों ने ही अब आपको परास्त किया है। खर के मरने पर ही मुझे विश्वास हो गया था कि राम कोई साधाराण मनुष्य नहीं है। मैं ने बारम्बार आपसे कहा था, रघुनाथ जी से बैर-विरोध न लें, किन्तु आप नहीं माने। उसी का आज यह फल मिला है। आपने महान तेजस्वी सीता का अपहरण किया।

वे संसार की महानतम पतिव्रता नारी हैं। उनका अपहरण करते समय ही आप जलकर भस्म नहीं हो गये, यही महान आश्चर्य है। आज वही सीता आपकी मृत्यु का कारण बन गई। हाय स्वामी! आपकी मृत्यु कैसे हो गई? आप तो मृत्यु की भी मृत्यु थे। फिर स्वयं ही मृत्य के आधीन कैसे हो गये? महाराज! पतिव्रता के आँसू इस पृथ्वी पर व्यर्थ नहीं गिरते, यह कहावत आपके साथ ठीक-ठीक घटी है। आपने युद्ध में कभी कायरता नहीं दिखाई, परन्तु सीता का हरण करते समय आपने कायरता का ही परिचय दिया था। मैं शोक से पीड़ित हो रही हूँ औ आप मुझे सान्त्वना भी नहीं दे रहे। आज आपका वह प्रेम कहाँ गया?"

इन शोकविह्वल रानियों को देखकर श्रीराम ने विभीषण से कहा, "हे विभीषण! इन्हें धैर्य बँधाओं और अपने भाई का अन्तिम संस्कार करो।"

श्रीराम की आज्ञा पाकर विभीषण ने माल्यवान के साथ मिलकर दाह संस्कार की तैयारी की। शव को भली-भाँति सजाकर शवयात्रा निकाली गई जिसमें नगर के समस्त लंकानिवासियों और अन्तःपुर की सभी रानियों ने भाग लिया। वेदोक्त विधि से उसका अन्तिम संस्कार किया गया।

36

विभीषण का राज्याभिषेक और सीता की वापसी

युद्ध की समाप्ति पर श्री राम ने मातलि को सम्मानित करते हुए इन्द्र के दिये हुये रथ को लौटा दिया। तत्पश्चात उन्होंने समस्त वानर सेनानायकों की भूरि-भूरि प्रशंसा करते हुये उनका यथोचित सम्मान किया। फिर वे लक्ष्मण से बोले, "सौम्य! अब तुम लंका में जाकर विभीषण का राज्याभिषेक करो, क्योंके इन्होंने मुझ पर बहुत बड़ा उपकार किया है।"

रघुनाथ जी की आज्ञा पाकर लक्ष्मण ने प्रसन्नतापूर्वक सोने का घड़ा उठाया और एक वानर यूथपति को समुद्र का जल भर लाने का आदेश दिया। उन्होंने लंकापुरी में जल से भरे उस घट को उत्तम स्थान पर स्थापित किया। फिर उस जल से विभीषण का वेदोक्त रीति से अभिषेक किया। राजसिंहासन पर विराजमान विभीषण उस समय अत्यन्त तेजस्वी प्रतीत हो रहे थे। लक्ष्मण के पश्चात् अन्य सभी उपस्थित राक्षसों और वानरों ने भी उनका अभिषेक किया। विभीषण को लंका के सिंहासन पर अभिषिक्त देख उसके मन्त्री और प्रेमी अत्यन्त प्रसन्न हुये। वे श्रीराम की स्तुति करने लगे। उन्होंने अपने निष्ठा का आश्वासन देते हुये दहीं, अक्षत, मिष्ठान्न, पुष्प आदि अपने नये नरेश को अर्पित किये और 'महाराज विभीषण की जय', 'श्रीरामचन्द्र जी की जय' का उद्घोष किया। विभीषण ने सभी प्रकार की मांगलिक वस्तुएँ लक्ष्मण को भेंट की और रघुनाथ जी के प्रति भक्ति प्रकट की।

जब लक्ष्मण विभीषण का राज्याभिषेक कर लौट आये तो श्री रामचन्द्र जी ने हनुमान से कहा, "महावीर! तुम महाराज विभीषण की आज्ञा लेकर लंकापुरी में जाओ और वैदेही को यह समाचार दो कि रावण युद्ध में मारा गया है और वे लौटने की तैयारी करें।"

रघुनाथ जी की आज्ञा पाकर हनुमान विभीषण की अनुमति ले अशोकवाटिका में पहुँचे और वैदेही को श्रद्धापूर्वक प्रणाम करके बोले, "माता! श्री रामचन्द्र जी लक्ष्मण और सुग्रीव के साथ कुशल हैं। अपने शत्रु का वध करके वे अपने मनोरथ में सफल हुए। रावण अपनी सेना सहित युद्ध में मारा गया। विभीषण का राज्याभिषेक कर दिया गया है। इस प्रकार अब आप निर्भय हों। आपको यहाँ भारी कष्ट हुआ। इन निशाचरियों ने भी आपको कुछ कम कष्ट

नहीं दिया है। यदि आप आज्ञा दें तो मैं मुक्कों, लातों से इन सबको यमलोक पहुँचा दूँ।"

हनुमान की यह बात सुनकर सब निशाचरियाँ भय से थर-थर काँपने लगीं। परन्तु करुणामयी सीता बोलीं, "नहीं वीर! इसमें इनका कोई दोष नहीं है। ये तो रावण की आज्ञा का ही पालन करती थीं। इसके अतिरिक्त पूर्वजनित कर्मों का फल तो मुझे भोगना ही था। यदि फिर भी इन दासियों का कुछ अपराध हो तो उसे मैं क्षमा करती हूँ। अब तुम ऐसी व्यवस्था करो कि मैं शीघ्र प्राणनाथ के दर्शन कर सकूँ।"

पवनपुत्र ने लौटकर जब दशरथनन्दन को सीता का संदेश दिया तो उन्होंने विभीषण से कहा, "भाई विभीषण! तुम शीघ्र जाकर सीता को अंगराग तथा दिव्य आभूषणों से विभूषित करके मेरे पास ले आओ।"

आज्ञा पाकर विभीषण ने स्वयं वैदेही का पास जाकर उनके दर्शन किया और उन्हें श्री राम द्‌वारा दी गई आज्ञा कह सुनाई। पति का संदेश पाकर सीता श्रृंगार कर पालकी पर बैठ विभीषण के साथ उस स्थान पर पहुँचीं जहाँ उनके पति का शिविर था। फिर पालकी से उतरकर पैदल ही सकुचाती हुई अपने पति के सम्मुख जाकर उपस्थित हो गईं। आगे वे थीं और उनके पीछे विभीषण। उन्होंने बड़े विस्मय, हर्ष और स्नेह से पति के मुख का दर्शन किया। उस समय उनका मुख आनन्द से प्रातःकालीन कमल की भाँति खिल उठा।

37

रावण के जन्म की कथा

अगस्त्य मुनि ने कहना जारी रखा, "पिता की आज्ञा पाकर कैकसी विश्रवा के पास गई और उन्हें अपने अभिप्राय से अवगत कराया। उस समय भयंकर आँधी चल रही थी। आकाश में मेघ गरज रहे थे। कैकसी का अभिप्राय जानकर विश्रवा ने कहा कि भद्रे! तुम इस कुबेला में आई हो। मैं तुम्हारी इच्छा तो पूरी कर दूँगा परन्तु इससे तुम्हारी सन्तान दुष्ट स्वभाव वाली और क्रूरकर्मा होगी। मुनि की बात सुनकर कैकसी उनके चरणों में गिर पड़ी और बोली कि भगवन्! आप ब्रह्मवादी महात्मा हैं। आपसे मैं ऐसे दुराचारी सन्तान पाने की आशा नहीं करती। अतः आप मुझ पर कृपा करें। कैकसी के वचन सुनकर मुनि विश्रवा ने कहा कि अच्छा तो तुम्हारा सबसे छोटा पुत्र सदाचारी और धर्मात्मा होगा।

"इस प्रकार कैकसी के दस मुख वाले पुत्र का जन्म हुआ जिसका नाम दशग्रीव रखा गया। उसके पश्चात् कुम्भकर्ण, शूर्पणखा और विभीषण के जन्म हुये। दशग्रीव और कुम्भकर्ण अत्यन्त दुष्ट थे, किन्तु विभीषण धर्मात्मा प्रकृति का था। दशग्रीव ने अपने भाइयों सहित ब्रह्माजी की तपस्या की। ब्रह्मा के प्रसन्न होने पर दशग्रीव ने माँगा कि मैं गरुड़, नाग, यक्ष, दैत्य, दानव, राक्षस तथा देवताओं के लिये अवध्य हो जाऊँ। ब्रह्मा जी ने 'तथास्तु' कहकर उसकी इच्छा पूरी कर दी। विभीषण ने धर्म में अविचल मति का और कुम्भकर्ण ने वर्षों तक सोते रहने का वरदान पाया।

"फिर दशग्रीव ने लंका के राजा कुबेर को विवश किया कि वह लंका छोड़कर अपना राज्य उसे सौंप दे। अपने पिता विश्रवा के समझाने पर कुबेर ने लंका का परित्याग कर दिया और रावण अपनी सेना, भाइयों तथा सेवकों के साथ लंका में रहने लगा। लंका में जम जाने के बाद अपने बहन शूर्पणखा का विवाह कालका के पुत्र दानवराज विद्युविह्वा के साथ कर दिया। उसने स्वयं दिति के पुत्र मय की कन्या मन्दोदरी से विवाह किया जो हेमा नामक अप्सरा के गर्भ से उत्पन्न हुई थी। विरोचनकुमार बलि की पुत्री वज्रज्वला से कुम्भकर्ण का और गन्धर्वराज महात्मा शैलूष की कन्या सरमा से विभीषण का विवाह हुआ। कुछ समय पश्चात् मन्दोदरी ने मेघनाद को जन्म दिया जो इन्द्र को परास्त कर संसार में इन्द्रजित के

नाम से प्रसिद्ध हुआ।

"सत्ता के मद में रावण उच्छृंखल हो देवताओं, ऋषियों, यक्षों और गन्धर्वों को नाना प्रकार से कष्ट देने लगा। एक बार उसने कुबेर पर चढ़ाई करके उसे युद्ध में पराजित कर दिया और अपनी विजय की स्मृति के रूप में कुबेर के पुष्पक विमान पर अधिकार कर लिया। उस विमान का वेग मन के समान तीव्र था। वह अपने ऊपर बैठे हुये लोगों की इच्छानुसार छोटा या बड़ा रूप धारण कर सकता था।

विमान में मणि और सोने की सीढ़ियाँ बनी हुई थीं और तपाये हुये सोने के आसन बने हुये थे। उस विमान पर बैठकर जब वह 'शरवण' नाम से प्रसिद्ध सरकण्डों के विशाल वन से होकर जा रहा था तो भगवान शंकर के पार्षद नन्दीश्वर ने उसे रोकते हुये कहा कि दशग्रीव! इस वन में स्थित पर्वत पर भगवान शंकर क्रीड़ा करते हैं, इसलिये यहाँ सभी सुर, असुर, यक्ष आदि का आना निषिद्ध कर दिया गया है। नन्दीश्वर के वचनों से क्रुद्ध होकर रावण विमान से उतरकर भगवान शंकर की ओर चला। उसे रोकने के लिये उससे थोड़ी दूर पर हाथ में शूल लिये नन्दी दूसरे शिव की भाँति खड़े हो गये।

उनका मुख वानर जैसा था। उसे देखकर रावण ठहाका मारकर हँस पड़ा। इससे कुपित हो नन्दी बोले कि दशानन! तुमने मेरे वानर रूप की अवहेलना की है, इसलिये तुम्हारे कुल का नाश करने के लिये मेरे ही समान पराक्रमी रूप और तेज से सम्पन्न वानर उत्पन्न होंगे। रावण ने इस ओर तनिक भी ध्यान नहीं दिया और बोला कि जिस पर्वत ने मेरे विमान की यात्रा में बाधा डाली है, आज मैं उसी को उखाड़ फेंकूँगा। यह कहकर उसने पर्वत के निचले भाग में हाथ डालकर उसे उठाने का प्रयत्न किया। जब पर्वत हिलने लगा तो भगवान शंकर ने उस पर्वत को अपने पैर के अँगूठे से दबा दिया। इससे रावण का हाथ बुरी तरह से दब गया और वह पीड़ा से चिल्लाने लगा। जब वह किसी प्रकार से हाथ न निकाल सका तो रोत-रोते भगवान शंकर की स्तुति और क्षमा प्रार्थना करने लगा। इस पर भगवान शंकर ने उसे क्षमा कर दिया और उसके प्रार्थाना करने पर उसे एक चन्द्रहास नामक खड्ग भी दिया।"

अगस्त्य मुनि ने कथा को आगे बढ़ाया, "एक दिन हिमालय प्रदेश में भ्रमण करते हुये रावण ने ब्रह्मर्षि कुशध्वज की कन्या वेदवती को तपस्या करते देखा। वह उस पर मुग्ध हो गया और उसके पास आकर उसका परिचय तथा अविवाहित रहने का कारण पूछा। वेदवती ने अपने परिचय देने के पश्चात् बताया कि मेरे पिता विष्णु से मेरा विवाह करना चाहते थे। इससे क्रुद्ध होकर मेरी कामना करने वाले दैत्यराज शम्भु ने सोते में उनका वध कर दिया। उनके मरने पर मेरी माता भी दुःखी होकर चिता में प्रविष्ट हो गई। तब से मैं अपने पिता के इच्छा पूरी करने के लिये भगवान विष्णु की तपस्या कर रही हूँ। उन्हीं को मैंने अपना पति मान लिया है।

"पहले रावण ने वेदवती को बातों में फुसलाना चाहा, फिर उसने जबरदस्ती करने के लिये उसके केश पकड़ लिये। वेदवती ने एक ही झटके में पकड़े हुये केश काट डाले। फिर यह कहती हुई अग्नि में प्रविष्ट हो गई कि दुष्ट! तूने मेरा अपमान किया है। इस समय तो मैं यह

शरीर त्याग रही हूँ, परन्तु तेरा विनाश करने के मैं अयोनिजा कन्या के रूप में जन्म लेकर किसी धर्मात्मा की पुत्री बनूँगी। अगले जन्म में वह कन्या कमल के रूप में उत्पन्न हुई। उस सुन्दर कान्ति वाली कमल कन्या को एक दिन रावण अपने महलों में ले गया। उसे देखकर ज्योतिषियों ने कहा कि राजन्! यदि यह कमल कन्या आपके घर में रही तो आपके और आपके कुल के विनाश का कारण बनेगी। यह सुनकर रावण ने उसे समुद्र में फेंक दिया। वहाँ से वह भूमि को प्राप्त होकर राजा जनक के यज्ञमण्डप के मध्यवर्ती भूभाग में जा पहुँची। वहाँ राजा द्वारा हल से जोती जाने वाली भूमि से वह कन्या फिर प्राप्त हुई। वही वेदवती सीता के रूप में आपकी पत्नी बनी और आप स्वयं सनातन विष्णु हैं। इस प्रकार आपके महान शत्रु रावण को वेदवती ने पहले ही अपने शाप से मार डाला। आप तो उसे मारने में केवल निमित्तमात्र थे।

"अनेक राजा महाराजाओं को पराजित करता हुआ दशग्रीव इक्ष्वाकु वंश के राजा अनरण्य के पास पहुँचा जो अयोध्या पर राज्य करते थे। उसने उन्हें भी द्वन्द युद्ध करने अथवा पराजय स्वीकार करने के लिये ललकारा। दोनों में भीषण युद्ध हुआ किन्तु ब्रह्माजी के वरदान के कारण रावण उनसे पराजित न हो सका। जब अनरण्य का शरीर बुरी तरह से क्षत-विक्षत हो गया तो रावण इक्ष्वाकु वंश का अपमान और उपहास करने लगा। इससे कुपित होकर अनरण्य ने उसे शाप दिया कि तूने अपने व्यंगपूर्ण शब्दों से इक्ष्व कु वंश का अपमान किया है, इसलिये मैं तुझे शाप देता हूँ कि महात्मा इक्ष्वाकु के इसी वंश में दशरथनन्दन राम का जन्म होगा जो तेरा वध करेंगे। यह कहकर राजा स्वर्ग सिधार गये।

"रावण की उद्दण्डता में कमी नहीं आई। राक्षस या मनुष्य जिसको भी वह शक्तिशाली पाता, उसी के साथ जाकर युद्ध करने करने लगता। एक बार उसने सुन कि किष्किन्धापुरी का राजा वालि बड़ा बलवान और पराक्रमी है तो वह उसके पास युद्ध करने के लिये जा पहुँचा। वालि की पत्नी तारा, तारा के पिता सुषेण, युवराज अंगद और उसके भाई सुग्रीव ने उसे समझाया कि इस समय वालि नगर से बाहर सन्ध्योपासना के लिये गये हुये हैं।

वे ही आपसे युद्ध कर सकते हैं। और कोई वानर इतन पराक्रमी नहीं है जो आपके साथ युद्ध कर सके। इसलिये आप थोड़ी देर उनकी प्रतीक्षा करें। फिर सुग्रीव ने कहा कि राक्षसराज! सामने जो शंख जैसे हड्डियों के ढेर लगे हैं वे वालि के साथ युद्ध की इच्छा से आये आप जैसे वीरों के ही हैं। वालि ने इन सबका अन्त किया है। यदि आप अमृत पीकर आये होंगे तो भी जिस क्षण वालि से युद्ध करेंगे, वह क्षण आपके जीवन का अन्तिम क्षण होगा। यदि आपको मरने की बहुत जल्दी हो तो आप दक्षिण सागर के तट पर चले जाइये। वहीं आपको वालि के दर्शन हो जायेंगे।

"सुग्रीव के वचन सुनकर रावण विमान पर सवार हो तत्काल दक्षिण सागर में उस स्थान पर जा पहुँचा जहां वालि सन्ध्या कर रहा था। उसने सोचा कि मैं चुपचाप वालि पर आक्रमण कर दूँगा। वालि ने रावण को आते देख लिया परन्तु वह तनिक भी विचलित नहीं हुआ और वैदिक मन्त्रों का उच्चारण करता रहा। ज्योंही उसे पकड़ने के लिये रावण ने पीछे से हाथ

बढ़ाया, सतर्क वालि ने उसे पकड़कर अपनी काँख में दबा लिया और आकाश में उड़ चला।

रावण बार-बार वालि को अपने नखों से कचोटता रहा किन्तु वालि ने उसकी कोई चिन्ता नहीं की। तब उसे छुड़ाने के लिये रावण के मन्त्री और अनुचर उसके पीछे शोर मचाते हुये दौड़े परन्तु वे वालि के पास तक न पहुँच सके। इस प्रकार वालि रावण को लेकर पश्चिमी सागर के तट पर पहुँचा। वहाँ उसने सन्ध्योपासना पूरी की। फिर वह दशानन को लिये हुये किष्किन्धापुरी लौटा। अपने उपवन में एक आसन पर बैठकर उसने रावण को अपनी काँख से निकालकर पूछा कि अब कहिये आप कौन हैं और किसलिये आये हैं?

“रावण ने उत्तर दिया कि मैं लंका का राजा रावण हूँ। आपके साथ युद्ध करने के लिये आया था। वह युद्ध मुझे प्राप्त हो चुका है। मैंने आपका अद्भुत बल देख लिया। अब मैं अग्नि की साक्षी देकर आपसे मित्रता करना चाहता हूँ। फिर दोनों ने अग्नि की साक्षी देकर एक दूसरे से मित्रता स्थापित की।”